A Linguistics Reader

GRAHAM WILSON

San Francisco State College

HARPER & ROW, PUBLISHERS

New York, Evanston, and London

A
Linguistics
Reader

Contents

Foreword

It is a rather depressing thing to be a linguist. One goes to a lot of expense and trouble to prepare oneself in the profession only to discover that the whole population has been practicing it all along, practically since birth. It must happen to a physician only occasionally that he meets some layman convinced that he knows more about medicine than any doctor does. To the linguist it is routine to be instructed in language not only by the man in the street but by the man who cleans it. There are few people who do not have strong views on language—what language is composed of, the relation of language and thought, how to learn languages. The intolerable thing, to the professional man, is that many of these views are correct.

The situation is favorable, of course, for the publication of a book like this one. The reader comes to it not in *statu pupillari,* as he might to a tome on mathematics, but as colleague, ready to dissect, approve, or denounce. He will find here material for all three operations.

The linguist Charlton Laird, in a book called *The Miracle of Language,* conceived of a character named Og who was the first being to speak a human language and therefore the first being to be human. Linguists have long since abandoned serious discussion of the origin of language: the topic has even been barred from the programs of some societies of linguists. We may not know much about language, but we know that we don't know how language originated and that we never will know. There isn't any data. Virtually all the languages of the world have become known by now to linguists, and there aren't any primitive languages among them. All human beings—even those who spend their active years doing nothing but stirring in the mud for worms—speak languages that are highly sophisticated and complicated systems. There are no traces of the steps that must have been taken between Og's first meaningful grunt and the actual languages of today.

Still there must have been an Og, or some Ogs. At some point, some of that species that was to become people must have begun to make sounds that were meaningful to their associates. But this wasn't yet human language. Certain animals can do this much. We are told, by those who have been there, that on the Malaysian Peninsula ape calls to ape, employing a repertoire of nine sentences with such meanings as "There is danger here," "You're asking for trouble," "I love you." This isn't yet human language, however. What the apes do not know how to do is manipulate the parts of their sentences so as to produce new, correct sentences that they had never heard before, like "There is trouble here," "You're dangerous," "Am I troubling you?" If they could just learn this trick, they would be as human as you and I, though of course markedly different in appearance and table manners.

Some Og did learn the trick once. Given "Mbu bork" and "Ho gluck," he made the brand new sentence "Mbu gluck," and some female of the species understood him. They moved shortly after that into a cave that Og had had his eye on and began raising children, who, as they grew to adulthood, were making new sentences like billy-o and wondering how they could use this power to do in their neighbors. And no doubt the senior Ogs were deploring the slovenly pronunciation and bad grammar of the children and reflecting on how all would be up with cave-dwelling culture if the degeneration continued.

Og's descendants have been deploring the degeneration of language ever since. Doubtless Socrates, though well aware that Plato was a bright young chap and a real comer, wished he wouldn't be quite so careless in the use of the aorist tense, and Marcus Antonius may have lost the battle of Actium because he disprized Octavius on account of the latter's bad Latin.

We have had examples in more recent times. In 1961, the Merriam-Webster company published a revision of its unabridged dictionary, the *Webster's Third International*. This company had been infiltrated by linguists, who reported the language as it was in 1961, not as they thought it should be. This radical departure evoked editorial wrath across the nation. The dictionary and its makers were pilloried in the Chicago *Daily News* and *The New York Times,* in *Life Magazine* and the *Atlantic* and the *New Yorker,* because they reported that respectable people sometimes say *ain't* and use *like* as a conjunction. To the writers of the editorials and articles, such admissions seemed a severe, perhaps a fatal, blow to western culture. There was a movement to have Merriam-Webster bought out by people more alive to the sacred responsibility of safeguarding our tongue, and we were urged meanwhile to use the *Second International* (1934) and not risk moral collapse by dipping into the racy and dangerous *Third.*

There are several interesting implications here: (1) that it was possible, without getting locked up, to speak and write in 1961 as people did in 1934; (2) that people learn to speak and write from dictionaries, however unabridged; (3) that the moral fibre of a nation is actually weakened if its citizens are allowed, without lexicographical reproof, to use *like* as a conjunction or to say *irregardless* instead of *regardless.* But this is now a long quiet battlefield, and I have no wish to roam it further. I use it merely as an example of the deep-seated feelings that people have about language.

A professor of English, a friend of mine with whom I had attended graduate school, once remarked to me that he was all for the scientific study of language *so long as the results were never applied to the teaching of English.* That was about twenty years ago, and I have been wondering ever since what he meant. He *could* have meant that the teaching of English was so bad that it couldn't survive objective appraisal; but I'm pretty sure he didn't think that, as I don't either. I think he felt rather that teaching English—the composition and literature part, that is—was a delicate and somewhat mystical enterprise. If one looks too closely at the flower, the petals fade. His attitude toward Leonard Bloomfield's *Language* might perhaps be compared to that of an enlightened minister to Renan's *Life of Jesus:* one might admire it as an interesting historical document, but naturally one wouldn't quote it in church.

Cherished as it is by so many worthy and eminent people, this attitude is hard to condemn, but it is equally hard to understand. Thomas Pyles, in a book called *Words and Ways of American English,* remarks that Americans, however much they pride themselves on being a free and easy folk, unconfined by tradition, are actually tight to the point of neurosis when it comes to language. They have conceived a correct English, spoken by a few members of the British upper classes and, with slight variations in pronunciation, by the better English teachers in America. This dialect is more for ostentation than for use. One doesn't really expect to speak it; it was given only to Galahad to see the Grail. Those of us with hearts less pure can only try to avoid the company of the better English teachers and members of the British upper classes. It's a point of view, of course, but it does seem to take a lot of fun out of life and literature.

It was with this attitude linguistic science collided when that science emerged in the early twentieth century and with which it is still in collission. In the hierarchy of science, linguistics is a branch of anthropology. Anthropology is the study of man, and one of man's most important attributes is the ability to make sentences. Linguistics studies the sentences that he makes, how he learns to make them, and the effect that making them has on his existence. The study may be said to have begun, in a disciplined way, around 1910 and to have been fostered mainly by American anthropologists interested primarily in the culture of American Indians. The best known names among these early anthropological linguists are Franz Boas and Edward Sapir.

Of course there had been linguists much earlier than Sapir and Boas. Perhaps Og was the first, but the first we have reliable information on was Panini, who described Sanskrit, and described it very well indeed, about four centuries before the birth of Christ. Aristotle had notions, some of them sensible, on language as he did on most other subjects, and he did not withhold them from his public. There were Greek grammars by the second century B.C., and these served as models for what came to be the main textbooks of the Middle Ages—the grammars of Latin.

There are several methods of teaching foreign languages in schools, but the one that seems to have met with most general success is Main Strength and Awkwardness. In the middle of the nineteenth century, Lord Macaulay, faced with the practical problem of how to teach English in India, came to the sensible conclusion that the best way was to start the children young and not teach them much of anything else. For about a century, those Indian childen who went to school studied not only English but history in English, science in English, all subjects in

English, with the result that millions of Indians today speak English—not very well, to be sure, but a great deal better than any significant number of Americans or Englishmen speak French.

Something like the same method was used for Latin in European countries during the Middle Ages. The school that one attended was called a "grammar school," and this meant specifically a school where one studied Latin grammar. That was essentially what one studied. No English Literature. No Driver Education. Just Latin grammar and the things that Latin might convey. As late as the 1880's, Winston Churchill, arriving at the age of seven at his first school, was set down the very first evening to learn the First Declension. If you start at the age of seven with the First Declension and keep plugging away along these lines until you are seventeen, you're bound to learn quite a lot of Latin, enough to read it with ease, correspond in it, write poetry in it—and educated Europeans were indeed able to do these things, for many hundreds of years.

In all these centuries of preoccupation with Latin, the structure of Latin came to be very finely known. This was what linguistics did in the Middle Ages: it described Latin. It had no truck with contemporary European languages and certainly not with non-European ones. Apart from Greek, which began to interest people in the later years of the Middle Ages, the focus was on Latin, and not just any old Latin, but specifically that of the last years of the Roman Republic and the first of the Empire. If one were to pinpoint it further, it was the Latin of Cicero that was deemed most worthy of study and emulation. Many people tried to emulate it in the Middle Ages, and a few succeeded fairly well.

Thus up to the Renaissance, linguistics was essentially descriptive but with a very small area for description to operate in. There were occasional philosophic speculations about the general nature of language, but they were of trifling importance and drew little attention. With the Renaissance, there was an opening up in several directions. For one thing, people became consciously aware of the vernaculars they spoke—of English, French, Italian, Spanish. Castiglione, in *The Courtier,* has a good deal to say about the kind of Italian a proper person ought to speak and why. In sixteenth-century England, there was much earnest discussion about English: how to spell it, for example, and how and whether to enrich its vocabulary by borrowing words from other languages. At the beginning of the seventeenth century, the first English dictionary appeared, the work of a man named Robert Cawdrey. Cawdrey was speedily plagiarized and improved upon. Other dictionaries followed, growing ever larger, and there were soon other works designed to conduce to a proper use of English the increasing number of people whose prosperity outran their breeding. English grammar was being born.

At roughly the same time, philosophers were beginning to pose more interesting problems, such as how people learn their languages in the first place. Descartes in the early seventeenth century and Locke in the later made suggestions which continue to beset and divide people who are interested in the nature of language.

Until the latter part of the eighteenth century, very little was known about languages other than European languages, and not much about the relationships among the latter. Presumably it was obvious that Italian and Spanish were related and both descendent from Latin, and that English was somehow or other connected with German. There was some knowledge of Old English, or Saxon as it was then generally called. Lexicographers displayed some interest and competence in simple etymology. But in general, awareness of language development and language relationships was slight. The Greeks and Romans had no notion that the Persians and Celts with whom they fought spoke languages related to their own. If put to it, they would no doubt have said that the Persians and Celts didn't really speak languages at all but just made barbaric noises like animals calling to other animals. No more did the educated European of 1750 have any notion that the language he spoke was directly related to languages of India, of Persia, of Russia, of Wales.

But toward the end of the eighteenth century, as scholars became conversant with Sanskrit, a religious language of India first written down around 1500 B.C., they noticed recurring correspondences of the consonants of Sanskrit with those of such languages as Greek, Latin, German, English. In the early nineteenth century, these correspondences were set forth by the Danish scholar Rasmus Christian Rask and a little later were formulated by Jakob Grimm in what came to be known as Grimm's Law or, more soberly, the First Consonant Shift. This demonstrated that such apparently dissimilar words as Latin *lupus* and English *wolf*, English *mother* and Sanskrit *mātṛ* were originally the same and had become differentiated by regular and ascertainable developments of the sound structure of the different languages. Such advances as these brought into being the variety of linguistics called *philology,* which concerns itself with tracing out the historical developments of languages and the relationships among them.

Throughout the nineteenth century and into the early twentieth, linguistics was essentially of this sort. It was historical and comparative and primarily concerned with establishing the facts of the language family to which most of the languages of Europe belong—Indo-European. The work done was enormous and the improvements in theory impressive. After Karl Verner showed that certain apparent irregularities in Grimm's Law weren't irregular at all but were the natural consequence of an ancillary law, people came to the view that, instead of there being no law without an exception, there was no exception without a law. Those who espoused this view, in the latter part of the nineteenth century, were called the Neo-Grammarians. They rode fast, and they rode far, and they filled massive volumes with the historical details of the Indo-European family of languages. They pretty well established linguistics, in its philological aspect, as a science.

But in all this time there was very little interest either in non-Indo-European languages or in the Indo-European languages themselves in their modern shape, and little also—among linguists, at any rate—in what languages are and how human beings learn them. A great many English grammars were produced, since by the nineteenth century, English had become a regular school subject, steadily making way at the expense of Latin. But the grammars were mostly amateurish, dashed off by people who did not in fact devote their lives to the nature of language or think very seriously about it. They often gave wholesome advice on how to use *who* and *whom,* but they did very little to illuminate the structure of English. It has often been said that one cannot really understand English without knowing Latin. Probably it is true that one must know Latin to figure out what the school grammars of English published in the nineteenth century are all about. Latin grammar was the only grammar their authors knew, and so English was presented as a kind of translation of Latin, a procedure that yielded results a good deal less than satisfactory.

There was much more sophistication, in the nineteenth century, in the field of lexicography. The principles developed in the eighteenth by such dictionary makers as Kersey, Bailey, and Johnson were extended and refined. The result was the greatest monument of lexicography of all time, the *Oxford English Dictionary,* first proposed in 1857, seriously undertaken in 1878, and completed in 1928. The late nineteenth century saw also much serious work in English phonetics by such scholars as Henry Sweet, said to be the prototype of the Henry Higgins of Shaw's *Pygmalion.* There began about this time as well what might be called scholarly traditional grammar, which flowered in the works of people like Jespersen, Poutsma, Kruisinga, Curme—multivolumed collections of types of English sentences, painstakingly gathered, arranged, and discussed. This sort of work continues, though with much abatement, and thus overlaps the two movements with which the present book is primarily concerned: structural linguistics and transformationalism.

Structural linguistics is a somewhat misleading term, since all linguistics is concerned with structure and since anyone who devotes himself professionally to the study of language is in some sense a linguist; but it is the most common designation for a kind of linguistic focus that started with the anthropologists early in this century, culminated in the nineteen forties, and then began, under the impact of newer ideas, to change its directions and abandon some of its goals.

The interest of anthropologists at the beginning of the twentieth century in the languages of the American Indian was very practically motivated. These languages were fast disappearing, and though it may not bother a scholar to see something disappear, he hates not to get a record of it before it does so. Accordingly, the anthropologists pursued the departing Indian, sat beside his deathbed, and took notes. The study proved fascinating. The anthropologists did not, of course, share the notion of the layman of the period that Indians communicated mostly by saying "Ugh" and "How" and waving their arms; but even the anthropologists were astonished by the intricate language systems that they found. Many Indian languages proved to be more highly inflected than Greek, though in vastly different ways. Some of their grammars compelled and made commonplace modes of thought not easily even graspable by speakers of Indo-European languages. Their sound structures disclosed that the human articulatory apparatus had capabilities not previously suspected. In short, it became apparent that human language was vastly more complex, diversified, and interesting than anyone in the nineteenth century could have supposed.

One immediate result was the realization that traditional procedures for language description would not serve the new purpose. You can describe Italian pretty well on the Latin model, and maybe you can get by describing English that way if you don't mind quite a few grotesqueries, but when you come to Algonquian, Potawatomi, and Kechua, Latin is largely irrelevant. You have to work out the structure without much help from traditional studies. Doing so, the anthropologist-linguist developed whole new techniques of language analysis.

The anthropologist was not the only one engaged in the endeavor. Equally important was the missionary. If one wishes to convert a people to Christianity, it is, if not indispensable, at least highly desirable to acquaint them with the Bible, and this means translating the Bible into their language, and *that* means learning their language. Many missionaries did this, from New Guinea to Tanganyika, and thus contributed to the growing knowledge of the languages of the world as well as to the technique of language description. Other people, primarily interested neither in religion nor culture but simply in language itself, entered the field, and before long something called linguistics or linguistic science or structural linguistics began to be recognized as a special academic discipline. The universities found themselves harboring professors of it.

It is not within the province of this foreword to describe the principles and practices of structural linguistics; the reader will find these ably set forth in the text itself. Attention may be drawn, however, to two important facets: the concentration on language as speech rather than as writing, and a different attiude toward correctness. The philologist, dealing necessarily with letters on page or stone, was interested, to be sure, in ascertaining the sounds they signified, but the structural linguist, working with notebook or tape recorder in Borneo or Carson City, Nevada, was interested in their immediacy and came to a much more profound understanding of them and the systems that contained them than had been attained before. It was this activity that led to refinement of the concept of the *phoneme,* which might be grossly defined as a bundle of similar sounds which seem identical to the native speaker of the language but which may sound quite dissimilar to a speaker of a different language. With the phoneme as a central unit, structural linguistics made extensive studies and inventories of the sound systems of a great many languages, went on to describe their morphological systems, and said something, but not so much that was startling and persuasive, about their syntactic systems. Structural linguistics started with phonology and worked up, so to speak, toward syntax, but it didn't always arrive.

Along with this descriptive and theoretical work went ideas about correctness which weren't exactly new but which tended to strike the layman as revolutionary and very likely dangerous. For reasons which a psychologist could most likely explain, people treasure the notion of a pure variety of whatever language they speak. Nobody is ever able to tell just what this purity consists of, what characteristics make it pure, but most people are sure that it exists somewhere. I was once told, by an educated Italian, that the purest Italian is to be found at a point just ten kilometers south of Siena, along the route of the Via Cassia. He was perfectly serious and thought himself communicating a fact analogous to a statement, say, about the boiling point of water. Always anxious to improve my understanding and extend my frame of reference, I stopped once at Kilometer Stone 214 on the Cassia, which is just ten kilometers south of Siena. There is a little settlement there, with a garage, a tobacco shop, a grocery store, and similar establishments. The residents speak a heavy Tuscan dialect barely understandable to the speaker of standard Italian who strains every auricular muscle. It is no doubt a very good and serviceable dialect, and I'm not saying it isn't. I just wonder what my mentor meant.

The structural linguists, dealing not, at first, with the sophisticated and self-conscious speakers of languages like English and Italian, but with languages of stone-age peoples with no literary tradition, were entirely free of this notion of correctness or purity of language. They did not titter when they heard Sitting Penguin say *ngungho* and tell him that he should say *ngunghu* like Laughing Mongoose. They simply noted that some speakers of the language said *ngungho,* whereas others said *ngunghu.* There was no way of determining that one of these was better or purer or more correct than the other. It could perhaps be ascertained which was the more common, but this was a matter of statistics, not of purity.

Had the structural linguists stuck to languages like Chamorro and Arawak, this century would have been much more peaceful, and the lanes of our universities would have run with far less blood. But they didn't. They got onto English and Italian and other languages which already had academic proprietors. With the disciplining experience of the prairie and the jungle under their belts, they looked with a cool and steady eye on the descriptions of the better known languages and found them sadly wanting. Worse, they said so publicly. Worse still, they said so with a good deal of humorous embroidery, pointing out with some insistence the donkey-like qualities of those to whom the instruction of the youth in their native languages had been entrusted. Very much worse still, they proposed to take over this instruction. The professor of English would be permitted to prattle about Shakespeare and Dickens if he wished, but all serious teaching of language should be confided to the structural linguist.

Naturally, the linguist was regularly clubbed and sometimes smeared, but he did gain enough footholds in the universities to keep the contest lively, and he became a formidable influence in such organizations as the National Council of Teachers of English, which the professor of Shakespeare and Dickens had too often considered beneath his notice. The linguist began to have an effect on teacher-training programs, on textbooks, on the curriculum of the lower schools. The effect was rather slight, actually, but it was enough to alarm the establishment, which launched a vigorous counterattack, oddly enough at the point at which the linguist was least culpable—the idea of correctness. Probably no linguist ever said that it doesn't matter how one speaks or writes, it is what one says that counts. The linguist knows better than most people that the how is at least as important as the what. But he knows also that the choice of one form over another is a sociological rather than a linguistic matter. That is, there are no linguistic reasons why, for example, "I brung it" should be eschewed. No arguments of logic or euphony or analogy can be adduced to establish *brought* as a purer form than *brung*. All that can be said is that, in the world of the closely shaved, the consequences of saying "I brung it" are very serious indeed and that the ambitious young man is well advised to avoid the expression.

Nevertheless, structural linguists were more or less successfully portrayed as champions of an anything-goes school of language. No doubt, they to some extent brought it on themselves. Books with titles like *Leave Your Language Alone* gave a somewhat false impression, and linguists, like stags at bay, often made reckless and inflammatory statements. At any rate, the impression was conveyed that linguists were bent on debasing and dismantling the language. It was suggested that this might be simply part of the permissive attitude that one saw everywhere, though some wondered whether international Communism was not involved in it somehow, and most of the guardians of our culture were quite sure that schools of education were part of the conspiracy. Articles began to appear in the national press about these anarchists who were saying dangerous things about *shall* and *will,* and the whole thing spilled over in the attack, mentioned earlier, on *Webster's Third.*

Ironically, by this time the problem had become, so far as linguists were concerned, largely of historical interest, for linguists had a much more important matter to worry about: generative transformational grammar. It has not been given to many people to change virtually single-handedly the whole course of a scientific discipline. One might think of Galileo, Lavoisier, Freud. If one doesn't rank Noam Chomsky with these, it could only be because one doesn't think linguistics as important as physics, chemistry, or psychology. Chomsky studied linguistics at the University of Pennsylvania and took his Ph.D. degree there. He spent the first part of the fifties thinking and studying and in 1957 published a book called *Syntactic Structures,* an excerpt of which appears in this text. Linguistics has not been the same since.

What Chomsky did in *Syntactic Structures* was to ask certain very general questions about language and language learning and to give some partial answers. What do we learn when we learn a language? One might be tempted to say words, or, if one were slightly more sophisticated, sentences. Indeed, most books designed for teaching foreign languages essentially produce words and sentences to be learned. Yet it can be shown that, apart from the simplest formulas and greetings, like "Hello" and "Thank you," and trite expressions of various sorts, like "A good time was had by all," the chances that any particular learner will have occasion to use any particular sentence are quite small. This is so even in cases where the needs of the learner are pretty well known in advance—those of tourists, for example. Countless British tourists preparing for continental travel have memorized the French, German, and Spanish equivalents of "I have two pounds of tea and three bars of chocolate for my own personal use," but it is doubtful that any considerable number have stammered out the sentences. What happens is that the customs man who boards the train at Modane, anxious to get back to his card game, says hopefully, *Rien à déclarer?* and you say *Rien à déclarer,"* and return to your study of the phrase book.

The views of people who write phrase books on what phrases might come in handy are sometimes peculiar. A Dutch book on *Useful English Words and Phrases* contains the sentence "Our postillion has been struck by lightning." One is not likely to find use for this, which is a pity, because it is a sentence with a certain euphony and a kind of dignity. But in fact the chances that a Hollander visiting New York will have occasion to say, for example, "Where are my suitcases?" are not much greater than they are for "Our postillion has been struck by lightning." They are a little greater, but not much. He would have to lose his suitcases, first of all, a thing not really easy to do, and then be in a situation in which "Where are my suitcases?" is the proper thing to say. Maybe "A thief just made off with my suitcases" or "Have you happened to see any unclaimed suitcases in the lobby?" would be more to the point. The orders of probability of "Where are my suitcases?" and "Our postillion has been struck by lightning" are quite similar. Both are near zero.

What, then, do we learn when we learn a language, if it is not words and phrases and sentences? Obviously, what we learn is a sentence-making mechanism of some sort. Chomsky pointed out that the number of possible sentences for any language is, if not infinite, at least on the order of magnitude of the particles of the universe. What is not so immediately obvious is that the number of sentence *types* is not appreciably smaller. The structures of syntax can combine and embed and intertwine and extend in such an endless number of ways that it is far beyond the power of any grammar, however multivolumed, to set them forth. One can come pretty close to listing the words of a language, if *word* is defined narrowly enough, but one can't even begin to list the sentences or the sentence types.

What one must therefore conclude is that we Ogs, in contrast to the Malaysian ape, have acquired a power to *generate* sentences—just those which will serve our unpredictable needs. The mechanism that enables us to do this is called grammar. Apparently every human child who is not deaf or functionally malformed builds himself a grammar. From the random sentences that he hears from the people around him, he builds a sentence-making system, going through some sort of process of theory construction. As Chomsky has pointed out, this goes to essential completion at a very early age—say around five or six years. The operation goes on indifferently to the particular language involved; that is, the Chinese child builds his grammar of Chinese with about as much ease or difficulty as the American child builds his of English and in about the same time. Also it goes on, apparently, indifferently to intelligence. You don't have to be bright to learn Chinese or French. All you have to have are Chinese or French parents. Once you have built your grammar, you can choose, among the trillion plus sentences at your disposition, just those which fill the need of the moment. You can locate the bathroom, complain about not being permitted to watch television, inquire about your suitcases, or report to the police a recent unpleasantness suffered by your postillion.

There are still a large number of unanswered questions about this grammar-building ability. One is whether the ability atrophies after a certain age. Little children are notoriously the most able learners of languages. Some tots build not just one grammar but three or four simultaneously and chatter with equal skill in English, French, Turkish, and Egyptian Arabic, according to the company in which they find themselves. Some psychologists feel that doing so is bad for their mental health, but nothing conclusive is known. Anyway, though the reasons are murky, it is certain that the older you get the harder it is to learn a new language. An English-speaking child of eight can learn French only laboriously if at all, but it isn't clear what the impeding factors are. Probably the self-conscious possession of a prior language is an important one.

People have often speculated on what would happen if a child were raised for a certain time in the absence of language—say six or seven years— and then confronted with it. Herodotus reports one such experiment, and King James the First is said to have made another, but in modern times it is hard to find a subject. Anyone who comes across a ten-year-old human child who has been raised by wolves should report at once to the nearest linguist.

All of these matters are in the realm of speculation and are unlikely to be understood soon, if ever. But if one can't very hopefully go about understanding the learning process, one can with more confidence try to figure out the thing learned, the grammar. Transformationalists have argued that a grammar consists of three components—the syntactic, the phonological, and the semantic. The syntactic component is in some sense prior to the other two in the setting forth of the grammar. (We may note that the point of entry for transformationalists is the opposite of that for structuralists and more in accord with traditional grammar.) This syntactic component is generated by two sets of rules. One set is called phrase-structure, or kernel, rules, the other transformational rules. The phrase-structure rules generate the elements of sentences in a simple order. The following might be said roughly to be generated by phrase-structure rules: "The suitcases are somewhere," "The children whine," "Lightning has struck the postillion." Transformational rules ring changes on such kernel sentences, reordering their parts, combining them, adding items and deleting others. The following are sentences to which transformational rules have been applied: "Where are my suitcases?" "I took steps to stop the whining of the children," "Our postillion has been struck by lightning."

The structures generated by phrase-structure rules are sometimes called deep structures; those generated by transformational rules are called surface structures. A pair of sentences may be quite similar in surface structure and yet quite different in deep structure. To employ a much used example, "John is eager to please" and "John is easy to please" have about the same surface structure but differ fundamentally in deep structure, since in the first John is the pleaser but in the second he is the pleasee. The other two components of the grammar, the semantic and the phonological, relate respectively to the deep structure and the surface structure. It is the deep structure that provides the basic meaning of sentences. It is the surface structure that has to be pronounced. The grammar might be diagramed as follows:

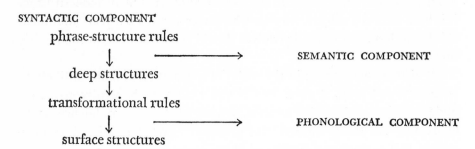

Thus transformational grammar provides a framework in which answers to the three basic questions one can ask of any sentence may be sought: (1) of what elements is it composed? (syntax), (2) what does it mean? (semantics), (3) how is it pronounced? (phonology).

All this may seem harmless enough, and even obvious, but it rocked the world of linguistics. Structural linguists had confined themselves, at least in theory, to describing the sentences found in corpora. A corpus might be a set of tapes of conversations by speakers of Navajo. Or it might be the complete works of Jonathan Swift. Whatever it was, the structuralist kept within it, describing the sentences as accurately as possible and making inventories of their elements. He never tried to predict what a Navajo or Jonathan Swift would have said if he had said something else. The transformationalist tries to do just that. His intent is to project, from a finite set of known sentences, an illimitable number of others and to show that these will be accepted as grammatical when and if they are ever used.

Along with this went a new view of correctness, or grammaticalness. The structuralist tended to take a whatever-is-is-right view of things. If a Navajo said something, it was accepted as correct Navajo. The transformationalist is more subtle, or more cautious. He would point out that interferences of many kinds might have derailed the Navajo from the track of Navajo grammar. He might have had a lapse of memory; he might have been drunk; one of his kids might have annoyed him just as he was getting into the predicate and made him forget what the subject was.

The transformationalist would say, in fact, that speakers of a language are ungrammatical more often than not, hitting near the mark but not often on it. Transformationalists make a distinction between *competence* and *performance*. The competence is the grammar itself which the speaker has internalized as a result of the theory-construction process mentioned earlier. The performance is what he actually does with it, beset by such distractions as screaming children, shyness, hysteria, LSD. Beyond this is the fact that we sometimes sport with the grammar, departing from it deliberately in order to be humorous or poetic. E. E. Cummings' "He danced his did," in which the grammatical "He did his dance" is deliberately inverted, is a frequently cited example. But also

"Are you the waiter?"

"No, I'm not. I'm a waitee."

Here the rule for forming words with the morpheme *ee* is pushed into new territory, and the expression is ungrammatical. Of course, if the usage became common, the grammatical rule would change in this particular to accommodate it. Transformationalists do not say, any more than structuralists did, that grammars are static.

Transformationalists differ from their predecessors also in their attitude toward the notions of rule and exception. Structuralists were pretty chary about rules, looking on them as somehow unscientific, whereas transformationalists take them to their bosoms whenever at all possible. The structuralists seem to have inverted the Neo-Grammarians' "There is no exception without a rule" to "If there is an exception, there can be no rule." For example, in English the ending *-ate* has a fairly regular effect on the placement of the primary stress: it tends to put it on the antepenultimate syllable: *démonstrate, víolate, cálculate.* But there are exceptions. Some people say not *rémonstrate* but *remónstrate.* Such irregularities led many structuralists not only to shrink from stating a rule for the stress effect of *-ate* but to adopt the much more far-reaching conclusion that stress is phonemic in English—that is, that, for any particular sentence you wish to say, you must learn previously which syllables have the various grades of stress. The transformationalist, on the other hand, would say that any rule, no matter how many the exceptions, is better than no rule at all, because if there is no rule, then everything is exception. If, confronted by a thousand items, he can take just ten of them together in a rule, the transformationalist joyfully does so, because that leaves him with only 990 exceptions, not a thousand. So naturally he gives a stress rule for *-ate:* it puts the stress on the antepenultimate syllable, with a few exceptions, like *remónstrate.* This leads him to the vaster conclusion that stress is largely predictable in English and hence, from his point of view, not phonemic.

As this is being written, we await the publication of *The Sound Pattern of English* by Chomsky and Morris Halle. Transformationalists were merely irritating to structuralists when they confined themselves to syntax, because structuralists had not travelled much in that realm anyway. But *The Sound Pattern of English* is, among other things, an attack on the concept of the phoneme, which has been the cornerstone of linguistics since about 1935. It will be interesting to see how the issue is resolved.

One may well ask what good linguistics is—transformationalist, structuralist, or other. How does it help us feed the chickens? There is, as a matter of fact, quite a large application. Linguistics contributes importantly to such sister disciplines as psychology, medicine, communication theory, as well as being the heart and soul of anthropology. But the most obvious application would seem to be to language teaching, whether to the teaching of foreign languages or to the improvement of the native one. The first time that linguistics was applied on a large scale to foreign-language teaching was during World War II. Leonard Bloomfield himself, sometimes called the Father of linguistics, was associated with the effort, and many of the great names of linguistics came to public attention at that time. Readers of newspapers learned of a marvelous new technology for language teaching. Our soldiers and sailors were being taught so efficiently and well that, after a short course of instruction, they could be dropped, say, behind Japanese lines in China and, with a little bit of makeup, pass as Japanese and steal secrets.

Undoubtedly, it was the journalists and not the linguists who were responsible for most of the exaggeration. When the war was over, Professors Frederick B. Agard and Harold B. Dunkel were commissioned to find out what had actually happened, to what extent the methods advocated by linguists had proved superior to traditional methods. Agard and Dunkel were linguists and would have been pleased to report that we had here a real cure for tooth decay, but they were also responsible scholars, and they stated that it was impossible to prove the fact one way or the other. The factors involved in language learning are so extraordinarily complex that it cannot be shown conclusively that particular methodologies contribute to or detract from the desired result.

It was certainly true that some of the language schools during the war achieved spectacular results, but it is impossible to know how much these results owed to techniques derived from linguistics and how much to Main Strength and Awkwardness. If you put a bright young soldier into a room with a native speaker of Japanese and keep them there eight hours a day for eighteen months, the soldier will learn quite a lot of Japanese, even if his text is just a Japanese translation of Cicero and his instructor is a nitwit. Unless, of course, the soldier simply goes mad, which also happened now and then.

Nevertheless, the euphoria felt during the war about new methods of language teaching survived the war and probably rightly so. It is no doubt true that linguistics has contributed importantly to language learning. It is hard to believe that one can teach something as well or better if he doesn't understand it than if he does. It would seem that the more we know about language, the more we are in a position to choose intelligently and effectively among methods of teaching it. This is not the same, however, as saying that we have a technology for foreign-language teaching in the sense that physics provides a technology for bridge-building. Linguistics has produced no simple and certain method for learning languages. It may some day, but it hasn't yet.

The problems of the application of linguistics to the improvement of the pupil in the use of his native language are more subtle and have been longer argued. Specifically, the problem is this: does it pay, if you are a native speaker of English and wish to improve your use of it, to study English grammar? In the twenties and thirties there were several investigations of this problem, and they were impressively unanimous in their conclusion: that it doesn't pay. Pupils who didn't study grammar seemed to improve as much or as little as those who did. It should be noted, however, that the grammar studied in the test cases was of a rudimentary type, unaffected by any doctrines of linguistics, and also that the variables are staggering. It is probably impossible to control an experiment of this type in any really effective way.

The essential question, actually, is this: how do people who write well learn to write well? And nobody really knows the answer. Obviously they must have a great deal of experience in reading and writing, but they must have other capacities as well—power of observation and of applying what is observed, intelligence, memory, willingness to take pains. It is quite possible that our best writers are not significantly assisted by what they learn in schools and that they would be just as good if they didn't go to school at all beyond the first few grades. This doesn't mean, however, that everybody would write just as well with little or no schooling. Indeed, the teaching and learning problem does not affect the Faulkners and E. B. Whites of this world but rather the great mass of citizens who, more and more in this age of paper, find that their careers and earning power and happiness are closely related to their ability to write sentences. The feeling persists in the schools that such people will do better in proportion as they understand the structure of the sentences they write. This may be a fallacy, but it is far from having been proved to be so. If a better method of teaching writing exists, it has yet to be demonstrated.

At any rate, the question is only whether or not the student in school or college should be subjected, or treated, to the study of his language, not what theory of the language should be presented to him. For this latter question eventually solves itself. Different theories contend in the forums of the Linguistic Society of America and the International Congresses of Linguists, in the classrooms of Berkeley, California, and University College, London. It doesn't really matter much, in the long run, how clever in debate the proponents of a particular theory are or how devastatingly they write. It is the theory that counts. If it gets us closer to a satisfactory notion of what language is like, it ultimately prevails; otherwise it doesn't. And when it prevails, those who deal with language in some professional way are stuck with it. The physicist might think that the world would be a happier place if neutrons behaved in some fashion different from the one they do, but he can't do anything about it. Neither can the language teacher—whether of a third grade in Mason City, Iowa, or of a Berlitz school in Vienna—do anything about the facts of language, except perhaps to avoid learning about them. It is hard to become unignorant, but it is nearly impossible, once unignorant, to become ignorant again. Linguistics may teach the teacher of language things that will make his work more simple or more difficult, more pleasant or more painful, more effective or less. However it is, there is nothing he can do about it. He has to accept what he knows, what he believes to be true, and operate from there.

It is to be supposed that most readers of this book are not expecting to become teachers of language and so are in no danger professionally of absorbing prickly and painful knowledge. They can relax and enjoy the ride down the rapids and perhaps even find some amusement in the imprecations that the boatmen scream at one another. Language ranks only slightly behind sex in the universal interest it inspires. If it is true that there is nothing like a dame (and it certainly is), it is equally true that there is nothing like a sentence. We who are descendants of Og cannot avoid speculation over the miracle of language. It is a great thing to have a grammar; it puts us one up on the Malaysian ape. And it's an even greater thing not to have to take the grammar too seriously, to be able to kick it around a little if we like. The only thing we have to fear is that some day linguists will know all there is to know about language, be able to lay it out completely and say it is just such and so, and there are no more questions. But we don't have to fear this very much.

PAUL ROBERTS

Preface

The content, attitude, and purpose of this book have been rehearsed in the Foreword, which may serve as both prologue and epilogue for the audience. The audience might be Freshman English students, upper-division English majors, or students preparing for teaching credentials. In fact, anyone interested in language and how it works should find here many things that are informative, stimulating, and amusing, and probably some things that are infuriating. Though the point of view of the book is admittedly biased, a number of current controversies in the field of language study are both acknowledged and aired.

The introductions to each section and to each essay are somewhat more extensive than is customary in a book of this kind, sometimes in order to give a partial explanation of what follows, sometimes to provide a historical context. The "For Discussion" material after each essay is largely self-contained, not because the editor disapproves of library research, but because most of the useful answers are available to a student willing to study the essay, to refer to a good dictionary, and to inspect his own language habits and those of the people around him. A manual with suggestions for the use of the book is available to instructors.

All editors owe something to others. This one owes quite a bit. A problem for any discipline is to get the best minds in it to write for the student as well as for other scholars. It is a less serious problem in linguistics, however, than it is in some fields of study. This book includes work by many of the most original, imaginative, and productive linguists now working in the United States or the British Isles. One's first debt then is to those scholars and their publishers who have generously—even charitably —allowed their work to be reprinted here. The collection itself was started some time ago by Paul Roberts, who chose most of the essays. He has read all the editorial material, but should not be held responsible for it. And finally, I should like to thank Rochelle Leszczynski of Harper & Row, who has edited the editor with sympathy and patience.

G. W.

A
Linguistics
Reader

The Student and the Language

As Albert H. Marckwardt and others indicate in the following essays, not much has yet been accomplished in applying the methods and insights of contemporary linguistics to the materials of the freshman English course, presumably language and literature.

The authors do, however, discuss some possibilities, and make some suggestions. The topics include the assumptions the linguist makes about language and how these assumptions are sometimes misunderstood by the unsympathetic, the necessary modification of these assumptions in the classroom, and some possible applications of linguistics to the teaching

1

of composition and literature. The authors in this section make the first of many observations about dialect variety and the consequent implications for what should be accepted as correct English. The essays as a whole suggest that an elementary knowledge of modern linguistics provides an excellent tool for working on the infinitely more complex problems to be found in the study of composition and literature. One essay emphasizes the ways in which we learn.

What to assume, what to teach, when to teach it, and how to test what has been taught are not questions confined to the United States. One of the essays in this section first appeared in an English journal. The reader will see that the problems of teaching, of testing, and, in general, of saving the younger generation from illiteracy—and even worse—are much the same, not only in kind (which we have always known) but in degree.

J . J . L A M B E R T S

Basic concepts for teaching from structural linguistics

LINGUISTS MAKE A NUMBER OF ASSUMPTIONS about the nature of language, which, when presented as a simple list of items, are sometimes puzzling, irritating, and even misleading. As a result, linguists and non-linguists seem frequently not to conduct a dialogue, but to endure a series of soliloquies.

This article invites the resumption of a dialogue. Professor Lamberts first mentions a couple of misunderstandings about what it means to be a linguist, then elaborates on four linguistic assumptions with which most of us might be persuaded to agree:

1. Language is a form of human behavior; like family or religion, it is one of man's culture systems. This seems obvious enough once it is said, but it does give language a broader base than most of us ordinarily assume. We are likely to limit our view of language to that which is written or printed.

2. The rules of language may be found in a description of it. They are not and cannot be legislated.

3. The resultant description, if skillfully made, will be orderly and possibly comprehensive. All our work indicates that language, however arbitrary, is systematic.

4. Every language has, in some ways at least, a unique structure. In working with one language, one cannot without qualification use the categories which have been set up in another one.

These are the first items in what will become a long list of assumptions that should be made when approaching the study of language.

J. J. Lamberts is Professor of English at the Arizona State University.

For the past thirty years or more, teachers of English have been aware of the presence of a group of peculiarly articulate and often provokingly self-assured grammarians who call themselves structural linguists, or descriptive linguists, to use the currently fashionable term. Within the past ten years or so there has been a vast mushrooming in the number of articles undertaking to apply structural linguistics to the teaching of

"Basic Concepts for Teaching from Structural Linguistics": From *The English Journal*, vol. 49, n. 3, March 1960, pp. 172–176. Reprinted with the permission of The National Council of Teachers of English and J. J. Lamberts.

English. Once again one encounters the same self-assurance, coupled with the delicately veiled suggestion that the golden age of student writing will be ushered in whenever the "old outmoded grammar" gives up the ghost and yields place to its linguistic counterpart which is even now standing on the threshold. As a result, many teachers of English have become seriously concerned and most of them would undoubtedly be willing to give it a try if they only knew where to begin.

The reader of the NCTE [The National Council of Teachers of English] journals who has attempted to keep up with the articles on linguistics no longer blinks at terms like *morphemics* or *juncture* or *pitch contour*. Indeed he may have turned for enlightenment to books like Fries' *Structure of English* or Paul Roberts' *Patterns of English* only to run into still more cabalistic nomenclature, including terms like *determiner* or *Class I word*. The persistent reader discovers that a determiner can be a word like *a* or *an* or *the* and that a Class I word is pretty much the same as a noun. Logic leads him to assume that there really is no significant change: the game and the players are the same, they simply have different names. And thus, in order to be a linguist one uses the "scientific" terms like *determiner* and *Class I* instead of the "unscientific" expressions like *article* and *noun*.

Other readers have encountered linguistics within the area of usage. If such a teacher has given heed to what the linguists have been saying on the subject of language correctness, he must have perceived that linguists are most consistent in advocating a "liberal" usage over against an older puristic tradition. Cause and effect are easily confused at this point, and there are persons who have concluded that a *sine qua non* of being a linguist is an attitude of flagrant defiance toward the customary niceties of language. That is to say, if a person insists on *It's me* instead of *It's I*, he is somehow nearer to being a linguist than the other way around.

Both of these are disastrous misunderstandings of what it means to be a linguist. Yet both notions are surprisingly prevalent and they have wrought more mischief than a single brief paper can remedy. But we can make a beginning. And we can sketch a sounder picture of language by outlining a few of the fundamental concepts of structural linguistics. These are ideas which the teacher ought to comprehend for the reason that they deserve to be part of the intellectual furnishings of an educated person. We anticipate, of course, that our intelligent citizens will know something about nuclear physics and missilery as recent developments in significant areas of science. We should be troubled to discover high school and college teachers in the physical and chemical sciences referring to phlogiston or the indivisibility of matter. Similarly in the important area of communication, whether by the spoken or the written word, we feel justified in considering a certain minimal acquaintanceship with linguistic science to be essential, particularly to the teacher of English. This is not because it will make theme grading less difficult or because it will settle with absolute finality all problems of usage, but because the older concepts have become so hopelessly out of date.

LANGUAGE AS AN ASPECT OF BEHAVIOR

The first concept is this: Language is a form or type or aspect of human behavior. Language is something which human beings produce and which in turn characterizes them as people. It is, so to speak, one of our most human activities, if not the most human. It is also the most complex, because all other human activities are channelled through it, which is to say, we use language to discuss everything we do and everything we can do. This means that language is to be thought of in a far broader sense than as an arrangement of black marks on the pages of books, magazines, or newspapers about which unapproachably learned persons called grammarians have laid down immutable pronouncements. The real language consists of vocal sounds which people produce when they talk to one another. That is to say, human talk is the subject matter of linguistic science. One should not gather from this that linguists favor teaching public speaking rather than literature, but simply that we regard the spoken language as primary and the written as derived from the spoken. Before we know how people write we must know how they speak, rather than the converse of this. We are constantly confusing written and spoken English and in practice we commonly identify the two. An extreme of such confusion is the delusion that written English is the only variety which is worthy of our notice, while spoken English is simply a de-

basement which becomes more gross by the day. Over against this we encounter enthusiasts who suggest that speech is everything and that the values of literature can have no interest to the linguistic scientist. Both are false.

A second concept of structural linguistics is that language as a form of human behavior may be studied objectively. This is not an easy thing to do. As something "out there" it is capable not only of being observed, but of being described with great minuteness in wholly objective terms. By habit we become so involved in talking and listening that we find it impossible to segment the flow of speech into significant and meaningful components. Yet it is a basic concept and a primary requirement of linguistic procedure. This "out there" is what children undertake to mimic exactly when they learn to talk like us, and it is what foreigners imitate with varying degrees of success. The structural linguist has putatively drawn an empirical statement from hearing thousands of utterances of English speakers, but in practice he may be limited to examining a variety of the written language, realizing however the restrictions this imposes on him.

We must bear in mind that the linguist's product constitutes a *description* of the language. Our grammar books still commonly employ *prescriptions*. The descriptive statement is based on the data of the language itself; the prescriptive statement attempts to impose on the language an external authority, presumably higher than the usage of the speakers and writers of the language. Or to put it still another way, the linguist says, "This is what users of Standard English do when they speak and write," the implication being that anyone who would like to sound like a speaker of Standard English is invited to do likewise, to the extent of using these persons as models. The old-time prescriptivist simply says, "Here is your rule. Obey it."

ORDERLY DESCRIPTION
OF LANGUAGE

A third concept is this: From an objective examination of the language it is possible to derive a comprehensive description of that language and moreover a description that will be orderly. In other words, language is inherently systematic and it can be studied with reference to such a system. Here is the essence of structural linguistics, namely, that for any language there exists an orderly system which can be discovered by examining the language in accordance with certain procedures. Now there are several ways of conducting such an examination. First of all, we can explore the language as a whole in order to discover recurrent patterns of configurations. During the 1930's and 40's linguists made intensive examinations of particular aspects of English, and as a result we have in phonetics such a classic study as John S. Kenyon's *American Pronunciation,* side by side with another classic, this one in morphology, C. C. Fries' *American English Grammar.* Over and above these there were of course scores of articles in various periodicals inquiring into specific instances of such patterning. Somewhat later, actually not until the close of the 40's,

structural linguists moved to another stage. Instead of looking for patterns, which linguists by this time had come to take for granted, they began to concern themselves with taxonomy or the problem of systematically classifying the facts of language. In *An Outline of English Structure* by George L. Trager and Henry Lee Smith, Jr., we have a remarkable effort toward making a complete systematization of the sounds of English, that is to say, to "structure" this part of the language. Fries' *Structure of English* seeks to do much the same thing in still another area, namely, the morphology or grammar of the parts of speech. Like zoologists or botanists, structural linguists accept taxonomy as a matter of course. The concept that a system or orderly structure is a dominating consideration in the study of any language is now linguistic dogma. The question presently being considered is whether the structure may be imposed on the details of the language, or whether the structure ought to be represented by complex statements which will include a variety of data which are neither systematic or readily classifiable. In other words, should we seek a basically simple statement and list the exceptions as such, or should we try to account for the exceptions in the statement itself? Sledd's *A Short Introduction to English Grammar* is one of the few studies which tend to advance the latter interpretation. The first view is the one generally advocated and it promises to remain important in popular treatments of linguistic science and particularly in such teaching materials as are available.

A fourth concept is that each language has its own unique system or structure, the totality of such structural features being the grammar of the language. Without doubt all of us have learned an apparatus of terminology which was derived in a loose way from the structure of another language, that is, from Latin. Many of us have also been persuaded that we can take this apparatus and leap nimbly from one language to another since it embodies the categories of universal grammar. To be sure, there are striking similarities in languages like English and German and French and Spanish, but these are more realistically explained as the results of historical accident than as conformity to any universal grammar, Latin or otherwise. We have been accustomed to coasting along gaily on this grammar as far as it will carry us and then explaining away any residue as vernacular or slang or idiom or simply as ungrammatical. Actually, every language calls for an independent and unique description. One that fits English will not fit German and vice versa. This raises some problems. To give an illustration: by tradition we have regarded an adjective as a word that modifies a noun. This is true as far as it goes, but all words that modify nouns are not adjectives, a fact we recognize at once in an expression like *dog biscuit* or *bird seed* and particularly *road house* side by side with *big house*. Structural linguists explain that in English an adjective is a word that can be compared for degree, a definition based not on the meaning of the word but on its form or physical shape. Modification, as Fries points out, is a function; it is something an adjective can do. But nouns can modify and so can verbs and so can just about anything

else. What are we to do about the unsophisticated people who have been convinced that any word that modifies a noun must be an adjective? Would it be wise for their sakes to start over and to compose a vocabulary of brand new terms? This is a real problem for the linguists. Most of them are sure that we should lose more than we stand to gain, and consequently the recent books contain conventional terms like *noun* and *verb* and *adjective*. But the definitions have been radically changed. And we must not forget that beyond such basic terms there is a large area in which the linguists are still working and classifying, as a result of which terminology is still often disappointingly unsettled. Several times a year linguists get together in the hope of achieving a uniform set of terms, but so far their success has been limited.

The fact is that terminology is not an important consideration to the linguist. In the older grammar you had to know your cases so you could translate properly into Latin. What we regard as important is an understanding of the system or structure of English and of the manner in which this structure operates. Many of the constructions we customarily classify as "errors" and attribute to original sin or other basic human frailty are nothing more than situations in which the structure has been operating in conflict with certain social conventions. Linguists have commonly been more lenient toward these failings than the traditional grammarians because they have comprehended the difficulty of overcoming structure, and they have also sensed the possibility of producing side-effects which are worse than the original ailment.

WHY TEACH STRUCTURAL
LINGUISTICS?

Here in very brief compass are a few basic concepts which ought to be in the intellectual tool-kit of every teacher of English. Yet it is obvious that unless one has had some training in structural linguistics with the assistance of a competent linguist, such concepts of themselves tend to be somewhat meaningless. One does not become a structural linguist merely by assenting to these concepts or admitting that they may contain a reasonable amount of truth. What is possibly even more calamitous is the person who wants to follow the mode, thus to "teach a little linguistics," and who seeks to pour the new wine of structure into the old wine-skins of the conventional grammatical approach. One is either scientific or one is not. An Indian medicine man conducting a dance around a sick patient may slip him a few sulfa pills, but that does not make the dance any more scientific.

What we have tried to say is this: structural linguistics is more than another set of names for the parts of speech or another way of diagramming sentences. It is a completely different way of looking at language, of sorting out the data, of classifying the findings. The emphasis is on the procedure rather than the results; on the quest rather than the goal. This is why linguists still seem so unreasonably casual about seemingly vast discrepancies in nomenclature. They want to give the student a tool for looking at his language so he can do the exploring for himself.

It is possible that linguistic science will not do all of the wonderful things which some of its more exuberant advocates have promised. It may help the teacher approach with more certainty some of the problems in sentence construction and in usage, both in speaking and writing, but this is only a by-product.

The fact that English is our language and the fact that language is our most important day-to-day activity are adequate motives for studying it. The structural linguist takes it for granted that these are more than sufficient motives also for studying it scientifically.

For discussion

A. Lamberts begins by discussing two current misconceptions about linguistics. What are they?

B. What is the distinction made between *prescription* and *description* in grammar?

C. On p. 6 Lamberts writes, "[F]or any language there exists an orderly system which can be discovered by examining the language in accordance with certain procedures." What different procedures does he discuss?

D. How does each of the following illustrate one of Lamberts' points in the discussion of language as "a form or type or aspect of human behavior."?

1. Man has been talking for hundreds of thousands of years. He has been writing for about six thousand years.

2. "They read the book."

3. Language is not inherited. It must be acquired again by each generation.
4. "Do you smoak?"
5. The average college student is exposed to about three-quarters of a billion words a year.

E. Assuming the following bit of Latin is all the Latin that exists, answer the following questions:
   1. Does Latin have articles?
   2. Do noun modifiers come before or after the words they modify?
   3. How many words does Latin need to indicate the passive voice?
   4. How does the position of the verb differ from the normal position of the verb in English?
   5. How does Latin indicate *in* in the passage "in language, in customs, in law"?

Gallia	*est*	*omnis*	*dīvīsa*	*in*	*partēs*
Gaul	is	all	divided	into	parts

trēs	*quārum*	*ūnam*	*incolunt*	*Belgae*
three,	of which	one	inhabit	the Belgae,

aliam	*Aquitānia,*	*tertiam*	*quī*	*ipsōrum*
the other	the Aquitania,	the third	who	of themselves

linguā	*Celtae,*	*nostrā*	*Gallī*	*appelantur*
in the language	Celts,	in ours	Gauls	are called

Hī	*omnēs*	*linguā,*	*īnstitūtīs,*	*lēgibus*
These	all	in language,	in customs,	in laws

inter	*sē*	*differunt.*
among	themselves	differ.

F. Rewrite the passage in what you consider to be normal English word order.

W . F . T W A D D E L L

Meanings, habits and rules

BY CONTRASTING what gets attention when we use our own language and what gets attention when we learn a new one, W. F. Twaddell, Chairman of the Department of Linguistics at Brown University, emphasizes two things: the habitual nature of native language practice, and what he calls "real meaning." He thus helps us to recognize the difference between habit and choice.

In one sense we can say what we want, but in order to do so, we must conform to an elaborate set of ground rules in our language. We are not conscious of this, for language is a game we've been playing all our lives, and its rules are at the very least second nature to us; except for certain literary peculiarities, we don't devise our own grammatical system and lexicon. Normally, we are no more aware of deciding whether an adverb of place should come between subject and verb than we are of noticing that a magazine is bound on the left as we reach to pick it up. But we do make certain decisions, such as whether we like something or not. Naturally, no declarations of approval or disapproval come forth untended. There is the matter of degree, of elegance, of length, and much else; but we know the rules of our own language so well that much of what we say is said without our having made conscious choices.

When conscious choices are made, however, we get "real meaning." For example, I have ten books or I have ninety books. The difference is eighty books, but it's all one to the grammatical system.

Twaddell explains how this changes when we take up a new language. Aside from the obvious implications for foreign language teaching, we find in this discussion the first mention of cultural relativity.

We are analysts and teachers of that odd human practice known as language. Whether we are working with grammar or literature, we are working with and through language. It is our business whenever one human being affects another by disturbing the molecules of the air or defacing some surface with marks.

This business of ours puts us at the ringside of an intricate and fascinating social activity. Language is one of

"Meaning, Habits and Rules": Reprinted from the October, 1948, issue of *Education* by permission of the publishers, The Bobbs-Merrill Company, Inc., Indianapolis, Indiana. [This was] a talk given before the New England Modern Language Association on May 8, 1948, in Providence, Rhode Island.

the points of intersection in that network of habit and choice which is the pattern of our human doings. Nowhere, probably, do we human beings act with quite so intimate a fusing of habits and choices as when we talk and listen, write and read.

In a sense, we can say what we choose: we can talk about the weather, or Aunt Susie's operation, or the scandalous behavior of Mrs. Applethwacker, or little Oswald's last test, or—so it seems to us—we can talk about anything else. Within the limits of propriety and discretion and the patience of our listeners we have complete freedom of choice to talk about anything we please, and to say what we please about it. But if we're talking American English, we are absolutely certain to do that talking in certain sentence types, making certain kinds of noises and no others, using certain combinations of those noises and no others.

We may choose to call Mrs. Applethwacker a hussy; we cannot choose to call her a *hwày-rén.* If we were talking Mandarin Chinese, we could choose to call her a *hwày-rén,* but we should neither be tempted nor be able to call her a hussy. Nor can we choose to tell the world that "Mrs. Applethwacker a hussy is." Nor can we choose to call Mrs. A. a "hoozie" or a "hassy." In sum, we can say what we please, but we have to talk in a particular way. There is an element of choice in language which we call meaning: that is an expression of the individual personality. But there is also an element of compulsion in language: that is the habitual aspect, which is predictable, which is below and above the control of the individual; it is a rule of the language.

In the practical affairs of social life, this habitual aspect of language is as much a matter of course as the air we breathe. The native speakers of a language talk and write in accordance with the rules of their language simply because that's the way they talk and write. They don't choose or invent a structure of pronunciation because they want to sound musical; they don't choose or invent a grammatical system because they want to talk logically; they don't choose or invent a repertory of words.

By the time we have learned to talk English, we don't have to think about using different pronunciations of *t* in "tin" and "still"; we do it right, every time, without thinking about it. We don't have to remember to set subject before verb in the statement sentence; that's the only sequence in statement sentences. We don't have to recall that the English word for "house" is "house" rather than *maison* or *casa* or *jyā* or *dom.*

We don't for example, apply the rules describing adverbs between subject and verb: Certain general adverbs of time occur between subject and verb—"I usually take a bath on Saturday," "We never serve horseradish on ice cream," "He always blames somebody else"; but adverbs of place do not occur between subject and verb, and we don't say "I there had a good time," "We here will build a campfire," "He everywhere gets into trouble." This is a rather complicated rule of English grammar; speakers of English are largely unaware of it, but the English they speak is consistent in conforming to it.

When we talk or write a language which we command, and when we hear it or read it, we pay no attention to these habitual practices. They are habits; they are taken for granted; we have learned both to conform to them and to ignore them.

In our practical use of language, all our attention is focused on the factor of choice. We decide whether to say "yes" or "no"; we don't worry about a monophthong in one answer and a diphthong in the other. We decide to assert that Senator Jumbo is a windbag; we don't have to plan to use the third person singular verb "is" rather than "are." When we hear that our alma mater has defeated Slippery Rock Teachers' College in basketball, we don't reflect that subjects precede verbs and deduce from that analysis which team was victorious.

All these habitual aspects of English are below the level of attention. Whenever, for some reason, our attention is required by such matters— an unfamiliar pronunciation, an unaccustomed combination of grammatical elements—we are distracted and usually annoyed or contemptuous. Our concern normally is meaning and meaning is a function of choice. What we pay attention to in listening and reading is the meaning, the speaker's or writer's choice of things to say.

How disturbingly different our procedure has to be in learning a new language! Here, everything attracts our attention, aspects of habit as well as aspects of meaningful choice. Precisely because we don't know the language, we are unable to take its habitual aspects for granted. We have to learn to ignore that which is habit in the new language, just as its native speakers have had to learn to ignore it; and some day we will be able to ignore it. But our skill in using our own language blinds us to the large element of habit in it; the only things

we notice in our own language are the meanings, the acts of choice.

So, whatever we notice is a meaning for us. And in the new language we notice everything, the habitual aspects as well as the aspects of choice. We notice unfamiliar sounds, and unfamiliar sequences of sounds; so we conclude that the rate of speech is extremely rapid. After we have learned to identify some individual words, we notice that the order of words is different from the habitual order in English; so we are aware of it, and therefore react as though the word order of the new language were an expression of meaning, an act of choice of some kind. We find in the new language nouns with cases, where our habits are prepositions; we find tenses and moods of verbs, where we are in the habit of using auxiliaries.

We find new word habits: the speakers of the language do not have separate word habits to correspond to a distinction between "swim" and "float"; but they have two different habits to correspond to our "know." Most perplexing of all, we find that the users of another language are addicted to idioms of a strange and alarming sort, whereas we are in the habit of just letting ourselves go and coming through with whatever we want to put across.

All these features are habits for the native users of the language, and they are as unaware of their habits as we are of the phonetic and grammatical peculiarities of English which we practice with unconscious skill. But in a foreign language we notice them; and when we notice something in language we are conditioned to assume a meaning, an act of choice.

This is incorrect, of course. And we teachers of language have learned better. We know that a speaker of French doesn't use a certain verb because he has decided to select a third person plural imperfect; he uses the verb ending because that's what you use when you're saying that particular thing in French. But our students assume that the Frenchman uses it for the same reason that the student would use it in a translation exercise: because there's a rule that requires it. The student has to make an act of choice to decide what ending to use; so he assumes that the Frenchman has to go through the same soul-searching experience.

The learner, that is, is hypersensitive to the habitual aspects of a new language; he sees meanings and choices where for the native speaker there is no meaning or choice. For the naïve learner, the foreign language represents a much greater density of meanings than his own, for he notices both real choices and also the habitual features which do not involve choice. So far as the naïve learner is concerned, the speakers of all other languages perform prodigies of split-second choosings from among intricate arrays of grammatical forms, add them to items in the dictionary, and then put the products together according to various patterns of word order. The innocent freshman naturally regards this as a hard fate—and one that calls for an explanation.

Alas, we have given him the explanation. We have told the freshman why the unhappy speaker of French or Spanish or German or Tibetan has to go to all this cruel and unusual trouble in order to talk: It is because of the rules of his language. We know what these rules are. We know that a "rule" of a language is the analytical statement of one of the habitual

aspects of that language. We know that the habit is the reality and the rule is a mere summary of the habit. We know that the rule describes how people talk and not why they talk that way. But our students are not as sophisticated as we.

So far as they are concerned, they notice something. And when they notice something, they assume that the speaker or writer meant them to notice it. So they have to endow the grammatical habits of speakers of another language with some meaning. I dare say many students pity or despise the ancient Romans as people who had to be constantly on guard for or against the ablative absolute and the subjunctive; the French are people whose recollections of history are forever filtered through past definite and past indefinite; and the conversation of Germans is hampered by the necessity of deciding whether a clause is independent or subordinate, so as to know where to put the verb.

It is quite natural for our students to have these absurd ideas. Not because the students are stupid; I have tried to show that these absurd ideas are a logical consequence of a skill in speaking any language and ignorance of the processes of language. It would be pleasant, to be sure, if our students had learned something of the body of knowledge we call modern linguistics. But they are by and large as ignorant of modern linguistics as the sixteenth-century peasant was ignorant of the Copernican theory. We have to take our student as we find him; and we find him predisposed to think about language in terms of rules rather than habits.

This makes our job harder; there is no doubt of that. A good many students simply find that the rules don't interest them, and the only meaning they can see in a foreign language is the rather unprofitable meaning of the disjunctive pronoun and the subjunctive verb. Without that meaning they think they can live; and they do.

We know that they are mistaken in regarding these grammatical habits as meanings; but we can't convince them. We know that the rules are only temporary substitutes for habits, and the sooner a rule is forgotten because it is absorbed and dissolved in a habit, the better. We want the student to get to the point where he can forget the rule and take the habit for granted, and give all his attention to the real meanings, to the real choices. But this takes time and practice, more time and practice probably than an Olympian curriculum committee has allotted us.

The sad result is that many of our students spend most of their language study time in this chrysalis stage, when they can't distinguish between meanings and habits, when they are still noticing unfamiliar habits and accounting for them as "rules," when they have not yet learned to ignore the habitual aspects and focus on the real meanings. It is those real meanings that we aim at; and, with the aid of Heaven and a long spoon, some of our students do get to the desired stage. But many of them don't; for *them* the study of a language is largely a study of rules—and that means that these students are not able to pay attention to the real things that are said and written in the language.

This is too bad, no doubt about it. We certainly prefer a student who can read a book to one who can only conjugate verbs. But we know that until he can take verb forms for granted he can't read the book and concentrate on the real meanings in it. This, of course, is the reason we spend so much time on the habitual aspects of a language: as a preliminary conditioning, to create the habit, so as the liberate the attention for the meaningful aspects of speech and writing.

Must we then resign ourselves to working with many students who will never emerge from this preliminary phase? Of course we must, just as all teachers must. The teacher of mathematics knows that most of his students will never read a mathematical treatise after the final examination. The teacher of chemistry knows that most of his charges will never perform any experiment more intricate than mixing a cocktail. The teacher of the social studies knows that most of his students will get their data from the radio, the newspaper, and gossip.

But the fact that these students do not reach the most productive, the most rewarding phase of their various studies does not mean that those studies are wasted. All those studies leave their residues in the little gray cells, and the world has more orderliness, more of the world is in the domain of the comprehensible, more of the actions of people are explicit and describable. Less of the world is irrationally magical, less of society is overlooked or attributed to individual caprice. The pupil product of even the preliminary phases is aware rather than stolid, rather more calculating and rather less excitable.

Just so, the preliminary phase of

language study, the "mere rules" phase, has a value in itself. That value may not be as great as the experience of communion with Racine, or Cervantes, or Goethe, or Lucretius, but it is still a value.

It is, among other things, the value of seeing the difference between a single language and universal reality. The price we pay for our prodigious skill in speaking our native language is what we do many things unconsciously. Those aspects of our language which are habitual are beneath our attention; they are wholly a matter of course, and it is always dangerous for anything human to be wholly a matter of course. English grammar is our way of talking, and our naïve students cannot help believing that it is *the* natural way of talking. An acquaintance with some other way of talking is salutary—solely because it is another way of talking.

Our students of course take the difference between "one" and "more than one" quite seriously; all their grammatical habits are enforcing the distinction between singular and plural, hundreds of times every day— and they don't know it. But only a minority of the human beings now talking are so channeled by their grammars; for many people, many millions of people, the distinction between "older" and "younger" is dinned into them oftener than a distinction between "one" and "more than one." Our students partition the flow of time in a certain way, because our grammar does—and they don't know it. A different partition of time by a different grammar is salutary.

These particular details are relatively unimportant, probably, but it is not unimportant that all of our habits of talking are only one of many possible sets of habits.

The rules of grammar, as the student suspects, do have a meaning. But they are not mere un-American perversities. They are indexes of non-American habits. And if there is any one thing which Americans in the second half of the twentieth century will need to recognize, it is precisely that there are *non-American habits* which are *not anti-American choices.* If we must use the jargon of the school catalogue, grammatical rules are a segment of social anthropology. Grammatical rules are our summary of a community behavior of societies; they are not the expression of the wisdom of academies, nor are they built into the structure of the universe, nor even into human nature, if there is such a thing.

Grammatical rules are likely to be the student's first introduction to cultural relativity. They should be taught as such. To be sure, the other West European languages are not ideal for this purpose; Cantonese Chinese or Eskimo would be better. But we are not only social anthropologists, we are also humanists and historians (and participants in West European culture). So we must compromise between the values of cultural relativity and the—for us—absolute values of Hebraeo-Graeco-Roman-Mediterranean-Northwest European-British-American cultural traditions.

Those cultural traditions, in the widest sense, are our major goals. The students for whom we can make those traditions accessible are the students with whom we have succeeded, just as the teacher of physics has succeeded with a student who subscribes to and reads the *Journal of the American Physical Society*. But we also have succeeded with the student who becomes in some degree more aware of how language works. In however modest degree, if one of our students begins to be aware of the habitual aspects of language, and draws some of the obvious conclusions, we have been socially useful.

For we are, I repeat, at the ringside of an intricate and fascinating social activity. Language is one of the points of intersection in that network of habit and choice which is the pattern of our human doings. Nowhere, probably, do we human beings act with quite so intimate a fusing of habits and choices as when we talk and listen, write and read.

He is a better human being who knows the difference between habit and choice. We teachers of language can probably be a bit more explicit in pointing out to our students what is so obvious to us along these lines. The study of the human activity of language can be made a constant reminder that we act as we do because we are at one and the same time members of the human race, members of a community, and individuals.

The range of possible noises that homo loquens[1] can produce is ultimately conditioned by the structure of the human vocal apparatus and hearing apparatus. Within these physiological limitations, the usage of a community imposes further restrictions: each language, each dialect has its phonemic structure, and only what is within that structure is possible for the speakers and listeners of the language or dialect. And, within the limits of structure imposed by the community, the individual speaker makes his choices. He who speaks and writes lives his social life along the network of his community's habits and his own choices among those habits. He sees his choices as free and he ignores the limitations. The beginning learner of a language sees that the choices are not free, and that is worth seeing. The advanced learner of a language comes to ignore the limitations and moves about among them comfortably, so that the real choices become the only choices he sees. And that is a skill of great value.

Meaning is our destination; the way to it, through rules, is a journey with its own rewards.

[1] "Speaking man."

For discussion

A. What does Twaddell mean by rules?

B. Normally the possible conflict between semantic and grammatical categories does not even come to our attention. This is just as well. We have "run fast" and "stand fast," and "burn up" and "burn down." Give five more examples of such pairs of possible contradictions.

C. Does Twaddell's description of what happens when you study a foreign language correspond with your own experience? Can you give a specific illustration?

D. Twaddell really brings grammar into the sphere of cultural anthropology. What are some of the implications of his statement that the rules of grammar in a foreign language "are indexes of non-American habits"?

E. Why do we think the rate of speech is rapid in other languages?

F. What does Twaddell consider to be the value of the "mere rules" phase in language learning?

ALBERT H. MARCKWARDT

Linguistics and English composition

LIKE MOST OF THE OTHER WRITERS in this book, Professor Marckwardt believes that a study of language is justified in its own right, whether it helps one's writing or not. Language is part of our cultural inheritance, and its structure may well control our way of conceptualizing the universe. Its study, then, is certainly proper in general education. He then warns of the dangers of misunderstanding some of the assumptions that the linguist makes.

Marckwardt makes it clear that in spite of a good deal of talk, until very recently, little had been done about practical applications of linguistics to one's native language, especially in achieving greater skill in the use of written language. He then suggests a striking number of possibilities, including some investigations into the relation between written and spoken English. His discussion, as did Twaddell's, uses a number of the findings of cultural anthropology.

Professor Marckwardt is now at Princeton University. He taught for many years at the University of Michigan.

From the very beginning of what might be called its modern period, the science of linguistics has been considered capable of practical application. In the foreword to the very first issue of the journal *Language,* Leonard Bloomfield asserted, that because of their ignorance of the real structure of language, teachers were wasting the time of their pupils and attaining poor results, and the last chapter of his own book, *Language,* bears the title "Applications and Outlook." Fries likewise concluded his

Structure of English with a discussion of practical application, suggesting that, "from . . . a descriptive display of the resources of the language," one might "provide the exercises, the actual activities by which a native speaker of English can develop a greater and greater control of these resources to the full."

Thus far, for reasons that need not be treated in detail here, the practical application of linguistics has been developed most fully in connection with the teaching of English as a sec-

"Linguistics and English Composition": From *Language Learning,* Special Issue, March 1961, pp. 15–23. Reprinted with the permission of the publisher, The Research Club in Language Learning of the University of Michigan.

ond language. About on a par with it is the employment of linguistic principles in the teaching of what have been variously termed the esoteric, the unusual, or the funny languages, by which we generally mean those which are non-Indo-European in structure. In two other areas the ground has scarcely been broken, even after thirty-five years: these are the teaching of the common foreign languages and the teaching of English as a native language.

Despite this rather pessimistic assessment of the current situation with respect to teaching the native language, it must be admitted that the last six or seven years have at least witnessed the appearance of a number of textbooks, the best known of which is Paul Roberts' *Patterns of English,* originally intended for secondary-school use. Moreover, meetings of the National Council of Teachers of English have featured some teaching demonstrations of a linguistic approach to English structure, and the Committee on College Composition and Communication meetings over the past several years have often had two concurrent discussion sessions or workshops on linguistics and its application.

Nevertheless, one has only to read the February, 1960 issue of *College English* for a disheartening demonstration of how little real understanding we have achieved. The articles by John C. Sherwood and A. M. Tibbetts reveal not only an emotional bias but a host of mistaken and ill-digested notions. Yet, a thoughtful consideration of these and similar displays of disbelief and dismay can be of value to us in pointing out both that which we must do more effectively than we have been doing, and that which has not been done at all.

Certainly, one place where we have failed almost completely is in securing an understanding of why the linguist gives his primary attention to the spoken form of the language. In part this has resulted from a misinterpretation of our use of the terms *primary* and *primacy*. We have been understood to mean that in our view, the spoken language is the only variety that merits any attention at all, either from the point of view of analysis or teaching. We have failed to convince our skeptical audiences of our belief that it is the spoken language which must be studied and described first so that the written language may be dealt with in terms of its deviations from the spoken pattern.

Not infrequently the logic of the opposition threads a tortuous path something like the following: the linguist's primary interest is the spoken language. As a consequence he is not concerned with the written language. The bulk of all literature finds expression in the written language. Therefore the linguist cannot be interested in literature. Moreover, literature is one of the humanistic studies. Since the linguist is not concerned with literature, he is of necessity anti-humanistic. And since he is anti-humanistic, he must also be anti-intellectual.

Fantastic as this may sound, I have not made it up out of whole cloth. This is actually a capsule account of a day's discussion on the part of the chairmen of the departments of certain of the modern languages in the various Big Ten universities, and I rehearse it here only to show how far short we have fallen from making a convincing case for a painstaking descriptive analysis of the spoken language.

For teachers of English the problem is further complicated by the fact that over the years there has been a decided shift in classroom emphasis from a highly formal style of writing to one decidedly less rigid and stylized. According to one current textbook, "Semiformal English is the language you will use for most of your college writing." Undoubtedly to many English instructors, who temperamentally enjoy fearing the worst, this seems like the first step down a perilous and giddy slide toward laxity and incoherence; to such persons the linguist's concern with the spoken language is a clear indication of a covenant with the Tempter.

Certainly, then, a clarification of the linguist's method in terms of his proper initial concern with the spoken language is basic to everything else that we want to accomplish, and obviously it must be done more cogently and more persuasively than it has been up to now. The outline of such an explanation need not be given here. We are all familiar with the arguments; what we need to do is to learn how to make them convincing to others.

It is by no means enough, however, for us to protest that we are not without interest in the structure of the written language. This must be demonstrated as well by studies which are calculated to show the structural differences between it and spoken English. We need to clarify the relationship between punctuation and the suprasegmentals.[2] Data on the

relative incidence of simple, compound, and complex sentence types in spoken and written English should be collected. The same would apply to appositive constructions. Comparative studies of the position of modifying elements, particularly adverbs, adverbial phrases, and subordinate clauses, should be undertaken. We also need to know how these two varieties of the language handle parenthetic expressions of various kinds. These are only a few of the worthwhile research topics on which we have as yet very little information. Henry Bradley barely began a treatment of this subject about forty years ago, and no one has really followed it up in a systematic fashion.[3]

The answers to the questions I have posed would have a dual utility. In the first place they would show what structural devices must be employed in writing as compensation for the lack of a systematic notation of stress, intonation, and juncture—to say nothing of a number of metalinguistic features. In addition, they would serve to suggest something of the stylistic potential of the written language. If information of this nature were to be considered along with data on the development of the student's ability to employ constantly expanding structural patterns, we would be much closer than we now are to the establishment of a pedagogical strategy.

This suggests another matter concerning which we have not been wholly convincing to our non-lin-

[2] See the introduction to George Faust's article, "Terms in Phonemics," p. 167.

[3] Dr. Henry Bradley (1845–1923) was, from 1915 until his death, the Senior Editor of the *Oxford English Dictionary*. The work referred to is *On the Relations between Spoken and Written Language, with Special Reference to English* (Oxford, 1919). It was originally a British Academy Lecture (1913).

guistic colleagues, namely the point at which, in the linguistic development of the individual, mastery of the language may be said to occur. The following quotation from Charles Hockett's *A Course in Modern Linguistics* (p. 360) is fairly typical of the kind of assertion made by many linguists. "By the age of four to six, the normal child is a *linguistic adult.* He controls, with marginal exceptions if any, the phonemic system of the language; he handles effortlessly the grammatical core; he knows and uses the basic contentive vocabulary of the language."

True enough, Hockett does go on to say that, "he may get tangled in trying to produce longer discourses, as in describing the activities of a morning at school, but clarity in extended exposition is a point on which older people also vary greatly." Hockett may well be correct in this, but clarity in extended exposition happens to be the principal aim of most composition teaching, and in the light of this, the linguist's claim that a child of six has a grasp of all the fundamental language patterns is quite beside the point as far as the teacher of composition is concerned.

Actually, I believe that insufficient consideration has been given to this whole matter. What, precisely, do we mean by a control of the fundamental language patterns? Undoubtedly the child of six has mastered most of the inflections. The chief exceptions will be some of the irregular verbs and possibly a few nouns of foreign origin. Moreover, we can assume that subject-verb-object and adjective-noun sequences are well established, and that simple adverbial placement will pose no problems. But this is by no

means the extent of the student's potential, even if we limit ourselves to the simple utterance. We need to know, therefore, much more than we do about the child's linguistic development after the age of six. For example, is there a clearly marked stage when the child frequently uses compound sentences prior to his mastery of patterns of subordination? In what constructions do students at various age levels use relative pronouns? When does apposition emerge as a structural device? If the linguist continues to insist that the kindergartner's achievement constitutes mastery of the fundamental language patterns, what the composition teacher will want to know is how these patterns are developed and expanded. And surely this is capable of linguistic description.

As we are all aware, there are some classic studies of the development of language in children, particularly those by Piaget, Grégoire, and the Sterns. These works contain a wealth of first-hand data but were written at a time prior to the development of what we regard today as acceptable techniques for describing linguistic structures. It would be illuminating, at the very least, to make an attempt to re-interpret these studies in the light of both present-day linguistics and modern psychological learning theory.

Recently some interesting research dealing with the development of language in the individual has been undertaken. Jean Berko has published in *Word* an account of the way in which English-speaking children learn to manipulate the morpho-phonemic variations in noun plurals and other English forms which take a so-called

-s inflection. Henry and Renée Kahane, in collaboration with Sol Saporta, have in effect carried out on a limited scale the suggestion that existing case studies of linguistic growth be re-interpreted structurally. Working with some of the materials that were mentioned earlier—the studies by Grégoire, the Sterns, etc.,— they have attempted to demonstrate the development of verbal categories in child language, arriving at the stage where contrasts in meaning are correlated with contrasts in form.[4]

Though as yet few in number, these are unquestionably important steps in the right direction. They must be increased in scope, so as to include all of the operational mechanisms of the language, and in range to cover at least the early adolescent years.

There is perhaps one other point of view from which the language-learning process needs careful study, namely in terms of its relationship to the learning of other culture patterns or systematized modes of behavior. In his challenging book, *The Silent Language,* Edward T. Hall repeats a differentiation that he has made elsewhere, namely the recogni-

tion of informal, formal, and technical learning as ways in which the individual absorbs different portions of the cultural heritage. Those forms of behavior which are acquired through sheer imitation of either elders or peers are said to be the result of informal learning. Whole clusters of related activities are learned at a time, in many cases without the knowledge that they are being learned at all or that there are patterns or rules governing them. In this way entire systems of behavior made up of hundreds of thousands of details are passed from generation to generation. The bright lower or middle class English youth who by dint of native ability and application wins a scholarship at one of the first-class public schools learns upper-class English from his classmates simply by the force of social pressure. He doesn't get it from his English master—at least not to any appreciable degree. This is informal learning.

Formal learning consists of that which is taught by precept and admonition. The adult mentor molds the young according to patterns he himself has never questioned. The burden of such teaching is that no other behavior is conceivably acceptable. In it, purposeful drill and repetition play an important part, but there is a conspicuous absence of any reasoned explanation. For most children, learning the catechism or any of the church services would be formal learning. So, too, would be the mastery of the multiplication tables. Many American children learn to master the strong verb forms through formal learning—at any rate those who hail from environments where such items are not in habitual use.

---

[4] Since the original publication of this article, much has been accomplished in the study of language acquisition. See George A. Miller's "The Psycholinguists: On the New Scientists of Language," the final article in this collection. Discussion, bibliography, and synthesis are provided by A. Richard Diebold Jr.'s "A Survey of Psycholinguistic Research" (1954–1964) in *Psycholinguistics: A Survey of Theory and Research Problems* (University of Indiana Press, 1965), edited by Charles E. Osgood and Thomas A. Sebeok. Diebold's survey is based on his earlier study, a review article (*Language,* vol. XL, n. 3, 1964, pp. 197–260) of *Psycholinguistics: A Book of Readings* (Holt, Rinehart, and Winston, 1961), edited by Sol Saporta with the assistance of Jarvis R. Bastian.

Ring Lardner's engaging character who regularly said, "Whom are you?" because he had attended night school is a striking example, but by no means the only one, of misdirected formal learning.

When the attempt to establish changed behavior is systematically placed in an intellectual context, the learning is technical. The person who attempts to improve his game of bridge with Goren in his lap and a bridge wheel on the table in front of him is engaging in technical learning. So is the language student who selects grammatical forms on the basis of paradigms and rules of syntax which he has mastered. The technology may be faulty, but that does not alter the case. The English-speaking child who avoids multiple negation because he has been taught that two negatives make a positive and are therefore incorrect is employing technical learning even though the particular rationalization is sheer nonsense.

It is a reasonable assumption, I believe, that each of these types has its place and function in the native language-learning process, that each is effective in some situations and futile in others. Would it not be desirable, therefore, to review the entire language-learning process of the American child, both in his home and his school experience in terms of these three kinds of learning activities? Nor can we expect to arrive at the same answer or set of answers equally applicable to all American children, for socio-economic and cultural factors will make for conspicuous variations.

It would be ideal, I suppose, if as much of the job as possible might be accomplished through informal learn-ing. I have already suggested that that is virtually what happens to the upper-class British child who goes to a well-established public school—that is public in the British sense. Such a child may require technical assistance at the time that he must learn to manipulate the written language in such a way as will enable him to express complex ideas and logical relationships, but beyond that, I am inclined to believe that his mode of learning is primarily informal. This might be equally true for a small minority of American children, and surely the percentage should increase generation by generation. The point at which we get into difficulty in this country is when the informal learning results in something other than the forms and usages of Standard English.

When this is the case, what has been characterized by Hall as formal learning would seem to be part of the answer. Certainly our first recourse would be drill on accepted or standard forms in an attempt to eliminate the unacceptable. In this connection, however, we need to remember several things. A vast amount of drill, along with systematic reinforcement, is required to fix the proper form as an instantaneous reaction, since we are in actuality seeking to replace one habitual response with another. In order to be successful, this requires a heavy concentration upon a small number of items at any one time, for certainly the number of forms or constructions which can be successfully altered in this manner is definitely limited in number. Moreover, if this is to be our procedure, the items to be attacked must be selected carefully and intelligently, with due regard for differences in regional standards. We must also be certain that what we choose belongs in a rigidly minimal program; we cannot afford to permit the petty and inconsequential linguistic prejudices held by one person or another to detract us from our major objective. It may well be that this is a point where some adaptation of the Skinner box[5] or teaching machine is capable of considerable assistance, inasmuch as it would permit each student to proceed at his own pace and would free the teacher for other activities.

It is probably in the expansion of language patterns rather than in the fixation of language forms that technical learning can play its most helpful role, both in warning the student of the dangers involved in inadequately controlled expression and in making him aware of resources and potentialities of the language, about which he might otherwise remain innocent. In short, what I am hinting at here is both a negative and a positive role for a soundly based knowledge of language structure.

The negative role consists, in considerable part at least, in the avoidance of structural ambiguities. It will be recalled that quite regularly throughout his *Structure of English,* Fries points to syntactic situations where the grammatical meaning is vague and unclear because of the lack of unambiguous formal markers. Following his lead, Norman C. Stageberg, in an article in the November, 1958, issue of *The English Journal* recognized some twenty constructions or construction types which he considered responsible for most of

5 A laboratory apparatus in which an animal is caged for experiments in operational conditioning.

the ambiguity in student writing. Although his treatment leaves something to be desired, both in the way of classification and in taking into account the differences between the spoken and the written language, nevertheless this is a move in the proper direction, and it is one which clearly involves what I have called technical learning.

Positively, most of us would like our students to achieve in their writing a greater degree of dexterity in the manipulation of the structural patterns of the language than is usual with them. In order to accomplish this, we must teach them the patterns as patterns first of all, and then the ways in which they may be expanded. Both the Lloyd and Warfel text, *American English in Its Cultural Setting* and Roberts' *Patterns of English* do this to a considerable extent, employing diagrams and formulas effectively to this end. Following some hints in Lloyd and Warfel, Sister Mary Aquin, writing in the February, 1960 issue of *College Composition and Communication* demonstrates a step-by-step procedure for expanding one of the basic patterns. Moreover, she then goes on to apply the same pattern expansion technique to the paragraph and to the whole theme as well. Although tactics other than those suggested in the article may come to mind quite readily, I believe that her strategy is essentially correct and that this is the way to get students to use the language more effectively. But our success here will depend upon an accurate and a skillful presentation of the basic language patterns.

This, however, raises the question, at what point in the student's education is this to be done. We have been unwise, I believe, in deferring a linguistically oriented approach to the language until either the freshman year in college or at the earliest the concluding years of the secondary school. In doing so we are forced to correct many of the notions and to revise the definitions that the student has already learned; in short, to alter radically his entire concept of language. It would be far preferable, I believe, to begin either at the end of the elementary school or the beginning of the junior high school, and to focus first on the behavior of the spoken language, possibly with such suprasegmental features as intonation patterns and accompanying terminal junctures—in short to demonstrate how sentences work and what their basic patterns are. Lest there be misunderstanding of my meaning here, let me say flatly that I am not recommending that we teach him the terminology of structural linguistics; I am recommending that we teach him a recognition of language structure. Definitions should be formally based, but I include here position in the sentence as well as liability to inflectional ending. The initial procedure should be largely inductive, but pattern drill should be employed, both as a means for assuring the recognition of and for expanding the basic patterns.

One advantage of beginning at this point lies in the circumstance that, according to my observation at least, the child is still writing pretty much as he speaks or else is just at the point of developing some differentiation between the written and the spoken language. This makes it possible, therefore, for the presentation of

structure to keep pace with the pupil's unfolding virtuosity and to develop within him a consciousness of what he is doing when he writes.

In this connection we need to study more carefully than we have the relationship between punctuation and the suprasegmentals in order to improve our presentation of the whole process of pointing, recognizing where correspondences exist and where they do not. A better understanding of morphemics would also enable us to present the whole matter of prefixes and suffixes as a means of promoting vocabulary growth. Phonemics and graphemics[6] provide us with the necessary roots for improving spelling. In short, the possibilities are almost unlimited, but I am convinced that in this, as in such subjects as physics and mathematics, the text or the presentation I am proposing here is a matter for group rather than individual endeavor. Recent educational history has furnished us with several striking examples of cooperative textbooks designed to break new ground in the presentation of a subject.

There is finally one other matter which must be dealt with briefly before I conclude: that is the study of language as a subject in its own right. The entire discussion thus far has been given over to the study and presentation of a sound language analysis as a means of enabling the

6 Since we frequently have a number of different spellings for the same sound (care*ful*, casu*al*, batt*le*, jonqu*il*) or a number of different sounds for the same spelling (ma*r*ine, f*i*t, eas*i*ly), the study of spelling in English should give special attention to the relationship between the sounds (the phonemes) and the written representation of these sounds (the graphemes). See Sir Archibald Sluter's "English Spelling" (p. 217).

student to achieve greater skill in his usage of language. Certainly this is one of the most important aims of elementary and secondary education, one which is not only characterized by social utility but is demanded by social necessity.

Yet, looked at from another point of view, language is possibly the most remarkable of all human achievements and an indispensable social tool. Its structure is the key of our classification and categorization of human experience, and as such reflects our entire Weltanschauung. In the light of all this, I fail to see how a competent understanding of the nature and structure of language can be excluded from our concept of general education. Indeed it is a basic element in it, vitally necessary for developing the breadth of vision and sensitivity of perception that will be demanded of the coming generation, if it is to meet successfully the manifold problems and situations that an evermore complex world will present.

For discussion

A. What does Marckwardt fear will result from the misunderstanding about why the linguist gives primary attention to the spoken language?

B. How might Lamberts explain why the linguist gives primary attention to the spoken language?

C. What are Marckwardt's doubts about the statement that a child of six controls the grammar of his language?

D. What does Marckwardt suggest would be the utility of the various studies he would make concerning the relationship between written and spoken English?

E. What part of your own acquisition of the mastery of English would you consider a part of informal learning? of formal learning?

F. Is Twaddell's discussion of the way we begin to learn a foreign language a description of informal, of formal, or of technical learning?

G. What does Marckwardt mean in saying that a soundly based knowledge of language structure has "both a negative and a positive role"?

H. At what point in the educational system would Marckwardt introduce a linguistically oriented approach to the study of language?

I. Marckwardt would not teach the terminology of linguistics, but he would use definitions of the parts of speech. Upon what would he base these definitions?

PAUL ROBERTS

The relation of linguistics to the teaching of English

PAUL ROBERTS HERE CONSIDERS the differences between linguistic grammar and traditional grammar, linguistic views on correctness, and the application of linguistics to the teaching of English. The process includes a summary of much that has been said in earlier essays and a number of fresh suggestions. He finds about as much to object to in definitions that are based upon a filled-in blank in a diagnostic frame (*The _____ man was very _____*) or upon inflectional characteristics (*fine, finer, finest*), as in the notional and functional definitions of traditional grammar. He makes the interesting suggestion that we replace our present definitions—but replace them with nothing. He also suggests that the contribution of linguistics to the study of English will not be a method, or a terminology, or even an attitude, but, rather, it will be a subject matter.

Paul Roberts, for many years Professor of English at San Jose State College, and more recently at Cornell University, is the author of *The Roberts English Series*, a set of texts for use in the elementary and junior high schools.

It is probably fair to say that linguistics is the hottest topic on the English teacher's agenda at the present time. It is the one topic almost certain to be on the program wherever English teachers come together, and articles on the subject claim an increasing share of the space in our professional journals. Linguistics is hot also in the sense that it gives off heat. Views tend to be extreme and to be extremely held. From one side we gather that linguistics is about to clear away all the problems of teaching English, to show us delightfully simple ways of bestowing literacy on the illiterate; from the other it is disclosed that linguists are satanically in alliance with progressive educationists bent on the destruction of humanism and the corruption of the youth. Whichever side you are on, it is perfectly clear to you that holders of opposing views are willful idiots and probably venal to boot.

The worst possible position to occupy in this struggle is that of the wise moderate, skillfully mediating be-

"The Relation of Linguistics to the Teaching of English": From *College English,* vol. 22, n. 1, October 1960, pp. 1–9. Reprinted with the permission of The National Council of Teachers of English and Paul Roberts.

tween the extremists. Such a person is certain to get clubbed mercilessly from all directions and is likely to end screaming louder than anybody. I have no intention of falling into this snare. Forsaking, if necessary, any claims to either wisdom or moderation, I must ally myself with the linguists and say that I think they have much the better of the argument—that, indeed, I can see no real argument against them. But I take this position at some cost. I have no natural bent for controversy and take no pleasure in being the object of attack either in school board meetings or in the pages of *College English*. I could wish for a cooling off, based on a greater measure of understanding than has so far been obtained.

Whether any great measure of understanding is actually obtainable seems sometimes doubtful. It may be that ultimately the differences are temperamental rather that rational, that those whose major professional commitment is esthetic can find no common ground with those whose commitment is scientific. Perhaps what is required for a lying down together of traditionalists and linguists is nothing less than the long-sought rapprochement of the humanities and the sciences, and this may be altogether beyond our powers. Still I cannot give up hope of persuading my colleagues in the humanities that linguists, though working in a different direction, may yet be friends to their ground and liegemen to the Dane.

It seems to me that the major points at issue may be indicated in a series of three questions:

1. What essentially are the differences between linguistic grammar (or whatever you call it) and traditional grammar (or whatever you call *that*)?

2. What is the linguistic view on correctness?

3. What exactly is the application of linguistics, supposing its views to prevail, to the teaching of English?

It is easy to exaggerate the weakness of traditional grammar and the superiority of linguistic grammar, as it is easy to exaggerate the differences between them. They are similar in the important sense that they come out with by and large similar answers. A traditionalist can tell an English verb or an indefinite relative clause when he sees one just as well as a linguist can. They may have different names for these categories, but surely we can agree that differences in terminology are trivial differences.

What is not trivial, however, is the framework in which the concepts are described and discussed. It has been traditional practice to describe such concepts as *noun, verb, subject, sentence* with what are called notional definitions—i.e., definitions based on the supposed meaning of the classes. These definitions have certain weaknesses. For one thing, they are invulnerable statements: one can never conclude an argument about their truth or falsity, and arguers must end by simply stamping their feet. It may be true that sentences are groups of words expressing complete thoughts, as it may be true that angels are incorporeal beings, but such statements can be pursued only to tautology: what is a complete thought?—that which a sentence expresses; what is an incorporeal being?—an angel.

What can, I think, be demonstrated is that such definitions are altogether unusable and that in fact nobody ever uses them. No one can learn the definition "a sentence is a group of words expressing a complete thought" and then use that as a criterion to sort out sentences from non-sentences in some particular language. Anyone who tried to apply it seriously would find himself instantly in serious perplexity. For instance, in what sense is the first sentence of this paragraph a complete thought? It could certainly not stand alone, since the word *such* necessarily implies a preceding statement. If we were to take this definition seriously, we would have to conclude that the sentences of a paragraph have no relation to one another and that there is no connection between paragraphs.

Similarly, no one can actually apply such a definition as "a verb is a word that expresses action." If he did, he would have to list as verbs such English words as *arrival, operation, action*. There must be some sense in which the word *action* expresses action. We do not count these words as verbs, not because they do not express action, but because they do not occur in what we recognize (somehow or other) as verb structures: we do not say "He will arrival," "They were afraid to operation," "I actioned."

Such traditional definitions as are not notional are relational, and these lead to another difficulty, that of mixing hierarchies in the analysis. *Adjective* and *adverb*, for example, are defined relationally, in terms of what is modified: an adjective is a word that modifies a noun. This leads us to conclude that "dirty sink" and "kitchen sink" are identical structures, each consisting of a noun modified by an adjective. But our intuition tells us that they are in some way different, that *dirty* is somehow a dif-

ferent kind of word from *kitchen*. If we were given a third structure, say "empty sink," we would I suppose not hesitate to say that it is more like "dirty sink" than like "kitchen sink." The traditional definition of adjective—anything that modifies a noun—simply buries and conceals a large and important part of English expression, throwing together such quite different structures as "our sink," "dirty sink," "kitchen sink," "leaking sink," "scrubbing sink," "repaired sink," "sink upstairs." All are different, and the difference is that in each case the modifying word belongs to a different class or subclass. I am aware that traditional grammarians can perceive and express such differences, using such terms as "limiting adjective," "descriptive adjective," "participle," "gerund," but they can do so only clumsily and with clear contradiction of earlier statements.

The basic fallacy here is a mixing of levels of description. English structures can be analyzed on the word–class level into such categories as *noun, verb, adjective*. They can also be analyzed on a relational level into such categories as *modifier of a noun, modifier of a verb, subject, object*. Both classifications are logical and both are necessary to a description of English syntax. But to mix them is like sorting the students of a college into the categories *men, women,* and *commuters*. To ask, in the traditional framework, whether *kitchen* in "kitchen sink" is a noun or an adjective is like asking whether John Jones is a man or a commuter.

To point out the weakness of traditional definitions is to invite the question—with what do you propose to replace them? The answer to this is—nothing. We must, I think, give up hope of finding definitions for such concepts as *noun, adjective, subject, sentence* which are both short and operable, which can actually be used to sort out the members of the categories. It is not hard to frame rational definitions for these concepts. A modern dictionary, for example, will give for *sentence* some such definition as this: "A structure in a language which is not shown by some grammatical feature to be a part of a larger structure." But this of course is not applicable as a criterion until we outline the grammatical features which do or do not make a structure part of another structure. To make the definition operable, we should have to describe such features as subject and predicate, modification, subordination, conjunction, transformation. In other words, we cannot really define the concept "sentence in English" short of describing English grammar.

Linguists have not, I fear, always been clear on this point. We have sometimes talked as if we had, or were on the point of getting, short and usable tests for determining whether items belong to one category or another. Thus we say "a noun is a word than can fill the blank in 'The _____ was interesting.' " Or "a noun is a word that forms a plural." But as definitions such statements fail in both directions. It is true that any item, any noise, that occurs in the blank in "The _____ was interesting" will be construed as a noun. But there may be nouns that do not occur there (some things may not be interesting) and there are many other positions in which nouns occur.

Definitions based on morphology—

inflectional endings and the like—seem to me to lead to error. If *noun* is defined as "any word that forms a plural," then *chaos* cannot count as a noun. This would appear to go contrary to our intuition as speakers of English. Adjectives have sometimes been defined as words that add the endings /-er/ and /-est/, as *small, smaller, smallest*. This also fails in both directions. It has been pointed out that if we were to apply it literally we would have to take *tear* as an adjective: *tear, terror, terraced*. Even worse, it requires us to put *beautiful, courageous, hopeful,* in a different class from *pretty, old, sad,* which, again, is contrary to our intuition.

What is true, it seems to me, is that in a real language it is only rarely that word classes or other structures are signaled by some simple and unique signal. If we were making up a language, creating an artificial language, we might wish to order things differently. We might, for example, make a rule that all nouns end in -*a* and that no other words end in this sound. Then we could always tell by the occurrence or nonoccurrence of -*a* whether a word was a noun or not.

But no real language has such a simple structure. In English, we must always know whether a word is a noun or not; otherwise we shall not be able to understand the sentence. But the signals which sort out nouns from the other classes with which they might be confused—verbs and adjectives, particularly—are multiple. The signal might be an inflectional ending, like the plural or the possessive; it might be a derivational ending, like -*ness* or -*ation*; it might be position; it might be the fact that our only previous experience with the word is in noun uses, so that we take it as a noun even when it occurs in a position in which other classes occur. Thus *Jones* in "It was Jones" is clearly a noun. But *Green* in "It was Green" could be taken, in speech, as an adjective. For any particular unambiguous sentence we could specify exactly how we know that a word is a noun and not an adjective or a verb, but there is no short and simple way of saying how we know in all sentences.

Similar remarks can be made about the concept *sentence*. One can imagine an artificial language in which sentences are marked in a simple way. Suppose that we had the custom, in English, of beginning every sentence with the expression *eek* and concluding it with the expression *awk:* "Eek, I ran into Sam Jones today, awk. Eek, he's been visiting his mother in Plainsville, awk. Eek, that's not far from Toledo, awk." Then we could easily define *sentence:* a structure that begins with *eek* and ends with *awk.* Students would memorize this definition at the age of six and never thereafter write comma faults or fragments.

Unfortunately, no real language has a simple and unique signal marking the sentence unit, either in the intonation or in the segmental structure. There is such a thing as "sentence in English," but it is marked as such in multiple fashion. "I have some" is a sentence; "if I have some" is not; "I have some—" (with the pitch staying level) is not; "I have some money" is; "Have some" is; "Is some" is not. There is simply no way of comprehending the concept "sentence in English" short of learning English grammar, either unconsciously, as a child learns it, or

through explicit instruction. Certainly nobody learns or teaches the concept "sentence in English" through steady repetition of the incantation "a sentence is a group of words expressing a complete thought."

Traditional teachers do teach the concept "sentence in English," as they teach such other concepts as *noun, verb, adjective, subject.* Some of their students, at least, come to recognize these structures and to be able to identify them in a more or less uniform way. A linguist should recognize this success. But he must point out that it is achieved not because of the definitional apparatus but in spite of it. The traditional teacher has the students learn the definitions, but must then take care that they never apply them. The learning comes not from definition and discussion of the concepts but from illustration, correction of mistakes, and the like. The whole burden of generalization is placed on the student, who must work through the examples to an understanding of what the teacher means when he says "a sentence is a group of words expressing a complete thought," "a verb is a word that expresses action, being, or state of being."

People nowadays frequently make remarks like "Linguistics may be all right but we had better not give up traditional grammar until we are provided with something to take its place." This is reasonable enough, unless by "something" is meant something similar, a comparable battery of short definitions. But neither linguistics nor anything else can ever provide such an apparatus. The classes English noun and English sentence are exactly as complicated as they are, and linguistics has no way of making them simpler. What linguistics does suggest is that the complexities be directly faced, not obscured in a fallacious philosophy. What a grammarian is—or ought to be—interested in is not meaning directly but the structure through which meaning is expressed, the mechanism by which meanings are distinguished. Every teacher of grammar must deal with structure and is therefore in some sense a structural linguist. But it is clear that the study could proceed much more efficiently, and infinitely more interestingly, if we could get through the philosophical fog and focus on the actual signals of the language.

The debate about correctness has been with us much longer than the debate about structure, but it seems no nearer conclusion. The difficulty seems to be at least partly a matter of misunderstanding, for which linguists are no doubt at least partly to blame. For one thing, linguists use the terms "correct" and "incorrect," but their usage departs considerably from the common one. By "incorrect English" a linguist is likely to mean such a mistake as might be made by a foreigner or a child learning the language. Thus both "I it bought" and "I buyed it" are incorrect sentences. But a linguist, as a linguist, would not say that "I done it" or "I brung it" are incorrect sentences. They are correct in relation to the dialects in which they occur, and the question of whether the dialects are admired in the nation as a whole is a sociological, not a linguistic, question.

Linguistics simply has to work in this way or it cannot operate as a science. To ask it to condemn "I done it" is like asking botany to condemn weeds. This is not to say that schools should not correct students who say "I done it." Those who go into college or into business saying "I done it" are clearly headed for difficulties which ought to be pointed out to them. There is a correlation, though not a perfect one, between the achievement of material success and the avoidance of expressions like "I done it," and therefore there is a strong sense in which "I done it" is incorrect. But the reason is purely sociological. The best people—so defined by wealth or education or some other criterion—don't say it, and that is all there is to it.

What more might be supposed to be to it, I simply can't figure out. We are not concerned here with "good" and "bad" sentences. If we are talking about good and bad, we can bring in such criteria as clarity, grace, euphony, economy, discrimination. But if we are talking about correctness, there is simply no criterion but somebody's usage. If a student asks me whether an expression is correct or not, I have no resource but to reflect on whether I use it or whether I hear it in the conversation of my friends, a small but select group of professors of English. If my answer does not satisfy, and it often does not, I am quite at a loss. There is no other principle I can invoke. Certainly not an historical one—I cannot suppose it proper that everyone speak Elizabethan English. Not an analogical one—if I insist on *bring/brought* on the analogy of *think/thought*, I should also, I suppose, have to campaign for *cling/clought* and *sting/stought*. So I answer according to the only principle I know—the usage of the best people, i.e., my friends and me. If the student persists—"I don't care what you and your friends say; what I want to know is which is *correct*"—I can only suppose him to be asking what God says.

If we knew what kind of English God speaks, we would have no problem, but we don't, and so we are reduced to figuring out who the best people are and reporting their English and persuading our students to emulate it. This is difficult, and perhaps linguistics will again be accused of destruction without replacement. But how is it a loss to be without what one never had? There has never been any criterion of correctness but somebody's usage. Linguistics does not create this complication; it merely points it out. Surely the first step in solving a problem is to discover the nature of the problem.

The problem is no doubt more complicated in the United States than it is—or at least than it has been—in England and on the continent of Europe. In countries with an aristocracy, it is relatively simple to define correct language: it is the language of the aristocracy, which is partly synonymous with the educated class. But in the United States, which has no visible aristocracy and where the tides of anti-intellectualism sometimes run strong, the situation is quite different. To decide what correct English is, we must in some sense decide who the best people are. I think this is what makes the subject explosive. Professors of English probably sometimes feel that linguists are somehow traitors to their class, pandering to the masses. I should like to point out that such a position is no necessary consequence of linguistics. It is possible to be both a linguist and

(in some sense) a purist. I myself am in no doubt about who the best people are. They are the intellectuals, like Jacques Barzun[1] and my friends and me.

It should be noticed that the problem of correctness becomes much simpler when we are careful to discriminate between speech and writing. Usage governs both, but in quite different ways. We must be forever in disagreement among ourselves and with our fellow citizens on what is correct in speech. It depends on who and what and where we are and on who and what and where we want to be. But in writing, and particularly in certain aspects of writing, we can achieve very considerable agreement. Nowhere are items more clearly right or wrong than in spelling. With a very few exceptions, all English words are correctly spelled in only one way. Like correctness in pronunciation, correctness in English spelling has no logical basis, but unlike pronunciation, spelling is uniform, and the agreed on system is knowable. The same is true, though to a lesser extent, of punctuation, word forms, sentence structures that occur in writing.

Yet in writing as in speech it is usage that controls, the difference being that in writing it is the usage of a relatively small and easily discernible group—the publishing industry largely—that matters. The question "Is this correct written English?" can be more specifically phrased: "Would a copy editor pass this?" "Does this accord with the style books of the publishing

[1] Jacques Barzun, Dean of Faculties and Provost of Columbia University, and a very productive and persuasive critic of literature and of culture, is represented in this collection by "The Retort Circumstantial" (p. 107).

houses?" One cannot change speech or retard its development by taking thought about it. It is doubtful that all the not inconsiderable efforts of mass education have had very much effect on the speech of the population as a whole. But the writing system is very largely controllable. It changes, but it changes very slowly, compared to speech. If we wanted to change it radically—e.g., if we wanted to reform our spelling—we could do that.

The last of the three questions posed was, what exactly is the application of linguistics, supposing its views to prevail, to the teaching of English? First of all, it must be said that this is a question that no linguist, as a linguist, can answer, just as no mathematician, as a mathematician, can say what the applications of mathematics should be. The application is a question for the teacher of English, and I speak from here on as a teacher of English and not as a linguist.

I think that the effect of linguistics on the teaching of English may be profound but that it will not be the sort of effect commonly expected. There seems to be a widespread hope that the teaching of grammar according to linguistic principles will lead directly to a great improvement in writing, a falling off in comma faults, fragments, dangling modifiers, and such errors. I think that linguistics might make some contribution in this direction, but I doubt that it will be substantial. Certainly I know of no way in which punctuation can be taught or in which "sentence sense" can be communicated to those who haven't got it, except through some kind of teaching of the grammar; and it is reasonable to suppose that a good grammar will serve better here than

a confusing one. But we must ask more fundamental questions. How much does the classroom teaching of any grammar contribute to improvement of writing? More generally, what are the processes through which people learn to write?

These questions must here be answered impressionistically, since the subject, oddly, has been very little studied. It is curious that it has not been, for the problem, though extremely complex, does not seem to be beyond the reach of ingenuity plus foundation money. It is nevertheless true that for the teaching of literacy we have built an elaborate and expensive educational system without really knowing whether it does much good or not. It is certainly true that millions of people in every generation learn to write passably well. What we do not know is whether this success is achieved because of English classes or in spite of them or irrelevantly to them.

One thing that is perfectly clear is that only in the first years of school can we see the teacher making obvious and consistent progress. We must all envy the first-grade teacher. She takes children who cannot shape the letters and shows them how. She receives in September youngsters who are largely illiterate and dismisses them largely literate in June. In the second, third, and fourth grade, similar progress is made, and we can see a clear connection between the instruction and the improvement.

In later grades, in high school, and in college, the connection is much harder to make out. The students—or some of them—continue to improve, but we don't really know whether to ascribe their improvement to reading habits, to correction, to practice in writing, to imitation of favorite authors, to interest, to growing older—or, perhaps, to instruction in grammar and the principles of composition. I myself am inclined to doubt that there is much connection between being able to analyze a sentence and being able to write one. I am a grammarian and I suppose more conscious of sentence structures than most people; yet when I write, I very rarely choose structures deliberately, very rarely say to myself, "I think a subordinate clause might serve my turn here rather better than a participial phrase." I do consider structure in punctuating. Probably punctuation can be taught only through some reference to structure, but there is a question to what extent it can be taught at all to those who are unable to learn it in some other way—e.g., through reading.

What has been said about grammar goes more than triply for rhetoric. Grammar is hard to teach and hard to learn because the sentence is so very complex; yet it is absurdly simple compared to the paragraph. When we say that a paragraph ought to be unified and coherent and meaty, we have said about all there is to say. The means of achieving unity, coherence, and meatiness are infinite beyond description. It seems to me perfectly obvious that nobody ever pauses in the heat of writing to think about Topic Sentences or Methods of Paragraph Development. Nobody, unless he is doing an exercise for a composition class, ever asks himself, "Now what would be a good topic sentence for this one?" or ever reflects, "I organized the last paragraph inductively, so I think I had better try a comparison-and-contrast this time." I would not say that

exercises in these matters are useless. Probably they are effective now and then in impressing on the students the need for order and logic. But I think that their effectiveness is limited and that returns diminish rather soon. It does not seem reasonable to spend a large part of each year, from the seventh grade through the first year of college, pondering the mysteries of the topic sentence, methods of paragraph development, and figurative language.

The dilemma that faces us as English teachers is that a great many students write quite badly and that the populace has the feeling that there is something we can do about it. We are to some extent to blame for the difficulty. In assuming responsibility for the improvement of writing, we have implied that we can improve it. And of course we can improve it, and we do, but only within rather severe limits. Given the situation—the necessity of educating all the children, dull as well as bright—given a nation not especially oriented toward reading and writing, not especially fond of intellectuals or intellect—given television and the other diversions that compete so successfully with the book—given a school system in which writing is done almost entirely in English classes and in which other teachers criticize English teachers because students misspell words on their objective tests—given these circumstances, we must realize, and make other people realize, that there is a point beyond which we cannot improve writing, no matter how many papers we assign, or how thoroughly we correct them, no matter how small our classes, no matter how powerful our methods.

I think that the only salvation for

teachers of freshman English or of high school English is to find a subject matter, and I think that the great contribution of linguistics is that it provides one. It gives us something that is teachable, interesting, and pertinent, and this is what most distinguishes it from traditional grammar. The chief trouble with classes in English composition (insofar as that means classes in rhetoric and traditional grammar) is that for interest they must depend entirely on the personality of the teacher; the subject contributes nothing. The traditional point of view is that grammar is useful but dull, and virtually no one has ever pretended to discern intrinsic interest in the topic sentence. The linguist has an entirely different notion. He is not at all certain that his grammar is useful, but he is dead sure that it is interesting, and he doesn't have much trouble in persuading students to the same opinion. There is nothing closer to us than our native language, nothing more important to us, more a part of us, and I see no reason why it is illegitimate to devote school time to studying it, objectively and dispassionately, and for its own sake.

I am well aware that such remarks as these are not likely to find favor with school boards or PTA's or with high school or college administrators. The layman is alarmed by the truly alarming illiteracy in the land, and he responds by wanting to put in more anti-illiteracy courses, by redoubling the effort in the teaching of writing. But this is a naive view, stemming from a misunderstanding of the problem. We might, by doubling the effort, get some improvement in writing, say five or ten percent. But it would be expensive. The most practical way of redoubling the effort would be to cut in half the student-teacher ratio, but this would cost millions of dollars annually in a large school system, hundreds of thousands in a large university. It is doubtful that many laymen are as alarmed about illiteracy as all that.

In suggesting that English classes shift their emphasis from composition to subject matter—and particularly to language and literature—I am not suggesting that they suspend their efforts to improve writing. I would have students in English classes write just as much as they do now, and I would have their papers as rigorously corrected. But I would have them write mostly on topics in the field of English—that is, on English literature and the English language. And I would hope that instructors in other departments would be giving similar care to writing in their fields. If a teacher in history or health education complained to me, "My students can't write," I should reply sympathetically, "I'm having trouble with mine too. What are you doing about yours?"

For discussion

A. Suppose we agree that a noun is the name of a person, place, or thing, and that a verb tells of an action. What, then, is the italicized word in each of the following?
1. The boys had a *fight.*
2. John made the longest *jump* of the day.

3. Elizabeth enjoyed Robert's *reading*.
4. The workers went on *strike*.
5. We watched the *blossoming* of the flowers.

B. What is the functional definition of each of the italicized words in the following?
1. *pretty* girl
2. *flower* girl
3. *dancing* girl
4. girl *upstairs*

C. How many signals of "nounness" are there for each of the italicized words in the following?
1. The *meek* shall inherit the earth.
2. The *living* is easy.
3. The *object* of my affection can change my complexion.
4. He saw all the *elephants'* trunks.
5. *Foolish* is the word for Carrie.
6. *Seeing* is believing.
7. *Chaos* will come again.
8. Three *men* were in the tub.
9. The *scissors* are dull.
10. His *trouser* leg was torn.

D. If you based your conclusion on inflectional characteristics only, to what form class would you assign each of the italicized words in C?

E. If you used a notional definition, how many would be nouns? Which would be nouns if you used a functional definition?

F. What does Roberts mean by the "mixing" of levels and what is his objection to it?

G. All of the italicized words in C except those in items 4 and 10 are subjects. What would be Roberts' objection to calling them all nouns?

H. How do Roberts' principles for determining correctness correspond with what has been said on the subject in earlier essays?

I. How does discriminating between speech and writing simplify the problem of correctness? What makes the writing system controllable?

JOHN HOLLOWAY

The "Use of English" and the use of literature

In THE FOLLOWING ARTICLE John Holloway, lecturer in English Literature at Cambridge University and a distinguished Shakespearean scholar and critic, shows among other things, that a controversy about what is to be tested and what is to be taught percolates in England as well as at home. Since this and other essays will refer to the English educational system, a word may be said about it.

School is obligatory from age five to fifteen, and continues to be free to age nineteen in the state system, in which more than nine-tenths of the students are enrolled. Primary school takes children to the fall of the year in which they have reached eleven years. At this time, on the strength of their past performance, an IQ test, and written examinations (the 11-plus), children are placed in one of three types of secondary school, of which the Grammar School is the most relevant for this discussion.

The English Grammar School has six forms (grades, though in some schools sixth-form work may take several years). At about the fourth form, students choose—or are chosen for—one of two major courses: classics or modern, terms that indicate language-literary or mathematics-science emphasis. At the end of the fifth form (at age fifteen or sixteen) most Grammar School students take state examinations in all the subjects they have studied. This is the GCE "O" level, the General Certificate of Education examination, "Ordinary" level. As a result of these examinations, in which English or English literature is compulsory, many students stop their general education, enter a special school (technical, medical, dental), or simply get a job.

At about the age of eighteen, the sixth-formers take the GCE "A" level examination, the General Certificate of Education, "Advanced" level, in their special subjects, and probably also the scholarship level examination. More than three-fourths of English university students have state scholarships, and about as many work for an honors degree.

Mr. Holloway is concerned with (1) the kind of questions that should be asked and (2) the subject of the instruction that will precede the asking now that the Latin paper, once a traditional part of the entrance requirement at Oxford and

"The 'Use of English' and the Use of Literature": From *Universities Quarterly,* vol. 14, n. 4, September 1960, pp. 337–344. Reprinted with the permission of the editor and the publishers, Turnstile Press, London, England.

Cambridge, is considered obsolete. His objections to a "General Education" paper, and his proposals for a course that would prepare a student for a "Use of English" examination, parallel many of Roberts's remarks in the preceding article.

"Where I come from, we are breaking English every day." These words were once uttered in my hearing by an American citizen from a Spanish-speaking enclave of California, when he was challenged over his "broken English." He may have been breaking English, but he was certainly using it; and those who (to simplify) have replaced a Latin by a "Use of English" requirement in entrance at Oxford and Cambridge now confront the problem of defining what "Use of English" it is that concerns them. Part of the process of definition, I believe, is to have regard to the argument of those who consider that a paper in "Use of English" is less desirable as part of the new arrangements than one in "General Education." To assess the force of this proposal is to advance in understanding what "Use of English" is truly at stake.

Those who press the claims of a "General Education" paper have a good deal on their side; but they seem (perhaps because they view the problem mainly from the point of view of the school) not to have sufficiently considered that between "general education" and what defines a university there is a fundamental divergence. Doubtless the ideal of a good average graduate (and the reality is not wholly different) is someone of high general education, and that in a broad, intelligent and liberal sense. But the good average graduate is also something else. He has studied his subject in a fundamental way. He is not an amateur, but a professional. No doubt, insofar as he has a trained sense of evidence, relevance and value, he can switch if challenged to fields other than his special field. A trained mind is a flexible mind. A history graduate brings a sharpened instrument to economics, or a classicist to a modern language. But in his own field, the good graduate offers more than this. His mind offers not merely a general development and sharpening, but a body of knowledge grounded in fundamentals, and a flexibility and authority of judgment which can come only from moving for some time, and familiarly, within that knowledge, and being to some extent acquainted with the direction and quality of its current movement forward.

It is at this point that the traditional position of Latin becomes relevant. Originally, Latin was an absolutely central and vital piece of equipment, in pursuing that advanced and fundamental knowledge which is what marks out study at university level. The need for it was a rigorous one. It was no form of cliqueish or obsolete elegance, but an indispensable tool for solid and advanced work. Here was its original and irrefutable *rationale*.

To replace that obsolete Latin requirement, however, by a "general education" paper, would be to introduce a shift, not very conspicuous, but exceedingly and disquietingly significant, in the standpoint taken up by the universities. It would be to replace a call for fundamental knowledge, rigorously a part of advanced study, by a call for something which of its very nature is not knowledge held in a fundamental way, but the knowledge of the intelligent and lively-minded amateur. It would be, so far as it went, to seem to take one's stand by a paper which of its very nature accepts a range, depth and quality of knowledge in radical contrast with the quality of knowledge that the student at a university is taught to pursue.

The special position of the "Use of English" paper now to be introduced, or whatever might be substituted for it, must not be forgotten at this point. It is not merely one paper among many. It cannot but seem to represent the universities' considered sense of what in our own world comes near to occupying that central place, in respect of the highest education, which Latin occupied in the days when its position was unassailable. But to turn to some of the "General Studies" papers of recent years, is to see something of fundamentally another kind. In these, a university entrant is asked to explain why one should keep a diary; to estimate the justice of a three-word judgment on Victorian England; to say how science has improved our domestic equipment "and how much more improvement is required"; to design a tea-pot. This is a genuine selection from a recent paper. The student whose mind is directed along these channels is indeed being invited to take a lively interest in his surroundings; but his attention is being turned away from the quality of study which makes a university education. Here are two catalogues in

another paper from which candidates had to choose their subjects: "brainwashing, brinkmanship, convertibility of the pound, cost-of-living index, deviationism, the Establishment, filibuster" . . . "Kafka, Mann, Priestley, Snow, Waugh." Each of these, in its different way, illustrates the point. The first shows how "general education" is easily seen as a lively assortment of the miscellaneous and transient, the second implies an alarming unawareness of relevant basic distinctions.

In university studies at present, changes of several different kinds are going on simultaneously: some of these are in the direction of stricter specialization, but others are connected with making courses broader and more topical; and they move in a direction for which "popularization," if not quite a fair name, is for all that a standing danger. This second kind of trend cannot but be strengthened by university expansion; and it is in such circumstances as these, that the replacement of Latin by "General Education" would have to be seen. There may be a place for such a paper somewhere within the whole range of papers. The quality of the knowledge which it invites is something about which every serious teacher probably feels a certain measure of regret. That is not altogether a decisive objection to it. There is a decisive objection, however, to its use as the paper which in effect replaces Latin. Or at least, it would be disastrous to use it for this purpose without the liveliest awareness that in so doing the universities had by no means merely replaced the out-of-date by the up-to-date. This is what they might seem to have done on the surface. In reality, they would have replaced the specialist by the popularizing; and since a university which becomes a Seventh Form ceases to exist, they would have created for themselves a new and serious danger.

Can a command of one's native tongue be regarded as central and necessary for specialist work, and as pointing authoritatively forward to it? The question is a large one, but in some sense of the phrase "command of one's native tongue" there would be agreement that the answer to it is, yes. Even so, several distinctions need to be borne in mind. The student's writing is one thing, his use of textbooks and other more or less plain sources of information is another, his powers in respect of literary documents or of original material calling for interpretation are a third. Again, the problems are different for the arts student, the scientist, and the social scientist. On the other hand, they may well be less sharply so than some might think. The mediocre work of social theory may fail for reasons which the literary mind could define with a special sharpness; and on the other hand, teachers of English must all be familiar with students who seek to sit in judgment as critics, but are debarred from this by a vocabulary which lacks range and clarity in the most humdrum dictionary sense.

When all this is said, however, there remains a fundamental rightness in the idea that, if attention is to be transferred from Latin, it should somehow be transferred to the native tongue. Yet although this decision may be right in theory, as things now stand it is very disquieting in practice. Why this is so becomes clear soon enough, if one goes over

"Use of English" papers which have been recently set, or over the drafts of proposed papers which run parallel to them. To do this is to undergo an experience at first amusing, and in the end profoundly alarming. Behind these papers, as the guiding idea which shapes and controls them, can be seen a sense of the use of English which is disablingly, disastrously, *anti*-English. "You may offer any solution that occurs to you in the light of the facts stated, or may simply associate yourself with opinions already expressed," writes one examiner in his instructions to the candidates. "The fate of the Bell Inn, a building of historical [should this be 'historic'?] interest, is under consideration . . ." writes another. Again, "you are living on the fringe of a growing industrial area, and are becoming acutely conscious of the smoke menace. You have consulted various sources of information, and have gathered the following facts . . ." The style is familiar enough. We can all easily lapse into it, and it goes with the incessant "indicate the characteristic qualities of," "estimate the consequences of the introduction of," "discuss the validity of the author's analogy," "might initially lack facilities," "investigate the possibilities" and so on, spattered over current "Use of English" papers, or general studies papers that go with them and might carry exemption from them.

Yet what can the reader do, but gape in horror and astonishment? What standard of English, what sense of the "Use of English," can lie behind papers which are set in this mummified diction of cliché and officialese?

Exasperation may break out at such

a spectacle, but no one has the right to speak of these papers in a merely supercilious spirit. At the present time, few things are more natural than to use English so; and here is the interest and value of the case. The fact is not, that these examiners merely happen to have a very indifferent style. Something more meaningful—and useful—is to be diagnosed. The style is exactly that which goes with the whole range of experience and subject-matter on which these papers steadily draw, their whole world of writing a letter to the Town Clerk or the Town Council, discussing the problem of university entrance, writing a speech for a Debating Society or a public meeting, commenting on a paragraph of popular science writing, and indicating "the general style or kind of writing you have chosen to follow, e.g., scientific paper, article in serious weekly or in popular press."

The fact seems inescapable, that this range of examination papers issues from the world of Current Affairs, Civics, "taking an intelligent interest in the world around us." This is the range of life towards which the papers are directed; and as a result, it follows naturally enough, though perhaps without intention, that the ideal of style, the ideal of English from which they start and which they accept, is the English in general use when these lively but ephemeral topics are engaged upon. It is the English, that is to say, of the committee-man, the local politician, the average journalist, the current affairs writer, the educationalist sometimes, and the popularizer of science.

The essential and melancholy fact comes out at last. The papers have in large part become the ally of the very menace against which they were set up to strive. At the present time, a veritable Dead Sea of diluted and colourless English, clotted throughout with officialese, jargon and cliché, rises about us on every side. These "Use of English" papers represent the same kind of interest in experience as this kind of writing serves in the popular media of the press, television, and vulgarization in book form. They represent that kind of interest; and they use English, and foster its use, that way. Abuse of our tongue has become so much the system of things that it has infected our very remedies against abuse; until these merely play their part in sustaining and perpetuating a kind of dreary competence in the accepted debilitation.

It seems, therefore, that behind these "Use of English" papers a quite coherent and intelligible story may be seen to lie: save that its outcome is a sorry one. Yet there is no great difficulty in locating the idea which offers guidance towards better papers; papers truly in the "Use of English," not in its misuse. First we must agree that to teach a student to use his native tongue well is a notable and difficult thing, and one which cannot be done with one hand while the other sustains a lively interest in current ephemeralities, or keeps us abreast of a changing world. Second, and probably more important, we must keep in mind the oldest principle of learning: that one learns to do something well, not from those who do it ill, but from those who do it best. On the one hand, we must jettison the idea that using English is something which can be taught, or tested, at the same time as we reap the harvest of a little civics, or a little popular science, or something lively and up-to-date about "the arts." Second, it must be perfectly clear that in learning the use of English, there are certain writers who have the standing of irreplaceable models: and these are the masters, in our literature, of plain prose in the highest sense.

A teacher of English Literature will wish, likely enough, to go further than that. He will wish to argue that plain prose, in the end, does not suffice; and that no one should engage in advanced and specialist work at a university without necessarily making contact, first, with a few literary works of the more imaginative and indeed poetic kind (again, not trivial if congenial current fiction, but what stands among the masterpieces of our literature). The teacher who has these views may well rub his eyes with bewilderment and pain, when he notices that neither at Oxford, nor at Cambridge, do the Boards of English seem even to have glimpsed how this might be the decisive moment for doing their subject justice. But there is no need to insist on these opinions, in order to make the vital point about "Use of English."

This vital point is simply that our ideal "Use of English" (in that plain sense in which its use is a matter for everyone) must be traced firmly back to the masters of plain prose in our literature. It throws into sharp relief the fact that if proficiency in the use of English is seen merely as the "acquiring of skills," it is travestied. We cannot so envisage, or teach, or test it. Certainly, it may include some more or less routine skills, or even ("use of words, grammar, and punctuation," as Oxford puts it) certain mere items

of knowledge. What important mental activities call for none, and who could wish that they did? But in the use of one's native language, these are the merest paste and scissors.

To turn to the masters of plain prose in English—I would name Bunyan, Defoe, Swift, Cobbett, and Newman among them—is not to be rewarded with any spectacle of teachable verbal skills, but to confront an achievement which in its unremitting energy, economy, precision and comprehensiveness, takes the attentive reader back to the full expanse, and the finest qualities, of the writer's mind. And so it is, more modestly, with ourselves, and with everyone, in the writing of the best that we have in us to write. We are steered clear of empty abstractions, tired cliché, limply festooning syntax, and ill-conceived or ill-sustained tone, by nothing short of our whole thinking on the subject about which we write, and our whole sense of the nature and responsibilities of the task of writing. And at the present time this is true twice over. In the past, a good prose was a natural heritage. A writer was innocent unless he was proved guilty. Today, on every hand, the unconscious or half-unconscious enemies of our language—from the societalist and stylistician at one extreme, to the pop-song writer at the other (happy terms, all of them)—stand armed and ready, waiting to infect language, or castrate it, at its birth. In these circumstances, the right use of English demands unfailing vigilance and conscientiousness, and a kindled awareness both of the true good in writing, and of all that incites us to settle for the sham.

If one's conclusions, then, are that "Use of English" can indeed reach to high qualities of mind, to the mind at work within sight of its full extent; and further, that it can claim a fundamental relevance in preparing for that advanced work which defines a university—these conclusions can stand only on a strict condition. The condition is, that the subject is to be defined from the standard of what is best in our plain prose literature. This is not to say that senior forms in schools must digest an undiluted diet of the authors mentioned above. Nothing at all is being said about the details of teaching programmes. What is said is that thinking about the problem starts there, and not elsewhere. These authors (and others as good, maybe) present the ideal, the standard. Any lower standard, taking and congenial though it may seem, is simply to be brushed aside.

This is why, although in my own files there is a sheaf of good prose passages (as I understand this term) from twentieth century authors, I am naming none of these. For the moment, they must go unnamed, if the central fact of the discussion is to be set in the light of day. Otherwise, before we realize it, we shall be half way back to prose which has a lively interest and a topical appeal, and is what the average boy or girl will take to (we shall be told) and find familiar. We are not likely to discover our weapons in these quarters. The terrain belongs to the enemy.

The actual process of teaching may largely be compromise. But there is an area of thinking about teaching which has no place for compromise; and I believe that those concerned with the paper now proposed must be absolutely uncompromising in their recognition that the ultimate model, and the point from which their thinking must start, is "Use of English" at its best and highest: the plain prose that has passed into our literature.

For discussion

A. What are Holloway's reasons for considering a "General Education" paper inadequate as a replacement for Latin?

B. Holloway points out the simultaneous demands in education today for both specialization and generalization. We are all familiar with the perils of specialization. What does Holloway consider to be the dangers of generalization?

C. What are the details of Holloway's answer to his own question, "Can a command of one's native tongue be regarded as central and necessary for specialist work, and as pointing authoritatively forward to it?" (See p. 41.)

D. Try to recall some of the subjects you have had to choose among for an examination in composition? How do they compare with some of Holloway's choices?

E. Why would Holloway make literature the subject matter of the English composition course? How does his idea correspond with Roberts's suggestions for a subject matter in a composition course?

F. Why would he exclude contemporary literature from such a course?

G. Both Roberts and Holloway are teachers, scholars, writers, and—implicitly at least—educational theorists. In what ways are their conclusions similar and in what ways are they different?

Correctness

To be correct is to conform, and we all conform. There are no communities of one. Indeed, so-called non-conformists are the fiercest conformers of all. Conformity demands a standard. We must conform to something. Some standards are very specific, giving us no choice (a stop light, for instance), while others are more general, condemning us to a certain amount of freedom (as does a Drive Safely sign). Some standards (for example, the word order of a sentence) are habits over which we ordinarily exert no conscious control. Some standards (like the wearing of dress, kimono, or sari) are imposed by custom. And some standards we choose

45

for ourselves. But always and everywhere there are standards, and always and everywhere we conform to them.

What is more, we conform to a variety of standards simultaneously. We are tuned to react to the manifold signals demanding conformity all around us. We behave—speech is a part of human behavior—in the company of our teacher, our father, our closest friend, our sweetheart, and the recruiting sergeant in quite different ways, and there is likely to be trouble if we get these ways mixed up. For our standards in these encounters, we probably try to duplicate the behavior of people we admire. We cannot actually duplicate it, of course. We approximate it. In terms of linguistics, this approximation is our individual dialect, our *idiolect*. Our real problem is to exercise as much freedom as we can within the standards, partly imposed and partly chosen freely. Without the standards there would be chaos, and without freedom there would be atrophy.

Although it is not so true as it once was, it is still reasonably accurate to say that for some groups, such as the members of the British Civil Service, there is a single standard of speech. Whether a young man originally came from Land's End or John O'Groats, by the time he goes to his first government post he speaks Received Standard English, a dialect which reflects the British public school, Oxford, and the BBC, but not his home county.

Things are somewhat different in the United States. Some distinguished Americans speak as the President does. Some speak like the Senior Senator from Arkansas. Some speak like the Junior Senator from Maine. Some speak like our Ambassador to the United Nations. Certainly, the young American cannot look to the national scene to find the proper accent in which to express his ambitions. The language of his home town is good enough to begin with, and it will be good enough in Washington, as almost any press conference in the capital will show. There is no single status dialect among us. Linguistic diversity is a fact of American life at all levels, social or geographical.

It is also a fact that the middle class is constantly expanding. There seems to be in the United States, however, more yeast than in other places. We expand faster and longer than they do anywhere else. We can't all be President, but we come to believe that we can—and should —all be correct speakers of American English. Influenced by the publishing industry and those who got to the middle class before we did, we also come to believe that there is only one way of being right. At this point we feel threatened by linguistic diversity and begin to feel as though we were walking on eggs. If we're lucky, we don't break any, but then, we can't walk very fast either, and we may ruin our nerves. To change the figure, we keep looking for stop lights when, in fact, we are on a freeway. In such a situation it seems worthwhile to elaborate upon the plural nature of linguistic protocol.

The following essays discuss the nature and sources of this protocol, observe in detail a number of specific problems in usage, and seem to indicate that correctness eventually is a combination of what is reasonable, what is conventional, and what is convenient.

ARCHIBALD A. HILL

Correctness and style in English composition

GIVEN THE PREVIOUS ASSUMPTIONS about the nature of language, and given the desirability of accommodating ourselves to the facts of usage, how can we best maintain rigorous standards in composition? Archibald A. Hill, Professor of English at the University of Texas, longtime Secretary of the Linguistic Society of America, and author of the most nearly complete phonologically-based grammar of American English, provides a linguist's answer.

By setting up a distinction between "correctness" and "style," Hill can maintain the descriptive linguist's insistence that any form is correct if it is current in the dialect of the user (or at least what should be the dialect of the user) since Hill keeps in mind the writer's intended audience. Thus "I could *of* danced all night" is incorrect because it is not current in any dialect of written American English, and "I went onto the fly-over flat out" would be incorrect in talking to most American motorists, though it would presumably be fine in England. With this view one may describe several kinds of incorrectness, and Hill does. His examples nearly all appear in simple declarative sentences.

Variations from satisfactory style, however, come from putting sentences—or parts of them—together in such a way as to create clear ambiguity, general uncertainty, or just plain shock. In this group appear such old acquaintances as vague reference and the dangling modifier. Though Hill finds some variations which he calls indifferent—six of one and half a dozen of the other—he considers aberrations in style, as he defines it, to be as subject to correction as violations of dialect, and he explains what is behind these aberrations.

The teacher of English is often accused by students of language of being unable to modify his teachings in accord with facts of usage no matter how well proved, and the linguist in turn seems to those of us who have to struggle with freshmen to be a wild libertarian who would accept the most shapeless writing on the ground that all linguistic forms are equally

"Correctness and Style in English Composition": From *College English*, vol. 12, n. 5, February 1951, pp. 280–285. Reprinted with permission of The National Council of Teachers of English and Archibald A. Hill.

good. Perhaps, as with other disputes, some of the differences may be resolved if the basic terms are more clearly defined.

I shall begin with correctness, giving a few well-worn statements of what it is not.

Correctness is not logic, since all languages are largely illogical. English says, "I see him," as if sight were a positive act of will comparable to that in "I hit him." Yet all of us know enough optics to realize that, if there is any action involved, it starts with *him* and reaches and affects *me*. Languages which happen, like Eskimo, to avoid this particular illogicality fall into others as great.

The basis of correctness is not beauty inherent in the forms used. Beauty in linguistic forms is due to the associations they arouse. Such a form as "goil" is ugly only if the hearer happens to dislike Brooklyn. To realize the truth of this statement, one has only to consider variants where we have no such associations. If a child in the New Mexican pueblo of Santa Clara puts the sentence, "I am going to town," in the form *bupiyeummang,* the "ugly" pronunciation is immediately corrected to *bupijeummang.* The Tewa parents are not being merely arbitrary; they are objecting to an unacceptable dialect. I doubt if any English speaker can seriously maintain that he finds one Tewa form more beautiful than the other.

The basis of correctness is not history; such a belief would contradict the results of linguistic science. Further, the belief that older forms are better than newer can readily be reduced to an absurdity. If only old forms are right, then we do not speak English but bad Old English—or bad Indo-Hittite.

Equally certainly correctness is not the result of an authoritative ruling by an individual or a book. A neat example of this last view is the statement of a columnist who once said that 98 per cent of Americans mispronounced a given word, since they failed to follow dictionary recommendations. Actually such a statement demonstrates that 2 per cent of America mispronounces the word or that the dictionaries had better catch up on usage.

A final view once widely held is that anything which is impossible in Latin is incorrect in English. The view hardly needs denial, baleful as its lingering influence may be on the analysis of English grammar. At least, no one would now seriously maintain that "Oh, father!" is a vocative case, incapable of being split into two words.

I can start my positive exposition with a quotation which puts clearly the idea that the composition teacher has a double task. Most of what will follow will be merely an attempt to sharpen the distinction set up in the quotation.

Competence . . . has to do with the organization of ideas . . . with putting words together . . . in such a way as to convey meaning easily and clearly. Decency may be regarded as the manners of discourse, and bears the same relation to speaking and writing that good table manners have to eating. The schoolboy who declares, "We ain't goin' to have no baseball team this year" is using language with competence, for his meaning is perfectly clear, but he is not using it with decency.[1]

[1] Clarence D. Thorpe (ed.), *Preparation for College English* (Ann Arbor: University of Michigan Press, 1945), p. 12 n.

For these terms I should like to substitute "correctness" and "style." Any form is correct if it is current in the dialect—to be defined, of course, beforehand—that the writer is using. A form is incorrect only if it has no such currency. It follows that it is possible to be incorrect in the use of other dialects than the rather vaguely defined Standard Written English with which teachers concern themselves. Professor Thorpe's schoolboy was using language incorrectly if he was speaking in the formal atmosphere of the schoolroom; but, if he was speaking to playmates across the tracks, he was speaking correctly enough. A more serious illustration is that the English department of one of our leading universities was recently taken to task because its training did not equip graduates to communicate with workmen. The point was well taken: it is as serious an error to use the forms of Standard English where they are socially out of place as it is to use Gullah[2] in the pages of a learned article. Incorrectness can result also, not merely from the use of a dialect in an inappropriate situation, but as well from the mixture of dialects or the improper imitation of a dialect. Readers of Galsworthy may remember that he sometimes makes an American character say sentences like, "If you've gotten a sense of humour, you've gotten it jolly well hidden up." Such sentences are grossly un-American at the same time that they are un-British; they are therefore incorrect.

The second term was "style." If forms A and B both occur in a given dialect, it is impossible to say that either is incorrect in that dialect. It may, however, be possible to show that A is better than B in the particular context in which it occurs. Such an evaluation will be based on the positive qualities of the passage under criticism; that is, A is better than B if it is clearer, more in accord with artistic conventions, or fits better with the structure of the utterance in which it falls. It should be stated emphatically that good and bad style are both possible in any dialect—Professor Thorpe's schoolboy was speaking with excellent style, since his statement left no doubt of the vigor of his denial. It should also be pointed out that, if a stylistic variant is condemned in one passage, it is by no means implied that it should be condemned elsewhere.

A third form of variant also exists. These are the indifferent variants. If A and B both exist, and no stylistic reason can be found for preferring one over the other, the variation is indifferent. The existence of indifferent variants is of some importance, since somehow the idea has gotten abroad that, if there are two ways of saying a thing, one must always be better than the other. English teachers are all too often called on to adjudicate between six and a half-dozen, though to devote effort to such decisions can only falsify what we so much need to tell our students.

From these rather generalized examples we can pass to discussion of variants such as actually appear in student themes. We will begin with

[2] Gullah is the local Negro dialect of the Sea Islands off South Carolina and Georgia. Although a few of its words are now used in the general American vocabulary (*gumbo, goober*), it is generally unintelligible outside the immediate area, and even to whites on the Sea Islands themselves.

variants which involve correctness, the first group of them springing from insufficient knowledge of the way in which writing represents the forms of speech. It is characteristic of these forms that, if read aloud with normal pronunciation, they immediately become acceptable Spoken English.

He couldn't *of* had a worse introduction.

Sentences like this have a sort of currency in dialect writing but have no currency in Standard Written English. The mistake consists in selecting the wrong spelling for a weak form which is homonymous for *have* and *of*. It is odd that the reverse mistake as in "a pair *have* shoes" seems never to occur.

Rooms for *Tourist*.

This is a type of form which is common in much of the South. What is back of it is an assimilation of *-sts* to *-ss* or simply to *-s*. It occurs at all levels of regional speech, and even teachers of English use it quite unconsciously. The mistake can be explained to students by giving the conditions under which the assimilation occurs and by pointing out that written forms do not recognize the change.

The next group of variants are incorrect because they employ local or social dialect forms not found in the Standard language.

Youse had better not do it.

This sentence will be recognized as belonging to uncultured New York City speech. Its badness, however, is altogether the result of its lack of currency in standard dialects of any type—it cannot be condemned as

illogical or out of keeping with the structure of the language, since it makes a contrast between singular and plural just as other pronouns do, and since it is parallel to the southern *you all*.

I want this *doing* immediately.

This sentence is not likely to occur in compositions by American students, but it is nonetheless instructive, since we are likely to think of anything British as all right. The form is northern British local dialect, which finds its way into occasional printed books, among them those of Hall Caine. It is certainly not correct in this country. Another local sentence type is the southern "I *might could* do it," which is common enough in colloquial speech, but which I have never seen in print. The sentence should be rejected in compositions, acceptable as it may be in less formal situations.

The next group of incorrect variants arises from an unsuccessful attempt to use the forms or vocabulary of a standard dialect and are thus comparable to the mistakes made by foreigners.

This phone broken. Do not *uses*.

This sentence appeared on a sign put up by a colored janitor in a government building. The writer presumably used a type of dialect in which the present forms of verbs are without variation. Knowing that an *-s* appears in many forms where he would not use it, he corrected a little too much.

Modern culture is *sadistic*. Its music, painting, and literature are all sad.

In these sentences from a doctoral examination it is amusing to watch what starts out to be a provocative statement evaporate into a merely un-fortunate attempt at elegance. The mistake is parallel to the student habit of describing modern poetry as "mystic" under the belief that this word is a critical term meaning "hard to understand."

A final type of incorrect variation is of rather common occurrence in student themes. This is contamina-tion of one construction by another, with consequent production of vari-ants lacking currency. A convenient if somewhat mentalistic explanation is to say that the writer intended one construction and then shifted his in-tention to another. Readers can readily supply other examples than the one which follows.

There are *a points* which I can make. . . .

The author of this phrase has mixed *are a few points* with *are points,* pro-ducing a mistake which at first sight seems quite improbable for a native speaker.

Our next group of variants are cor-rect but are examples of bad style. All but the first are actual examples of composition.

John met Jack, and *his* wife spoke to *him.*

In English, as in many languages, we have no way of distinguishing the reference of pronouns when there are two nouns of the same class, so that ambiguity often results. The sentence above must be condemned as bad style, though similar sentences can be found by the hundreds in all sorts of writing.

Record the pronunciation on the lists in capital letters.

This sentence is drawn from a set of directions made up by a professor of English, who will, I hope, pardon my use of it. The sentence seems clear enough, but unfortunately the in-tended meaning was: "Record the pronunciation of only those words which appear in capital letters on the lists." Such ambiguities pursue us all.

This factory is two miles beyond Lynch-burg, going south.

This sentence is the only really bad example of our old friend the dan-gling participle which I collected in two sessions of theme-reading. You will note that I have called it bad style, not an example of incorrectness. First, it produces ambiguity, not per-haps of a sort dangerous to real un-derstanding, but sufficient to give a comic effect. Thus the sentence has positive badness. Second, dangling participles are surprisingly common in Standard Written English, though the handbooks do not admit it. Gen-erally, no matter what our rationali-zations, we do not notice danglers unless the stylistic effect is bad.

The next sentence may strike the reader as wildly improbable, though it comes from an actual composition.

Mrs. Jackson devoted many years of endeavor to establishing and supporting a home where unfortunate women who had made mistakes (which they often sincerely regretted) could go to have their bastards.

The stylistic fault is obvious, since the final word comes with a distinct shock, the stronger for the vaguely elegant verbiage which precedes it.

The next variants are some which seem to me indifferent, though occasionally a particularly puristic handbook condemns one or more of them.

He *dove,* OR *He dived.*
It's *me,* OR It's *I.*
We carried it in a *burlap bag* (OR *croker sack,* OR *gunny sack*).
Let him do it if he *dares* (OR *dare*).

The first three of these are regional variants or are regional variants sometimes crossed with social variation. Yet since both forms appear in Standard writing, no matter what the origin, none of them can be condemned as incorrect. The second set is perhaps the most interesting, since *It's I* seems to occur as the natural form around Boston, though elsewhere it is a schoolmastered product not to be recommended. Shelley's line, "Be thou me, impetuous one!" is a helpful quotation in dealing with the overmeticulous, since, though it may be a trick, it is always possible to point out that no one would wish the line changed to "Be thou I." The last set shows variation between an older and a newer form, both of which occur in formal writing.

There follow some forms of wide currency, which seem to me also defensible stylistically, though they are nonetheless often condemned.

The mail is all delivered by plane, *which* is not only remarkably efficient, but is the chief weekly excitement.

This sentence violates the frequently expressed rule that *which* must have a definite antecedent. Yet vague antecedents are common in modern writing and have been common at all periods of the language. There is no ambiguity in the sentence above, and *which* seems a convenient device for avoiding a clumsily exact rephrasing.

The sentence comes from the *Saturday Evening Post.*

We might assume that Standard Oil is going to sponsor a news program. *They* will select a commentator with political views which coincide with *their* own.

This example comes from a student theme discussed by a panel of English teachers, a majority of whom regarded the indefinite *they* as incorrect. The sentence is of a type similar to the one above, has wide currency, and is certainly convenient. The stylistic effect of *it* would be quite different in this passage, and some such periphrasis as "the board of directors of Standard Oil" would be awkward. In the opinion of one person at least, illogical suppleness has always been one of the beauties of English.

I hope that I have by now given enough examples to make it clear that skepticism toward handbook rules does not mean undue libertarianism. To sum up, that part of a composition teacher's activity which concerns itself with correctness is grammar—normative grammar if he is telling students what to use; descriptive grammar if he is himself finding out what forms are current. That part of his activity which concerns the excellence of forms is a part of literary criticism. Both activities are difficult, and both important. On the one hand, it requires investigation rather than mere acceptance of authority to determine whether a given form is right or wrong. For instance, I recently wanted to know whether students should be graded down for writing "the table's leg" or "the story's climax." I went to a national periodical and found there about a hundred examples of both the *-s* genitive and *of* phrase, about equally divided between living beings and inanimate objects. The handbook rule is clearly false, and students should not be corrected for genitives which break it. As for stylistics, on the other hand, it is not my task to try to cover the subject, though it is obvious that we must bring to the reading of themes the same sort of detailed analysis which we give to understanding the literature we teach. I am aware that teachers are overworked and that it is perhaps too much to expect them to devote even an hour a week to investigating usage, or that they criticize their themes in the same spirit in which they analyze a paragraph of Swift or Arnold. There is only one answer to such an objection, arrogant as the answer may sound. It is surely better, and in the long run easier, to find the facts and teach them than to rely on a merely convenient myth.

For discussion

A. Hill lists and illustrates five things which correctness is not. Give one further illustration for each of his five points.

B. How does Hill distinguish between "correctness" and "style"?

C. Of the four ways in which student themes may vary from correctness, which does each of the following represent?
1. Smile awhile, and bid me sad ado.
2. He brung down the house.
3. Their purpose was to bring off a *coup d'être*.
4. Parallels are odorous.
5. Where will we find the writers to fill the cry and need?
6. I could of danced all night.
7. It seems to me it was funny, don't you?

D. Hill's examples of bad style would simply be called examples of ambiguity and violation of tone by most people. Why, then, does he distinguish these examples from his earlier examples of incorrectness?

E. What would you do to improve the correctness or style of the following?
1. When Claudius suggests that Hamlet not return to school, he is somewhat upset.
2. Hemingway once landed a 468 pound marlin without a harness.
3. LEFT TURN ONLY ON GREEN LIGHT
4. The evidence would prove Banquo's ghost to be a good one because he was very well-mannered with the exception of swiping Macbeth's place at the banquet table.
5. The missionary came after the whiskey.
6. Albert enjoys surfing, dancing, and racing cars.
7. We need more conscientious officials.
8. Gloria left the reception with her new husband suited in winter white wool with black and gold.
9. Do not take pictures of moving trains or bridges.
10. Some men like food better than their wives.
11. After receiving this notice, your regular garbage collection day will be on Monday.

F. Read an article of five pages or more in a current issue of *Harper's, The Atlantic Monthly, The New Yorker, The Reporter, Holiday,* or *Ramparts,* and record all examples of (a) *which* that do not have a definite antecedent (b) *they* that do not refer to a clear plural.

G. On p. 51 Hill writes that in evaluating which of two correct dialectical variations is preferable, the decision should be based upon "the positive qualities of the passage under criticism." What does he mean by "positive qualities"?

H. When, according to Hill, does the instructor use normative grammar? When does he use descriptive grammar?

I. A current widely-read book about English grammar contains what is called a test of grammatical ability, in which items analogous to the following are included. Take the test yourself.
   1. Why does Gertrude have such a tremendous (affect, effect) on you?
   2. How does one go about (effecting, affecting) a reconciliation between ex-friends?
   3. Polo's is one of the (principle, principal) eating places in town.
   4. The murderer will be (hung, hanged) tomorrow.
   5. Are you trying to (imply, infer) that I am flirting with your wife?
   6. (It's, Its) the spirit that counts.
   7. Phil Persky has a little (stationery, stationary) store on North 9th.
   8. I'm (uninterested, disinterested) in hearing about the question.
   9. His (fiancée, fiancé) deserted him.
   10. (Who, Whom) do you think you are, anyway?
   11. Have you (drank, drunk) all your apple juice?
   12. Cats are generally (sensuous, sensual) in their approach to life.
   13. You should (of, have) arrived sooner.
   14. What do you want for (dessert, desert)?
   15. (Who, Whom) did you see at the party?

J. How many of the above items involve a distinction between speaking and writing? How many items are a vocabulary test?
   How many would be perfectly acceptable if read aloud?
   Does your dictionary list either choice as non-standard in items 4 or 11?
   Does your dictionary provide a clear choice in 5, 8, or 12?
   What do you think is the most reasonable explanation of the fact that *who* would be a very common choice in 15?
   Which items would Hill probably call matters of correctness?

DONALD J. LLOYD

Our national mania for correctness

ALTHOUGH WE TALK a good deal about cleaning up the writing of students, most readers of ordinary English prose would agree that it is characterized not so much by its grammatical ineptness as by its lack of variety: its repetitiveness, its lack of imagination, its timidity. Vigor, warmth, and wit congeal as we face a blank page of paper, and a demon seizes us. Professor Lloyd says this demon is a "mania for correctness," an ill that is propagated by books on correctness. He does not indicate that a good style is available upon application from nature, but he insists that it eventually must seem natural. Professor Lloyd, for many years at Wayne State University in Detroit, is now in private business.

Every now and then the editors of the university presses let out a disgruntled bleat about the miserable writing done by scholars, even those who are expert in literary fields; and from time to time there are letters and editorials in our national reviews bewailing some current academic malpractice with the English language. At present, even *PMLA* (The Publications of the Modern Language Association), traditionally the repository of some of the worst writing done by researchers, is trying to herd its authors toward more lucid exposition. And at two recent meetings of the august Mediaeval Academy, one at Boston and one at Dumbarton Oaks, bitter remarks were passed about the failure of specialists in the Middle Ages to present their findings in some form palatable to the general reader, so that he can at least understand what they are writing about.

Even admitting that a really compelling style is the result of years of cultivation, much scholarly writing is certainly worse than it needs to be. But it is not alone in this. Generally speaking, the writing of literate Americans whose primary business is not writing but something else is pretty bad. It is muddy, backward, convoluted and self-strangled; it is only too obviously the product of a task approached unwillingly and accom-

"Our National Mania for Correctness": Reprinted from *The American Scholar,* vol. 21, n. 3, Summer, 1952, pp. 283–289. Copyright © 1952 by The United Chapters of Phi Beta Kappa. By permission of the publishers.

plished without satisfaction or zeal. Except for the professionals among us, we Americans are hell on the English language. I am not in touch with the general run of British writing by non-professionals, but I suspect that it is nothing to make those islanders smug, either.

Furthermore, almost any college professor, turning the spotlight with some relief from himself and his colleagues to his students, will agree that their writing stinks to high heaven, too. It is a rare student who can write what he has to write with simplicity, lucidity and euphony, those qualities singled out by Somerset Maugham; far more graduating seniors are candidates for a remedial clinic than can pass a writing test with honors. And freshman writing is forever the nightmare of the teachers of composition, as it would be of their colleagues if the latter could not escape to the simple inanities of their objective tests.

Yet it was not always so. I have on my desk a little manuscript from the fourteenth century written by an unknown author, which I am in the process of editing. When I read it to one of my classes, as I occasionally do, with no more modernization than my own Great Lakes pronunciation and the substitution of a word for one which has become obsolete, it is a simple, clear and engaging document. "Where is any man nowadays that asketh how I shall love God and my fellow-Christians?" it begins. "How I shall flee sin and serve God truly as a true Christian man should? What man is there that will learn the true law of God, which he biddeth every Christian man to keep upon pain of damnation in hell without end? . . . Unnethe [scarcely] is there any lewd

man or lewd woman that can rightly well say his Pater Noster, his Ave Maria, and his Creed, and sound the words out readily as they should. But when they play Christmas games about the fire, therein will they not fail. Those must be said out without stumbling for dread of smiting. But if a lewd man should be smited now for each failing that he maketh in saying of his Pater Noster, his Ave Maria, and his Creed, I trowe he should be smited at the full." And so on, to the beautiful poetic line, "Then think it not heavy to dwell with thy mother in her wide house, thou that laist in the strait chamber of her womb." The spelling in the original is hectic, and the capitalization and punctuation sporadic, to say the least.

Yet there was a man who knew what he had to say and set out about saying it, with no nonsense and no fumbling. He aimed for his audience and, judging by the dog-ears and sweat-marks on the book, which is about the size of one of our pocket books, he hit it. Why cannot we do as well in our time? Indeed, the eighteenth century was about the last age in which almost any man, if he was literate at all, could set down his thoughts—such as they were—so that they did not have to be excavated by the reader. We have an abundance of letters, diaries, pamphlets, and other papers from that period, and they are well written. It was the age, we may recall, not only of Boswell and Johnson, but of Pepys and Franklin as well, and of a host of other men whose main legacy to us was a simple, direct, workmanlike style, sufficient to the man and to the occasion, which said what it had to say and said it well. With the end of that century we go into the foggy, foggy darkness, and God knows whether we shall ever find our way out of it—as a people, that is, as a nation of thinking men and women with something to say.

Nevertheless, there is no question what makes our writing bad, or what we shall have to do to better it. We shall simply have to isolate and root out a monomania which now possesses us, which impedes all language study and inhibits all mastery of our native tongue—all mastery, that is, on paper; for as speakers of English, we Americans are loving and effective cultivators of our expression. I recall the gas station attendant who was filling my car. The gasoline foamed to the top of the tank, and he shut off the pump. "Whew" I said, "that nearly went over." "When you see white-caps," he replied, "you better stop." "You better had," I said, lost in admiration. But if you had given him a pencil, he would have chewed the end off before he got one word on paper.

The demon which possesses us is our mania for correctness. It dominates our minds from the first grade to the graduate school; it is the first and often the only thing we think of when we think of our language. Our spelling must be "correct"—even if the words are ill-chosen; our "usage" must be "correct"—even though any possible substitute expression, however crude, would be perfectly clear; our punctuation must be "correct"—even though practices surge and change with the passing of years, and differ from book to book, periodical to periodical. Correct! That's what we've got to be, and the idea that we've got to be correct rests like a soggy blanket on our brains and our hands whenever we try to write.

This mania for correctness is another legacy from the eighteenth century, but it did not get a real grip on us until well into the nineteenth. Its power over us today is appalling. Among my other tasks, I teach advanced courses in the English language to students preparing to teach. Most of these are seniors and graduate students, and in the summer especially, there is a sprinkling of older men and women, experienced teachers, who are sweating out a master's degree. They have had courses in "English" throughout their schooling. But of the nature and structure of the English language, the nature of language habits, the relation of speech to writing, and the differences in usage which arise from dialect and from differing occupational and educational demands—of all these, they know nothing at all. Nor do they come to me expecting to learn about these. They want to know two things: what correct usage is and how you beat it into the kids' heads. That there are other considerations important to an English teacher is news to many of them. What they get from me is a good long look at their language.

To trace this monolithic concentration on usage is to pursue a vicious circle, with the linguists on the outside. The literate public seems to get it from the English teachers, and the teachers get it from the public. The attitudes and pronouncements on language of a Jacques Barzun,[1] a Wilson Follett, a Bernard De Voto, or a Norman Lewis ("How Correct Must Cor-

[1] Some "attitudes and pronouncements" on language by Jacques Barzun appear in "The Retort Circumstantial" (p. 107). The work of a scholar with a different approach, Charles Carpenter Fries, is discussed in Karl Dykema's "Progress in Grammar" (p. 158).

rect English Be?") mean more to English teachers than anything said by the most distinguished professional students of language—such as Leonard Bloomfield, Robert Hall or Charles Carpenter Fries. Correct usage is pursued and discussed, furthermore, without much reference to the actual writing of literary men. Now and again I amuse myself by blue-penciling a current magazine such as the *Saturday Review* . . . against the rules. I have to report that error is rampant, if variation is to be considered error. The boys just don't seem to pay attention to the rules. Moreover, having seen some of their first drafts, I am pretty sure that what conformity they do display is the work of their wives, secretaries, editors, proofreaders and typesetters, rather than their own. It takes a determined effort to beat the old Adam out of a readable manuscript.

Thus it is only the determined, consciously creative professional who can build his work on the actual language of men. In a recent issue of the *Saturday Review,* I stumbled on a quotation from Wolfgang Langewiesche. "Well, it isn't crowned by no castle, that's for sure," he wrote, "and by no cathedral either." My eyes popped, and I read it again. I liked it. It looked right; it sounded right; it had a fine Chaucerian swing to it. But I bet it cost him some blood and a fifth of Scotch to get it into print. In my own limited publication, I find "a historical" changed to "an historical," all my "further's" changed to "farther" and all my "farther's" to "further," "than us" watered down to "than we," and many, many more. How E. M. Forster got by with "the author he thinks," and got it reprinted in a freshman handbook a few pages

along from the prohibition of such locutions baffles me. A phony standardization of usage appears in print, the work of editors unconscious of the ultimate meaning of what they do.

The result of all this is that a wet hand of fear rests on the heart of every nonprofessional writer who merely has a lot of important knowledge to communicate. He writes every sentence with a self-conscious horror of doing something wrong. It is always a comfort to him if he can fit himself into some system, such as that of a business or governmental office which provides him with a model. It is thus that gobbledegook comes into being.

I once braced a distinguished sociologist, a student of occupational myths and attitudes, about the convoluted, mainly nominal turgidity of his writing. He apparently admitted verbs into his sentences the way we admit DP's into the United States, reluctantly and with pain. In speech he was racy, confident and compelling, a brilliant lecturer. "It's the only way I can get my work into the periodicals," he told me blandly. "If it's clear and simple, they don't think it's scholarly." With what relief the pedagogues subside into pedagese!

If we really want to get good writing from people who know things, so that we can come to learn what they know as easily as we learn from their talk, we can do it in a generation or so. In school and out, in print and out, we can leave usage to its natural nurse, the unforced imitation of the practices which are actually current among educated people. We can use our English courses in school and college, not to give drill on questionable choices among common alternatives, demanding that one be taken as right and the others as wrong, but to give practice in reading and writing. We can learn to read and write for the idea, and go for the idea without regard for anything else. Then our young people will come to maturity confidently using their pencils to find out what they think and get it down on paper; then our scholars will come to write simply, clearly and brilliantly what they brilliantly know.

In our speech we have arrived, I think, at a decency of discourse which is conducive to effective expression. We listen, with a grave courteous attention, to massive patterns of speaking different from our own because they come from differences in dialect and social status; we listen without carping and without a mean contempt. Furthermore, we participate; we go with a speaker through halts and starts, over abysses of construction, filling in the lacunae without hesitation; we discount inadvertencies and disregard wrong words, and we arrive in genial good will with the speaker at his meaning. In this atmosphere, our speech has thrived, and the ordinary American is in conversation a confident, competent expressive being. In writing he is something else again.

No one flourishes in an atmosphere of repression. It is possible, of course, for a person with special aptitudes and a special drive to bull his way past the prohibitions and achieve an individual style. But with the negative attitude that attends all our writing, those whose main interest lies elsewhere are inhibited by fear of "error" and the nagging it stirs up from setting pen to paper, until the sight of a blank white page gives them the shakes. It is no wonder that their expression is halting and ineffective. They cannot fulfill the demands of a prissy propriety and trace the form of an idea at the same time. They thus arrive at adulthood victims of the steely eye of Mr. Sherwin Cody, whose bearded face stares at them from the countless ads for his correspondence school, demanding, "Do YOU make these mistakes in English?" The locutions he lists are not mistakes, and Mr. Cody knows they are not; but his readers do not know it, and they do not know that they don't matter anyway.

For usage doesn't matter. What matters is that we get done what we have to do, and get said what we have to say. Sufficient conformity is imposed upon us by the patterns of our language and by the general practices of its users so that we do not have to run the idea of conformity into the ground by carping about trivial erratics in expression. Why in this matter of language alone complete conformity should be considered a virtue—except to typists, printers and typesetters—it is difficult to see (unless, perhaps, we are using it as a covert and pusillanimous means of establishing our own superiority). In our other concerns in life, we prize individuality; why in this one matter we should depart from a principle that otherwise serves us well is a puzzle for fools and wise men to ponder, especially since there is no general agreement on what to conform to, and one man's correctness is another's error. Not until we come to our senses—teachers, editors, writers and readers together—and stop riding each other's backs, will the casual, brisk, colorful, amused, ironic and entertaining talk of Americans find its way into print. We should all be happy to see it there.

For discussion

A. How does Lloyd's idea of correctness apparently differ from Hill's?

B. Is Lloyd referring generally to the written or spoken language when he speaks of a "mania for correctness"?

C. Lloyd finds the source of the great concern with correctness to be in the eighteenth century. What are the steps by which this concern reached us?

D. What relationship does Lloyd think discussions of correctness have with what good writers actually write?

E. Whom does Lloyd hold responsible for standardization of usage in printing?

F. What don't Lloyd's summer school students know, and what do they want to learn?

G. What is Lloyd's solution for the monomania about correctness?

H. On p. 61 Lloyd writes that ". . . the ordinary American is in conversation a confident, competent, expressive being." Would you agree or disagree with this statement?

I. What might Archibald Hill say about the correctness and style of this article?

DORA JEAN ASHE

One can use an indefinite "you" occasionally, can't you?

HILL HAS told us that whatever correctness is, it is not logic. Yet logic has deprived us of the double negative on the grounds that two negatives make a positive. We scorn "I don't know nothing about it." No proper modern Mercutio would be allowed to say, "I will not budge for no man's pleasure." Logic has not yet gone so far as to say that "No. No," means "Yes," though given the special circumstances of the romantic quest, one might make an argument for double negation meaning affirmation even here. Such an argument would not, of course, be logical.

Logic has also deprived us of the double superlative, and this is one of the most unkindest cuts of all. And yet another nick is the idea that since *you* refers to the second person, singular and plural, one cannot use it as an indefinite. You can't be much more logical than that. One can't be much more unrealistic, either. This does not mean that you do not frequently find use for the indefinite *one*. Just when you use the indefinite *one* and when one uses the indefinite *you* concern Dora Jean Ashe of the College of Lynchburg as she finds herself instructed in the development of a number of skills by her students.

One has it on the impeccable authority of English grammar textbooks that the pronoun "you" is the exclusive property of the so-called second person, both singular and plural. One also knows that the third person, a much more important personage than the mere second person, has undisputed authority over all matters not directly concerned with the more personal pronouns "I," "you," and "we." In practice, however, this grammatically undisputed realm is being invaded with increasing frequency by a second person who simply does not know his place. Almost any college freshman will unwittingly further the upstart's cause by writing blithely, "We went outside around nine o'clock, and it was so dark you couldn't see your hand in front of your face." In another theme from the same group a student is likely to remark earnestly, "You have to study hard when you come to college," and a third will admonish lugubri-

"One Can Use an Indefinite 'You' Occasionally, Can't You?": From *College English*, vol. 14, n. 4, January 1953, pp. 216–219. Reprinted with the permission of The National Council of Teachers of English and Dora Jean Ashe.

ously, "Milk your cows at the same time every day, or your milk production is sure to go down." One wonders how this situation came about, when one's grammar books seldom permit this upstart "you" to be admitted even colloquially as an indefinite pronoun. So one muses awhile on this lamentable situation, allowing one's red pencil to rest before one proceeds to the next indefinite "you" which in the course of one's theme-reading will inevitably appear soon.

One recalls (at least this one does) that no less a literary celebrity than Rebecca Rowena Randall, of Sunnybrook Farm fame, had her difficulties with indefinite pronouns. Kate Douglas Wiggin records that Rebecca's teacher, the somewhat ineffectual Miss Dearborn, found fault with an essay of Rebecca's on "Solitude," saying, "There are too many 'yous' and 'yours' in it; you ought to say 'one' now and then, to make it seem more like good writing." The revised essay "hardly satisfied either teacher or pupil," which is understandable. It read in part: "Does one ever feel bereft when one picks up one's chips to light one's fire for one's evening meal? Or when one washes one's milk pail before milking one's cow? One would fancy not." Is it possible that the impeccable "one" can be overdone? One fancies, from this illustration and others that one knows, that it can. What guiding principles can be established which will aid both the college essayist and his harassed teacher in dealing with the Scylla and Charybdis of "one" and "you"?

It can be immediately established that the average college student has little use for the indefinite "one." He can nearly always be counted upon to strike out boldly with the indefinite "you," except in discouraging cases where the indefinite "they" gets his nod. And at times his writing gains in vividness when the "you" is thus employed. For example, when the student is struggling with the exposition of a process, he finds it much more familiar to say to the reader, "Now you take the long end of the tie and pass it under the short end," than to state pedantically, "The long end of the tie is now passed under the short end," or, more personally, to confide, "I now take the long end. . . ." Often he may find support for his preference of the pronoun "you" in the expository selections he reads in textbook models. In *Modern English Readings,* for instance, he will note that Oliver La Farge, in the excerpt called "Rowing," drops quite naturally into the "you" idiom in explaining the nature of the stroke: La Farge writes, "You are sitting on a slide. . . . Your two hands are on the loom of your twelve-foot oar. . . ."

Vividness and a sense of reader-participation are often gained by the use of "you" in such expository writing. Most teachers will permit this use but will insist that the "you" must be made to refer definitely to the reader, so that he, like the listener in conversation, knows that the "you" is directed at him, giving him information of interest and perhaps benefit.

There are other cases, however, where the "you" refers only indirectly to the reader and still others where it cannot be interpreted as referring to him unless exceptional circumstances are granted. The reader customarily —and with reason—takes the use of "you" personally; the teacher, who is the usual reader, naturally resents being told that he must study to keep his grades up and that he must milk his cows at regular times. Under severe provocation, as in the matter of the cows, he may write a sarcastic marginal note in which he reserves the right to milk his nonexistent cows when it pleases him to do so. But even here the student, by exercising ingenuity, could justify his use of the "you" by making it clear that his remarks were addressed, say, to a 4-H Club group engaged in studying dairy production. The teacher in all probability will insist that this special situation be clearly explained in the theme, so that he will be cleared of all complicity in the matter of the cows' milking time.

It seems possible to establish two facts about the indefinite "you": one is that the college freshman will use this pronoun instinctively in all kinds of situations; the other is that his teacher will try to restrict such wholesale usage to cases where the pronoun demonstrably refers to the reader. Thus the student, the teacher, and the pronouns may engage in a running battle all term, with the student being forced finally to adopt a few formal trappings. He will almost never use "one," but he may begin to say, "The farmer should milk his cows . . ." or "Cows should be milked. . . ." The teacher may well congratulate himself that he has eradicated many troublesome "you's" and has fitted the student out with a pronoun usage that could perhaps at times be considered "formal" in its correctness. But has he in so doing improved the student's literary style, or has he merely removed it a few paces farther into the Lethe-like region of "formal written English," a

style which there are few to praise and almost none to love? We know that colloquial usage is customarily twenty or thirty years ahead of formal usage and that the border marauders of today may well be the solid grammatical citizens of tomorrow. The fact that the pronoun "one" sounds archaic to today's student bodes ill not only for its future existence but for its present-day existence. Writers of considerable repute, as well as students, play fast and loose with the indefinite "you." Somerset Maugham in *The Summing Up* uses both "you" and "one" with apparently little distinction in reference. At one point he says, "The prestige you acquire by being able to tell your friends that you know famous men proves only that you are yourself of small account." Two pages farther on, he writes, "One does not die immediately one has made one's will; one makes one's will as a precaution. To have settled one's affairs is a very good preparation to leading the rest of one's life without concern for the future."[1] In both situations the pronouns are meant presumably to mean people in general, and it is noteworthy that the use of "you" in the first quotation seems less stiff than the "one" of the second quotation.

It is this "you," the "you" of universal application, that has definite merit and that is increasingly being employed by good prose writers. Examples of its use can be found significantly at all levels of spoken and written English. There is, for instance, the almost proverbial statement, "You can't take it with you." Its effectiveness is lost if it is changed mincingly

[1] Somerset Maugham, *The Summing Up* ("New American Library" [New York: Mentor Books, 1951]), pp. 7 and 9.

to "One can't take it with one" or ploddingly to, "The world's inhabitants cannot take their material possessions with them." And the "you" *does* refer to the reader; it has perfect reference because, without qualification, it can refer to *any* reader. The reader may not have cows or college grades, but he is bound to have earthly possessions that he can't take with him when he departs this life. Proverbial sayings customarily employ the "you"—or imply it in imperative constructions—to make sure that every reader knows that he specifically is meant to profit by the advice. Just as the Uncle Sam of the recruiting posters points his finger directly at the reader when he thunders, "I want YOU!" so statements of universal application gain pointedness when they are addressed to "you" and not to a namby-pamby "one."

It seems reasonable to conclude that the pronoun "you" can be used effectively and correctly both when it is carefully made to refer to a specific reader or group of readers, as in various types of exposition, and when it refers to the reader and all other members of the human race. Of course, you can never be quite sure when you are safe in addressing humanity in general, because some segment of humanity can always be counted upon to retort scathingly, "Speak for yourself, John!" But more can be gained by ignoring these doubting Thomases than by heeding them. Since, as Donne has so well told us, we are involved in humanity to such an extent that a funeral bell tolls as much for us who remain as for the individual who is dead, there must be many situations in which a single reader and a world full of potential readers can be lumped together as "you." You wouldn't feel offended, would you, if a writer full of temerity wrote, "You need as often as possible to be made to feel your own active participation in what someone else has written because then the words, if they have any value at all, will belong peculiarily to you and to all other human beings who read them"? And can you never be quite sure that a "you" couldn't mean you? After all, you may even own cows someday!

For discussion

A. What does the author consider to be the dangers of the indefinite *you?*
B. What are the two facts the author thinks can be established about the indefinite *you?*
C. The author speaks of one kind of indefinite *you* which, as employed by good writers, has real merit. What is it? Give five examples.
D. What is the other effective use of the indefinite *you?*
E. Write a paper of about 250–300 words in which you give specific directions, with examples, for the most effective use of the indefinite *you* and the indefinite *one.*

S . I . H A Y A K A W A

Contexts

IN THE SUMMER of 1964, newspaper reporters and radio and television newscasters and commentators started using the verb *escalate*. If people looked it up in any dictionary but *Webster's Third International* dictionary, they were wasting their time—it wasn't there. And even the definition in *Webster's Third* didn't seem sufficient. But probably few people looked it up; they didn't need to. There was increasing danger in the quickening pace of the crises in Southeast Asia, and one didn't need to know what a back-formation was to realize that *escalate* had something to do with *escalator*. Besides, the specific meaning was fortified every time the word was used—in a context.

Someday, when they catch up with the language of the summer of 1964, dictionaries will illustrate this new meaning. In the following article, Professor Hayakawa tells how in describing part of the process by which dictionary makers decide what a word means. It turns out that they find out from us, the users of the language.

S. I. Hayakawa is Professor of English and Language Arts at San Francisco State College and editor of *ETC*, the magazine of general semantics.

HOW DICTIONARIES ARE MADE

It is widely believed that every word has a correct meaning, that we learn these meanings principally from teachers and grammarians (except that most of the time we don't bother to, so that we ordinarily speak "sloppy English"), and that dictionaries and grammars are the supreme authority in matters of meaning and usage. Few people ask by what authority the writers of dictionaries and grammars say what they say. The writer once got into a dispute with an Englishwoman over the pronunciation of a word and offered to look it up in the dictionary. The Englishwoman said firmly, "What for? I am English. I was born and brought up in England. The way I speak *is* English." Such self-assurance about one's own language is not uncommon among the English. In the United States, however, anyone who is willing to quarrel with the dictionary is regarded as either eccentric or mad.

Let us see how dictionaries are made and how the editors arrive at definitions. What follows applies, incidentally, only to those dictionary offices where first-hand, original research goes on—not those in which editors simply copy existing dictionaries. The task of writing a dictionary begins with reading vast amounts of the literature of the period or subject that the dictionary is to cover. As the editors read, they copy on cards every interesting or rare word, every unusual or peculiar occurrence of a common word, a large number of common words in their ordinary uses, and also the sentences in which each of these words appears, thus:

---

pail
The dairy *pails* bring home increase of milk

        Keats, *Endymion*
        I, 44–45

That is to say, the context of each word is collected along with the word itself. For a really big job of dictionary writing, such as the *Oxford English Dictionary* (usually bound in about twenty-five volumes), millions of such cards are collected and the task of editing occupies decades. As the cards are collected, they are alphabetized and sorted. When the sorting is completed, there will be for each word anywhere from two or three to several hundred illustrative quotations, each on its card.

To define a word, then, the dictionary editor places before him the stack of cards illustrating that word;

each of the cards represents an actual use of the word by a writer of some literary or historical importance. He reads the cards carefully, discards some, rereads the rest, and divides up the stack according to what he thinks are the several senses of the word. Finally, he writes his definitions, following the hard-and-fast rule that each definition *must* be based on what the quotations in front of him reveal about the meaning of the word. The editor cannot be influenced by what *he* thinks a given word *ought* to mean. He must work according to the cards or not at all.

The writing of a dictionary, therefore, is not a task of setting up authoritative statements about the "true meanings" of words, but a task of *recording,* to the best of one's ability, what various words have *meant* to authors in the distant or immediate past. *The writer of a dictionary is a historian, not a lawgiver.* If, for example, we had been writing a dictionary in 1890, or even as late as 1919, we could have said that the word "broadcast" means "to scatter" (seed and so on) but we could not have decreed that from 1921 on, the commonest meaning of the word should become "to disseminate audible messages, etc., by radio transmission." To regard the dictionary as an "authority," therefore, is to credit the dictionary writer with gifts of prophecy which neither he nor anyone else possesses. In choosing our words when we speak or write, we can be *guided* by the historical record afforded us by the dictionary, but we cannot be *bound* by it, because new situations, new experiences, new inventions, new feelings, are always compelling us to give new uses to old words. Looking under a "hood," we should ordinarily have found, five hundred years ago, a monk; today, we find a motorcar engine.[1]

VERBAL AND PHYSICAL CONTEXTS

The way in which the dictionary writer arrives at his definitions merely systematizes the way in which we all learn the meanings of words, beginning at infancy, and continuing for the rest of our lives. Let us say that we have never heard the word "oboe" before, and we overhear a conversation in which the following sentences occur:

He used to be the best *oboe* player in town. . . . Whenever they came to that *oboe* part in the third movement, he used to get very excited. . . . I saw him one day at the music shop, buying a new reed for his *oboe*. . . . He never liked to play the clarinet after he started playing the *oboe*. . . . He said it wasn't much fun, because it was too easy.

Although the word may be unfamiliar, its meaning becomes clear to us as we listen. After hearing the first sentence, we know that an "oboe" is "played," so that it must be either a game or a musical instrument. With the second sentence the possibility of its being a game is eliminated. With each succeeding sentence the possibilities as to what an "oboe" may be are narrowed down until we get a

[1] *Webster's Third New International Dictionary* lists the word "hood" also as a shortened form of "hoodlum."

The time that elapsed between *Webster's Second Edition* (1934) and the *Third* (1961) indicates the enormous amount of reading and labor entailed in the preparation of a really thorough dictionary of an language as rapidly changing and as rich in vocabulary as English.

fairly clear idea of what is meant. This is how we learn by *verbal context*.

But even independently of this, we learn by physical and social context. Let us say that we are playing golf and that we have hit the ball in a certain way with certain unfortunate results, so that our companion says to us, "That's a bad *slice*." He repeats this remark every time our ball fails to go straight. If we are reasonably bright, we learn in a very short time to say, when it happens again, "That's a bad slice." On one occasion, however, our friend says to us, "That's not a *slice* this time; that's a *hook*." In this case we consider what has happened, and we wonder what is different about the last stroke from those previous. As soon as we make the distinction, we have added still another word to our vocabulary. The result is that after nine holes of golf, we can use both these words accurately—and perhaps several others as well, such as "divot," "number-five iron," "approach shot," *without ever having been told what they mean*. Indeed, we may play golf for years without ever being able to give a dictionary definition of "to slice": "To strike (the ball) so that the face of the club draws inward across the face of the ball, causing it to curve toward the right in flight (with a right-handed player)" (*Webster's New International Dictionary, Second Edition*). But even without being able to give such a definition, we should still be able to use the word accurately whenever the occasion demanded.

We learn the meanings of practically all our words (which are, it will be remembered, merely complicated noises), not from dictionaries, not from definitions, but from hearing these noises as they accompany actual situations in life and then learning to associate certain noises with certain situations. Even as dogs learn to recognize "words," as for example by hearing "biscuit" at the same time as an actual biscuit is held before their noses, so do we all learn to interpret language by being aware of the happenings that accompany the noises people make at us—by being aware, in short, of contexts.

The definitions given by little children in school show clearly how they associate words with situations; they almost always define in terms of physical and social contexts: "Punishment is when you have been bad and they put you in a closet and don't let you have any supper." "Newspapers are what the paper boy brings and you wrap up the garbage with it." These are good definitions. They cannot be used in dictionaries mainly because they are too specific; it would be impossible to list the myriads of situations in which every word has been used. For this reason, dictionaries give definitions on a high level of abstraction; that is, with particular references left out for the sake of conciseness. This is another reason why it is a great mistake to regard a dictionary as telling us all about a word.

For discussion

A. How does Hayakawa show that the writer of a dictionary is a historian, not a lawgiver?

B. How is it possible always to use a word accurately and yet not be able to define it?

C. If you were compiling a dictionary and had before you only the following quotations, what definitions would you write for the word *shrdlu?* Don't just try to find a one-word synonym but write out a ten- to twenty-word definition.
1. He was exceptionally skillful with a shrdlu.
2. He says he needs a shrdlu to shape the beams.
3. I saw Mr. Jenkins yesterday buying a new handle for his shrdlu.
4. The steel head of Jenkins' shrdlu was badly chipped.
5. Don't bother with a saw or an ax; a shrdlu will do the job faster and better.

D. From the following quotations make up a definition in less than twenty words of *wanky*.
1. He seems to be perpetually wanky.
2. Some people feel most wanky in the early morning, but I get that way just before supper.
3. If you want to get over that wanky feeling, take Johnson's Homogenized Yeast Tablets.
4. Everybody feels more or less wanky on a hot, humid day.
5. . . . the wanky, wanky bluebell
   That droops upon its stem . . .
6. I am not cross, just wanky.

E. Ablation (n), apogee (n), gantry (n), jet (v), pad (n), and scrub (v) have all extended their meanings in the last few years. Not all of these new meanings have yet been recorded in dictionaries, but you almost certainly know what they all mean. How? What is a recent meaning for each?

ROBERT L. COARD

The possessive apostrophe in names

WHEN DO YOU USE periods after each letter in abbreviations? It doesn't seem to matter with NATO, but how about WHO for the World Health Organization? Do you add another -*s* to form the possessive when a word ends in -*s*? It seems all right in "Charles's Wain" but how about "Moses's Tablets"?

Some say one may leave out the periods in NATO, but that it might avoid confusion to put them in with W.H.O. Most style books and dictionaries call for -*'s* after a word ending in -*s*, though few of us ever pronounce it. But when the sibilants multiply, even the style books allow us to omit the last -*s*. In short, the regulations for a variety of minor traffic problems in writing are a combination of historical convention and linguistic convenience. After all, no style maker wants to recommend a hiss.

And so it is generally with the use of the possessive apostrophe in names, as Robert L. Coard of St. Cloud State College, Minnesota, demonstrates in the following article. The apostrophe has been used in English since the year of the Spanish Armada, and it has been used as an indicator of possession since shortly thereafter. Its use with names has varied with time, place, circumstance, and the individual contemplating its immediate relevance. Professor Coard examines the use of the apostrophe as an indicator of possession in the names of cities, topographical features, colleges, books, magazines, associations, and businesses. He explains a good deal, finds some order, and points out certain clear trends in contemporary American English.

An associated press news item indicates that the conflict over Hell's Canyon has now spread from the issue of public versus private power to the question of the use of the apostrophe. Sam Fretwell, of Parma, Idaho, chairman of the Idaho–Oregon–Washington's Hell's Canyon Association, is quoted: "We always spell it Hell's Canyon," But Gilbert Stanton, public relations director for the Idaho Power Company, states: "It's Hells Canyon as far as we're concerned." Though indexed with an apostrophe, the titles collected in the *Readers' Guide to Periodical Literature* display both forms. A check of seven periodicals during the first week of July, 1957, showed them preferring the form without the apostrophe five to two.

"The Possessive Apostrophe in Names": From *American Speech*, vol. 33, n. 3, October 1958, pp. 176–179. Copyright 1958 by Columbia University Press and reprinted with their permission.

The question whether to use an apostrophe in the names of cities, topographical features, colleges, books, magazines, associations, and businesses is indeed troublesome. A word of this kind may take an apostrophe, and then again it may not. *Webster's New International* (with the apostrophe) lists *Devil's Bit Mountains* and *Devil's Island,* but also *Devils Lake* and *Devils Tower National Monument.* Some conflict exists between forms recommended by standard reference works. The *Columbia Lippincott Gazeteer of the World* lists *Devilsbit Mountains* or *Devil's Bit Mountains* in that order, but *Webster's Geographical Dictionary* lists only *Devil's Bit Mountains. Columbia* lists *Devils Island, Saint Mary's Peak* (Australia), *Kings Peak* (Utah), and *Land's End* or *Lands End;* but *Webster* records *Devil's Island, Saint Mary Peak, King's Peak,* and *Lands End* or *Land's End.*

Although usage has varied widely ever since the first introduction of the apostrophe as an indicator of possession in the seventeenth century, certain current trends in its use or omission may be detected. In the United States, for example, the apostrophe in place names seems faced with extinction since the Board on Geographic Names of the United States Government discourages its use. *Harper's Ferry* appears as a secondary form in the *American College Dictionary* and *Webster's New World Dictionary* and may still be seen in print occasionally as in Allan Nevins's *The Emergence of Lincoln,* but most editors and atlas makers, following the decision of the Board, consistently omit the apostrophe. Only in a relatively few instances like *Martha's Vineyard* and

Lee's Summit (Mo.) has the Board admitted an apostrophe. In the *United States Official Postal Guide* one must pass over scores of names like *Devils Elbow, Carters Bridge, Lees Creek, Browns Store,* and *Hells Half Acre* before he finds a few with the apostrophe like *Lincoln's New Salem* and *Boy's Ranch.* This omission of the apostrophe represents a sharp break with American usage of the nineteenth century as Civil War forms like *Harper's Ferry, Stone's River,* and *Drewry's Bluff* show. Today when one sees an apostrophe in a name list in a gazeteer, there is a likelihood that the form is British, since the British have been far more tenacious in retaining the apostrophe than Americans.

The possessive apostrophe is found more frequently in the names of American colleges than in American place names. For example, it's *Paul Smith's College* at *Paul Smiths,* New York. The numerous colleges named after saints generally take an apostrophe as the half dozen or more colleges called *St. Joseph's College* demonstrate, but even here the tendency to use the uninflected form appears as in *St. Joseph College,* West Hartford, Connecticut. Especially when the result would be harsh or cumbersome, the apostrophe and the *s* may be omitted in colleges named after saints as in *St. Francis College* or *St. Mary-of-the-Woods.* When a college is named after any one except a saint, the apostrophe is rare. As with associations, colleges having the word *woman's* in their name regularly take an apostrophe (*Woman's College of the University of North Carolina, Colorado Woman's College*).

A handy rule to remember is that

not one of the teachers colleges in the United States takes an apostrophe in its name. True, most of those that have not already done so are feverishly trying to change their names to colleges of education, state colleges, or universities, but a good many of them still remain in the unregenerate form (*State Teachers College,* Minot, North Dakota: *General Beadle State Teachers College*). Years ago the apostrophe seems to have been employed in the form *teachers college,* though then they were generally called normal schools. Older editions of the *Encyclopaedia Britannica* write of *Teachers' College* of Columbia University. As usual in linguistic matters the Canadians have been more conservative and still generally speak of such institutions as normal schools, but *Webster's New Collegiate* does record an apostrophe in the single Canadian one with *teachers* in the name (*New Brunswick Teachers' College*).

Books and magazines whenever circumstances permit its insertion cling to the apostrophe with great fidelity. Though it is possible to find exceptions like *Finnegans Wake, American Peoples Cookbook,* and *Funk and Wagnalls New Standard Dictionary* (names ending in *s* tend to resist the apostrophe), one has to search for them. *Grove's Dictionary of Music and Musicians, The Publishers' Trade List Annual, Ulrich's Periodicals Directory, The Old Wives' Tale,* and *Readers' Guide to Periodical Literature* represent the customary practice in books.

Magazines, though generally following book practice, show a somewhat greater freedom in dispensing with the apostrophe. Most of the well-known magazines, however, keep it: *Harper's Magazine, Ladies' Home Journal, McCall's, Nation's Business, Parents' Magazine,* and *Today's Health. Harper's Magazine* apparently made a tentative effort to abandon the mark, for in the 1930s the apostrophe was omitted on the outside cover though retained on the inside. Now *Harper's* is consistent in using the apostrophe in all places. Less well-known magazines listed in *Ulrich's Periodicals Directory* generally follow the practice of the better known ones: *National Bottlers' Gazette, Farmers' Elevator Guide, Publishers' Weekly, Arborist's News,* and *Agricultural Leaders' Digest.* But some use no apostrophe: *Bankers Monthly, Brewers Digest, Brewers Journal, Manufacturers Record,* and *National Bowlers Journal and Billiard Revue.*

In contrast to books and magazines, which generally employ the possessive apostrophe, the names of associations are usually free of the mark. Most of the possessive apostrophes in the names of associations listed in the *Encyclopedia of American Associations* (1956) occur only when the words *men, woman, women,* and *children* are employed in the name. Then an apostrophe and an *s* are invariably used. Two examples of each follow: *American National Cattlemen's Association, Textile Salesmen's Association; Woman's International Bowling Congress, National Woman's Christian Temperance Union; Women's Veterinary Medical Association, Women's Joint Congressional Committee; Children's Book Council, Infants and Children's Wear Salesmen's Guild.*

Excluding the forms *men's, woman's, women's,* and *children's,* I found just thirteen others in the *Encyclopedia of American Associations* using an apostrophe, though hundreds, such as the *National Farmers Union* and *American Tramp Shipowners Association*, might have theoretically done so. The thirteen employing the apostrophe are as follows: *National Cotton Ginners' Association, Fur Dyers' Guild, Fashion Originators' Guild of America, Rice Millers' Association, National Sheriffs' Association, United States Shellac Importers' Association, American Electroplaters' Society, Lepidopterists' Society, American Dental Hygienists' Association, Committee for the Nation's Health* (defunct), *Boys' Clubs of America, United Boys' Brigades of America*, and *International Order of the King's Daughters and Sons*.

The apostrophe is also generally omitted in the names of state associations, local labor unions, and other organizations, though it appears much more often than in the names of the national associations. Usage as recorded in telephone directories shows considerable variation. Generally, of course, there is no apostrophe (*Bookbinders Union Local No. 60*), but sometimes one finds a singular possessive (*Hoisting Engineer's Local Union No. 101, Barber's Local No. 192*), and sometimes a plural possessive (*Bricklayers' Union No. 4 of Mo., Insulation Production Workers' Local Union No. 1*).

Any statement about the use of the apostrophe in the names of business firms would require an enormous amount of qualification, and even then one could note variation in the way a given firm writes its name. In a poster at the back of the store the apostrophe may be present; in the neon sign on the façade it may be

missing. This inconsistency is also noticeable in printing. I have before me a communication from Illiana Teachers' Service, which employs an apostrophe in its name in two places and omits it in the third. Probably the average business firm does give its name without either an apostrophe or *s* (*C. B. Buffalow Bicycle Shop, Frank Pierce Body Shop*). Less frequently, though often enough on signs, the *s* is given without an apostrophe. The apostrophe seems to enjoy its greatest vitality in the names of small businesses or in businesses that wish to give that impression, such as gift shops, beauty parlors, service stations, grocery stores, restaurants, and taverns. The tendency to use the apostrophe is especially strong when the person's first name is used. Thousands of small American businesses show these forms: *Lucille's Flower Shop; Hazel's Gift and Card Shop; Mabel's Beauty Shop, Mr. John's Beauty Salon; Ward's Service Station, Thomas' Gulf Service Station; Kelly's Grocery, Lazenby's Food Fair; Pete and Pauline's Chicken Dinners, Tommy's Silver Skillet; Pat's Tavern, Oscar's Lounge.*

The apostrophe and the *s* cause difficulties in many other places besides those discussed above. Usage in such a combination as *St. Marks Methodist Church* fluctuates greatly. In general, the name of a saint in a church follows the pattern outlined in the treatment of the names of saints in colleges. Other perplexing situations frequently arise. The writer may be tormented by the question whether he should use an apostrophe in *Apostles' Creed* (the lexicographers say yes), or in *Peasants' Revolt* (the lexicographers say yes).

The agonies of writers hesitating over the question of using an apostrophe have often been matched by the sufferings of sign painters. On a sign above a bookstore on a university campus the painters decided on *Charle's Book Store.* A few weeks later ladders were again visible, and the apostrophe traveled about twelve inches to the right. Probably the painters share the sentiment of Steven T. Byington expressed in *American Speech* in February, 1945: "The fact is, the apostrophe is a morbid growth in English orthography, and our language would be none the worse for its abolition."[1]

1 "Certain Fashions in Commas and Apostrophes," XX, 27.

For discussion

A. Why is the apostrophe disappearing in place names in the United States?

B. Under what circumstances is there a tendency to omit both the apostrophe and the -*s?*

C. Stop by your neighborhood magazine stand and make a record of which magazines do and which do not use the apostrophe.

D. Look in the "Yellow Pages" of your phone book at the list of names of magazine subscription agents, restaurants, and drug stores. For each group, note how many names use the apostrophe to indicate possession and how many omit it. Then write a short report on the uses of the possessive apostrophe in these three groups.

E. Under what circumstances do you use the hyphen with *re-?*

F. Under what circumstances do you use the hyphen with *ex-?* (e.g., *ex officio, ex cathedra, ex champion, ex post facto, ex President*). Any good dictionary will provide an answer to this and to the following questions.

G. Write a general rule for use of the hyphen after checking the following: *life buoy, life line, life boat, life guard, life time, police car, police man, three mile hike, navy blue shirt, small business man, foreign aid plan, pay as you go bill, devil may care attitude.*

H. Write a general rule for the use of -'s in the plurals of abbreviations, letters, and figures, after checking the following: *M.D., C.P.A., vets, Amvets, co-op, Ph.D., G.P.O., I.Q., G.I., apt., hr.*

NORMAN C. STAGEBERG

Some structural ambiguities

ANY CHILD WHO HAS LEARNED that you can say *longer* but not *gooder, grouchy* but not *ouchy, two causes* but not *two chaoses,* and *friendly* but not *cryey* may suspect that there is something arbitrary about language. By the time he has learned the difference between *day off* and *off day,* between *body English* and *English body* and between *I am going* and *Am I going?*, he knows that the way you put words together has a lot to do with the meaning you take away. He also knows that there are some ways in which you don't put words together at all, such as *house white, goes there he?*, and *and man the of.*

But this, according to Norman C. Stageberg of State College of Iowa, is not all. Sometimes you can put the words together in a proper American English pattern, and still have trouble. It's not that you haven't said anything; on the contrary, you may have said two different things at the same time. In short, acceptable English patterns frequently permit semantic ambiguity. There seems to be nothing incorrect— at the very least in Hill's sense of the word—with "She wore a rose in her ear which collapsed as the evening wore on." The trouble is that we don't know whether this sentence is an observation about botany or zoology.

Stageberg explains and illustrates a number of these ambiguities. To make it simpler to refer to them, an example of each situation is listed below:

1. . . . a dull boy's knife . . .
2. . . . modern language teaching . . .
3. German teachers visit Greensboro.
4. Give more realistic details.
5. . . . Cream cheese cake . . .
6. . . . good vision, coordination and speed . . .
7. . . . heather gray, red, and blue . . .
8. . . . heavy padded coat . . .
9a. U.S. Sabre jet pilots today shot down one Communist MIG-15 and damaged another in clearing North Korean skies.
9b. . . . the standing committee . . .

"Some Structural Ambiguities": From *The English Journal,* vol. 47, n. 8, November 1958, pp. 479–486. Reprinted with the permission of the National Council of Teachers of English and Norman C. Stageberg.

10. . . . artificial ice and fuel . . .
11. He used an arm stroke and a kick which propelled him through the water.
12. After choosing the college I thought I would attend, the Student Adviser at my high school arranged an interview with a former student.
13. We believe in doing what we do well.
14. The club will be open to members only from Monday to Thursday.
15. The loud speaker wakes everyone up in the hall.
16. His job is to post changes in address, telephone numbers, and performance ratings.
17. She has cute ideas for parties that are easy to plan.
18. I like my roommate as well as Janice.
19. The hostess greeted the girl with a smile.
20. He had never gone ice-fishing from a hut like that.

Many native speakers believe that our language can be manipulated like a boy's mechanical-builder set—with its interchangeable parts that can be put together in every which fashion —and that in English one can say any old thing in any old way. Such a belief is naive, for English is structured with a large number of syntactic patterns that we are compelled to follow. As a quick example, consider this noun group: *Our first large authorized class party.* Each of the five modifiers belongs in a class by itself and takes its predetermined position in the pattern.[1] If you change the order of these modifiers in any way, you will get a non-English sequence. And with many other patterns the same is true. We are pattern-bound in language just as we are culture-bound in mores. Now one would think that the numerous patterns of English, after centuries of development, would have become so refined as to be clear and unequivocal vehicles of thought. But such is not the case. On the contrary, there are many syntactic pat-

[1] There is nothing "natural" about the order of pre-noun modifiers. In Russian, for example, one says "gray two horses" and "two my friends."

terns that are open to ambiguity. It is these ambiguous patterns that I propose to describe—not all of them to be sure, but those that may be of greatest interest to the teacher of composition. At the outset we must be clear on one point: we are dealing with ambiguities in the written, not the spoken, language.

First, it may be useful to distinguish between two kinds of ambiguity, lexical and structural. In lexical ambiguity the multiple meaning resides in the words themselves, as in this news item from a California paper: "Rev. Keith Hammond was congratulated on being able to get his parish plastered." Structural ambiguity, on the other hand, results from the arrangement of the words, that is, from the structure of the utterance. It is sometimes known as syntactic ambiguity and, in older logic books, as amphiboly. Here is an example from a New York paper: "Whatever her thoughts, they were interrupted as the hotel lobby door swung open and a young woman carrying a baby and her husband entered." Our concern here is with the latter type of ambiguities, and I will present them in a series of structural situations.

SITUATION 1: *Adjective + noun in possessive case + noun.* As an example we may take *a dull boy's knife.* The trouble here is that the adjective may modify either the noun in the possessive case or the second noun. It is true that in English we tend to interpret an adjective as modifying everything that follows it up to and including the headword; but despite this tendency we often meet ambiguities like a *blond artist's model, a clever reporter's story,* and *a plain man's necktie.* An advertisement in the *New Yorker* played upon this pattern with this legend: "A handsome man's shirt? No, a man's handsome shirt."

SITUATION 2: *Adjective + noun + noun.* A good example occurs on a sign beside an Iowa highway reading *Little Charm Motel.* This is similar to the first situation in that the adjective may modify the immediately following noun or the second noun. We meet ambiguities of this kind often in such expressions as *modern language teaching, big building owners, basic English text, hot evening drink, fresh strawberry ice cream, hot bed covers, heavy hog production,* and *deep love movies.*

SITUATION 3: *Modifier (noun or adjective) + noun.* In this situation the reader must know whether the modifier is a noun or an adjective if he is to understand the sentence. A convenient example is furnished by a headline in the *Waterloo [Iowa] Daily Courier:*

Fleet planes told shoot snooper jet.

What kind of planes do we have here, speedy planes or planes of the fleet? The sentence is ambiguous because we do not know the form-class of the modifier *fleet.* From a trade journal called the *Tire Review* comes a similar case:

A keen edge quickly on rubber knives with Branick electric knife sharpener.

Or suppose you read this headline:

German teachers visit Greensboro.

Would you take this to mean teachers of German or teachers from Germany?

SITUATION 4: *More or most + adjective + noun.* The ambiguity lies in the two possibilities—that the *more* or *most* may modify the adjective or the noun. Of the examples which follow, the first is a comment I once wrote on the paper of a freshman, who demanded clarification:

Give more realistic details.
The defense system should have fewer troops with more modern arms, including field missiles.

Occasionally the words *less* and *least,* because of their use in the sense of *fewer,* and *fewest,* will cause a similar difficulty:

This soap has less harmful effects on the hands.

SITUATION 5: *Noun + noun + noun.* When this pattern occurs it may raise a question of modification, as it does in this newspaper headline:

Study of fish blood system may aid cancer research.

Does the first noun *fish* modify the compound noun *blood system,* or does the compound noun *fish blood* modify *system?* And how do you interpret the next:

Cream cheese cake.

Is this cheese cake with cream or cake with cream cheese? The list of ingredients below the label does not help a bit: "Cheese, sugar, fresh eggs, cream, graham crackers, flour. . . ." Usually when we meet a collocation of three nouns, the sense operates to prevent ambiguity, as in *hand garden plow* and *coil bed springs*. When more than three nouns pile up, the result is likely to be confusion, as in this:

New Moscow bus student travel officer.

SITUATION 6: *Adjective + series of nouns*. Here is an example from a student paper:

A baseball player must have good vision, coordination, and speed.

Does the adjective *good* in this sentence modify only *vision*, or the whole series of nouns? If one insists that of course it modifies only *vision*, then what can be said about this sentence, which has exactly the same pattern?

She raised wonderful tulips, hyacinths, and crocuses.

Does *wonderful* here modify only tulips? Thus it seems apparent that the situation itself makes for ambiguity. Of course the lexical compatibility of the words may keep the reading from going wrong. For instance, the first sentence would be clear if the adjective were compatible only with *vision:*

A baseball player must have sharp vision, coordination, and speed.

Here are two more instances:

Bulletin No. 7 contains only a few items on French literature, theology, and philosophy.

For sale: Handwoven towels, table mats, wool shirts, and wool stoles.

SITUATION 7: *Noun + series of adjectives*. This is like Situation 6. It can be illustrated by a quotation from a *New York Times* advertisement. The words describe three colors in which men's socks are available: *heather gray, red,* and *blue*. If one ordered red socks on the basis of this description, what color would he get, red or heather red?

SITUATION 8: *Modifier + past participle + noun*. In this pattern the question is whether the first term modifies the past participle or the noun. Students write expressions like these, without punctuation: *steep pointed gables, heavy padded coat,* and *clean swept room*.

SITUATION 9: *ing verb + noun*. This pattern may sometimes be construed in two ways: as modifier + noun, or as verb + noun object. An AP Story gives us a good example:

U.S. Sabre jet pilots today shot down one Communist MIG-15 and damaged another in clearing North Korean skies.

From E. A. Nida's *Synopsis of English Syntax* we get another:

. . . two systems of outlining notation are employed.

A second interpretive possibility for the *-ing verb + noun* pattern is that it may be looked at as either adjective + noun, or as noun + noun. This is fundamentally the same as Situation 3. The following examples will illustrate:

So you think you have moving problems!

He joined the standing committee.

She maintains an entertaining apartment.

SITUATION 10: *Adjective + noun + conjunction + noun.* The question in this pattern is whether the adjective modifies only the first noun or both nouns. An example will make the question clear:

A new company was formed to handle artificial ice and fuel.

SITUATION 11: *Series of words + modifying word or word-group.* The series usually consists of nouns. The question that arises is whether the modifier refers to all items in the series or only to the last item. A few examples will show the problem:

. . . a conservative, a Fascist, and an atheist who might be excluded from the teaching profession because of non-conforming beliefs.
He used an arm stroke and a kick which propelled him through the water.
Red, yellow, blue, navy, or white with trim.
At the dress rehearsal she sang, danced, and tumbled very expertly.

SITUATION 12: *Modifier + subject of sentence.* The reader tends to associate an opening modifier with the closest following word, which is usually the subject, whereas this modifier may relate to something further on in the sentence. This is more often a misleading construction than a genuine ambiguity, as these examples will show:

After choosing the college I thought I would like to attend, the student adviser at my high school arranged an interview with a former student.
Whether religious or humorous, the church plays a great part in everyone's Christmas activities.

SITUATION 13: *Modificand[2] + intervening material + modifier.* The difficulty here is that the modifier may appear to modify some part of the intervening material. Here are some cases from student papers:

We must show the world how fallacious the Communist Party is by democratic means.
Zola was able to describe the characters, the places they went, and the things they did very well.
We believe in doing what we do well (motto of Tuskegee Institute).

When the intervening material consists of a noun + relative clause, we have a pattern that frequently occurs:

Every child awaits the time he can go to school with great excitement.
When applying the clay coil to the base, roughen the parts you are joining with a comb.

SITUATION 14: *Modificand + modifier + modificand.* This is our old friend, the squinting modifier, which looks before and after and pines in both directions, as in this sentence:

The club will be open to members only from Monday to Thursday.

A writer sometimes gets into this pickle when he tries to wriggle out of a split infinitive. In the next example a *New York Times* writer placed the modifier before the *to:*

. . . one-way streets had failed completely to relieve cross-town traffic.

And the writer who puts the modifier after the infinitive runs the same risk, as the next exhibit will show. It is from a textbook by a Browning scholar who eschews a split infinitive like ginger ale in his whiskey:

2 The *modificand* is the word modified.

The university man or woman learns to examine critically conflicting points of view.

The last example is from a well-known college textbook of speech:

What we believe profoundly influences our ability to listen fairly to any subject.

SITUATION 15: *Verb-adverb, or preposition.* By *verb-adverb* is meant such verbs as *put up with* (endure), *turn up* (appear), *turn down* (refuse), *look up to* (admire), *look down on* (scorn), and *prevail on* (induce). Sometimes a reader cannot be sure whether the second word is part of the verb or a preposition. These two instances will illustrate:

The loud speaker wakes everyone up in the hall.
The amphibious truck will carry over its rated capacity when crossing a stream.

SITUATION 16: *Dual parallel structure.* A sentence element may sometimes be taken to go with either one of two structures already established in the sentence. This ambiguity occurs frequently in student writing, from which these sentences are taken:

We overheard the same cleaning woman who cleans the Rose Lounge and another one.
Some persons, after consuming alcohol, want to fight and become hard to manage.
It seems as though the commander of the ship put very little foresight into a problem which faced him and endangered both men and ships.

This situation not infrequently forms the basis of cretinous humor, as in this TV exchange: "I've always wanted to see Lake Louise and Banff." "Sounds great, but how do you banff." A special case of this kind that students find hard to see occurs with a prepositional phrase which contains a series of nouns:

His job is to post changes in address, telephone numbers, and performance ratings.
The course includes the theory of procurement, property accounting, and requisitioning.

SITUATION 17: *Modificand + two modifying word groups.* If we consider the modifying words groups may be of three kinds—prepositional phrases, relative clauses, and verbal phrases—then it is evident that this situation contains nine different patterns. Each of these nine lends itself to possible ambiguity. In all of them the trouble lies in the third term— what does it refer to?

A. *Modificand + prepositional phrase + relative clause.* In this pattern the writer often intends the relative clause to modify the modificand; but when this clause appears to modify the last word of the preceding phrase, then the sentence is ambiguous. There is no ambiguity, of course, when ties in agreement prevent us from misreading. This is a standard pattern of modification in English, and students frequently run afoul of it. Here are three examples culled out of many:

The life of a movie star that the public sees does look glamorous.
She has cute ideas for parties that are easy to plan.
He has a blue satin ribbon around his neck which is tied in a bow at the top.

The menu of a restaurant in Marshalltown, Iowa, proudly makes this ambiguous pronouncement:

We have a reputation for fine food, quick service, and a friendly atmosphere which amounts to a tradition.

The remaining eight patterns are fundamentally the same, except that only two of them can be protected from ambiguity by ties in agreement. Hence a mere listing, with a single example each, will perhaps suffice to show what they are.

B. *Modificand + prepositional phrase + verbal phrase.*

There was a spotted dog in the group barking at the speeding car.

C. *Modificand + prepositional phrase + prepositional phrase.*

This restatement of the central idea serves as a review for the audience of the entire speech.

D. *Modificand + relative clause + prepositional phrase.*

I was talking about the books I had read in the library.

E. *Modificand + relative clause + verbal phrase.*

We watched the old miner, Maheu, who was feeding his horse, begrimed with dust from the mine.

F. *Modificand + relative clause + relative clause.*

Fred had a second-hand car that he later traded for a motorcycle which he loved to tinker with.

G. *Modificand + verbal phrase + prepositional phrase.*

They stood watching the fireworks in the back yard.

H. *Modificand + verbal phrase + relative clause.*

There is also a theater located near the business district which is crowded every night.

I. *Modificand + verbal phrase + verbal phrase.*

I saw the rake lying against the box stuffed with leaves from my last raking.

SITUATION 18: *Elliptical constructions.* Sometimes the omission of words from a structure will result in ambiguity, as in these cases:

Serve meat when thoroughly stewed.
For sale: Two Dutch rabbits, does, low cost. Breeding age. Will breed if requested.

In this respect *than* and *as well as* are especially troublesome. Here is an example from Noah Webster:

. . . we are less under the influence of reeson [*sic*] than our ancestors.

And students will write sentences like these:

It is more important for me to enter the activities in high school than college.
I like my roommate as well as Janice.

SITUATION 19: *Movable adverbial modifiers.* The different kinds of adverbs and adverbial modifiers have allowable and non-allowable positions in various types of sentences, though this matter has never, to my knowledge, been thoroughly studied. At any rate, such modifiers do move around rather freely, and it is this freedom that betrays students into putting them in positions where they are ambiguous. Student writing contains many ambiguities of this sort:

I repaired the car and returned the following day.
The hostess greeted the girl with a smile.

The crew chief will drive the truck, choose a suitable site, and unload the ammunition with the assistance of two helpers.

The bottle on the table there.

SITUATION 20: *Reference of pronouns, relatives, and demonstratives.* This kind of ambiguity might be considered lexical rather than structural. Words like *he, it, they, her, which, who, this,* and *such* are a constant source of ambiguity in student writing because they often refer to more than one antecedent. The instances that follow are taken from both professional writings and student papers:

At 10 a.m. today the anchor will be carried out into Lake Ontario aboard a naval craft and consigned to the waters. The three chaplains will accompany it.

The local weather bureaus are not permitted to dispute the predictions of the central weather bureau, regardless of whether they are right or not.

The Graf Zepplin was leaving Lakehurst Airport. Among the last to enter was Mrs. J. D. Smith, lone woman passenger. Slowly her huge nose was turned into the wind. Then, like some huge beast, she crawled along the grass.

Men like Brodie and Kolmer discovered vaccines and gave them to the public, but they were not successful. . . .

He had never gone ice-fishing from a hut like that.

The words *this* and *which* are a special source of confusion because they may refer not only to individual words but to word groups. The following cases are typical:

He was always bringing into the room a strange dog which he had found. This was a nuisance when I was trying to study.

She told me that Joe had come, which pleased me.

Biologists have discovered that fragments of chromosomes attach themselves to another chromosome which is called translocation.

Each room has two study desks and only one study lamp. This is very inconvenient because of poor lighting on one of the desks.

The foregoing twenty situations seem to be the ones responsible for much of the structural ambiguity that we find in student writing.[3] Of those that remain we should take into account one set of situations which need not be described in detail and which can be lumped together in a single omnibus group of form-class ambiguities. These have been emphasized by Professor C. C. Fries in his *Structure of English*.[4] He points out that if one does not know the form-class, that is the part of speech, of a word, then one does not recognize the pattern and as a consequence the word is ambiguous. We have remarked this condition above in situations three, nine, and fifteen. Even the basic sentence pattern of subject-verb-object, Professor Fries reveals, can be ambiguous, as in *Ship sails today,* where we do not know the form-class of *ship* and *sails.*

We frequently meet form-class ambiguities of various types in newspaper headlines, where the demands of space-saving cause the usual signals of form-class to be left out. Here are a few miscellaneous examples: *PW's 1st item on agenda—call girl; baby-sitter demands rise; police raid gatherings; digs well with bulldozer; complete 31-piece drill outfit.* Now

---

[3] Sometimes one finds interesting permutations of them, as in *a manned missile launching base,* and in this description of shirts—*blue, tan, or gray stripes or checks.*

[4] New York: Harcourt, Brace, 1952.

and then form-class ambiguities other than those we have classified will turn up in student papers. Here are a few:

At last they heard the boat whistle.
The storm was striking.
Unlike other Shakespearean plays, *Othello* offers no real complicated personality.
Students have important experiences in college that prepare them for the future. They are meeting people, gaining new friendships, and learning to get along with different types of people.

The presence of ambiguity in student writing is easy to understand. In high school the student does not always write to communicate to a known class of readers, as we do in normal writing situations. Instead he often writes writing to fulfill an assignment. The consequence is that he does not develop a reader-awareness: he does not learn to step outside himself and survey his words as with the mind of another person. When he reads over what he has produced, the words mirror exactly what was in his mind as he wrote, and he fails to realize that other readers might get other meanings from these same words.

One way to sensitize the student to the dangers of multiple meaning is to make a direct attack on the structural situations liable to ambiguity. For instance, the teacher can present the situations described above and then have the class write original examples of them with double-track meanings. These examples will furnish material for lively discussions and will offer heady and challenging problems of restatement. Such a procedure will help the student to tool his sentences to a closer tolerance in meaning and to write with greater clearness and precision.

For discussion

A. What distinction does Stageberg make between lexical and structural ambiguity? Would Hill call lexical ambiguity a matter of correctness or of style? Add one example to each kind of structural ambiguity noted by Stageberg.

B. What is Stageberg's explanation for the presence of ambiguity in student writing, and what does he suggest as a solution?

C. In "Correctness and Style in English Composition," Hill's first group of incorrect forms results from the student writer's not knowing enough about how writing represents speech. If the forms are read aloud, they become acceptable spoken English. Hill gives as an example, *He could of had a worse introduction.* Perhaps this principle can be applied to some of Stageberg's ambiguities. Read aloud examples from Situations 2, 3, 4, 8, 14, and 15. Can you remove the ambiguity? How? Can you make the statements clear in the written form without rewriting? How?

D. Hill gives the following as examples of bad style:
1. John met Jack, and his wife spoke to him.
2. Record the pronunciation on the lists in capital letters.
3. This factory is two miles beyond Lynchburg, going south.
Which of Stageberg's ambiguities is each an illustration of?

E. Which situation does each of the following illustrate?
1. plastic belts and suits
2. He was obliged more than to double the price.
3. smoked turkey, salmon, and olives
4. an old English grammar
5. He smiled at the elephant in his calico shirt.
6. When she got to the restaurant, Carol requested a hot plate.
7. Rose Exterminator Company
8. Having reached the age of five years, my parents moved me to Montana.
9. a dull girl's explanation
10. He caught a 468 pound marlin with a harness.
11. The two students seemed to be in a failing contest.
12. more wholesome meals
13. He conceded that she was attractive with great difficulty.
14. a paper flower girl
15. Forgetting his appointment, he drove to San Francisco and endangered his job.
16. the woman on the horse that needs attention
17. He refused to work out the problem which was such a nuisance.
18. A drive against sex and race bias in want-ads was begun by the Federal Government.
19. He likes short women, cars, and card games.
20. a pretty girl's dress
21. Fleeing Germans proved a nuisance yesterday for the Eighth Army.

STANLEY RUNDLE

Language and dialect

THE NEXT TWO essays are about "dialect," a word which frequently carries a good deal of emotional impact. Persons who happily endure such perversions of sense and logic as "When did the chink begin to pierce the armor?" or "Don't fail to miss tomorrow's doubleheader," will wince—and judge—at the omission of an *r* (/bətə/) when they think it should be kept, or at the addition of one (/sowdər/) when they think it shouldn't be there. Occasionally we find a foreign accent charming or romantic or both, though we more generally tend to find it opaque and therefore undesirable. Native deviators from standard English—ours—are suspected of being vulgar, uneducated, or simply rustic.

However, when we discuss language, "dialect" should be a neutral word. We simply mean "the form or variety of a spoken language peculiar to a region, community, social group, or occupational group." *Fatwood* is not a part of most American vocabularies, but it is used by many people in and near South Carolina. Few of us use the word *cavitation,* but many people do in Houston, Texas and at Cape Kennedy, Florida. *Cot* and *caught* are pronounced the same way by some people, especially if they grew up in southwestern Pennsylvania. And if they did grow up there, they probably know what *smearcase* is. Some people pronounce the *t* in *often* or say *a quarter till eight.* Others regularly use *finalize,* as, for instance, three Presidents of the United States and two Secretaries General of the United Nations.

To get us started, Stanley Rundle answers a reader's query in the British Magazine *The Linguist,* elaborating upon what a dialect is and finding his illustrations among the languages of Europe.

. . . There is certainly a great deal of confusion centring around the idea of "dialect." People tend to study and patronize dialects as though they were some odd form of folklore persisted in by certain communities. Dialects to most people are deviations from the standard speech of a country, and might even be regarded as corruptions of it: the men of Cornwall and Scotland are considered to mutilate standard English when they speak it.

That may be so—when they at-

"Language and Dialect": From *The Linguist,* January 1949, pp. 8–9. Reprinted with the permission of the publishers and Stanley Rundle.

tempt to speak standard English. In fact, often a stage impersonation of dialect is nothing more than an attempt to give an impression of a person who is used to speaking a local dialect speaking standard English, which is deeply influenced by his habitual mode of speech. If a stage Scotsman, for example, spoke in a truly local form of Scots, he would probably not be understood at all on an English stage, so that he has to use a sort of stage Scotch, which is standard English with a certain admixture of Scottish words, all pronounced—yes, let me say it—with a foreign accent.

What we have to get clear in our mind is that dialects are not deviations from an accepted modern standard, but all have a history stretching right back through the centuries. In other words, the English dialects include the modern standard *dialect* which for cultural, political and geographical reasons has become the accepted standard today. This is a process which has taken place all over the world, and at many stages in history. Each of the cities of ancient Greece had developed a very fine literature before there was any political union between them, and it was only when Athens took precedence that Attic speech became the literary language of Greece and was in fact the language of Plato, Aristotle, Euripides and many others. By this time, however, there was already a great deal of high-class literary work in the other dialects, such as the Homeric poems.

The same process took place in the case of Sanskrit, which was an artificially perfected literary language. The natural dialects were known as

Prakrits, and as these Prakrits developed literatures of their own, even they became influenced by the literary Sanskrit. In fact, the grammarians of the day developed special rules for turning Sanskrit into Prakrit, so that the real Prakrit tended to be lost to the written language and the literary Prakrit became a definite mutilation of Sanskrit.

In most of Europe the languages of the people developed freely until the Middle Ages because they were mainly spoken languages, while all learned writings were made in Latin. Then certain people began to write things in their own vernacular. Some of the earliest of these were the troubadours singing their songs of the great romances. When a number of very great men using one particular vernacular started to write in their own dialect and their works achieved immortality, that usually meant the beginning of the precedence of one dialect over the others and the coming into being of a national language. It was in this way that Dante and others lifted the dialect of Tuscany to the status of an Italian language. At the time of the Moorish conquest there were many great dialects in use in Spain: Catalan, Arragonese, Galician and Castilian. The last-mentioned dialect was only spoken in one small area, but suddenly spread its influence until it became accepted as the standard language in Spain. This does not mean that it ousted the others. Galician and Catalan are still very strong.

There were many dialects spoken in Germany, but for political and cultural reasons one of the High German dialects became accepted as the standard speech of the country, and Platt Deutsch is now regarded as a dialect, a mutilated form of standard German. In the same way in Holland, High Dutch became the standard language, while a form of Low Dutch, which is much nearer to English than standard Dutch, has lingered on as Frisian, which is regarded by the Dutch as a local aberration.

When a particular dialect assumes the role of standard language, the result on writers of dialect may be either to influence their dialect considerably so that it tends to become more standardized, or to goad the dialect writer into trying to make his writing as individual as possible and into keeping as clear as he can from the usage of the standard language. If he takes the latter course, his writing can only have a very limited appeal. What he usually does is to use the method of achieving a compromise between dialect and standard speech, so that his writings will be read more widely. The language of the poems of Robert Burns is not a local language of any part of Scotland whatever. If it had been, very few people would have understood it. What it is is a judicious mixing of standard English with a large number of "Scotchifications." This explains to some extent how these words could have such a wide appeal.

I was very interested during the war when attending certain performances of Shakespeare where the audience contained a large proportion of American soldiers, because I was reminded very forcibly of the problem of language versus dialect. It seemed that the American section of the audience chuckled and chortled in very many places where I could see nothing funny. However, on marking these places in a copy of Shakespeare and studying them later, it was possible to note certain quips which could be shared between American English and Shakespearian English, but which pass unnoticed in modern, standard, southern English. In Shakespeare's time the vowel in *calf, half,* etc., was still pronounced in the same way as the vowel in *cat* and *hat.* The change to the long-vowel sound in these words took place later, and only in a very limited part of southeast England. This was in the dialect which was to become accepted as standard English. However, in the dialects preserved in the remainder of this country *calf* and *half* still retain the vowel sound of *cat* and *hat.* The English of America did not undergo this change which took place in the particular region of southern England, so that the Americans retain the pronunciation of these words as Shakespeare knew it.

* * *

It is really amazing how much vitality dialects possess, in spite of modern methods of unification and communication. The very smallest features and the finest details remain very firmly fixed in the language of the people of a particular district, and people with a good ear can usually tell from which part of the country a person comes "as soon as he opens his mouth." In fact, with great care this division is not merely a division from one country to another, one province to another or even one town to another, but dialects can occur within a particular city. With practice it is possible, for instance, to tell on which side of the river Tiber a native Roman was brought up.

But now we are encroaching into the realm of linguistic geography, and that must wait for someone else's query.

For discussion

A. According to Rundle, what does *dialect* mean to most people? What does it mean to Rundle?

B. Using a standard desk dictionary look up, list, and illustrate the meanings of *dialect*.

C. Under what three possible circumstances does a dialect achieve status? Illustrate.

D. Why would it be difficult for a single dialect to achieve status in the United States?

E. When a particular dialect has assumed the role of national language, what might the writers of other dialects do?

F. Why did American soldiers understand some of the language of Shakespeare which Rundle himself did not?

G. Television has exposed us to a great variety of dialect usage—in pronunciation, in vocabulary, and in syntax. Our top government officials come from many parts of the United States, and speak in somewhat different ways; show business personalities share a special vocabulary; and so on. List some items which vary from your own speech patterns which you have noticed.

HANS KURATH

Area linguistics and the teacher of English

HANS KURATH, Professor Emeritus of English at the University of Michigan, the director of the Linguistic Atlas of New England, author of *Word Geography of the Eastern United States, A Phonology and Prosody of Modern English,* and the Editor Emeritus of the *Middle English Dictionary,* here applies his immense knowledge of the English language and especially of dialect geography to some problems of English usage in the classroom. After pointing out that the average textbook is inadequate in its treatment of area linguistics, he discusses a number of examples of linguistic diversity, some of which should be accepted and some of which should be corrected.

Dialect geography is the branch of linguistics which works with differences within a language area, whether of pronunciation (/šrimp/ or /srimp/), vocabulary (*veranda* or *porch*), or syntax (*he hadn't ought to, he ought not to . . .*). Kurath's discussion is devoted principally to differences in pronunciation, with a brief discussion of dialect differences in syntax. Dialect geography has naturally developed its own techniques and its own shorthand. Small "n," "e," "s," or "w" preceding an area designation means "north," "east," "south," or "west." MNY stands for Metropolitan New York, AE for American English, and South Midland for an area covering parts of Pennsylvania, Delaware, Virginia, West Virginia, Kentucky, Western North Carolina, and Eastern Tennessee. The /j/ in the transcriptions stands for the sound which shows the difference in pronunciation between *booty* and *beauty.*

It should be obvious that the teacher of English in grade school, high school, or college should know the usage of the area in which he does his teaching before he undertakes to "mend" the speechways of his pupils. If there is a class cleavage in usage within the area, he should be aware of it, so that for the good of his students he can set "better" or "cultivated" usage over against socially less desirable practices. If several regional dialects are current within the area (as for instance in Detroit, with its large groups of recent immigrants, black or white, from south of the Ohio), he

"Area Linguistics and the Teacher of English": From *Language Learning,* Special Issue, March 1961, pp. 9–14. Reprinted with the permission of the publisher, The Research Club in Language Learning of the University of Michigan.

should be familiar with them in order to deal sensibly with his wards.

How does the teacher of English get the information he needs to do a good job? Can he rely upon the ordinary textbooks, the desk dictionaries, Kenyon and Knott's *Pronouncing Dictionary*, Craigie and Hulbert's *Dictionary of American English*?

Yes, to some extent. However, the *DAE* deals with American vocabulary without identifying regional usage or the social standing of the expressions, though a check of the quotations often permits an inference; Kenyon-Knott is adequate for Northern pronunciation, including Eastern New England's, but fails to deal satisfactorily with usage in Metropolitan New York and the South; the desk dictionaries, though registering some variant cultivated pronunciations, give no indication of their habitat; the ordinary textbook is tailored for the national market and is apt to gloss over regional differences, even if the author knows better.

Two recent textbooks on AE [American English] (Hill and Francis[1]) practically obliterate regional differences current in cultivated use by imposing Trager's "over-all" nine-vowel system. Only "incidental" differences are admitted, and rather effectively concealed by the transcription at that.

Clearly, the teacher of English must be given better information than he now has at his disposal. What can area linguistics, the study of regional and social dialects, do to help him? I shall try to show, by dealing with differences in pronunciation current in the

[1] A. A. Hill: *Introduction to Linguistic Structures* (Harcourt, Brace & World, Inc., 1958) and W. Nelson Francis, *The Structure of American English* (The Ronald Press, 1958).

Eastern States, how a useful body of information can be made available, and how this sort of information can be instrumental in developing a scholarly, and therefore salutary, point of view.

Some sections of the Eastern States (all of the South and the South Midland) have a /j/ after the initial alveolar consonant (as in *tube, due, new*) on all social levels, others not (as Pa and eNE). Should a teacher in Boston or Philadelphia make his students adopt the /j/? In other sections usage is divided, as in MNY: should the teacher insist upon one or the other of these pronunciations in such a community?

In eNE, MNY, Va, and SC postvocalic /r/, as in *ear, care, four, poor*, is not pronounced as such by a considerable majority. Should the minority be urged to "drop the /r/," i.e., substitute unsyllabic /ə/, in this position when no social stigma attaches to pronouncing the /r/? What should be done when /r/ is an index of rusticity, as in most of eNC and parts of SC and Ga?

In the greater part of the South and the South Midland the dipthongal vowel in *down, owl, crowd* begins like the vowel of *man* on all social levels, whereas in NEngland and elsewhere this pronunciation is confined to folk speech. How should a teacher behave under such diverse circumstances? What should he do in Michigan, where [æu] is uncommon, except among recent immigrants from south of the Ohio?

Eastern NEngl and wPa have the same vowel in *law, caught, salt* and in *lot, cot, rod*, whereas all other sections of the Eastern States have contrasting vowels in these two sets. If a Michigan student lacks the contrast, as many do, should he be taught to distinguish *caught* from *cot*, *taught* from *tot?*

On the Atlantic seaboard, the vowel in *care*, *chair*, *stairs* ranges regionally all the way from the /æ/ of *cat* to the /ɛ/ of *get* and the /e/ of *gate* without social implications. Should one insist upon one of these pronunciations in view of the fact that, except for parts of SC and Ga, no regional dialect has more than one vowel phoneme between high and low before historical /r/, pronounced regionally as /r/ or unsyllabic /ə/?

Hoarse and *horse*, *mourning* and *morning* are homophonous in an area extending from the Potomac northward to MNY and westward throughout Pa, but not elsewhere in the Eastern States. For the sake of a few homonyms, or for some other reason, should one undertake to teach contrasting vowels in *four* and *forty* in the schools of Michigan, if usage is divided among the student body?

If a student pronounces *Mary* like *merry*, and *fairy* like *ferry*, or rimes *story* with *sorry*, should he be urged to differentiate them, as Southerners, New Yorkers, and most New Englanders do? Or is Pennsylvanian usage good enough?

When a Michigan student says *he et* (= *ate*) *it*, *he dove* (= *dived*) *right in*, and *he hadn't ought to* (= *ought not to*) *talk so much*, like his Yankee forebears, should the teacher "correct" him or merely point out to him that others say *ate*, *dived*, and *ought not to?* If his own usage is in line with that of well educated New Englanders, why should he change his ways? On the other hand, if he says *he eat it all up*, *he clumb a tree*, *he driv in the nail*, he should be told to avoid these past tense forms if he wants to appear to advantage, since they are strictly folk forms, though they are of venerable vintage, being derived by normal phonemic change from standard forms of earlier English.

These examples and queries have probably suggested to you the drift of my thinking in this matter. Unless a variant is clearly marked as "low class" or "rustic" within the area in which one teaches, it should be tolerated. To fight it is not only a waste of time, but an insult to students coming from well educated families or from other sections of the country. It breeds confusion, if not resentment, in the student body. On the other hand, a teacher who can say: "Your family must come from New England," or "Did you grow up in New York City?" or "That's the way they say it in Virginia," will command the respect of his class. In any event, he will stimulate the interest of his better students in our language, if he can tell them that well educated New Englanders, New Yorkers, Pennsylvanians, and Virginians don't talk exactly alike (although they understand each other quite easily), and point out some of the salient differences.

To put the teacher of English into a position to make pertinent comments on usage, we need better textbooks; and before we can produce better textbooks we must have more adequate information on regional and social differences in usage than we now possess. We are making progress in that direction, but we still have a long way to go.

We must realize that the linguistic situation in this country is rather different from that in England and France, and even from that in Germany. The former have *one* unquestionably dominant social dialect, and German-speaking Europe has at least the *Bühnenaussprache* (stage pronunciation) as a guide, though Bavarians, Austrians, and Swiss don't hew exactly to the line. On the other hand, we have rather well marked regional types of cultivated speech, and there is no reason for assuming that in matters of pronunciation Virginians will bow to New Yorkers, or Detroiters to Bostonians, within the foreseeable future. It is equally unlikely that the Ohio Valley will conform in usage to the Great Lakes Basin. Though postvocalic /r/ is fairly regularly used in both of these major areas, there are many differences in the incidence of the vowels and in their phonic character, as Professor Marckwardt can tell you, the common fiction of a "General American" type notwithstanding.

[Professor Kurath's preceding remarks were originally a lecture at the University of Michigan, at the conclusion of which he answered a number of questions. The discussion follows.]

Discussion

QUESTION: If we base acceptable pronunciation of American English on what would be used by educated speakers in a given area, what should the teacher of English in a foreign country do?

ANSWER: That is a practical question, and a very important one. I should say that in Europe Standard British English will continue to be taught, and for good reasons. If any type of American English is also to be taught, I would suggest using one in which postvocalic /r/ is preserved, either that of the Great Lakes Basin or that of the Ohio Valley. These differ the most from British English and are spoken over wide areas. However, if your teacher is a cultured New Yorker or Virginian, let him have his way. All varieties of cultivated American English are mutually intelligible.

QUESTION: I wish to ask about the English used in our mass media, radio and television. Might this be considered standard pronunciation?

ANSWER: What we hear on the radio are all the varieties of more or less cultivated American English, and some British English. Even if the announcers were all trained in one and the same dialect, they would have little influence on our youth, who are much more fascinated by cowboy talk and the lingo of the jokesmith. The chief contribution of the radio is to familiarize the listeners with a great variety of regional and social dialects.

QUESTION: Is there any way of knowing how quickly people who move from one area to another acquire the local dialect?

ANSWER: This is a problem that needs investigation. Detroit would be a wonderful place for making such a study. How long do the Negroes from south of the Ohio retain their dialects in that city? Do Negroes born in Detroit talk two dialects, one in their homes and another in school? How about the second

Detroit-born generation? I have had some experience with the Irish in New England. They adapt their speech completely to the local Yankee types in the first New England-born generation, though they remember some of the Irishisms of their parents.

COMMENT: You were speaking of the Negro boy as speaking two dialects. I teach quite a few Negro children and I notice that not only do they talk differently at home, but the minute they are out of the school building and are walking along the street with their playmates they immediately begin to talk the way they had first learned to talk.

QUESTION: I wonder if you've ever speculated on the causes of these regional distinctions.

ANSWER: Well, yes, and in my *Word Geography* I have suggested some things, partly by implication. Of course, the Atlantic seaboard is much more highly subdivided than areas farther west. There are various factors involved. First of all, the early colonies, strung out along the Atlantic seaboard, had little contact with each other. Their contact was with back home, with England. Even in New England it took nearly a century and a half before the Massachusetts Bay settlement expanded far enough to the west to meet the settlements on the lower Connecticut River. In three or four generations different dialects, more or less uniform, had developed in the Boston area on the one hand and in the Hartford area on the other; and to this day eastern and western New England have noticeably different dialects. Other dialects came into being in the several Middle and Southern Colonies before the Revolution and were carried westward in the nineteenth century. It is a complicated and fascinating story. Will anyone predict that one day Richmond will bow to New York or Boston to Chicago?

For discussion

A. Why cannot the interested person get all the information he might want about dialect differences in the U.S. from an ordinary textbook or desk dictionary?

B. Pronounce *Tuesday, dew, steward, tube, nuisance,* and *tune.* What geographical areas do your pronunciations of these words exclude you from?

C. How would the following pronunciations be judged in eastern North Carolina: /hir/, /ber/, /yur/, /kar/, /harvərd/?

D. What are the acceptable pronunciations of *care* along the Atlantic seaboard?

E. *Webster's Seventh New Collegiate* and *Webster's Third International* dictionaries indicate regional restrictions for standard words based loosely on Kurath's *Word Geography of the Eastern United States.* Check in one of these dictionaries for the regional restrictions on the following words: *hammock, bree, clabber, groundnut, lightwood, poke, smearcase.*

F. Why, according to Kurath, are there so many regional distinctions in pronunciation?

G. When, and why, would Kurath correct a student's use of a variant pronunciation?

H. Why does Kurath call General American a fiction?

I. Using Kurath's article and your own speech as your authorities, indicate the probable pronunciation of the following words in the places listed:

	Boston	Charleston	Pittsburgh	Your town
care				
caught				
dot				
down				
fairy				
ferry				
four				
Italian				
tube				

Linguists and Their Critics

We have now read a good deal about the nature of language, about the doctrine of correctness, and about current approaches to language analysis. It would be a mistake, however, to assume that everyone agrees with everything that has been said so far. In fact, a number of people disagree with quite a lot that has been said so far, as two of the articles in the following section make abundantly clear. We shall sample the controversy. The arguments are real, and the reader may judge their effectiveness for himself. They will not be neutralized by casual asides, but a few general observations may be made.

For one thing, there is some difference between the nature of language and the nature of the classroom. The linguist may quite properly say that correctness depends upon usage, though this statement needs explanation, if not qualification. It does not necessarily follow that an English teacher with some knowledge of contemporary linguistics is ethically prohibited from making judgments about the way his students use the language. The linguist wants to find out what people actually say. The English teacher presumably is familiar with what his students might say, and is therefore concerned with providing standards with which they may eventually safely—and with some comfort—make their own linguistic choices. Since standards are not easily established, an English teacher frequently provides specific choices, choices which his greater knowledge entitles him to make. At this point, the teacher who follows some of the insights of contemporary linguistics, and the teacher who scorns them as milestones on the way to linguistic chaos, may really be acting quite similarly, their public arguments notwithstanding. One may suspect that it is their philosophies, not their practices, that differ.

For another thing, in the present state of the study of English grammar, it is increasingly difficult to determine what is desirable about the traditional and what is traditional about the desirable. It is not, however, difficult to determine that no student of English grammar can ignore what the working linguist has to tell. If he does so, he must argue, not from his knowledge, but from his ignorance. He is still not certain just how current work in the discipline of linguistics will eventually affect the art of teaching English. What is certain, is that the effect will be powerful.

DONALD J. LLOYD

Snobs, slobs and the English language

PROFESSOR LLOYD'S TITLE is abrasive, no doubt intentionally. It is a challenge to Professor Barzun, who will retaliate in the article following this one.

The linguistic arguments involved are by now familiar to you. It is interesting, though, that both the impurist and the purist speak with comparable eloquence. The linguistic philosophy that divides Professors Lloyd and Barzun is not analogical to ignorance versus learning or science versus the humanities. Perhaps we may equate it with change versus permanence, and the delights of the uncertain versus the satisfactions of the settled. The rigor of the arguments should not obscure the point of view.

Professor Lloyd, for many years at Wayne State University, is now in private business Professor Barzun is at Columbia University.

There is at large among us today an unholy number of people who make it their business to correct the speech and writing of others. When Winston Churchill says "It's me" in a radio address, their lips purse and murmur firmly, "It is I," and they sit down and write bitter letters to the New York *Times* about What is Happening to the English Language. Reading "I only had five dollars," they circle *only* and move it to the right of *had,* producing "I had only five dollars" with a sense of virtue that is beyond the measure of man. They are implacable enemies of "different than," of "loan" and "contact" used as verbs, and of dozens of other common expressions. They put triumphant exclamation marks in the margins of library books. They are ready to tangle the thread of any discussion by pouncing on a point of grammar.

If these people were all retired teachers of high-school English, their weight in the community would be negligible; but unfortunately they are not. They are authors, scholars, businessmen, librarians—indeed, they are to be found wherever educated people read and write English. And they are moved by a genuine concern for the language. They have brought us, it is true, to a state in which almost anybody, no matter what his education or the clarity of his expression, is likely to find himself attacked for some locution which he has used. Yet their in-

"Snobs, Slobs, and the English Language": Reprinted from *The American Scholar*, vol. 20, n. 3, Summer, 1951, pp. 279–288. Copyright © 1951 by The United Chapters of Phi Beta Kappa. By permission of the publishers.

tentions are of the best. It is only that their earnest minds are in the grip of two curious misconceptions. One is that there is a "correct" standard English which is uniform and definite and has been reduced to rule. The other is that this "correct" standard can only be maintained by the vigilant attention of everybody concerned with language—indeed, by the whole body of educated men and women.

The enemy these self-appointed linguistic sentries see lurking in every expression which stirs the correcter's instinct in them is something they call illiteracy—which is not a simple state of being unlettered, but something more. This illiteracy is a willful and obstinate disregard for the standards of civilized expression. It stirs anger in them when they think they see it, because it seems to them a voluntary ignorance, compounded out of carelessness and sloth. When they think they find it in men who hold responsible positions in the community, they feel it to be a summation of all the decline of the graces of culture, the last reaches of a great wave of vulgarity which is eroding the educated and literate classes. It seems to them to be a surge of crude populism; they hear in each solecism the faint, far-off cries of the rising mob. It is really a sort of ringing in their ears.

In view of the general agreement among the literate that a "correct" standard English exists, and in view of the vituperation directed at anyone suspected of corrupting it, one would expect some kind of agreement about what is correct. There is little to be found; the easy utterance of one educated man is the bane of another. "For all the fussiness about *which* and *that,*" remarks Jacques Barzun in the *Nation,* "the combined editorial brass of the country have feebly allowed the word "disinterested" to be absolutely lost in its original sense. One finds as careful a writer as Aldous Huxley using it to mean uninterested, so that by now a "disinterested judge" is one that goes to sleep on the bench." And on the subject of what surely is a harmless word, *whom,* Kyle Crichton [formerly] editor of *Collier's* is quoted in *Harper's:* "The most loathsome word (to me at least) in the English language is 'whom.' You can always tell a half-educated buffoon by the care he takes in working the word in. When he starts it I know I am faced with a pompous illiterate who is not going to have me long as company."

Probably only a cynic would conclude from the abundance of such comments that those who demand correct English do not know it when they meet it; but some students of language must have been led to wonder, for they have made up lists of disputed locutions and polled the literate on them. So far, the only agreement they have reached has to be expressed in statistical terms.

The latest of these surveys, a questionnaire containing nineteen disputed expressions, was reported by Norman Lewis in *Harper's* Magazine for March, 1949. Lewis sent his list to 750 members of certain groups chosen mainly for their professional interest in the English language: lexicographers, high school and college teachers of English, authors, editors, journalists, radio commentators, and "a random sampling of *Harper's* subscribers."

If we count out two groups on the basis of extremely special knowledge and interest—the college professors of English and the lexicographers—we find all the others accepting about half the expressions. The authors and editors (book and magazine) were highest with about 56 per cent, and the editors of women's magazines lowest with about 45. (The expression which was least favored was *less* in the sense of *fewer*—"I encountered *less* difficulties than I had expected"—but even that received an affirmative vote of 23 per cent.) The distinguished electors seem individually to have played hop, skip and jump down the column, each finding among the nineteen expressions about ten he could approve of. If any two fell on the same ten, it was merely a coincidence.

A person innocent in the ways of this controversy, but reasonably well-informed about the English language, noticing that the disputants ignore the massive conformity of most writers in most of their language practices, in order to quibble about fringe matters, might assume that they would welcome the cold light of linguistic science. This is a naïve assumption. In response to an attempt of mine to correct some of the misapprehensions I found in Mr. Barzun's article—among them his curious notion that "detached" and not "uninterested" was the original meaning of "disinterested"—he replied by letter that I represented a misplaced and breezy scientism, and that what I said struck him as "the raw material of 'populism' and willful resistance to Mind. . . . All dictionaries to the contrary notwithstanding, the word disinterested is now prevailingly used in the meaning I deprecated. . . . The fact that an illiterate mistake may become

the correct form . . . is no reason for not combating it in its beginnings. . . ." This rejection both of the professional student of language and of the dictionary, when they disagree with the opinions of the writer, has the effect of making each man his own uninhibited authority on language and usage—an effect which I do not believe was exactly what Mr. Barzun had in mind.

What he did have in mind he stated clearly in one distinguished paragraph:

A living culture in one nation (not to speak of one world) must insist on a standard of usage. And usage, as I need not tell you, has important social implications apart from elegance and expressiveness in literature. The work of communication in law, politics and diplomacy, in medicine, technology, and moral speculation depends on the maintenance of a medium of exchange whose values must be kept fixed, as far as possible, like those of any other reliable currency. To prevent debasement and fraud requires vigilance, and it implies the right to blame. It is not snobbery that is involved but literacy on its highest plane, and that literacy has to be protected from ignorance and sloth.

It is a pity that these sentiments, so deserving of approval, should receive it from almost all educated people except those who really know something about how language works. One feels like an uncultivated slob when he dissents—one of the low, inelegant, illiterate, unthinking mob. Yet as a statement about the English language, or about standard English, it is not merely partly true and partly false, but by the consensus of most professional students of language, totally false. It is one of those monstrous errors which gain their original currency by being especially plausible at a suitable time, and maintain themselves long after the circumstances which give rise to them have vanished. Mr. Barzun's remarks are an echo from the eighteenth century; they reek with an odor mustier than the lavender of Grandmother's sachet. They have little relevance to the use of the English language in America in our day.

In actual fact, the standard English used by literate Americans is no pale flower being overgrown by the weeds of vulgar usage: it is a strong, flourishing growth. Nor is it a simple, easily describable entity. Indeed, it can scarcely be called an entity at all, except in the loose sense in which we call the whole vast sum of all the dialects of English spoken and written throughout the world a single language. In this sense, standard American English is the sum of the language habits of the millions of educated people in this country. It is rooted in the intellectual life of this great and varied people. Its forms express what its users wish to express; its words mean what its users think they mean; it is correctly written when it is written by those who write it, and correctly spoken by those who speak it. No prim and self-conscious hoarding of the dead fashions of a superior class gives it its power, but its negligent use by minds intent on stubborn and important problems. There is no point in a tiresome carping about usage; the best thing to do is relax and enjoy it.

There are five simple facts about language in general which we must grasp before we can understand a specific language or pass judgment on a particular usage. It is a pity that they are not more widely known in place of the nonsense which now circulates, for they would relieve the native-born speaker of English of his present uncertainty, and give him a proper authority and confidence in his spontaneous employment of his mother tongue. They arise from a common-sense analysis of the nature of language and the conditions of its use.

In the first place, language is basically speech. Speech comes first in the life of the individual and of the race. It begins in infancy and continues throughout our lives; we produce and attend to a spoken wordage much greater than the written. Even the mass of writing which floods in upon us today is only the froth on an ocean of speech. In history, also, speech comes first. English has been written for only about fifteen hundred years; before this, it is of incalculable antiquity. In speech its grammar was developed; from changes in the sounds of speech, changes in its grammar come. The educated are inclined to feel that the most important aspect of language is the written form of it, and that the spoken language must and should take its standards from this. Actually, the great flow of influence is from speech to writing. Writing does influence speech somewhat, but its influence is like the interest a bank pays on the principal entrusted to it. No principal, no interest.

In the second place, language is personal. It is an experience and a pattern of habits of a very intimate kind. In the home, the family, the school and the neighborhood we learn the speechways of our community, learning to talk as those close to us talk in the give and take of daily life. We are at one with our nation in our easy command of the pitch, tune and phrase of our own home town. Language is personal, also, in that our grasp of it is no greater than our individual experience with it. The English we know is not that vast agglomeration of verbal signs which fills and yet escapes the largest lexicons and grammars, but what we have personally heard and spoken, read and written. The best-read man knows of his native language only a limited number of forms in a limited number of combinations. Outside of these, the wealth which a copious tongue has as its potential is out of his world, and out of everybody's, for no dictionary is so complete or grammar so compendious as to capture it.

The third fact about language is that it changes. It changes in its sounds, its meanings and its syntax. The transmission of sounds, words and meanings from generation to generation is always in some respects imprecise. Minute differences add up in time to perceptible changes, and changes to noticeable drifts. Difference in changes and in rates of change make local speech sounds, pitches, tones and vocabularies draw subtly and persistently away from one another. And all it takes to produce an identifiable dialect is sufficient segregation over a sufficient length of time.

The fourth great fact about language, then, is that its users are, in one way or another, isolated. Each has with only a few others the sort of familiar relationships which join them in one language community. Yet there are upward of two hundred million native speakers of English in the world. Obviously they cannot all be in close touch with one another. They congeal in nuclei—some stable, some transitory—which by a kind of double-action draw them together and enforce isolation of many more-or-less shifting kinds: the isolation of distance, of education, of economic levels, of occupation, age and sex, of hobbies and political boundaries. Any one of these will be reflected in language habits; any two or three will bring about, in one community, speech differences as great as those caused by oceans and mountain ranges.

The fifth great fact about language is that it is a historical growth of a specific kind. The nature of English is one of the absolutes of our world, like air, water and gravity. Its patterns are not subject to judgment; they simply are. Yet they have not always been what they are; like the physical world, they have changed with time, but always in terms of what they have been. *Boy loves girl* means something different from *girl loves boy*. It is futile for us to prefer another way of conveying these meanings: that is the English way, and we must live with it. Yet students of the language see in this simple pattern the result of a cataclysmic change, great and slow like the geologic upheavals that have brought old salt beds to the very tops of mountain ranges, and as simple. Each is what it is because of what it has been before.

Language as a social instrument reflects all the tides which sweep society, reacting in a local or surface way easily and quickly—as a beach changes its contours to suit the waves—but it offers everywhere a stubborn rock core that only time and massive pressures can move. The whim of a girl can change its vocabulary, but no will of man can touch its essential structure; this is work for the long attrition of generations of human use. Ever lagging a little behind human needs, it offers a multitude of terms for the things men no longer care about, but keeps them improvising to say what has not been said before.

Spoken English is, then, by its own nature and the nature of man, a welter of divergences. The divergences of class and place are sharpest in Britain, where the same dialects have been spoken in the same shires and villages for more than a thousand years. Although these can be heard in America by any traveler, no matter how dull his ear, they are relatively slight, for our language is essentially and repeatedly a colonial speech. Each of the American colonies drew settlers from various parts of Britain; each worked out a common speech based mainly on the dialect of its most influential group of immigrants (which differed from colony to colony); each remained in relative isolation from the others for about a hundred years. Then many colonists began to move to the interior: wave after wave of settlers traveled along rather distinct lines of advance until the continent was covered. Everywhere there was a mingling of dialects, with a composite speech arising, based mainly on the speech of the dominant local group. And so we have a Northern speech fanning out from the Northeastern states, a Midland speech fanning out from the Mid-Atlantic states, and a Southern speech in the land of cotton-raisers, all crossing and merging as the pioneers moved west. Local differ-

ences are greatest along the Atlantic coast.

Wherever our people settled, they worked out local ways of talking about the things of common experience, and found their own verbal symbols of class distinctions. Here and there are areas where foreign-speaking groups clung together and developed special exotically-flavored dialects, but otherwise most speech patterns in America can be traced back to the dialects of Britain. Everywhere there is a common speech used by the multitude which works with its hands, and a slightly different dialect spoken by the professional and leisure classes.

The standard English written by Americans is not, however, the written form of educated speech, which shows great local variation. Its spellings have only a rough equivalence to the sounds we make; its grammatical system, which has nationwide and even worldwide currency, had its origin in the educated speech of the Northeastern states, and before that in the dialect of London, England. The concentration of schools, colleges, publishing houses and print shops in early New England and New York had the same effect in this country as the concentration in England, for centuries, of political power, commercial activity and intellectual life in London: it established a written standard, native only to those who grew up near the Hudson River or east of it. Elsewhere in America this written standard has been a learned class dialect—learned in the schools as the property and distinguishing mark of an educated class. Like many of its spellings, it is itself a relic of the past, an heirloom handed down from the days when the whole nation looked to the schoolmasters of New England for its book-learning.

The present controversy about usage is simply a sign that times have changed. The several vast and populous regions of this country have grown self-sufficient and self-conscious, and have taken the education of their youth into their own hands. Where the young once had to travel to the East for a respectable education, they receive it now in local public systems of rapid growth and great size. From local schools they may go to local universities of fifteen to fifty thousand students, where they can proceed to the highest degrees. Yale University is overcrowded with some six thousand students; in the community colleges alone of California more than 150,000 are enrolled. Most of these young people take their diplomas and go to work among their own people. They form a literate class greater in numbers and in proportion to the total population than the world has ever seen before. Speaking the speech of their region, they mingle naturally and easily with its people. When they write, they write the language they know, and they print it, for the most part, in presses close at hand. Everywhere they speak a standard literate English—but with differences: a regional speech derived from the usages of the early settlers.

Standard written English is, after all, an abstraction—a group of forms rather arbitrarily selected from the multitude offered by the language as a whole—an abstraction which serves the peculiar needs of the intellect. It achieves its wide currency because the interests of its users are the common interests of the educated, which transcend frontiers and negate distances—

law, literature, science, industry and commerce. It is the tool of intelligence. Any thinking person must use it, because only this form of the language provides the instruments of delicate intellectual discrimination. And it is not static. As the needs of the intellect change, standard English changes. Change is its life, as anyone can see who picks up a book written only a little time ago, or examines almost any old newspaper.

The common speech of the uneducated, on the other hand, is comparatively static. Though it varies greatly from place to place, it is everywhere conservative; far from corrupting the standard language, it follows slowly after, preserving old forms long ago given up by literate speakers. "Them things" was once standard, and so were "he don't," "giv," and "clumb" and "riz." Its patterns are archaic, its forms homely and local. Only its vocabulary is rich and daring in metaphor (but the best of this is quickly swiped by writers of standard English). Seldom written because its speakers seldom write, it is yet capable of great literary beauties, uncomplicated force, compact suggestion, and moving sentiment. But it will not bear the burden of heavy thinking, and anyhow, heavy thinkers have a better tool to use. It is about as much danger to the standard language as an old house cat.

I have often wondered at the fear of common English and its speakers which the cultural aristocracy display, at their curious definition of illiteracy, and at the intemperance of their terms, which verges on the pathological. A Freudian should have a picnic with them. They use such epithets as *illiteracies, crudities, barba-*

risms, ignorance, carelessness and *sloth.* But who is not negligent in language, as in the mechanics of driving a car? They mutter darkly about "inchoate mob feelings." They confess themselves snobs by denying that their attitudes are snobbish. The stridency of their self-assurance puzzles the mind.

We might better adjust our minds to the divergences of usage in standard written English, for time, space and the normal drift of culture have put them there. We need not raise our eyebrows at a different twist of phrase, but enjoy it as an echo of a way of life somewhat different from our own, but just as good. We could do more than enjoy these things; we could recognize that the fixed forms of the language which do not come to our attention were developed in the past. We have come too late for the show. It is the changing forms that evidence the life in our language and in our society; we could learn much about our people and their ways by simply and objectively observing them.

If there is one thing which is of the essence of language, it is its drive to adapt. In an expanding culture like ours, which is invading whole new realms of thought and experience, the inherited language is not wholly suited to what we have to say. We need more exact and expressive modes of utterance than we have; we are working toward finer tolerances. The fabric of our language is flexible, and it can meet our needs. Indeed, we cannot stop it from doing so. Therefore it would be well and wholesome for us to see, in the locutions of the educated which bring us up sharply as we read, not evidences of a rising tide of illiteracy (which they are not), but marks of a grand shift in modes of expression, a self-reliant regionalism, and a persistent groping toward finer distinctions and a more precise utterance.

JACQUES BARZUN

The retort circumstantial

Mr. Lloyd's article is the culmination of a lively correspondence between him and me, in the course of which I feel sure that I repeatedly cut the ground from under his feet. Since from the outset he hadn't a leg to stand on, my efforts were bound to be useless, but we were both having such a good time that neither of us noticed his plight. At my suggestion he has consented to display his miraculous position in public, and I must therefore return to the charge. The public will judge.

It seems clear in the first place that by preaching the attitude of the mere recorder, the *registrar* of linguistic fact, Mr. Lloyd disqualifies himself for remonstrating with me or anybody else. I, as a writer, am his source, his document, his *raison d'être,* and he can no more logically quarrel with me than he can with a piece of papyrus. Nevertheless, I am willing to concede his human (and very modern) right to inveigh against my moralism in the tones of an outraged moralist.

What then does his objection come to? That in seeking to criticize certain tendencies in current literary English,

I am usurping an authority I do not possess, and interfering with the natural evolution of the language. This is the prime fallacy in his case, which rests on a chain of reasoning somewhat as follows: English has greatly changed through the ages; many of these changes were resisted by purists; but the evolution was irresistible, and the result is something we now consider correct and natural. Hence Mr. Barzun's attitude is *contra naturam;* he is an old fogey, a snob, and an ignoramus who thinks he can set his face against the future only because he is blind to the past.

The truth is, of course, that one does not obtain "nature" by merely removing opposition, wise or unwise. Nor can we know what is inevitable until we have tried good and hard to stop it. The whole analogy with nature is false because language is an artificial product of social life, all of whose manifestations, even when regular, bear only a remote likeness to the course of nature. Being a social product, language is everybody's football, and that is precisely what gives me, as well as Mr. Lloyd, the right to push

"The Retort Circumstantial": Reprinted from *The American Scholar*, vol. 20, n. 3, Summer, 1951, pp. 289–293. Copyright © 1951 by The United Chapters of Phi Beta Kappa. By permission of the publishers.

it this way or that by argument.

And here it is important to remember that resistance to change is by no means futile. The history of the language is not what the gallant liberals make out—a struggle between the dauntless Genius of England and a few misguided conservatives. It is a free-for-all. At this point it is for the advocates of the "Hands Off" policy to trot out the word "mob," which Swift[1] attacked with several other curtailed forms, and pretend that it was ridiculous of the Dean to boggle at it, "in the light of what came after." Well, what came after is that we deodorized "mob," and abandoned altogether the other vulgarities he was deprecating: we no longer use *rep, pozz, phiz, hipps,* or *plenipo.* The future, in short, belonged as much to Dean Swift as to his opponents—and rather more if we count the hits and misses.

So much for the pseudo-naturalism of the linguistic registrars. Their vow not to judge among words and usages is a fine thing as long as it expresses a becoming sense of incapacity, but it must not turn into a union rule enforceable on those who have taken precisely opposite vows—namely, to exploit, preserve, and possibly enrich

the language. This is the duty of the writer, it calls for judgment, and it brings us to that blessed word "disinterested" which seems to have acted on Mr. Lloyd like a whiff of mustard to the nose.

My simple and meritorious deed as regards "disinterested" was to draw attention to its widespread misuse as a duplicate of *un*interested. Examples abound, and the fight against the plague may already be lost without the confusion being anything like over. Every piece of printed matter exhibits it, and nearly every conversation. Just the other day I heard this sentence, spoken to identify a stranger: "He is an impresario, but when it comes to art, he's completely disinterested." Did the speaker mean, X has no interest in art? Or: he is so much interested in it that money is no object? According to current usage this is impossible to determine without questioning the speaker. Not even his presumed degree of education will settle the matter, for the wrong use has affected all ranks.

At the phrase "wrong use," Mr. Lloyd twitched his non-existent leg, and with his hands made the motions of a man taking to earth in a dictionary. A few American, and especially collegiate, dictionaries do give the meaning "uninterested" as a second choice—which is a sufficient reason for me to view with a lack-luster eye Mr. Lloyd's naïve faith in lexicographers. The one work that seems relevant to the argument is the *O.E.D.*,[2] which

---

[1] Jonathan Swift (1667–1745), English satirist, included among his many targets those whom he felt were contributing to the degeneration of the English language. He proposed an academy to maintain linguistic purity, and in a famous essay (*Tatler* No. 230, 1710) attacked those who pronounce only the first part of a word and let the rest go, as in the list cited by Professor Barzun: *re*putation, *posi*tive, *phy*siognomy, *hypo*chondriacs, and *plenipo*tentiary. A couple of these survive in informal speech, and the device itself is common, as any *prep* school student under*grad.* or even *piano* player, knows.

[2] The *Oxford English Dictionary*, also known as *O.D.* (*Oxford Dictionary*), *H.E.D.* (*Historical English Dictionary*), and *N.E.D.* (*New English Dictionary*), begun in the 1850's, completed in 1928, and bound in ten, twelve, or twenty volumes, is widely considered the finest dictionary in any language.

gives us the history of the word. It tells us that the meaning *un*interested is obsolete and it lists five separate earlier forms, going back to the French of Montaigne, all connected with the idea of "removing the self interest of a person in a thing." As an English adjective, examples are given from 1659 to Dr. Livingstone in 1865, with the meaning: "not influenced by interest, impartial, unbiased, unprejudiced." My original remark was to the effect that nowadays the "disinterested judge" is probably taken to mean one who sleeps on the bench. My final remark is: As a writer concerned with the precision and flexibility of the language I use, I cannot regard the return to an obsolete and ambiguous form as useful or in any other way justified.

I now carry the war into the enemy's camp. If instead of complacently taking notes on the growing confusion, and protecting under pretext of "science" the vagaries of modern usage, Mr. Lloyd and his compeers would reflect upon their data, they might be able to safeguard the complex instrument of our speech by telling us when and why these deplorable losses occur, and how they might be repaired—loss of clarity and exactness at large, absolute loss of meaning in a word such as "disinterested" and in another such as "connive." Everyone has seen this last used as a synonym for "conspire" and "contrive"; I have heard it in the intransitive sense of "manage" about some trivial business: "How did you connive?" Hitherto, when you escaped from the concentration camp because the guard deliberately looked the other way, it was he who *connived* at your escape, no one else. Can it be that the action is ob-

solete and we no longer need the word?

These instances are not isolated, and I shall accept statistical refutation only from someone who can show that he reads each year more written matter than I, and hears a greater variety of local uses from a larger body of students.

Meantime, the generality which I hazarded, and which Mr. Lloyd assails as undemocratic and tainted with ethical feeling, is that with the rapid extension of educational opportunities, many persons of otherwise simple hearts are snatching at words half understood in order to bedeck their thought. Only the other day I read in a "literary" review about a distinguished American critic who was so full of insight that he could be called a *voyeur*. The writer meant *voyant*, if anything, but he could certaintly be sued for slander before an educated court.

Foreign words are always treacherous, but what of the newspaper editorial which states that Mr. So-and-so's election is "highly fortuitous" (meaning "fortunate"), or the college dean who tells parents that his institution gives the students "a fulsome education"? Then there are those who believed that "to a degree" means "to a certain extent," instead of just the opposite. Have not the oil and drug companies been forced to change their labels to flammable" because many users of their products took *"in*flammable" to mean non-combustible? At that stage, the issue ceases to be comic or inconsequential. With the tremendous output of verbiage by air and print to which we are all subjected, the corruption of meaning is rapid and extensive. We are at the mercy of anyone who thinks the sense of a word is discoverable by inspection, and whose misuse consequently liberates an echoing error in the minds of his peers.

To put it differently, the danger to English today is not from bad grammar, dialect, vulgar forms, or native crudity, but from misused ornaments three syllables long. The enemy is not illiteracy but incomplete literacy—and since this implies pretension it justifies reproof. There is no defense against the depredations of the brash except vigilance and no quarter given. I am certain that in this regard Mr. Lloyd, who writes with so much felicity and force, does exactly this in his capacity as a college teacher of English. Why then does he not square his precepts with his practice? I cannot answer for him, but to help his amputated philosophy to its feet, I want by way of conclusion to quote from a writer who, being anonymous and attached to both journalism and business, can hardly be suspected of flaunting pedantry and preciosity. The extract is from *Fortune* for November, 1950:

"Language is not something we can disembody; it is an ethical as well as a mechanical entity, inextricably bound up in ourselves, our positions, and our relations with those about us."

For discussion

A. In 1673 Lucius Waddingham condemmed the use of the following words: *cumble, incalamity, nefandous, piacle,* and *transfulation.* None are used today. How much credit should we give to Waddingham?

B. What is Lloyd's explanation for his statement that standard written English changes fairly rapidly, but that the common speech of the uneducated is comparatively static?

C. The following passage probably sounds old-fashioned. Why?
   Almost all their tragedies will afford us examples of the like nature. Tragedies and comedies were not written as they are now, promiscuously, by the same person. This is so plain that I need not instance to you that Aristophanes, Plautus, Terence, never any of them writ tragedy; Aeschylus, Euripides, Sophocles, and Seneca never meddled with comedy; the sock and buskin were not worn by the same poet. Having then so much care to excel in one thing, very little is to be pardoned them if they miscarried in it.

D. What is Barzun's standard of usage? What is Lloyd's?

E. Discover in your own dictionary how the following words have been downgraded in the English-speaking world: *wench, silly, sly, counterfeit, lust, lewd, respectable.*

F. What does Barzun mean by the "pseudo-naturalism of linguistic registrars"?

G. Barzun feels that when a word like "disinterested" shifts connotation, a useful distinction has been lost. What, in fact, happens in language when such distinctions disappear? What words have replaced those in question E?

BERTRAND EVANS

Grammar and writing

MOST PEOPLE WOULD no doubt be hard put to believe that grammar teaching can be a thoroughly sanguinary pursuit. The polemics of the next two articles should convince them otherwise.

Both authors are teachers of grammar; both are Professors of English (Evans at the University of California at Berkeley, and Sledd at the University of Texas). Evans has written an important book on Shakespearean comedy, and Sledd, an important book on Samuel Johnson as a lexicographer. This mutual interest in learning, however, has not culminated in a sharing of views upon either the content or teaching of English and grammar. The differences that divide them are really greater than those that divide Professors Lloyd and Barzun, not only because Evans and Sledd disagree more vehemently about what the facts of the matter are, but also because they cannot agree on how these facts should be interpreted.

As everyone knows, the study of English grammar in the public schools has had a precarious existence for at least twenty-five years. It has been suspect from contrary directions, on quite opposite grounds.

I

On the one hand, college English professors who have had anything to do with freshman composition have charged, often and hotly, that the study of grammar has simply been neglected or omitted entirely—for otherwise how could high school graduates possibly write with such utter disregard for discipline? All over the nation the problems of dealing with the grammatical incompetence of freshmen entering college have been numerous and severe. Along with those of the colleges, voices of the public have been raised in anger and dismay also—voices of parents who remembered the drilling *they* had in school, which surely *must* have been good for them because it was so exacting and so tedious, and voices of businessmen whose office workers did not prove notably grammatical. From this side, then, the din has been loud and continuous. The voices have often been confused, but the general sense has always been unmistakable: the study of grammar has been neglected and should be restored.

On the other hand, especially during the late 1920's and 1930's, professional educationists challenged the basic assumptions of the study of grammar, partly because their tests proved to them—if not to everyone else—that grammatical knowledge had no appreciable value and partly because the arduous kind of study that has always been associated with grammar did not fit the pattern of the new child-centered, activity conscious, experimental "progressive" school. And, in fact, in some high schools—where there prevailed a coalition of avid educationistic administrators, self-expressionistic young English teachers fresh from teachers' colleges whose English departments had surrendered responsibility for teacher training to departments of Education, and core-curriculum-minded young social studies teachers, early embracers of Educationism—the study of grammar was put aside, along with whatever else carried a taint of the "traditional." Then, more recently, taking up where the most enthusiastic educationists left off, the professional linguists—perhaps more aptly called "linguisticists," that eager band of anti-traditionalists in language studies whose zeal to prevail sorts so oddly with their claim of disinterested, scientific observation—have been carrying the battle against the old-fashioned study and teaching of old-fashioned grammar.

Thus, between charges that it was *not* being taught and *should* be taught and charges that it *was* being taught and should *not* be, grammar has had a very bad time of it for more than a quarter of a century. And, frankly, its

troubles are likely to get worse before they get better.

During this unstable, often chaotic, always trying period, however, in nearly all of the English classrooms with which I have had direct or indirect acquaintance, the teaching of the same old grammar has continued in essentially the same old way. English teachers trained before the mid-1930's, and therefore taught to believe in the values of traditional grammar and in traditional methods of teaching it, have remained dominant forces. They have stood off the educationists; though waves of "progressive" theory lapped high on their classroom walls, the doors held firm. And of late they have been standing off the linguisticists, whom someone has called "kissing-cousins of educationists." These, replacing the gross-sounding jargon of educationism with the high-sounding jargon of linguisticism, flushed with victories over old-fashioned philologists in colleges and universities, and affecting the dispassion that more conspicuously marks true scientism than true science, are urgently, even fanatically, storming the classroom in order to persuade the old-fashioned grammar teacher that she, too, should be dispassionate in her attitude toward language so that the attitude of linguisticism can prevail: let her just accept the view that there are merely "different" levels of usage—*not* "good" and "bad," "acceptable" and "unacceptable"—and all will be well.

The reader will possibly have guessed by now, correctly, that I am neither educationist nor linguisticist, and he may have assumed that the present essay is to be an attack on the attackers of the beleaguered teacher of grammar and a defense of the matter and methods that she has continued to use. But although my sympathies are wholly with grammar and the grammar teacher, my purpose just now is not to dissipate my own energies or to suggest that she dissipate hers by swatting at her swarming assailants, but to urge her to take a long and uncompromisingly honest look at what she has been and is doing in her teaching. For what is even more disturbing than the fact that such highly mobile forces are allied against her is the fact that though she has been teaching grammar faithfully throughout the years, the results, observed by college professors and employers, have given rise to the belief that she has *not* been teaching it. I shall certainly not go so far as to suggest that unless she mends some of her ways she will deserve to become extinct, but I have no choice other than to predict that unless she does so, she *may*.

But how to mend them? And, harder than that question, will mending them really do any good? The implications of many charges made in the past quarter of a century are that grammar would not do any appreciable good no matter how it might be taught. I have taught grammar in high school and junior college and to future English teachers undergoing their final year of preparation, have observed many teachers and student teachers in action, and, by means of freshman classes in college composition, have had a dozen years of steady necessity to examine the results of the teaching of grammar in high school. My variety of experiences has tempted me to a number of conclusions, which I will try to boil down to a single one. Let me say, first, that it seems to me there can be only one of

two possible reasons why students who have been exposed to a great deal of grammar nevertheless continue to write so ungrammatically that even friendly critics of the schools have concluded that they surely must have been exposed to none at all: either grammatical knowledge really has little connection with problems of writing, or it has latent bearings which our methods of teaching have failed to exploit and which our students have therefore failed to translate into practice. I take the latter view. My conclusion is that *grammar has failed to do what, at best, it can do because our methods have not been designed to establish and maintain a sufficient connection between grammatical knowledge and the practice of writing.* I make this statement in full awareness, I believe, of the efforts of the so-called "functionalists" of the past twenty years.

My use of "sufficient" implies, inevitably, a conviction that if such a degree of connection *were* maintained by our methods, the study of grammar would produce appreciable results. That is in fact my conviction. But, now, what is it that grammar can, "at best," do for students? I am not prepared to make such claims as the following, which were made by an early nineteenth-century grammarian in his introductory remarks addressed "To the Young Learner":[1]

You are about to enter upon one of the most useful, and, when rightly pursued, one of the most interesting studies in the whole circle of science. If, however, you, like many a misguided youth, are under

[1] My copy of the book from which these excerpts are quoted lacks a title page, and the covers are so worn that no lettering shows. The owner's name appears in ink, along with "Genoa, 1817."

the impression that the study of grammar is . . . a matter of little consequence, I trust I shall succeed in removing from your mind, all such false notions and ungrounded prejudices; for I will endeavour to convince you, before I close these lectures, that this is not only a pleasing study, but one of real and substantial utility; a study that directly tends to adorn and dignify human nature, and meliorate the condition of man. Grammar is a leading branch of that learning which alone is capable of unfolding and maturing the mental powers, and of elevating man to his proper rank in the scale of intellectual existence;—of that learning which lifts the soul from earth, and enables it to hold converse with a thousand worlds.

After asserting categorically that "Nothing of a secular nature can be more worthy of your attention, then, than the acquisition of grammatical knowledge," the same grammarian continues:

You are aware, my young friend, that you live in an age of light and knowledge; —an age in which science and the arts are marching onward with gigantick strides. You live, too, in a land of liberty —a land on which the smiles of Heaven beam with uncommon refulgence. . . . These considerations forbid that you should ever be so unmindful of your duty to your country, to your Creator, to yourself, and to succeeding generations, as to be content to grovel in ignorance. . . . Go on, then, with a laudable ambition, and an unyielding perseverance, in the path which leads to honour and renown.

Beside these nineteenth-century claims, the only claim that I wish to make for the power of grammar will seem very modest. Though I recognize the possibility that the higher claims may contain more truth than we are now likely to suppose, I want the reader to understand that I am not writing in support of them. As a matter of fact, I shall not argue that the study of grammar will enable students to write interestingly, effectively, elegantly, eloquently, logically, persuasively, or even clearly and intelligently. My claim is only that the study of grammar *can* enable students to solve certain problems of form and order that inevitably occur whenever they write: in short, that grammatical knowledge, applied, enables students to write—grammatically. Moreover, I believe that the study of grammar is much more likely to equip students to write grammatically if the teacher holds only to this lower expectation and manages her teaching accordingly. I believe that our first and greatest mistake in the past has been our assumption that if we could just force students to "learn" it, all of it, a knowledge of grammar would somehow, miraculously, transform them— "dignify human nature, and meliorate the condition of man." I believe that if grammar is taught with that high but obscure purpose, it may not even help anyone to write more correctly.

The possession of grammatical knowledge will not enable students even to write grammatically unless a deliberate working relation between grammatical knowledge and the practice of writing has been maintained during the study of grammar. It should really not have been surprising that during the 1920's and 1930's tests devised and conducted by educationists seemed to prove that there is little demonstrable correlation between training in formal grammar and the ability to write. But these tests did not prove that there is not a potential correlation. What they proved was that the application of grammatical knowledge to problems that occur during the process of writing is not an *automatic* application, made inevitable by the mere possession of the knowledge. In order to maintain a working relation between grammatical knowledge and the practice of writing, the teacher must, I believe, do two things. The first of these can be stated briefly; the second will require the remainder of this discussion.

II

The first requisite is only to make certain that the study of grammar is not widely separated *in time* from the practice of writing. It is difficult to imagine what kind of reasoning ever led us English teachers to fragmentize our subject as we have done, so that we have treated each part as a distinct entity not related to the others. At the worst, we have taught spelling on Monday, grammar on Tuesday, vocabulary on Wednesday, "theme writing" on Thursday, and reading on Friday. We have also taught grammar during one semester and writing during another, vocabulary one year and reading another. As often, particularly in recent years, we have presented a "unit" on grammar for a week or two, one on reading for another week or two, another on writing, and then another on vocabulary. There can be no doubt that it is difficult to keep all phases of English study constantly involved as integral parts of the same subject, and perhaps some separation of parts in order to allow concentrated study is inevitable. But it is clear that deliberate physical

separation of parts, as if they must be kept apart at all costs, is an error. The study of grammar should not be weeks, months, or semesters away from the practice of writing; it should be only minutes away. The study of grammar apart from or without steady practice in writing is as tedious and wasteful as the study of vocabulary apart from or without steady reading in good books.

The second necessity calls for more than the avoidance of separation in time. What it calls for is something positive and highly complex: the discovery, through investigation and analysis, of the specific connections between grammatical knowledge and problems that occur in the act of writing, and thereafter the teaching of these connections together with the grammatical elements themselves. Let me now attempt to make clear what is implied by this statement.

Not only the old-fashioned grammar teacher of the old-fashioned school, but the typical grammar teacher of the typical school is going at her work—not yesterday, but today —as though she meant that once grammar is *learned,* that is the end of it. She is using grammar textbooks and workbooks. She is having her students learn the eight parts of speech by heart so that they can recite the definitions. She is having them identify these eight parts in workbook sentences. She is having them learn the names and descriptions of the several kinds of phrases, clauses, and sentences. She is having them prove their knowledge of these by underlining the correct portions of sentences in a workbook series. She is having them identify subjects, objects, predicate nominatives, objects of prepositions, and appositives in these same workbooks. She is having them—but there is hardly need to continue: the system is well known to everyone who has been through it as a student and to everyone who has visited English classes in operation.

Who has ever stopped a child, busy at his set task of underlining all of the prepositional phrases contained in the sentences on a workbook page, and asked him just what good he thinks it is going to do him to be able to recognize prepositional phrases? And who, of those who have asked this question, has received an answer that made real sense? At the very most, the student's reply is a halting and uncertain "If I learn about grammar, it will help me write better."

It is not now, and I trust it never will become, my purpose to argue that grammatical knowledge is not a *good* in itself. But, then, I believe that *any* knowledge is a good. But I suggest that grammatical knowledge taught as an end in itself, taught without a calculated, relentless focus on its applicability to problems that occur in writing, will have no appreciable value to a student in his writing.

Let me try another way of making my meaning clear. Whenever I have talked with teachers of English on the subject of grammar and writing, I have made a point of asking them, first of all, whether they do in fact give time to the study of grammar. I have invariably had an affirmative answer to this question from a very large majority of the particular group. Next, I have pressed them about some details: Do they have students underline prepositional phrases? infinitive phrases? gerund phrases? participial phrases?—and so on, until I have

sampled the full range of descriptive grammar. I have never asked these questions but that I have not been assured that most English teachers do in fact cover the forms and functions of all but the most obscure grammatical elements.

So far, so good. But then I have gone on: "You tell me that you teach your students to recognize prepositional phrases, for example. But now can you tell me just what difference it would really make if students did *not* recognize prepositional phrases?" And I have asked the same for infinitive phrases, adjective clauses, noun clauses, and so on. The very worst kind of answer I have received to this question is something like this: "Why, if a student has not been taught to recognize prepositional phrases, infinitive phrases, and so on, he will be unable to pick them out on an examination." The very best kind of answer I have received to the question is the same as that I have received from students who were actually engaged in underlining sentence elements in workbooks: "If they learn grammar, it will help them to write better."

But when, after receiving this answer, I have put the question more specifically, I have never received a reply at all, but only a strained silence: "If grammatical knowledge will indeed, as you say, help students to write better, then it follows that if they *lacked* grammatical knowledge they would fall down in certain ways. Now, can you tell me exactly how a student might go wrong in his writing because he was ignorant, for example, of the form and function of a prepositional phrase? How might his ignorance of gerunds and gerund phrases actually *show itself* in his writing? What problems that do actually occur in writing will knowledge of adjective clauses equip a student to solve?"

After asking these questions, I have been greeted only with silence, with startled and then distrustful looks: my fellow English teachers take me for an anti-grammarian who is bent on arguing them out of teaching grammar on the grounds that grammar will not do students any good when they write. They are, of course, quite mistaken: I am possibly the very last person who would try to argue teachers out of teaching grammar. But it does seem highly desirable to argue them out of teaching it in such a way that, later, to teachers of college freshmen, employers, and other observers, it appears that no grammar has been taught, and in such a way that, to still others, it appears that grammar would not improve writing no matter how it was taught. Between teaching grammar in such a way that no one will believe it has been taught and not teaching grammar at all, there would not seem to be much choice.

It is in the fact that teachers of grammar—on being asked bluntly what problems that occur in writing are solvable by a knowledge of gerund phrases, for example—look startled and lapse into silence that I find, or think I do, the basic reason why the teaching of grammar has failed to have significant effect on students' writing. If teachers themselves cannot say just what problems the knowledge of a specific element of the sentence will enable the student to solve when he is writing—just what grammatical blunders it will enable him to avoid by solving these problems

correctly—then it is quite unrealistic to suppose that the student will perceive the connection and make the application at the crucial moment. If there is anything at all certain about the relationship between grammatical knowledge and the practice of writing, it is that there is very little in it that is *automatic*. The connections between knowledge and practice need to be forged by the teacher in her teaching and by the student in his study.

III

Undoubtedly, at the very beginning of the study of grammatical elements, in the elementary school, when students are first learning the names of the parts of speech, a good deal of mere memorization of names, descriptions, functions, and definitions is unavoidable. But after that early confrontation with these terms, I believe there should never be anything quite like it again. Instead, I suggest that the teacher who is about to embark on a study of grammar with students, by means of workbooks or otherwise, might take a long step in the right direction by offering her class a proposition just before the work begins: "Whenever you do not see any connection between knowledge of a particular element that we are studying and any problems of writing, ask me to explain. If I cannot explain and demonstrate a connection, we shall omit that element from our study."

This is a bold offer, which puts every element under an obligation to prove its value in the very most pragmatic sense. It is only fair to warn the teacher that unless she has given the matter some hard and systematic thought in advance, she will soon find herself "skipping" much more grammar than she had intended. For if she is not prepared—and if she holds to her bargain literally and does not make use of empty arguments such as "You will need to know prepositional phrases in order to be able to underline them on examinations" and "A knowledge of gerund phrases will help you write more correctly"—she will certainly fail to see connections that in fact do exist, and, failing to see them, will be unable to demonstrate them. On the other hand, it must seem perfectly right that she and her class omit the study of elements whose connections with problems of writing she finds herself unable to explain—for surely if her mature mind, after consideration, can establish no honest connections it is quite unlikely that the immature minds of students would do so, and if they established none would hardly put their knowledge to use in their writing.

But the teacher who offers her class this kind of proposition cannot count on students to press very hard or insistently for explanations. When I first made this very bargain with a class, I expected to be challenged anew on every element that the students were assigned to study. But the faith of children in a teacher's wisdom is blinder than I could possibly have imagined. Accustomed to assuming that whatever they were ordered to do must in *some* mysterious way be good for them—and, in a general way, perhaps it is—my students fell at once into the old routine of unquestioning learning, underlining this, labeling that, with never a pause to ask—

"Why?" It was I, therefore, who had to remind them of our bargain, not once but repeatedly: "Here you have underlined all the adjective clauses on this page and can repeat the definition of an adjective clause. Do you know what good this knowledge can do you when you write?" No one could say, of course; it seemed very odd to everyone that I had even asked. It was not until a week or two later that a bright girl raised her hand, as we were about to underline a page of infinitive phrases, and asked pointblank *just how "knowing" infinitive phrases could help her to solve any problems she would meet in writing.* After that, questions came more regularly: what problems of writing does ability to recognize gerund phrases enable one to solve? what can go wrong with one's writing if one is ignorant of adverbial clauses? of direct objects? of appositives? and so on.

Answering such questions required more thought than I had given to them in the past, and more than I had time to give on the spur of the moment, while the class sat waiting. Sticking to my bargain, I threw out more grammar during that semester than I should have thrown out. Impatient to get on with their underlining, children in the class were themselves satisfied with any sort of vague, dubious, dishonest answer I chose to try on them; but I learned in that semester to be absolutely honest in my teaching of grammar. I ended by omitting the study of elements about which I could utter only general, pious assurances that they would somehow be useful things to know. I could *not,* at the moment I was asked to do so, demonstrate in unequivocal terms just how ability to recognize prepositional phrases would be usable in writing. I could not make explicit the applicability of knowledge of gerunds to writing. It was right to throw these out of our study, since the students would make no use of the knowledge if none of us could see a specific application for it; but I was also wrong in throwing them out, because knowledge of these elements *does* bear directly upon certain problems that occur in writing, and I should have been prepared in advance to make these clear.

At the very least, then, I believe that a teacher of grammar should make the bargain with a class that I made, and I believe that she should keep to it, even though it may mean that she will throw out three-fourths of the matter contained in her workbooks. But at the very most, I believe that she should set about a patient, thorough, systematic, and painfully honest examination of each separate grammatical element in the entire battery of parts, forms, and functions. Her question of each should be the same: "What problems that occur in writing will knowledge of this one element solve or help to solve?" Her purpose should not be to find excuses to "justify" the teaching of all the elements listed in the index of a textbook on grammar; on the contrary, her purpose should be to seek the indispensables of grammatical knowledge.

The present essay is obviously not the place in which to outline or to describe in detail the connections between particular grammatical elements and particular problems that occur in the course of writing sentences, paragraphs, and essays. The full analysis requires an elaborate representation that should be tedious and unsightly here. But there is a better reason for omitting a full analysis here. I do not believe that my analysis would help another teacher very much. I believe that the individual teacher of grammar and writing needs to work out these relationships of grammatical knowledge and writing for herself, by herself in her own way. I do not believe that it is a job to be left to writers of textbooks and workbooks. My purpose in the remainder of this essay, therefore, is only to suggest ways of proceeding that the teacher may want to try—and, of course, to reject when she finds sounder ones.

IV

The immediate aim of the investigation, then, is to find, not excuses for teaching a vast amount of grammar that tradition or blind faith tells the teacher she must teach, but precisely what grammatical knowledge is necessary and at what points it is applicable. The ultimate aim, of course, is to make oneself ready to explain and demonstrate to students, *while they are learning the elements themselves,* just how the knowledge of these elements enables them to solve problems that occur in the course of writing.

There are two possible approaches to the investigation. First, one can take the parts of speech, the word-group elements, and the "uses," such as subject, direct object, and so forth, and put the same direct question to each in turn: "Just what problems of writing are solved by knowledge of this element?" (Or, of course, one can put the same question in a blunter way: "What grammatical blunder may the student make if he lacks knowledge of this element?") Second, one can start from the other end, with the major characteristic ways in which writing does in fact go wrong grammatically, and can put this question to each in turn: "Just what knowledge of what element or elements is needed to solve this problem?" (Or, more baldly: "Just what grammatical knowledge is needed to avoid this gross blunder?")

The first approach is slower, less certain, involves far more repetition and duplication of data. Let me illustrate briefly by using one part of speech, one word-group, and one "use." How, for lack of knowledge of the *adjective,* may one blunder in writing? The possibilities are not numerous: one can get the wrong degree ("It is the best of the two"), and one can use adjective where he should use adverb ("This car runs real good"). I would not set children to underlining the adjectives on a workbook page unless they understood that these are the immediately demonstrable reasons for their learning to identify adjectives. For the word-group, let us take the *participial phrase* and ask the same basic question of it. So far as I can ascertain, the major demonstrable "faults" that can be directly associated with lack of knowledge of participial phrases are only three: dangling modifier, fault in parallelism, and fault in comma punctuation. Finally, for the "use," let us consider the *subject* of a sentence or clause. The major grammatical faults that result from failure to identify a subject are only two: improper case of a pronoun as subject ("Give the book to *whomever*

wants it") and faulty agreement of the verb with the subject ("A pile of books *were* on the table"). It would seem to me that if students have underlined ten workbook pages of subjects without realization that these are the main reasons for recognizing subjects, they have wasted their time.

The second approach to the analysis means starting from the "surface spots" in writing at which lack of grammatical knowledge betrays itself and working back to discover precisely what knowledge of what elements is applicable at these points. One of the most obvious of these focal centers is that at which it becomes necessary to choose between the case forms of pronouns, and the teacher may wish to begin her research by examining some sentences in which the problem occurs. Her immediate purpose will be to find just what must be known—and, therefore, taught—before one can choose knowingly between, for example, *whoever* and *whomever*. Let her take an ordinary sentence: "Give the book to (whoever-whomever) you believe will like it." The bare outline of grammatical knowledge that must be called into play in solving this problem includes recognition (1) that "whoever" is the subjective and "whomever" the objective form; (2) that "whoever you believe will like it" is a dependent clause; (3) that a dependent clause can perform offices of the noun—and in this instance serves as object of the preposition; (4) that "whoever" serves as subject of its clause. If the teacher will go on to examine a dozen such sentences in which it is necessary to choose between forms of pronouns, she will discover that at one time or another a writer needs to use knowledge of a considerable body of that grammar which some have scrapped too hastily and which others have "taught" without advising either themselves or their pupils in what precise ways it will be useful. She will discover also how to make connections in the minds of students between their knowledge of particular elements and these particular problems. And, finally, she may glimpse, in the act of doing this research, profound implications for her method of teaching grammar.

The necessity to choose between case forms of pronouns, then, is one of the villains that make knowledge of numerous grammatical elements, facts, and principles indispensable. Clearly, if distinctions of this kind "did not matter," as some linguisticists assert, it would be possible for us to put aside a good deal of grammar that we must otherwise teach; but I assume that the reader who has read thus far into the present essay agrees with me that these distinctions do matter, and that equipping students to make them is a part of the responsibility of the English teacher: If that supposition is accurate, the reader will agree that we must ferret out the particular portions of total grammatical knowledge that bear on the problem.

But even though we could be freed from the necessity of choosing between case forms of pronouns, we should still have to deal with problems of a structural kind whenever we write, and a second "surface spot" from which the teacher can work backward, or inward, to discover what grammatical knowledge she should give her students is the complex, but fairly well defined, assortment of places in the sentence at which these problems arise. Wrongly solved, or slipped over

naively, as though no problem were present, these problems manifest themselves as structural faults, in the forms of sentences run together, fragments set down as whole sentences, modifiers that dangle or are misplaced, pronouns that refer to the wrong noun or to two nouns or to none, subjects and verbs that do not agree in number, nonparallel elements that should be parallel, and so forth. Let us take only two examples from this assortment of characteristic ways in which students go wrong structurally when they either lack the right knowledge to solve the problem or fail to apply the right knowledge at the right time.

First, what knowledge of what elements do students need to have in order to solve correctly the problem that, incorrectly solved, expresses itself in the form of a dangling modifier? Three rather similar elements lend themselves most readily to the vice of dangling: the participial phrase, the prepositional phrase containing a gerund, and the elliptical clause; once in a great while a student contrives to dangle an infinitive phrase also. Danglers persist in the styles of students who have been taught a great deal of grammar, including recognition of participial and prepositional phrases and elliptical clauses; indeed, it is a fair guess that they persist in the styles of such students every bit as much as in the styles of those who have been taught little or no grammar. Mere ability to recognize these elements, then, is next to useless: *it is necessary to teach students at the time they are learning to recognize them that a major reason for learning to recognize them is the problem of proper modification.* I believe that the student who has learned only to identify a participial phrase has learned only the half of his lesson that, alone, will not do him any good; he must learn also *why* he has learned to identify it.

Second, what knowledge of what elements do students need to know in order to solve correctly the problem that, incorrectly solved, shows up as a fault in parallelism? Of all the major structural blunders, the fault in parallelism is the most tenacious. It hangs on even in rather sophisticated styles, long after the writer has ceased to commit such barbarities as dangling modifiers, agreement errors, reference errors, and case-form errors. The reason it is most tenacious is not hard to find: the problem of maintaining grammatical parallelism requires knowledge of a greater number of elements of the sentence than does any other single problem of sentence construction. In fact, equipping students to solve problems of parallelism necessitates the teaching of *all* elements of the sentence, for all elements of the sentence are capable of being compounded with their likes, and every problem of compounding elements is a problem of parallelism. Conversely, if we have "taught" all the elements of the sentence and failed to relate the students' knowledge of them to the problem of parallelism, we have failed to focus on one of the very largest single reasons for teaching grammar. Grammatical parallelism is of course a matter of balance, of coordinating like elements that perform like functions. We compound two nouns, two verbs, two adjectives, two adverbs— indeed, even two prepositions, two interjections, and two conjunctions. The problem of compounding all these

simple parts of speech is easy enough: only the true dullard needs any instruction in compounding these properly and in avoiding coordinating, say, a noun and a verb, an adverb and an adjective. But we also compound prepositional phrases, participial phrases, gerund phrases, infinitive phrases, absolute phrases, noun clauses, adjective clauses, adverb clauses, independent clauses—and in order to be sure of compounding these likes with one another, one must be capable of distinguishing them. So long as a writer is unable to distinguish one from another, he is certain occasionally, if not frequently, to cross them up. The possibilities of "going wrong" in solving the problem of parallelism are as numerous as the elements of the sentence, and the only sure way of enabling students always to solve the problem correctly is to teach them to recognize every element of the sentence and to distinguish it from every other. But, again, the ability to do so will have no significant effect on the way in which students solve the problem of parallelism unless they have also been taught the application of their knowledge. I do not believe that a student should ever be set to underlining prepositional phrases, infinitive phrases, participial phrases, or any of the other phrases or clauses, unless he is made aware, and ideally kept constantly aware while he is doing so, that the greatest single application for his knowledge of these elements is in solving the problem of parallelism that occurs every time he compounds two elements.

Finally, the teacher who is searching out the precise connections between grammatical knowledge and the practice of writing may want to look at the "surface spot" of punctuation, particularly comma punctuation. During the past twenty-five years much strange advice has been given students about comma punctuation: "Use commas where they are needed to make your sentence clear" —a certain way to invite students to write miserably sprawled sentences and then attempt to make them "clear" by punctuation; "Use commas where there is a natural pause"—but the most masterful oral readers of prose pause before, on, and after single words and phrases according to nuances of meaning and special emphases of personal interpretation, and to use commas at all these places would simply be a lunatic practice. The "clarity" and "natural pause" directives are possibly useful for sophisticated writers who have already mastered the art of writing, including punctuation; given to the unsophisticated, they merely become a license for indulgence in a foolish sort of stylistic anarchy. The fact is that sufficiently exact directives for punctuation can be given to students only in the terms of the grammar of the sentence: "Use a comma between independent clauses joined by a coordinating conjunction," "Use a comma after an introductory participial phrase," and so on. If these directives are to have any meaning, the student must obviously be able to identify the sentence elements that are employed in them: there is no way, really, of circumventing that necessity.

V

Possibly I have now sufficiently illustrated the two approaches by means of which the individual English teacher can work out for her own use the specific connection between grammatical knowledge and the practice of writing. I do not know which is better—to start from a list of the parts of speech and the several forms and functions of sentence elements and to attempt to state the precise applicabilities of each to problems of writing, or to start with the major problems of grammatical writing as these show in the "surface spots" at which sentences most often "go wrong" in the hands of the inept and to work back from these points to the particular grammatical knowledge that is useful in solving them. I suspect that both approaches are needed, each complementing the other; in working out this huge problem, the teacher will probably find herself playing one against the other.

The finished analysis is not likely to be very tidy; it is likely to be sprawling and gigantic, if not monstrous. It is likely to be filled with repetitious detail. It may not be perfectly complete or perfectly accurate. In the midst of her undertaking, surrounded by sheets of paper bearing portions of uncertain outlines, the teacher may sometimes fear that she is caught in a messy bad dream. She may very likely find herself wishing that she had never started, and she is almost certain to despair of ever finishing. But in the end, if she persists, she will emerge from her experience much wiser about the teaching of grammar than before. She will have a healthier respect for grammatical knowledge than before. In place of what may have been a growing uneasiness about it in the pit of her stomach—"What if, after all, the educationists and the linguisticists *were* right, and there *was* no really honest value in the study of grammar?"—she will have gained an insight into the indispensability of grammatical knowledge for solving certain problems that occur in writing.

Her study will probably make instant, drastic differences in her method of teaching grammar. She will probably want fewer workbook sentences in which students endlessly underline elements without knowing why. She will certainly not spend weeks getting students to underline subjects and verbs without making sure they understand, every step of the way, that one of the very greatest reasons for being able to identify subjects and verbs is that when we write or speak we have to make these agree in number. She will probably want to replace most of her old drill sentences with others in which it is possible actually to demonstrate to students the usefulness of the knowledge that they are being made to acquire: for example, she may want to eliminate drill on objects of prepositions in sentences like "Give it to *John*," in which there is no immediately demonstrable reason for recognizing the object of the preposition, since it is a noun, and to do all or most of her teaching of objects of prepositions through sentences like "Give it to *him*," in which there *is* demonstrable reason for recognizing them. She may no longer be content with having students underline gerund phrases in the usual workbook sentences in which it is impossible to demonstrate that a knowledge of gerund phrases has any earthly use; she may want sentences in which gerund phrases are involved in a problem of parallelism, in a problem of punctuation, and in a pronoun which "possesses" the gerund. These are random samples only: she will unquestionably want to reconsider her means of teaching every element.

If the student needs more than merely to "know" grammar in order to make use of his knowledge in his practice of writing, clearly it is even more important that the teacher who directs his learning be prepared not only with knowledge of grammar but with knowledge of the specific uses of grammar: to make that point has been the main purpose of my discussion here. If my notion of the usefulness of grammar looks small and mean beside the grand conception advertised by the nineteenth-century grammarian whom I quoted earlier—a conception which sets grammar second only to religion as a proper influence on young lives—perhaps teachers can believe more honestly in my claim than in his, and if their methods are devised to implement the lesser purpose for which I have argued, grammar may be made to do more good in more immediate and obvious ways than it has been doing hitherto in our time. If it can be made just to help students write more grammatically, I, at least, will settle for that objective.

JAMES SLEDD

Grammar or gramarye?[1]

*I wald cause the universities mak an Inglish grammar
to repres the insolencies of sik green heades.*

ALEXANDER HUME

Grammarians are accustomed to humiliation. It is their heritage. They are dry, they are plodding, they are mere: at their funerals no one weeps. Grammarians make, indeed, no loud pretenses to high status. In the great chain of academic being there is a place for regents, a place for coaches; there are places for vice-chancellors, publicity directors, maintenance engineers, careerists, critics, hollow men, and teachers of teaching; there is even a place, though an inferior one, for grammarians. That station, with its duties, is all they claim.

Yet not even a grammarian should always be meek. Like a rat-catcher, a word-catcher has worked hard to master the secrets of his trade. Not every man can catch a rat or define a noun, and if the grammarian has abandoned all foolish hopes of a place at the top of the totem pole, at its foot he wants no amateurs shouldering him aside. He is a professional. It took a long

time to separate grammar from astrology and magic, grammar from gramarye; and an honest grammarian cannot keep his peace when he sees knowledge and superstition once again confused.

That confusion was exemplified in an article in the *Educational Forum* for January 1959. Under the title "Grammar and Writing," Professor Bertrand Evans offered a defense of English grammar which was more damaging to that ancient study than any attack he could have made. And Evans' theory, it now appears, is not the solitary aberration of an isolated individual. He is a leading member of a small group within the College Eng-

[1] In 1966 Mr. Sledd believes that in 1959 he was too severe in his judgment of traditional grammar, too favorable in his judgment of structural grammar, and unaware of the full significance of transformational generative grammar. He believes that he was right in his opposition to the dogmas of gramarye.—*J.S.*

"Grammar or Gramarye?": From *The English Journal*, vol. 49, n. 5, May 1960, pp. 293–303. Reprinted with the permission of The National Council of Teachers of English and James Sledd.

lish Association of the San Francisco Bay Area which has recently sold a remarkable bill of goods to that association and to the English departments of California's colleges and universities. According to this group, education is by its very nature dictatorial, and there is just one way by which the high school teacher of English can achieve "real integration" in his "total work with language" (James J. Lynch in *College English,* November 1959). Evans' statement may therefore be taken as a kind of semi-official appendix to the communal manifesto of California's educators for unfreedom; and since these would-be dictators have gained powerful support for their doctrine, the potential influence of the statements makes it imperative that it receive an answer which its quality would not deserve.

The theory is not abstruse; it may be stated in a single paragraph. In order to help students avoid "grammatical blunders" in their writing, Evans would have teachers in the schools teach the old-fashioned grammar of the schoolroom to its full extent. He would have them teach students "to recognize every element of the sentence and to distinguish it from every other," but he would have them insist always on practical applications. Each bit of grammar should be presented as a means to correct a specific blunder. The result would be that students would write more grammatically.

So simple an argument is appealing to a simple conservative mind, particularly when it is accompanied by stern denunciation of a mythical academic monster branded "linguisticist": the old-fashioned teacher can go on teaching the same old grammar in much the same old way, and she can take pride in her ignorance of everything that she might otherwise feel bound to learn. But the argument really will not do. Evans has systematically begged every important question which his subject raises, and his fourteen pages succeed only in revealing him (if I, too, may rudely neologize) as a sophisticist. The meekest grammarian must defend himself against such defenders.

LINGUISTS AND STANDARDS

Let me begin my self-defense by disposing of Evans' mythical monster, the "linguisticist." To amateurs, the monster must be fearsome, since he is characterized, at his introduction, as a professional, one of "the professional linguists." Moreover, he is eager, he is convinced he is right, he believes in "disinterested scientific observation," and he strongly attacks "the old-fashioned study and teaching of old-fashioned grammar." So far, the description applies quite well to a substantial number of the most learned, able, and responsible professional students of the English language in the United States and elsewhere in the English-speaking world; many grammarians might be proud to answer "present" to such a roll-call. The description even remains accurate (though no longer a matter of pride) when Evans complains of the jargon of the linguist. Technical terms are necessary, and inevitably distressing to those who cannot understand them; but the linguist has certainly gone too far, as his colleague the literary critic has gone too far, in coining awkward phrases: the linguist has only the advantage that *morphophonemics* has a precise meaning, while *dissociation of sensibility* is vague. When Evans goes on, however, to repeat the old slander that linguists have no standards, he has turned his back on reality. A livelier respect for fact would have constrained him to say rather that many linguists have standards different from his own and that this difference places upon each party the responsibility for a reasoned statement of its views.

Both Evans' own standards and the precise nature of his charges against the linguist should therefore be examined. In general, he says, the linguist takes "the view that there are merely 'different' levels of usage—*not* 'good' and 'bad', 'acceptable' and 'unacceptable'"; as a particular example of this heresy, Evans alleges an assertion by "some linguisticists" that distinctions among the case forms of English pronouns "do not matter." He rounds out his indictment with the surprising assertion that linguists believe there is "no really honest value in the study of grammar."

A harsh answer to these charges could very easily be given: the man who makes them is either culpably ignorant or maliciously deceitful. I have studied linguistics off and on for twenty years and have taught it for ten, my acquaintance with linguists studying English is wide and representative, and I do not know a single linguist who holds the views which Evans attributes to his unnamed bogeyman. Is it not suspicious that the bogey *is* unnamed? Linguists would not write grammars if they saw no value in the study of grammar; they would not describe pronominal forms and their uses if such distinctions did not matter; and they do not believe that in language anything

goes. To say they do is to say that which is not.

What charitable explanation might be given of the origin of Evans' gross misstatement? I can think of only one. It is true that many linguists see no way of judging the system that is a language, or an element in that system, as in itself either good or bad. I say *bucket* where my Northern friends say *pail;* I pronounce *mother* without a final *r;* I use *you all* as a plural pronoun; and in humorous conversation I revert to my childhood ways and *I used to could.* I have no means of deciding, in absolute terms, whether these expressions, simply as expressions, are good, bad, or indifferent. They are just some possible ways of saying certain things in one variety of English, and I would not waste time in fruitless discussion of the absolute merits or demerits of postvocalic *r.* This is not to say, however (and here may be the source of Evans' blunder), that the *use* of these expressions may not be good or bad. On the contrary, outside the South I deliberately drop a number of my Southernisms, since they are not always understood; and I distinguish sharply between those forms which are appropriate for serious exposition and those which are fit for laughing talk. The writer's or speaker's task is precisely such choice among the available resources of his language, and he will best accomplish that task if he defines good English as that English which will best do, in the given situation, what a good man would want his English to do there. To deny the necessity of linguistic choice, or to make that choice mechanically, is the part of fools.

What Evans' own standards are is

not quite clear. He wants students to write "grammatically"; he wants stenographers to write in a way that will please their employers; but he never clarifies his measure of grammaticality. One may be pardoned for suspecting that to write "grammatically" is to follow the unreasoned and perhaps unreasonable rules of some outmoded handbook, to surrender one more small part of that responsibility for rational choice which makes us human. I say this for two reasons. First, Evans himself perpetrates bad sentences with obvious pride in their "correctness": "The full analysis requires an elaborate representation that should be tedious and unsightly here"; "I have never asked these questions but that I have not been assured . . ."; etc. No one could write so badly without working at it. Second, Evans condemns as grossly ungrammatical at least one sentence which outstanding grammarians for the past seventy years (Curme, Jespersen, Kruisinga, Palmer, Sweet, Zandvoort) would have accepted: "A pile of books *were* on the table." Often and properly, a collective noun may stand as the subject of a plural verb, especially when it is followed by a prepositional phrase whose object is plural; but presumably, for Evans, the chastity of the singular subject is violated if it lies down with a plural verb. Such scrupulosity is vice, not virtue, and the linguist who derides it is no enemy of standards but of *low* standards. Man, if not reasonable, at least is capable of reason.

PURPOSE OF GRAMMATICAL INSTRUCTION

So much for the "linguisticist" and his sins against the dark light of schoolroom grammar. It is confessed that his jargon is ugly, but nothing else is proved against him by Bertrand Evans. It must also be admitted, however, that the insulting attack on linguists is only one part, and that a minor part, of Evans' argument. His principal contentions must still be examined. As I have said, they are very simple. The teacher in the schools, he argues, should reconsider her teaching of grammar (I do not know why Evans' teacher is always feminine). The main purpose of her teaching should be to improve her students' writing, to make them write "grammatically"; and to this end she should teach only those elements of grammar whose relevance to specific writing problems she is prepared to demonstrate. At best, "she should set about a patient, thorough, systematic, and painfully honest examination of each separate grammatical element in the entire battery of parts, forms, and functions. Her question of each should be the same: 'What problems that occur in writing will knowledge of this one element solve or help to solve?' Her purpose should not be to find excuses to 'justify' the teaching of all the elements listed in the index on grammar; on the contrary, her purpose should be to seek the indispensables of grammatical knowledge." Yet this "painfully honest examination," it happily turns out, will not place the teacher in the ranks of the technologically unemployed. She has only to think of the problem of parallelism, and her job is saved. "The possibilities of 'going wrong' in solving the problem of parallelism are as numerous as the elements of the sentence, and the only sure way of enabling students always to solve the problem correctly is to teach them to recognize every element of the sentence and to distinguish it from every other." The upshot is that the teacher may begin—or continue—to teach the whole of some traditional description of English but that she will teach her traditional description with just one narrow purpose in her mind: "to help students write more grammatically." She will present all the familiar paraphernalia of rules and analysis, but she will make her teaching effective by reminding the students that the purpose of the analysis is to enable them to follow the rules.

To avoid misunderstanding, let me say at once that I am as eager as any one else to improve the quality of student writing, that I share the conviction that more grammar than is usually taught today should be taught not only in our schools but in our colleges and universities, that I believe the teaching of more grammar *might* make for better writing, and that at the very least I do not see how a teacher can discuss a student's use of language without some set of grammatical terms and distinctions. To these aims and propositions, so stated, I believe I can guarantee the assent of a large number of Evans' despised linguisticists. But when all these things have been said, the big questions are still unanswered. What is the purpose of grammatical instruction? Is it only the narrowly practical purpose of enabling students, in their writing, to conform to some arbitrary set of rules, or is it also the humanistic purpose of advancing the study of man as proper to mankind? There are many grammars of English, not just one; which grammar, or which grammars, should prospective teachers learn, and which grammar or grammars should practicing teachers teach? It is quite impossi-

ble, in one year, or two, or twelve, to teach students to "recognize every element of the sentence and to distinguish it from every other" (Jespersen's grammar runs to seven volumes, and Curme's to some thousand pages); since there is no such thing as a "complete grammar" of English and since we have neither time nor teachers to teach one if there were, how shall we determine and how shall we teach the real "indispensables of grammatical knowledge"? What real evidence is there that extensive and intensive grammatical training is a necessary condition of better writing or even the best means to achieve it? These are some of the questions which articles on "grammar and writing" should attempt to answer, but Evans' only answer is to pretend the questions are not there.

I can finish my self-defense, and turn it to some constructive purpose, by offering my own answers. Admittedly they are incomplete, and they may be worse than incomplete: they may be wrong; at least they are answers, my best efforts to face some of the issues which Evans has evaded; and argument, not bluster, will be needed to refute them. *Linguisticist* is only a sophisticistic word.

In stating the purpose of grammatical instruction, I shall take, with some circumspection, the highest ground I can. The teaching of writing is a mysterious process. For myself, I often doubt that I can teach a student to write better; I sometimes hope that I can help him learn. But my uncertainty does not extend to the teaching of English grammar. I know I can teach grammar, and I teach it for a good reason. The proper study of mankind *is* man, and there is nothing so basic to our humanity as our language. That, and the fact that people will pay me for innocently amusing myself by studying and teaching English, are my reasons for doing what I do. I could not prove, and I know no one else who could prove, that the vast sums devoted to the teaching of English grammar pay off in terms of better student writing. I know expert linguists who write badly, and I know students who write well but could no more define an auxiliary verb than they could lay an egg. Maybe the best way to make a student write well is to get him born into an educated family where good books are cherished, but neither linguisticist nor classroom teacher can play God. Given a man, they *can* help him to understand what he is and what makes him so, and if in the process they may help him to become a writing man, they should be thankful for an added blessing.

WHAT GRAMMAR TO TEACH

My statement of the reason for grammatical instruction thus differs widely from Evans' statement, and my choice of grammars to be taught differs yet more widely. Evans writes as if English grammar were a fixed and unalterable body of knowledge which he controls but is willing to share with the uninitiate. In his questioning of teachers, he says, he has "sampled the full range of descriptive grammar" and has been assured "that most English teachers do in fact cover the forms and functions of all but the most obscure elements." What can he mean? The claim seems preposterous on the face of it, and concrete evidence seems to refute it. "The full range" of a fairly traditional descriptive gram-

mar of English includes phonology, morphology, and syntax. An adequate phonological statement involves, among other things, the distinction between phonetics and phonemics and the description of the English vowels, consonants, stresses, pitches, and junctures. The morphology can be separated from the syntax only by some kind of definition of the word as distinct from larger forms, and within the morphology one must deal with such thorny questions as the distinctions between inflection and derivation and between the native and foreign derivational patterns. In the syntax, one must establish a number of "parts of speech," some of them large open classes like nouns, others small closed classes like prepositions; one must somehow relate these syntactic classes to morphological classes defined in terms of inflection or derivation or both; one must establish a concept of modification or expansion and state the positions of modifiers of noun heads and verb heads; one must describe the favorite sentence patterns for statements, questions, and requests; etc., etc. The barest outline of such a description is a lesson in modesty, and the rash amateur who lightheartedly begins to fill up the outline is quickly overwhelmed. To cite a few problems quite at random: How can one change the meaning of an alternative question by changing its intonation? How shall a compound word be defined? What subclasses of nouns and of determiners need be recognized, and how are they related? What distinguishes the *keep* of *to keep going* from the *be* of *to be going?* What subclasses of adverbs are necessary in order to deal with such various forms as *then, there, thus, not, never, very, so?* What order-classes are represented in a monstrous phrase like *not quite all those same two extremely bad architects' own first four very markedly inferior brown French stone houses over there on Main Street that are being remodeled?* Are all the objects of *take* alike in the old sentence *He took umbrage, alarm, his hat, his departure, no notice of his pursuers, a pistol from his pocket,* and finally, *his life?* Why will every reader happily accept Bertrand Evans' phrase *the very best kind of answer* although many will reject as un-English or effeminate his similar phrase *the very most pragmatic sense?* It is easy to talk about "sampling the full range of descriptive grammar" or about "teaching students to recognize every element of the sentence"; I have yet to meet the teacher who has accomplished such wonderful things.

Some of the teachers, indeed, whom I have met in the last twenty years could not even understand a statement of the problem of describing English. I know one noisy teacher of teachers who conducts advanced classes in English grammar yet boasts that he knows no linguistics and means to learn none, and when I examine teacher candidates on traditional grammatical problems I get astounding answers. For example, in a Middle English class in the spring of 1959, I asked a group of thirty-two candidates for the M.A. in English to tell me what is meant by *case*. These students were probably better informed than most, since I had explained some of the traditional terms to them in lectures and since they had been instructed to read a Middle English grammar. Eight of the thirty-two victims gave such bad definitions of *case* that I preserved them in a mimeographed horror sheet. Here are the first three specimens:

(i) "Case refers to the form or usage of a noun in a sentence. Cases in English are: (1) Nominative. . . . (2) Genitive. . . . (3) Dative. . . . (4) Accusative. . . . (5) Ablative. . . ."

(ii) "Case refers to nouns, as to whether they are subject form, object form, possessive or indirect object form. Hence, nominative, genitive, dative, accusative are cases. There are other forms as the vocative (imperative) or instrumental which is the case for issuing a command."

(iii) "Case: refers to a noun as it functions in a sentence. There are three cases in ME—genitive, dative and accusative—all of which reflect spelling changes in the noun. Genitive used to indicate possession, dative the object of the verb, and accusative the subject."

I hasten to assure the reader that the illiteracies are not mine; they are not unexampled among the students who as teachers, according to Evans, will shortly "cover the forms and functions of all but the most obscure grammatical elements."

I can only conclude, after analyzing Evans' claim and some of the evidence bearing on it, that his concept of descriptive grammar must be pathetically limited. I suppose he hopes and thinks that most teachers know and teach some traditional handbook of grammar and that such a handbook treats "the forms and functions" of all the important grammatical elements in English. I can share neither these hopes nor these beliefs. The biggest of all the questions which Evans begs is just the question of which grammar shall be taught, and until it is answered the plea for grammar in the schools is almost meaningless. Does grammar mean Lowth[2] in Victorian dress or Jespersen's *Essentials*[3] or Paul Roberts' *Patterns?* My own experience with traditional grammars (they are not all alike) was so bad that I should not like to repeat it or to inflict it on other students. Precisely because the conventional handbooks that I know are mainly intended for the correction of errors in student writing, they overemphasize those elements of English structure where usage is divided, and underemphasize those elements where divided usage is impossible for native speakers and writers. For instance, some good speakers and writers may prefer Evans' *was* in "A pile of books *was* on the table," others "A pile of books *were* on the table"; some use the forms interchangeably; others use now one and now the other, with a difference in meaning. Certainly a student should be aware of the different practices and should have some principles to guide his own choices in such matters: presumably to use *were* in a paper for Bertrand Evans would be bad English, since it would produce an unfortunate effect. But who would build a teaching program on a foundation of pedantry? If Evans would, then indeed he is upholding standards, but bad standards. By way of contrast to the disagreement about the pile of books, one

[2] Robert Lowth (1710–1787), English cleric and scholar, wrote *A Short Introduction to English Grammar* (1762), a thoroughgoing prescriptive approach to English syntax.
[3] Harry Otto Jens Jespersen (1860–1943) was one of a number of great European scholars of the English language. His *A Modern English Grammar on Historical Principles* (seven volumes) was reprinted as recently as 1961 (George Allen and Unwin, Ltd., London).

might point out that no native speaker or writer would have the least hesitation in determining the proper order of the six forms *dogs, big, the, black, ten, same;* but the statement of that order is a much more important part of a descriptive grammar than the rules for the agreement of verbs with collective nouns. It is much more important, that is, if the purpose of grammatical instruction is primarily the humanistic purpose of inculcating a conscious and organized knowledge of the mother tongue. Naturally the technologist who is concerned to make secretaries acceptable to tired executives will pass a contrary judgment, for he is neither humanist nor scientist but a social manipulator.

FAULTS OF TRADITIONAL DEFINITIONS

Let us assume, however, that the purpose of grammatical instruction is not to teach men to understand their humanity but to teach mice to scurry through mazes in record time. Even on that assumption the traditional grammars that I have known are less useful than they might be, since their terms and distinctions will confuse the mice. The traditional grammars order students to write complete sentences, which are defined as groups of words that express complete thoughts; but the student gets little help if he complains that that definition applies as well to a book, a chapter, or a paragraph as to a sentence and that the definition does not tell him how to judge thoughts as complete or incomplete. If "the subject of a sentence is that word or group of words of which something is said or asserted," then both *dog* and *man* are subjects of the sentence. *The dog bit the man;* if "a modifier is a word or group of words that adds to the meaning of another word," then *he* modifies *rat* in *He's a rat*, since *he* indicates that *rat* means "a dirty, treacherous man" and not "a rodent"; since *thing* can mean *"any* thing" or "no thing," the casual definition of a noun reduces to the statement that a noun is a name, and that in turn is much the same as to say that a noun is a noun. And so it goes. The simple truth is that the traditional definitions are definitions that do not define. Teachers who defend them do not really use them, because they cannot be used. Instead, both teachers and students rely on the examples which follow the pseudo-definitions. When a teacher tells a student that a noun is the name of a person, place, or thing, she has told him little or nothing; but she gives a native speaker a good deal of information if she says, "Look here. *Man* is a noun. I say *one man, two men;* I say *the man's hat, the men's hats;* I say *The dog bit the man, Man is mortal,* and *Socrates is a man.* Words that behave like that are nouns." It would seem the part of wisdom to recognize the fact that we identify nouns by the positions they occupy in morphologic and syntactic forms: since mice need cues to get through mazes, even the mouse-trainer should give them the cues.

What Evans, then, has flatteringly called "old-fashioned grammar" might just as well be called antediluvian grammar, or hardshell grammar, or gramarye. In the schools, as he says, "the teaching of the same old grammar has continued in essentially the same old way"; prostitution is the oldest profession. On the other hand,

Evans' new-fangled linguisticists are not so new as he would make them. I have known many teachers who were shocked when someone told them their definition of a noun was useless, but it was in 1891 that the great English grammarian Henry Sweet contemptuously dismissed "the quibbling etymological definition of a noun as 'the name of anything.' " In the same preface, Sweet passed a truer judgment on gramarye and gramaryeans than Evans can manage a lifetime later: "Practical teachers, who generally confine themselves to one book and one method, are often hardly able to realize how unsettled grammar still is." Forty years after Sweet, a great American grammarian, George O. Curme, delivered to the Modern Language Association a presidential address which Bertrand Evans might profitably read. It is entitled "Are Our Teachers of English Adequately Prepared for Their Work?" and it is much more destructive of pseudo-grammar than anything I could hope to say. Since my conclusion will be rather like Curme's, and since I do not wish to seem either new-fangled or unduly severe, I will prepare for my peroration by quoting a few of his remarks:

It never occurs to many grammarians to study the language which they are describing. They probably think that this has been done and that the school grammars contain the infallible records of these investigations.

We find queer statements in our school grammars because their authors know little about the English language.

Our school grammarians are not scholars. They do not inform themselves upon the subjects that they teach. They are helpless if the little antiquated school grammars do not give them information.

For many years there has been a remarkable interest in our language both in Europe and America, and now after a great period of English study there is a rich literature at their disposal. If only they might become aware of it!

Many teachers of English represent good idiomatic English as bad usage. They are not sufficiently trained to know what good English is. This is an intolerable condition of things.

The correction of a few errors of speech will not give them [our students] the training they need. They must become acquainted with the inner nature of their mother tongue. A large number of our teachers of English have had such a meager scientific training that they cannot give their students what they need.

TEACHER EDUCATION ESSENTIAL

At this point, amen does not stick in my throat. Evans' proposed remedy for the precarious situation of English grammar in the schools will do nothing but harm. The worst feature of that situation is that "the teaching of the same old grammar has continued in essentially the same old way." Teachers whose own teachers have not known what they were teaching can only perpetuate the folklore and superstition which reputable students of our language exploded long ago. To be sure, more grammar should be taught in the schools, but it should be the best grammar available—a grammar constructed by professionals, not an amateurish mishmash. I grant that in any given case, the practicing teacher must resort to casuistry. She (or he, if Evans' Miss Bessie can be allowed a male companion) must consider what her pupils have learned in earlier grades, what she herself has learned and is competent to teach, what textbooks are available, and what pressures will be exerted by supervisors, colleagues, boards of education, parents, businessmen, and teachers of teaching in state universities. She cannot always do what ideally she might hope to do. The ideal must still be always clear: to teach the best available grammar, to teach it for humanistic and not technological reasons, and always to confront her students, as they write, with the necessity for rational choice among the resources which their language richly provides them.

That ideal can never be realized by doing the same old thing in the same old way. The first step toward its realization, better training of teachers, cannot even be taken in the schools. It must be taken, instead, in the colleges and universities, in the departments of English and the schools of education. A student who intends to teach English grammar and composition in the schools must first learn his subject, and he cannot learn it if ignorant men teach him only one kind of grammar. The field is too unsettled for that, as Sweet said; and the profession cannot stand it. A teacher candidate should learn the schoolroom grammar since he will have to live with it; the knowledge of evil may be a good, for grammatical virtue cannot be fugitive and cloistered. He should also learn at least one of the systems devised by the great European grammarians of English; Jespersen's *Essentials of English Grammar,* or Zandvoort's *Handbook,* would be a good choice. The candidate should know, too, some one or more of the recent American books, such as Roberts' *Patterns* or Francis's *Structure of American English.* Most important of all, he should understand the methods of the various grammarians, the merits and defects of the various systems, and he should be able to translate, where translation is possible without distortion, from one system to another. The unexamined grammar is not worth teaching.

These ambitions are not too high. They could be realized in a one-year graduate course. But they can never be realized so long as the blind continue to lead the blind. Bertrand Evans denounces the linguisticists as "kissing-cousins of educationists." It is hard to say, in the present darkness, who is kissing whom. At any rate, Evans has aligned himself quite squarely with those who believe that even the teachers of teachers do not need to know the subject to be taught. He sides with the amateurs against the professionals. He lays our present troubles at the door of the teacher in the schools, whose "methods have not been designed to establish and maintain a sufficient connection between grammatical knowledge and the practice of writing." A greater responsibility lies with Evans and his like. The purposes of their grammatical instruction are too low, their methods of grammatical description are amateurish, their grammatical prescriptions are unreasoned, their cures will kill.

If I must choose, then, between the sophisticist and the linguisticist, I will choose the linguisticist every time. But he has no panaceas either. Though any grammar which is taught in the schoolroom should ideally be a grammar which linguists have constructed, and though schoolroom teachers of grammar should get their basic training from linguists, linguists alone are not equipped to say exactly how much grammar should be taught, or where, or when, or how. On subjects like these, their voices should be heard, but so should the voices of educationists and classroom teachers. As a grammarian, I can no more answer questions of educational engineering than Evans has answered them. Hence a final plea. There is danger at the present time, when educationists are under sharp attack, that their real knowledge and accomplishments will be forgotten; and there is always danger, when professors are throwing their weight around, that the best expert on teaching, the teacher who does it, will get lost in the shuffle. Is it too much to hope that linguists, educationists, and schoolteachers may combine their efforts, as they already have done in some few places, to produce textbooks which are linguistically respectable and pedagogically usable? Well-taught teachers with good textbooks could do much more than chase the same old pig round the same old pen. A need exists, a market is prepared, and publishers are crying for texts. Here is a chance for virtue to be rewarded, and much of the reward belongs rightfully to the great number of teachers and teacher-trainers who do *not* prefer darkness to light.

I cannot include, in that honorable though too often unhonored group, either Professor Bertrand Evans or his fellow pontificators of the Bay Area English Association. They believe that education can only be dictatorial and that there is just one way to teach. I believe that education can never be dictatorial and that there are many ways of teaching. They believe in gramarye. I believe in grammar.

Well-bred silence is sometimes the greater absurdity.

For discussion

A. What is the implication of Evans's statement that linguists might more aptly be called "linguisticists"?

B. What does Evans give as the two possible explanations of the fact that students can have studied a great deal of grammar and still write ungrammatically?

C. Evans wants to maintain "a working relation between grammatical knowledge and the practice of writing." What does he consider to be the two things the teacher must do to achieve this?

D. What might the authors in the first two sections of this book reply to the argument in the second part of Evans's article?

E. What is Evans's idea of the relationship between grammar and composition? What is Sledd's?

F. In what two ways does Evans think a teacher can discover "precisely what grammatical knowledge is necessary and at what points it is applicable"?

G. What does Evans mean by "surface spots"?

H. How would you define Evans's conception of grammar? How would you define Sledd's?

I. What is "gramarye"?

J. To what extent does Sledd agree with Evans? Sledd suspects that to write "grammatically" (in Evans's sense of the word) means simply to follow handbook rules. What are the two reasons he gives for this suspicion?

K. What is the purpose of instruction in grammar according to Sledd? To Evans?

Grammar

It is not necessarily true that facts and figures speak for themselves. The great drama of classical Greece was written before Aristotle could write his analysis of its nature in the *Poetics*. Like other thinkers and investigators— before and since—Aristotle brought order to a complex set of facts.

To place the modern grammarian in the company of Aristotle is not entirely fanciful. The grammarian too seeks the system lurking in the data. His search is the subject of the following articles concerning grammar: what it has meant and stood for in the past, and what it represents today. The later essays in this section discuss briefly two current emphases in grammatical research, the *structural* and the *transformational*. These articles are presented more or less in the order of when they were written. Such an arrangement can blur any lack of continuity of development in the study of grammar and unduly emphasize the idea that we stand today at the apex of a pyramid. The work of the transformational grammarians is, however, a discontinuity. If it is revolutionary, it is counter-revolutionary. It is a good deal more traditional than most serious grammatical study of the second quarter of this century. Their work is of the greatest importance for any student of language, but the culmination of the efforts of thousands of years is not yet here. We are simply at another point in time. The grammarian is not about to fold his tent and silently steal away, his work completed.

In a sense, the essays in this section make up an incomplete report on work in progress. There are approaches to language analysis not discussed in this book at all which find different answers for the questions about grammar asked here. In fact, some grammarians even ask different questions.

KARL DYKEMA

Where our grammar came from

THERE WAS A TIME—with the Greeks, of course—when grammar was a philosophical inquiry into the nature of language. A good grammarian was as treasured as a winning discus thrower. In Rome, grammar drew the attention of the highest ranks, and emperors fiddled with alphabets and spelling. Today, for most people, grammar is a utilitarian list of rules for keeping one's syntax and one's phonemes acceptable. Though he is not particularly sympathetic with the present fact, Karl Dykema of Youngstown University, documents the transformation.

We have learned that English grammar is based upon Latin, which in turn is based upon Greek. We have read that language structure is amenable to Aristotle's logic, and we have read that it isn't. Usage has been declared the ultimate arbiter of correctness, but we are told that we must judge among usages. It should not be surprising that the attitude of modern man toward language is an ambivalent one.

Though the bulk of Dykema's discussion carefully documents how these assumptions developed, he also indicates why they did. He suggests first that young teachers, whether Roman or Texan, have a tendency to expose the student to notes from their own graduate courses. Thus, what had been the culmination of one man's educational process becomes almost the introduction for that of his students. The other problem comes from the difficulty of reconciling the methodology of a discipline with a procedure for the classroom. Some educational psychologists today believe that almost any idea can be presented to almost anybody in an intellectually respectable way. But they have not yet suggested that doing so is easy. What is easy is to tell others what one has been told. After awhile, the result becomes tradition.

The title of this paper is too brief to be quite accurate. Perhaps with the following subtitle it does not promise too much: A partial account of the origin and development of the attitudes which commonly pass for grammatical in Western culture and particularly in English-speaking societies.

The etymology of *grammar* shows rather sharp changes in meaning: It starts with Greek *gramma, letter* (of the alphabet), itself a development

"Where Our Grammar Came From": From *College English*, vol. 22, n. 7, April 1961, pp. 455–465. Reprinted with the permission of The National Council of Teachers of English and Karl W. Dykema. Some of the footnotes from the original article have been omitted here.

from *graphein, draw* or *write*. The plural *grammata* develops in meaning through *letters* to *alphabet* to the *rudiments of writing*, to the *rudiments of learning*. The adjective form *grammatike* with *techne* meant the art of knowing one's letters. From this form comes the Latin *grammaticus*. The medieval vernacular forms with *r* are something of a mystery, appearing first in Old Provençal as *gramaira* and developing in English with a variety of spellings, often with only one *m* and ending in *er*. One of the more amusing forms is that with the first *r* dissimilated to *l, glamour*.

In present usage at least four senses can be distinguished which have an application to language: (1) The complete structural pattern of a language learned unconsciously by the child as he acquires his native tongue; (2) an attempt to describe objectively and systematically this fundamental structure, usually called descriptive grammar; (3) a partial description of the language based on puristic or pedagogical objctives, usually called prescriptive grammar, (4) a conviction held by a good many people that somewhere there is an authoritative book called a grammar, the conscientious memorization of which will eliminate all difficulties from their use of language. This I call grammar as remedy. It is mainly with the last two of these notions of grammar that I shall concern myself, prescriptive grammar and grammar as remedy, and how the earlier conceptions of grammar were metamorphosed into them.

As the etymology of the word suggests, Western grammar begins with the ancient Greeks. As early as Plato we find in the *Sophist* the statement

that a word describing action is a verb (rhema), one which performs the action is a noun (onoma). Aristotle adds conjunctions (syndesmoi), recognizes that sentences have predicates, and is aware of three genders and of inflection (*Rhetoric*, etc.). The Stoics attempted to separate linguistic study from philosophy and made important contributions to the discipline. In their writings we find terms which are approximately equivalent to *noun, verb, conjunction, article, number, gender, case, voice, mood,* and *tense*.[1] But the direct source of most of our widely used grammatical terms is Dionysius Thrax's little *Techne Grammatike*, which Gilbert Murray recollects his great-uncle still using at the Merchants Taylors' School in the nineteenth century to learn Greek from.[2]

A few quotations from this little work will illustrate how close many of our school grammars still are to their source of more than 2000 years ago:

A sentence is a combination of words, either in prose or verse, making complete sense. . . . Of discourse there are eight parts: noun, verb, participle, article, pronoun, preposition, adverb, and conjunction. . . . A noun is a part of discourse having cases, indicating a body (as 'stone') or a thing (as 'education'), and is used in a common and a peculiar way (i.e., is common or proper). . . . A verb is a word without case, admitting tenses, persons, and numbers, and indicating action and passion (i.e., being-acted-upon). . . . A pronoun is a word indicative of definite persons and used in place of a noun. . . . The adverb is an uninflected part of discourse, used of a verb or subjoined to

[1] R. H. Robins, *Ancient and Medieval Grammatical Theory in Europe* (London, 1951), pp. 20–35.
[2] Gilbert Murray, *Greek Studies* (Oxford, 1946), p. 181.

a verb. . . . The conjunction is a word conjoining or connecting thought in some order and filling a gap in the expression.[3]

The few examples I have given emphasize analysis by meaning, because that is the aspect of classical grammar which our traditional grammar has dwelt upon. But the definitions of noun and verb, it should be observed, begin with formal distinctions—case and tense—and throughout the work there is clearly an awareness of the importance of structure in the functioning of the language. The contribution of the Greeks to linguistics was a great one, as Gilbert Murray and others have pointed out. But for twenty centuries their work was carried on by slavish and unimaginative imitators incapable of developing the work of their predecessors. Especially in the less highly inflected languages like English and French it did not occur to them that the inflectional devices of Latin and Greek must have some counterpart in the structure of the modern language.

Though today there are a few scholars in universities who assert that they pursue grammar for its own sake as an academic discipline, most people conceive of grammar only as a utilitarian thing, as a means of learning to use a language correctly. This notion was certainly completely absent from the thinking of Plato, Aristotle, and the Stoics, and probably from that of Dionysius Thrax. Grammar began as a philosophical inquiry into the nature of language. Now, for most people, it is merely a dogmatic

means of achieving correctness. It is this transformation that I am mainly concerned with.

How the transformation took place is not easy to document. Perhaps the most plausible explanation lies in the familiar desire of younger teachers to regurgitate undigested fragments of what they have swallowed in the course of their higher education. All too often a high school teacher just out of college will use his college lecture notes as the foundation of his high school teaching, or a teacher of undergraduates tries to give them exactly what he got in his graduate seminar.

Then there is the fundamental difference between the prevailing purposes of elementary and advanced instruction. Primary education is severely utilitarian; and though it can hardly be denied that, especially in our society, graduate instruction is often infected by utilitarianism, the speculative approach does persist, and inquiry for its own sake plays a major role. The curriculum at all levels of education is and has been determined partly by tradition, partly by immediate utilitarian objectives, partly by a desire to perpetuate the best elements of the cultural heritage. The application of these criteria is of ascending difficulty. Easiest is to accept without question the practice of one's predecessors; not much harder is to accept a limited practical goal and provide instruction intended to achieve it. Most difficult is to select critically what is most valuable in the cultural heritage, and the Romans weren't up to it.

Because of Greek prestige in the ancient world, less developed cultures borrowed extensively from that of

---

[3] "The Grammar of Dionysius Thrax," translated . . . by Thos. Davidson, *Journal of Speculative Philosophy*, VIII (1874), 326–339.

Greece. The influence of Greek art, philosophy, and literature on Rome is familiar, but Greek grammar was quite as influential and became the model not only for grammars of Latin but of Syriac, Armenian, Hebrew, and possibly Arabic as well.

It could not be a good model. The structure of every language is peculiar to itself—though there are, of course similarities between members of the same linguistic family—and the best description of it derives from a careful examination of the language itself, not from an attempt to fit it into the pattern of another. To be sure, both Greek and Latin are rich in inflections and the Latin of Varro was not much further away from the parent Indo-European than was the Greek of Dionysius Thrax; so the deformation imposed by the model was less distorting than when the same procedure was followed many centuries later and attempts were made to straitjacket the modern vernaculars of Europe within the model of Latin grammar. For example, Greek had a definite article, Latin had none, though in Varro's *De Lingua Latina,* the term *articuli* is applied to the demonstratives *is* and *hic* (VIII, 45, 51). Latin has more cases but a different tense system and no dual. English has only two inflected active tenses against six for Latin, but many more periphrastic verbal constructions than had Latin.

The attention given to grammar by the ancients seems to have been considerable. Susemihl in his *History of Greek Literature in the Alexandrian Period* discusses over fifty grammarians. One of them, Aristophanes of Byzantium (ca. 257–ca. 180 B.C.), was librarian to Ptolemy Epiphanius, who

imprisoned him to prevent the king of Pergamum from hiring him away.

Among the Romans, grammarians were also in demand. The slave Lutatius Daphnis, a grammarian, was bought for 700,000 sesterces, perhaps $35,000, which puts him about in the class of a lesser baseball player. Caesar put this Lutatius Daphnis in charge of the public libraries, though it was not until much later, according to Suetonius, that a regular salary of 100,000 sesterces was paid from the privy purse for Latin and Greek teachers of rhetoric (Suetonius, *Lives of the Caesars,* VIII, xviii). Caesar himself took part in one of the persisting grammatical quarrels of the time, that of the analogists and the anomalists, by producing a work called *De Analogia,* known to us only in fragments. Though he favored the analogists, who demanded complete inflectional consistency, it is significant that he wanted no radical departures from usage.[4] Suetonius also states that Claudius "invented three new letters and added them to the [Latin] alphabet, maintaining that they were greatly needed; he published a book on their theory when he was still in private life, and when he became emperor had no difficulty in bringing about their general use" (Suetonius, *Lives of the Caesars,* V, xli). Theodore Roosevelt was less successful when he tried to impose a few spelling reforms on the Government Printing Office; Congress refused to permit the changes.

Though Caesar favored the analogists, he was unwilling to depart from established usage. His position was that of many of his cultivated con-

---

4 Jean Collart, *Varron, Grammairien Latin* (Paris, 1954), pp. 10, 19, 146; Robins, p. 58.

temporaries, as it has been of many cultivated people ever since. The appeal of analogy is the appeal of logic, a creation of the Greeks and a tool that has been used with interesting and surprising effects in most areas of Western thought ever since. The foundation of Aristotelian logic is the syllogism. As the analogists applied the syllogism to language it worked like this: The form of the personal pronoun determines the form of the verb of which the pronoun is the subject. The form *you* is plural; therefore the form of the verb *be* which follows it must be plural; hence *you were,* not *you was.* So we have in cultivated English today only *you were.* But the cultivated dare not apply this syllogism to the intensive or reflexive, where the eighteenth-century practice of agreement with the notional number of the pronoun still persists. The eighteenth century had both *you was there yourself* and *you were there yourselves;* while we have *you were there yourselves* when the notional number of *you* is plural, but *you were there yourself* when it is singular.

Language has its own logic, which it is the function of the descriptive grammarian to discover if he can. Whatever it may be, it is not Aristotelian logic. But for two millennia our attitudes toward language have been colored by the assumption that the system of a language can be analyzed and prescribed by an intellectual tool that is inapplicable.

Conformity to a standard, or correctness if you like, is, of course, socially of the greatest importance. There is a long record of the penalties imposed on those who deviate from the standard, the earliest I know of being the account given in *Judges* (12, 4–6) of the forty and two thousand Ephraimites who were slain by the Gileadites because they pronounced *shibboleth sibboleth.* Later examples are less gory. Aristophanes in the *Lysistrata* (lines 81–206) ridicules the dialect of the Spartan women, though they are the allies of the Athenian women in their campaign of sexual frustration. Stephen Runciman in his *Byzantine Civilization* says "the Patriarch Nicetas in the Eleventh Century was laughed at for his Slavonic accent, and the statesman Margarites treated with disrespect in the Thirteenth because he spoke with a rough rustic voice."[5] And Chaucer's nun spoke the provincial French of the Benedictine nunnery of Stratford-Bow, the French of Paris—standard French—being to her unknown.

Conformity to the standard is what matters. But how is the standard to be determined? Quintilian, whom Professor T. W. Baldwin calls "The Supreme Authority" in his *Shakespeare's Small Latine and Lesse Greeke,* provides a most illuminating basis for discussion. In the *Institutes* Quintilian tells us that:

Language is based on reason, antiquity, authority and usage. Reason finds its chief support in analogy and sometimes in etymology. As for antiquity, it is commended to us by the possession of a certain majesty, I might almost say sanctity. Authority as a rule we derive from orators and historians. For poets, owing to the necessities of metre, are allowed a certain licence. . . . The judgment of a supreme orator is placed on the same level as reason, and even error brings no disgrace, if it results from treading in the footsteps of such distinguished guides.

5 Stephen Runciman, *Byzantine Civilization* (Meridian Books, New York, 1956), pp. 173, 176.

Usage however is the surest pilot in speaking, and we should treat language as currency minted with the public stamp. But in all cases we have need of a critical judgment, . . . (I.vi.1–3).

This is fuller than Horace's neater statement: "Use is the judge, and law, and rule of speech" (*De Arte Poetica*, 72: *Quem [usus] penes arbitrium est et ius et norma loquendi.*) and shows more clearly why we have troubles. Usage "is the surest pilot" but "we have need of a critical judgment."

Quintilian has more to say on the matter:

Usage remains to be discussed. For it would be almost laughable to prefer the language of the past to that of the present day, and what is ancient speech but ancient usage of speaking? But even here the critical faculty is necessary, and we must make up our minds what we mean by usage. If it be defined merely as the practice of the majority, we shall have a very dangerous rule affecting not merely style but life as well, a far more serious matter. For where is so much good to be found that what is right should please the majority? The practices of depilation, of dressing the hair in tiers, or of drinking to excess at the baths, although they may have thrust their way into society, cannot claim the support of usage, since there is something to blame in all of them (although we have usage on our side when we bathe or have our hair cut or take our meals together). So too in speech we must not accept as a rule of language words and phrases that have become a vicious habit with a number of persons. To say nothing of the language of the uneducated, so we are all of us well aware that whole theatres and the entire crowd of spectators will often commit *barbarisms* in the cries which they utter as one man. I will therefore define usage in speech as the agreed practice of educated men, just as where our way of life

is concerned I should define it as the agreed practice of all good men. (I.vi. 43–45)

But Quintilian makes it quite apparent from the many examples he cites that educated men are not entirely agreed on their practice, and that they lean heavily on the authority of Greek usage:

More recent scholars have instituted the practice of giving Greek nouns their Greek declension, although this is not always possible. Personally I prefer to follow the Latin method, so far as grace of diction will permit. For I should not like to say *Calypsonem* on the analogy of *Iunonem,* although Gaius Caesar in deference to antiquity does adopt this way of declining it. Current practice has however prevailed over his authority. In other words which can be declined in either way without impropriety, those who prefer it can employ the Greek form: they will not be speaking Latin, but will not on the other hand deserve censure. (I.v. 63–64)

A thorough knowledge of Greek, learned from slave-tutors, had long been common among educated Romans, but it was Varro who transferred the entire body of Greek grammatical scholarship to Latin in his *De Lingua Latina,* written between 47 and 45 B.C. Though of the original 25 books of that work only V through X survive relatively intact, we have a fairly good account of what was in the rest because Varro is the source which all later Latin grammarians follow, and they have apparently borrowed from him most faithfully.

Greek grammar, is, then, a development of Greek philosophy, an attempt to treat systematically an important aspect of human behavior.

It is a late development which in Alexandrian culture is given a practical application through its use in the editing, elucidation, and interpretation of texts, especially that of Homer; and in the correction of solecisms. Since there was little of the speculative in the Romans, Varro's encyclopedic treatment of Latin language and literature was the ultimate source of a host of school texts.

What has been presented so far is a partial account of the development of philology, though this ancient term has been an ambiguous one for almost as long as it has existed—naturally enough, since it derives from the Greek roots usually translated as *love* and *word*. Some people love words as the means of argument, others because they are the foundation of literature, others still for their forms and relations in discourse. All these senses have been designated by the word since it first appeared in Greek, and in nineteenth-century France and Germany it normally included literary history, textual and literary criticism, and linguistics. (We might well revive the word; it would provide a single term by which we could describe ourselves along with chemists, historians, and the rest; we are philologists.)

The ancients called the various aspects of this study by a variety of names: *philologos, grammatikos, grammatistes, kritikos* in Greek; *philologus, grammaticus, litterator, criticus* in Latin. They were evidently no more certain of exactly what the terms signified than we are today with similar terms. Suetonius writes:

The term *grammaticus* became prevalent through Greek influence, but at first such men were called *litterati*. Cornelius

Nepos, too, in a little book in which he explains the difference between *litteratus* and *eruditus* says that the former is commonly applied to those who can speak or write on any subject accurately, cleverly and with authority; but that it should strictly be used of interpreters of the poets, whom the Greeks call *grammatici*. That these were also called *litteratores* is shown by Messala Corvinus in one of his letters, in which he says: "I am not concerned with Furius Bibaculus, nor with Ticidas either, or with the *litterator* Cato." For he unquestionably refers to Valerius Cato, who was famous both as a poet and as a grammarian. Some however make a distinction between *litteratus* and *litterator,* as the Greeks do between *grammaticus* and *grammatista,* using the former of a master of his subject, the latter of one moderately proficient. Orbilius too supports this view by examples, saying: "In the days of our forefathers, when anyone's slaves were offered for sale, it was not usual except in special cases to advertise any one of them as *litteratus* but rather as *litterator,* implying that he had a smattering of letters, but was not a finished scholar."

The grammarians of early days taught rhetoric as well, and we have treatises from many men on both subjects. It was this custom, I think, which led those of later times also, although the two professions had now become distinct, nevertheless either to retain or to introduce certain kinds of exercises suited to the training of orators, such as problems, paraphrases, addresses, character sketches and similar things; doubtless that they might not turn over their pupils to the rhetoricians wholly ignorant and unprepared. But I observe that such instruction is now given up, because of the lack of application and the youth of some of the pupils; for I do not believe that it is because the subjects are underrated. I remember that at any rate when I was a young man, one of these teachers, Princeps by name, used to declaim and engage in discussion on alternate days; and that sometimes he would give instruction in the morning, and in the afternoon remove his desk and declaim. I used to hear, too, that within the memory of our forefathers some passed directly from the grammar school to the Forum and took their place among the most eminent advocates. (*On Grammarians,* iv)

[A] writer who provides evidence of the Roman attitudes towards language is Aulus Gellius in his *Attic Nights.* Gellius represents the aristocrat's conviction that what he himself does must be right coupled with the conservative attitude that older practice is to be preferred:

Valerius Probus was once asked, as I learned from one of his friends, whether one ought to say *has urbis* or *has urbes* and *hanc turrem* or *hanc turrim.* "If," he replied, "you are either composing verse or writing prose and have to use those words, pay no attention to the musty, fusty rules of the grammarians, but consult your own ear as to what is to be said in any given place. What it favours will surely be the best." Then the one who had asked the question said: "What do you mean by 'consult my ear'?" and he told me that Probus answered: "Just as Vergil did his, when in different passages he has used *urbis* and *urbes,* following the taste and judgment of his ear. For in the first *Georgic,* which," said he, "I have read in a copy corrected by the poet's own hand, he wrote *urbis* with an *i.* . . .
But turn and change it so as to read *urbes,* and somehow you will make it duller and heavier. On the other hand, in the third *Aeneid* he wrote *urbes* with an *e:* . . .
Change this too so as to read *urbis* and the word will be too slender and colourless, so great indeed is the different effect of combination in the harmony of neighbouring sounds. . . .
These words have, I think, a more

agreeable lightness than if you should use the form in *e* in both places." But the one who had asked the question, a boorish fellow surely and with untrained ear, said: "I don't just understand why you say that one form is better and more correct in one place and the other in the other." Then Probus, now somewhat impatient, retorted: "Don't trouble then to inquire whether you ought to say *urbis* or *urbes.* For since you are the kind of man that I see you are and err without detriment to yourself, you will lose nothing whichever you say." (XIII, xxi, 3–8)

And his attitude towards grammarians is expressed quite as explicitly in this passage:

Within my memory Aelius Melissus held the highest rank among the grammarians of his day at Rome; but in literary criticism he showed greater boastfulness and sophistry than real merit. Besides many other works which he wrote, he made a book which at the time when it was issued seemed to be one of remarkable learning. The title of the book was designed to be especially attractive to readers, for it was called *On Correctness in Speech.* Who, then would suppose that he could speak correctly or with propriety unless he had learned those rules of Melissus?
From that book I take these words: "*Matrona,* 'a matron,' is a woman who has given birth once; she who has done so more than once is called *mater familias,* 'mother of a family'; just so a sow which has had one litter is called *porcetra;* one which has had more, *scrofa.*" But to decide whether Melissus thought out this distinction between *matrona* and *mater familias* and that it was his own conjecture, or whether he read what someone else had written, surely requires soothsayers. For with regard to *porcetra* he has, it is true, the authority of Pomponius in the Atellan farce which bears that very title; but that "matron" was ap-

plied only to a woman who had given birth once, and "mother of the family" only to one who had done so more than once, can be proved by the authority of no ancient writer. . . . (XVIII, vi. 1–7)

By the Middle Ages the aristocrats were unlikely to have had much education, and the classical heritage was perpetuated by the grammarians, whose dogmatic victory was complete. Donatus (fl. 400) and Priscian (fl. 500) are the dominating figures. The name of the first, shortened to Donat or Donet, became synonymous with "grammar" or "lesson" in Old French and Middle English, and the grammar of the second survives in over a thousand manuscripts.[6] He also has the distinction of being consigned to Hell by Dante (*Inferno,* 15:110).

As an example of Priscian, here is the beginning of an analysis of the *Aeneid*—this is not from his big grammar, which was in eighteen books, but from a smaller one, *Partitiones Duodecim Versuum Aeneidos Principalium:*

Scan the verse. *Arma vi/rumque ca/no Tro/iae qui/primus ab/oris.* How many caesuras does it have? Two. What are they? Semiquinaria (penthemimeral) and semiseptenaria (hephthemimeral). How? The semiquinaria is *arma virumque cano* and the semiseptenaria is *arma virumque cano Troiae.* How many figures are there? Ten. For what reason? Because it consists of three dactyls and two spondees. How many parts of speech has this verse? Nine. How many nouns? Six: *arma, virum, Troiae, qui, primus, oris.* How many verbs? One: *cano.* How many prepositions? One: *ab.* How many conjunctions? One, *que.* Discuss each word; *arma,* what part of speech is it? Noun. Of what

sort? Appelative (or common). What is its species? General. Its gender? Neuter. Why neuter? Because all nouns which end in *a* in the plural are unquestionably of neuter gender. Why is the singular not used? Because this noun signifies many and various things. . . .[7]

And this is not the end of the catechism on the opening line of Virgil. Evidently this sort of drill was to accompany the study of the poem from beginning to end, if the end was ever reached.

Increasingly in the Middle Ages the written heritage of Greece and Rome was accepted unquestioningly because literate men did not have a cultural background which would permit them to ask pertinent questions. We learn, for example, that one of the best sources for the text of Diogenes Laertius is a manuscript of about 1200 written by a scribe "who obviously knew no Greek."[8] To be sure, there were sometimes conflicts between the Christian heritage and the classical, usually resolved in favor of the Christian. In a medieval manuscript is this comment: "Concerning the words *scala* (step), and *scopa* (broom), we do not follow Donatus and the other who claim they are plural because we know that the Holy Ghost has ruled that they are singular." And it was comforting when the traditions of classical grammar could be given divine corroboration. For example: "The verb has three per-

---

[6] John Edwin Sandys, *A History of Classical Scholarship* (Cambridge, 1920), vol. 1, p. 230, note; p. 274.

[7] Heinrich Keil, *Grammatici Latini* (Leipzig, 1859), vol. 3, p. 459.

[8] Diogenes Laertius, *Lives of Eminent Philosophers,* with an English translation by R. D. Hicks (Loeb Classical Library) (Cambridge & London, 1925), vol. 1, p. xxxv. (The quotations from Suetonius, Varro, Quintilian, and Aulus Gellius are from the translations in the Loeb Classical Library editions.)

sons. This I hold to be divinely inspired, for our belief in the Trinity is thereby manifested in words." Or this: "Some maintain that there are more, some that there are fewer parts of speech. But the world-encircling church has only eight offices [presumably Ostiariat, Lektorat, Exorzistat Akolythat, Subdiakonat, Diakonat, Presbyterat, Episkopat]. I am convinced that this is through divine inspiration. Since it is through Latin that those who are chosen come most quickly to a knowledge of the Trinity and under its guidance find their way along the royal road into their heavenly home, it was necessary that the Latin language should be created with eight parts of speech."[9]

On the other hand, St. Boniface's (675–754) "sense of grammatical accuracy was so deeply shocked when he heard an ignorant priest administering the rite of baptism *in nomine Patria et Filia et Spiritus sancti* [that is, with complete disregard of the required case endings] that he almost doubted the validity of the rite."[10]

Up to about the twelfth century Donatus and Priscian, whose grammars were based ultimately on classical Latin, were followed unquestioningly except where there seemed to be a conflict with sacred texts. The Vulgate and various theological writings were in a later Latin which might disagree with classical grammar, as in the more frequent use of the personal pronouns.[11]

But in the twelfth century the reintroduction of Greek philosophy had a tremendous impact on medieval thought, as is best illustrated by the Aristotelianism of Aquinas. And St. Thomas, as might be expected, deals with philological matters in the *Summa Theologica,* and again as might be expected through the syllogism:

It seems that in Holy Writ a word cannot have several senses, historical or literal, allegorical, tropological or moral, and anagogical. For many different senses in one text produce confusion and deception and destroy all force of argument. Hence no argument, but only fallacies, can be deduced from a multiplicity of propositions. But Holy Writ ought to be able to state the truth without any fallacy. Therefore in it there cannot be several senses to a word. (First Part, Question One, Article 10, Objection 1)

A more explicitly grammatical example is this one from the thirteenth century:

For a complete sentence, two things are necessary, namely a subject and a predicate. The subject is that which is being discussed; it is what determines the person of the verb. The predicate is that which is expressed by the subject. Nouns were invented to provide subjects. . . . Verbs were invented to provide predicates.

This concept of grammar being something created is found in another thirteenth-century writer:

Was he who invented grammar a grammarian? No, because the creation of grammar cannot be based on teaching since that would presuppose its existence. Grammar was invented. For the invention of grammar must precede grammar. So it

[9] J. J. Baebler, *Beiträge zu einer Geschichte der lateineschen Grammatik im Mittelalter,* (Halle a. S., 1885), p. 22/Hans Arens, *Sprachwissenschaft, der Gang ihrer Entwicklung von der Antike bis zur Gegenwart* (Munich, 1955), pp. 30, 31.

[10] Sandys, p. 469.

[11] Baebler, p. 22.

was not the grammarian but the philosopher who created grammar, for the philosopher studies the nature of things and recognizes their essential qualities.[12]

The authority of the grammarian was occasionally challenged. In a seventeenth century German satirical treatment of schoolmasters is this account of a fifteenth-century episode:

> The Emperor Sigismund came to the Council of Constance and said: "Videte patres, ut eradicetis schismam Hussitarium." There sat an old Bohemiam pedant in the Council who was convinced that with this box on the ear to Priscian the Emperor had sinned against the Catholic Church as gravely as had John Hus and Hieronymus of Prague. So he said [in Latin]: "Most Serene Highness, *schisma* is neuter gender." The emperor said [in German]: "How do you know that?" The old Bohemian pedant answered [now in German]: "Alexander Gallus says so." The emperor said: "Who is Alexander Gallus?" The Bohemian pedant answered: "He is a monk." "Yes," said Sigismund, "I am the Roman emperor, and my word is worth at least that of a monk." (Joh. Balthaser Schupp, *Der Teutsche Schulmeister,* 1663)[13]

It now remains to consider the transfer of these attitudes to the modern vernacular languages. But first a brief review of the three preceding stages. The first is the unique situation in Greece, which differed from that of any of the succeeding cultures in two significant ways: It was essentially a monolingual society, and at least during the period of its greatest intellectual and artistic achievement it knew nothing of formal grammar. Rome differed in both essentials.

12 Arens, pp. 34, 32.
13 Baebler, p. 118.

The cultivated Roman was educated in Greek, and formal grammar was a part of his Latin education, though this does not mean that he learned Greek through formal grammar. In the Middle Ages the two-language requirement for the educated, which was characteristic of Rome, was continued, but with an important difference. Whereas for the Roman, Latin was a respectable language with a respectable literature, for the educated man of the Middle Ages his native vernacular was not respectable and at least at first had no important literature. Also he learned the language of scholarship and literature in a way quite different from that used by the Roman. He learned it with the aid of formal grammar.

Of these three stages, the third, the medieval, is much the longest; in formal education and scholarship it lasts well into the eighteenth century and therefore has a duration of well over a thousand years. Of course during the last two or three hundred of those years a great change had come over Europe, due partly to an intimate reacquaintance with the heritage of Greece and Rome. But in the field of philology this meant largely a return to the attitudes of the ancients. It also meant the transference of the whole philological approach—ancient and medieval—to the modern vernacular languages.

The history of vernacular grammars and of English grammars in particular comes next in this development, but there is no space for it here.

One consequence of this transfer must be illustrated: The ambivalence it has given us toward language. Here are some examples. Trollope in his *Autobiography* writes:

The ordinary talk of ordinary people is carried on in short sharp expressive sentences, which very frequently are never completed,—the language of which even among educated people is often incorrect. The novel-writer in constructing his dialogue must so steer between absolute accuracy of language—which would give to his conversation an air of pedantry, and the slovenly inaccuracy of ordinary talkers, which if closely followed would offend by an appearance of grimace—as to produce upon the ear of his readers a sense of reality. If he be quite real he will seem to attempt to be funny. If he be quite correct he will seem to be unreal.[14]

The nineteenth-century German philologist Wilhelm Scherer, discussing the great dramatist Heinrich Kleist, remarks that "he did distinguished work in all forms. There dwells in his language an individual magic, though he has an uncertain control of German grammar."[15] And in a recent review in the *TLS* is this sentence: "He [Leonard Clark] died after completing the first draft of his book, *Yucatan Adventure,* which would have gained some grammar, while losing some of the punch of its author's virile enthusiasm, if it had been more carefully revised."[16]

In a detective story, Rex Stout has Archie Goodwin make this comment after one of the principal characters has said, "Yes. . . . We shall see.":

But what really settled it was her saying, "We shall see." He [Nero Wolfe]

will always stretch a point, within reason, for people who use words as he thinks they should be used.[17]

But in another story Wolfe is made to say, "If it's her again . . ."[18]

And Mark Twain, who took Cooper severely to task for his "ungrammatical" English, did what was perhaps his best work, in *Huckleberry Finn,* by using a narrative device which relieved him of all responsibility for conforming to standard usage.

One of the most eloquent and emphatic in condemnation of the Latin grammatical tradition was Macaulay, but, as you might guess, he is much too long to quote here.[19]

To conclude by returning to the four senses of the term grammar outlined at the beginning. Contemporary philologists who specialize in linguistics have, it seems to me, attempted to strip away the accretions of two thousand years and are turning to a rigorously descriptive approach, the seeds of which are to be found in the Greeks. Other philologists have other interests, such as literary history, literary criticism, and, of course, the problem of getting freshmen to write better. As an inescapable burden of their academic heritage, they have to bear the weight of the ancient and medieval grammatical tradition, which survives in

[14] Anthony Trollope, *An Autobiography* (World's Classics, Oxford, 1953), p. 206.
[15] Wilhelm Scherer, *Geschichte der deutschen Literatur* (Knaur, Berlin, n. d.), p. 752.
[16] *Times Literary Supplement,* March 20, 1959, p. 156.

[17] Rex Stout, "Murder Is No Joke," *And Four to Go, A Nero Wolfe Foursome* (Viking, New York, 1958), p. 155.
[18] Rex Stout, "Too Many Women," *All Aces, A Nero Wolfe Omnibus* (Viking, New York, 1958), p. 237.
[19] T. B. Macaulay, "The London University," Edinburgh Review, February, 1826, in *Critical, Historical and Miscellaneous Essays and Poems* (Porter and Coats, Philadelphia, n. d.), vol. 3, pp. 631–634.

the other two senses, prescriptive grammar and grammar as remedy. What I have tried to do is to give some account of how that tradition developed, how it was transmitted, and why much of it is essentially irrelevant to the problems the philologist faces today.

For discussion

A. Dykema gives four senses in which "grammar" is used in application to language. What are they?

B. Traditional grammar has emphasized the analysis by meaning in classical grammar. What evidence does Dykema give of formal definition in classical grammar?

C. According to Quintilian, language is based, among other things, on reason. "Reason," he writes, "finds its chief support in analogy and sometimes in etymology." What would the argument from etymology tell us is the reasonable meaning for the following words: *advertise, amanuensis, atom, cosmos, hysteria, manufacture, matrimony, research, religion, vegetarian?*

D. What is Quintilian's definition of usage in speech?

E. What was the "practical" application of grammar in Alexandrian culture?

F. Aulus Gellius lived in the second century after Christ; he was a Roman aristocrat and a judge, who studied his grammar in Rome and his philosophy in Athens. What was his attitude toward language and toward grammarians? How do these attitudes compare with those expressed by Lloyd in "Snobs, Slobs, and the English Language," and by Barzun in "The Retort Circumstantial"?

G. In the Middle Ages the aristocracy in effect abdicated their right to be educated. What were the results for ideas about grammar and its use?

H. On p. 149 Dykema divides the development of attitudes toward grammar into three stages. What are these three stages?

I. What was the effect upon the general attitude toward language of transferring the combined ancient and medieval philological approaches to the study of modern languages?

J. How would Dykema like to define "philologist"?

HUNTER DIACK

A re-examination of grammar

EARLY IN 1956 some research experts in England concluded that the teaching of grammar is a waste of time. Shortly thereafter, Hunter Diack of Nottingham University concluded that what the experts meant was that teaching grammar badly is a waste of time.

After a few comments about what teaching the grammar of one's native language should *not include,* Diack suggests that every child is a grammar "machine." By this, he does not mean that every child is a grammarian. Although what comes off the top of a child's head may be ignorant or foolish, what comes off the top of his neck is likely to be understandable without effort by other native speakers of English. This is a startling and wonderful thing, and our grammar courses should take advantage of it. Diack goes on to indicate that grammar and thought are two parts of the same process, and he proposes a program to replace those courses or parts of courses, now known as "Grammar."

Many of the most constructive thinkers in education during the past few decades have been against the teaching of grammar and many of the stodgiest and least creative teachers of English have been for it. Research as usual has an answer, and it is that the teaching of grammar is a waste of time. There is, so far as I have been able to discover, unanimity among research-workers about this. When, however, there is something approaching unanimity in research on a complicated subject like this it is time to sit up and take notice because one of two things has probably taken place: (1) a definite and perhaps very important truth has been established or (2) people (including research-workers) are no longer thinking but have succumbed to the magic of phrases or have taken to the mere parroting of words.

One cannot off-handedly dismiss the results of research as a collection of airy nothings, but on the other hand a decent scepticism should be maintained. There is a certain parallel between developments in the teaching of reading and those in the

"A Re-Examination of Grammar": From *The Use of English,* vol. 7, n. 4, Summer 1956, pp. 251–255. Reprinted with the permission of the publisher, Chatto and Windus, Ltd., London, England, and Hunter Diack.

teaching of grammar during recent years. Throughout the English-speaking world the teaching of reading and the reproduction of reading schemes has been dominated by a phrase which everyone in the business seems to have accepted without question: "seeing words as immediate wholes." And yet there are few people who have not driven past a newspaper placard,[1] say, too quickly to be able to see more than a letter or two. The phrase counted: the experience did not. In the teaching of grammar there is no single phrase to which one can point, but there are three words which have been so loosely used as to enable anyone to put forward his prejudices as though they were proven generalised truths. These words are "grammar" itself, and "formal" and "functional." In numerous discussions with teachers about grammar, I have frequently found that teachers who rail against the teaching of "formal grammar" teach a great deal of the most formal grammar with the idea that because it is taught in an "incidental way" it is no longer formal. The word "grammar" itself is also frequently used as though it meant, purely and simply, Nesfield,[2] or Latin grammar to an English base, and the word "functional" is often used as though "grammar" ceased to be "formal" and became "functional" just because examples were taken from the pupils' work.

Take the statement: "An adjective

describes a noun." This is a statement often made in formal grammar books (though not in Nesfield); and certainly often made by teachers in both junior and secondary schools. In my experience there are teachers who would object to teaching a lesson on the "adjective"—*that* would be formal grammar—but who would claim to be teaching "functional" grammar if they made that statement about the adjective during an informal discussion of pupils' writing. But the statement is a plain falsehood—in the phrase "crescent moon" the word "crescent" plainly does not describe the noun "moon" but the thing called "moon." The word "describe" itself needs critical examination for which there is no space here.

In numerous grammar books still being published and in numerous lessons still being taught some very inaccurate things are said about the sentence. The commonest of these is the statement that a sentence is the expression of a complete thought. What is a complete thought? Is this a complete thought? "It crept along the wall." What crept? A cat? A shadow? Or just an ordinary creeper? Yet that is a sentence.

Such definitions are worse than meaningless; they confuse pupils instead of clarifying matters for them.

One of the main criticisms one can legitimately make of most research into this subject is that it has done little to eradicate such inaccurate verbalisms from grammar teaching. Since that is so, the most that can be claimed is that research has proved that it is not profitable to teach grammar badly.

It is also true that some of the investigators have shown more knowl-

---

[1] A sheet of paper with a headline on it, placed beside newspaper vendors in England.

[2] J. C. Nesfield: *English Grammar, Past and Present* (Macmillan, London: 1898 *et seq.*). This is a widely used English school grammar, the first chapter of which sets up Latin grammar "to an English base."

edge of statistics than of the structure of language.

There have been three main reactions recently to the conclusions of research.

1. There is a considerable body of opinion, particularly in the grammar schools and universities, in favour of bringing grammar back into the schools more or less as it was before. This showed itself in the recent sponsoring by the English Association of a new but rather old-style grammar book.

2. More progressive opinon, those, shall we say, who want to see English taught *creatively* in the schools have campaigned against the teaching of grammar in the belief that all the grammar any pupil is likely to need will be picked up incidentally.

3. There has been some attempt by writers of textbooks to produce brighter grammar books with such titles as *Grammar Made Gay*. Often it is still the old grammar and seldom is it very gay. One such book states that verbs have moods just as people do— and who, teacher or pupil, is any wiser for that?

I suggest that the answer to the problem is neither to abolish grammar from the schools nor to make the old grammar gay but to re-examine the whole concept of grammar in relation to education.

To set down in detail the lines which such a re-examination would follow is not possible in the space of an article such as this. It is possible, however, to point out the broad outline and to indicate certain facts which must be considered before one reaches the conclusion that grammar should be thrown out of the schools altogether.

The first point I would make is that certain matters which bulk largely in "incidental" grammar teaching are not fundamental questions of grammar at all. The pupil who says, or writes, "They was" is, of course, not using correct grammatical English; it is a grammatical error but generally he makes it by sheer imitation of what he has heard and the question of thinking about grammar has not come into it. There is a kind of grammatical error, then, which is hardly to be called a grammatical error but simply a bad habit of speech. With this aspect of grammar I am not in this article concerned.

Then it is necessary to point out that whether a teacher is specifically teaching grammar or not pupils are inevitably learning the grammar of their mother tongue. This process begins at the mother's knee. Children are far more logical beings than some modern theories of education would lead us to think. The child who wiped a steamed-up window and exclaimed, "I can see betterly now" had begun to learn by analogy with other sentences something about the grammatical form of the adverb. It is what I might call a half-conscious knowledge. I suggest that it is one of the fundamental aims of education to make such twilight knowledge clear and articulate.

One of the most difficult things to do in thinking about grammar is to keep constantly in one's mind the fact that in all this business one is not concerned principally with print on a page nor even sounds in the air. An adjective is not a set of letters on a page nor is it a pattern of sound waves; what we signify by "adjective" and all other grammatical terms is a particular type of mental occurrence. Grammar is something that goes on inside people's heads and not on printed pages. I go further and say that this something is very important indeed; it is part of the very process of thinking. During a grammar lesson a pupil should be studying his own mind at work and he should know that that is what he is doing. There does not seem to me to be any place in school for a grammar lesson which is not directed in this way. But when it is so directed, since it is a study which is teaching pupils something about how their own minds work, it must be regarded as one of the humane studies.

A grammar course designed with these ideas in mind will differ greatly from the usual grammar course. It would perhaps be called a language course. At the beginning of such a course there would be nothing of what is usually thought of as school grammar. Pupils would be concerned at the first stage not with the relationships between words but with what a word is in its simplest form—the common noun. They would be led by easy stages towards the idea of language as the index of experience and a fair amount of work would be done on the nature of communication with a diagram of this sort as the basis.

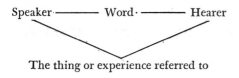

Speaker ——— Word· ——— Hearer

The thing or experience referred to

The essential point about the diagram is that it gives a means of showing that when the two lines meet communication is successful, otherwise not. A discussion of the reasons for failure of communication leads inevitably to a consideration of levels of abstraction in, of course, a very simple form. The simple distinction between "concrete" and "abstract" nouns is of very little value, since the most concrete of nouns is to a certain degree abstract. One shows, for example, that the word "animal" is more abstract than the word "cow." This matter is well handled in S. I. Hayakawa's *Language in Thought and Action.*

The first part of the course, then, deals with the relationship between words and things. This seems to be a necessary prelude to the study of the relationships between words. These relationships form the content of traditional grammar, and rightly so. But here, too, mere verbalism—that is, the failure to get down to the processes words stand for—has wrought havoc with the teaching of grammar.

The teaching of grammar is in one important respect different from the teaching of such a subject as geography. The content of geography has by some means or other to be brought to the pupil. No amount of thinking about what goes on inside his own head will tell a pupil the chief export of Brazil. But the mere fact that a pupil can speak, write and read with a fair degree of accuracy means that he has already a fair amount of grammatical knowledge. The grammar is there. This is one of the main arguments of those who would not teach grammar in a planned sort of way: that children pick it up incidentally. Indeed it is true that without any specific grammar lessons children on the whole can speak and write grammatically correct sentences, and the grammatically incorrect sentences are far fewer than the correct ones.

Surely, however, it is the very fact that the content of grammar is already there which gives the study of grammar—the proper study!—its peculiar value. Here, as in no other subject whatsoever, the pupil is, in however rudimentary a manner, thinking about thought. But it is necessary that mere words should not get in the way. Let us take again the adjective as an illustration. In discussions about the relations between words and things, which is the first phase in the teaching of grammar, pupils will have become acquainted with the idea of the noun, though not necessarily with the various kinds of "work" which can be called "noun-work." They will also have learned that a word which is limiting the area of reference of a noun is doing adjective work. Most of them will then be able to pick adjectives out of a piece of connected prose with a fair degree of accuracy, and that is usually all that is required of them. But the most important thing of all has been omitted in such practice.

Pupils who pick out the two adjectives in the sentence: "Fat men should not skate on thin ice" have not necessarily completed the process of gram-

matical thinking even in connection with the simple adjective. They should be able to see that what they have done in describing the words "fat" and "thin" as adjectives is to state that "fat" is to "men" as "thin" is to "ice." It is only when pupils realize that grammatical terms mean relationships of that simple kind that they can see past the obstacles which traditional presentations put in their way and begin to have insight into what it is all about.

And what is it all about? First, it is a study of precision in statement—for that consists very largely in knowing at what level of abstraction words are used and in putting words in such a way that there can be no doubt as to which one goes with which. But if, in addition, the subject is taught so that the pupil becomes thoroughly aware that in studying grammar he is studying his own habits of thought, then surely it is not too wild a claim to say that it can be one of the most humane of studies. There is something in Whitehead's definition of the aim of education: to bring what is unconscious to the level of consciousness. The fact that grammar lessons have so often appeared to be and indeed have been mere drill in verbalism is no justification for throwing the whole subject overboard.

For discussion

A. What are Diack's objections to the way the words "grammar," "formal," and "functional" are frequently used?

B. What is his objection to defining the sentence as the expression of a complete thought?

C. There are a number of very close parallels between this article and Roberts' "The Relation of Linguistics to the Teaching of English." What are some of them?

D. What is Diack's explanation of why a pupil writes "They was"? Would this be an error in correctness or in style as judged by Hill in "Correctness and Style in English Composition"?

E. What does Diack mean by "twilight knowledge"?

F. Starting with one, number the following statements in order of increasing "abstraction" as Diack uses the term:

1. I like (American literature).
2. I like (Mailer's *The Naked and the Dead*).
3. I like (the last chapter of Mailer's *Advertisements for Myself*).
4. I like (books).
5. I like (all American novels about the Second World War).

G. Recognizing the varying degrees of abstraction in the above sentences indicates an awareness of the relation between words and things. Yet some relationships among the five phrases in parentheses are very close. They all have the same function in relation to "like," and they are all basically the same structure. What is the function, and what is the structure?

H. How does Diack explain his idea that in studying grammar the student is studying his own habits of thought?

KARL DYKEMA

Progress in grammar

WE TURN NOW to structural grammar, though it is probably well to remember that these identifying labels are generally assigned with greater certainty by the people who talk about grammars than they are by those who write them. In the following essay, Karl Dykema discusses Charles Carpenter Fries's *The Structure of English: An Introduction to the Construction of English Sentences* (1952), one of two books which accelerated the use of recent findings of American linguistics in the preparation of high school and college textbooks. This review was written shortly after the publication of the book, and its very title, "Progress in Grammar," describes the feeling of many teachers of English who were interested in linguistics.

The Structure of English provides one answer to the demands of the anti-Roman legions that have patrolled the earlier pages of this collection. It analyzes English without the aid of Latin categories, definitions, or terminology. Its basis is about a quarter of a million words of contemporary American English as it was used over the telephone in an academic community, presumably Ann Arbor, Michigan, the residence of its author. Fries uses the sentence as his unit of analysis, and bases his definitions principally upon the way or ways a word fits into sentence patterns, not upon the notion of what the word might mean. The assumption is that we don't know what to call a word until we see it operating; take, for instance, the various /reds/ in *Red read the red book*. Fries also makes some use of the intonation system of English.

His analysis of his recorded telephone conversations produced four form classes, numbered—not named—primarily because they are not co-extensive with older lists of nouns, verbs, adjectives, and adverbs. He does use such terms as "subject" and "object," but the fact that he puts them within quotation marks indicates that he considers an item to be a subject because of its *formal position,* not its *notional function.* In addition to large expandable form classes, Fries notes a number of small classes, which cannot easily be added to. These are very similar to such things as we have traditionally called prepositions, conjunctions, and so on.

Fries's major criterion for assignment of a word to a form class is its arrangement—or possible arrangement—in a sentence pattern, which he establishes through a set of diagnostic frames. However, he uses a number of formal characteristics, among which

"Progress in Grammar": From *College English,* vol. 14, n. 2, November 1952, pp. 93–100. Reprinted with the permission of The National Council of Teachers of English and Karl W. Dykema. Some of the footnotes from the original article have been omitted here.

are derivational endings, (*act, active, actively, activity*), inflections, and patterning in smaller-than-sentence groups with function words. If you hear a word like *the,* you know a word more or less like *apple* is coming. When the various ways of signaling a form class conflict, Fries gives priority to position within a frame. In "The meek shall inherit the earth," *meek* is assigned to a list which includes *people,* not one which includes *fine, finer, finest.*

Charles Carpenter Fries in *The Structure of English* has made significant progress in English grammar, though the term "grammar" is probably intentionally avoided in the title because it has become so ambiguous.

Grammar illustrates one of those etymons which in most European languages still show their Greek form. But for *Grammar* we have not only preserved much of the Greek spelling but also much of the Greek descriptive system that the word came to denote. Our modern Western culture is grammar-conscious, and the present complex of concepts for which *grammar* stands in the minds of Western people had its origin more than two thousand years ago in ancient Greek culture.

If grammar means different things to different people today, it is hardly surprising because it was conceived in varying ways within a few centuries of its birth. Grammatical terminology had its origin in the philosophical speculations of Greek thinkers; at first it had neither normative nor pedagogical implications or applications. Gradually, however, linguistic speculation became a systematic field, and grammar—in our sense—became a part of the curriculum of Hellenic Greece and Rome.

It is not clear just where and when in the Western cultural tradition grammar became primarily a means of learning the correct use of a language—at first usually a foreign one—

and ceased to be a part of logic and hence of philosophy. The break, of course, was never complete, and the Middle Ages continued the idea of grammatical concepts as universals. But certainly in the period since ancient times grammar has generally come to be thought of as the means of achieving correctness in language. And since Western culture accepts correctness in language as vastly important, Western culture is preoccupied with grammar.

But the ancient difference in objective lingers on. There are grammarians who are primarily concerned with the essential structure of a language, and there are grammarians who are primarily concerned with the correct use of a language. Both kinds, to be sure, are likely to give some attention to the primary concern of the other. The latter, the normative grammarian, must get his prescriptive system somewhere, and, though he generally inherits it from an earlier grammarian, he usually makes some attempt to show a relationship between his system and the way people actually do talk. The former, the descriptive grammarian, discovering discrepancies between what he observes and what the prescriptionist teaches, is often exasperated to the point of trying to get his grammar applied to the teaching of correctness.

For many hundreds of years the speculative and descriptive grammarian had no place in Western culture. To the medieval scholar no language except Latin was worth serious attention, and he had inherited authoritative grammars of that language which made further investigation of it unnecessary. Latin and grammar became often synonymous terms; to know one's grammar was to know Latin. By implication, then, Latin grammar was a complete and perfect description of the Latin language itself. And this conviction that a book labeling itself a grammar of a language was a complete and perfect description of that language was carried over to the vernacular languages when grammars of them were devised on the model of classical grammar.

When the nineteenth-century scholars began to examine languages as phenomena, they were confronted with these grammars of the vernacular constructed on the classical model and sometimes as much as two centuries old. Only gradually did they discover the inadequacy of the classical system for describing languages other than Greek. Acquaintance with the works of the ancient grammarians of Sanskrit was a revelation as was also the impossibility of fitting some non-Indo-European languages into the classical system. Still the nineteenth century made relatively few innovations in grammatical description because of the tremendous task of gathering and systematizing historical phonological and morphological material.

The crucial problem in grammar is syntax; that is, the crucial problem in understanding how a language works —and also simply in understanding it —is to grasp the structure of that language. In English, at least, it is apparent that we have two kinds of linguistic units. The first can be quite easily identified and even, by the convenient if arbitrary system of spelling, classified for ready reference in a dictionary. But words as isolated units are insufficient for communication; they must be part of another unit which we have agreed to call a sentence. It is this unit that reveals the essential structure of English.

But what is a sentence? Fries is at some pains to show that careful descriptive grammarians have failed to give a satisfactory definition. He believes that the reason for their failure is their dependence on meaning as a criterion. In the earliest Western grammar extant, that of Dionysius Thrax (b. *ca.* 146 B.C.), the sentence is defined as "a combination of words, either in prose or verse, making complete sense."[1] But the decision as to what complete sense is, is a subjective one and therefore one on which no satisfactory agreement can be reached. Fries determines to reject meaning as a criterion. His book is a description of his methods and procedures for identifying the sentence. It is therefore a formal grammar of English but strictly in the sense of formal as a description of form and structure.

For perhaps two centuries now, English-speaking students have been taught to believe that the classical formal grammars of English give us an accurate description of the structure of our language. In the past twenty years—say, since Leonard's *Current English Usage* (1932)—there has been some doubt as to the accuracy in detail of this formal grammar, and in

[1] "The Grammar of Dionysius Thrax, Translated from the Greek by Thos. Davidson," *Journal of Speculative Philosophy*, VIII (1874), 326–29.

the practical matter of teaching correctness it has in varying degrees been abandoned in favor of what is now often called the grammar of usage or just usage. But, as Fries points out, an acceptance of usage as the basis for teaching correctness does not necessarily mean the abandonment of faith in the essential adequacy of classical grammar as a description of English. An examination of the more recent college handbooks will verify this assertion. In varying degrees they all accept the conclusions on good usage of the various studies of the last two decades, particularly Leonard's. But also in varying degrees they give some account of the classical formal grammar of English.

Professor Fries believes that this position is untenable. The rigorously descriptive technique has been applied with devastating effect to individual usage items. Scarcely a handbook any longer argues, for instance, that *It's me* is wrong. The handbook writers have been forced to bow to the overwhelming evidence of the descriptive approach. This has been the easier for them to do because the pedagogical descriptionists have for the most part concerned themselves only with minute aspects of the total structure of the language and have seldom insisted upon the relationship of the particular item to the total structure. The classical formal grammar has therefore been tacitly left unchallenged.

Professor Fries now challenges it. He believes that this same rigorous descriptive approach when applied to the total structure of English will have as devastating an effect as it did with individual usage items. "From the point of view underlying this study, the principles, the procedures, the definitions, of 'formal grammar' are unsound. [It] is, like the Ptolemaic astronomy, falsely oriented . . . [and] . . . cannot be expected to provide any satisfactory insight into the mechanisms of our language or any grasp of the processes by which language functions."[2]

A strong statement, indeed! Yet largely true. But he does seem to forget sometimes how heavily he leans on the thousands of grammarians who are his predecessors. The statements quoted above might suggest that Fries has completely rejected the principles, procedures, and definitions of formal grammar. Not at all. Many of them he finds useful, as far as they go. But they don't go far enough. They are insufficient. His quarrel with classical formal grammar is that it is unsound because falsely oriented. False orientation may result not only from false description but from incomplete description. The trouble with classical formal grammar as a description of English is not so much that it is wrong as that it is incomplete. Worst of all, it is an incomplete description which pretends to completeness, and that is its fatal weakness.

Fries accepts the traditional system to the extent that it applies to the phenomena he finds in English. He finds, for example, that the concept of parts of speech can be applied to four kinds of words. But the traditional means of defining parts of speech are undependable because inconsistent in vacillating between function and form, on the one hand, and meaning, on the other. Fries rejects meaning, finding that on the basis of structural considerations alone four

[2] Fries, *The Structure of English* (Harcourt, Brace & World, Inc., New York, 1952), p. 277.

parts of speech emerge. I shall equate these with nouns, verbs, adjectives, and adverbs, though Fries quite rightly insists that there is necessarily no exact correspondence because his definitions do not apply to words except in actual utterances. Similarly he uses terms such as "subject," "object," "appositive," "modifier," etc., in a structural sense which is much more narrowly definable than the traditional one because he eliminates meaning entirely as an identifying factor and relies entirely on "contrasting formal arrangements."

Fries begins his quest of the sentence by isolating an *utterance unit:* "any stretch of speech by one person before which there was silence on his part and after which there was also silence on his part."[3] He then defines a sentence as "a single free utterance, minimum or expanded; i.e., that it is free in the sense that it is not included in any larger structure by means of any grammatical device."[4] Here is the significant addition which Fries has made to the classical procedure. Dionysius depends on meaning to identify his group of words as a sentence; Fries rejects meaning and depends entirely on formal considerations.

Fries's sentence is, then, a word or group of words performing a linguistic function but having no grammatical connection with other linguistically functioning words. Here we find two limitations on the classical procedure. First, he never invents his material, as older grammarians have been all too prone to do when they wanted a convenient illustration of a point. In

fact, he feels that objectivity can be achieved only by using recordings of speech which was spoken solely to perform its linguistic function. Second, the sentence is identified by its having no connections with other words through formal grammatical devices. The bulk of Fries's book is devoted to describing the grammatical devices which English uses to show the relations of words in sentences. "The grammar of a language consists of the devices that signal structural meanings."[5]

Fries's book makes significant progress in English grammar because of a number of important procedures which he carries through more rigorously and systematically than have others. First, he follows most rigorously the principle so much insisted on by the nineteenth-century linguistic scholars that the grammatical description of a particular language must be derived solely from it, not imposed upon it through preconceived grammatical categories derived from another system. This is a simple injunction but almost impossible to follow because grammarians have always absorbed classical grammar in the course of their regular education and tend therefore to find examples of the classical grammatical concepts in the language they are studying. Fries feels that, though he can go so far as to name four groups of words parts of speech, each individual group is best labeled by a number rather than noun, verb, adjective, adverb. The remaining words he refuses even to call parts of speech. Instead he labels them "function words" and classifies them into fifteen subdivisions.

3 *Ibid.*, p. 23.
4 *Ibid.*, p. 25.

5 *Ibid.*, p. 56.

Second, he depends entirely upon living language. The material of his study is mechanical recordings of "some fifty hours of . . . conversations on a great range of topics—conversations in which the participants were entirely unaware that their speech was being recorded."[6] The author believes that this record of 250,000 words of three hundred different speakers supplies a body of material sufficient to permit an analysis which will be "an *introduction* to the structure of English utterances—not a complete descriptive treatment of all the features of that structure."[7] This use of nonliterary material as the basis for grammatical analysis may at first be disturbing, but, though the literary artist's use of language is that which most impresses us, his use of it must be based on the same foundations as our own, or we could not understand him. The essential structure of a language is to be found therefore in the practice of the ordinary user, preferably in his spontaneous, unedited oral practice. Throughout the history of Western grammatical analysis, the grammarian has found it difficult to get at the essential grammatical structure of the language because he has had to use as his material the consciously contrived written products of the literary artist. Dionysius in his definition of grammar went so far as to exclude by implication the structure of the spoken language: "the usages of the language as generally current among poets and prose writers."[8] Nevertheless, grammarians have recognized the weakness of their dependence both on

literary material and on the transcription of the language, but they have not been able to obtain a usable body of spoken language in any sense comparable to the inexhaustible supply of printed material. By using modern recording equipment to provide him with the material, Fries is able to base his study exclusively on spoken English—on a record which faithfully reproduces every characteristic of the original, undistorted by editors or the vagaries and inadequacies of English spelling.

Third, he recognizes grammatical structure only in sentences. For example, in the sentence *The bird flies after flies*, the two *flies* have identical phonetic form and are therefore formally ambiguous as isolated units. To isolate them is therefore to give an incomplete grammatical description of them; only in the sentence can their structural meaning be properly analyzed. "Another of the basic assumptions of our approach here to the grammatical analysis of sentences is that the formal signals of structural meanings operate in a system—that is, that the items of form and arrangement have signalling significance only as they are parts of patterns in a structural whole."[9] The temptation to make morphology a separate part of grammatical analysis results, no doubt, from the sets of paradigms so familiar to students of Latin, though even in Latin many of the inflected forms are ambiguous except in structural units. Fries insists that structural devices are significant only in contexts, and he holds rigorously to this principle.

Fourth, he uses evidence which is

---

6 *Ibid.*, p. 3.
7 *Ibid.*, p. 3.
8 "The Grammar of Dionysius Thrax," *op. cit.*

9 Fries, *Structure*, pp. 59–60.

apparent only to the ear, which would not be indicated in a transcription in ordinary spelling. He points out, for example, that intonation is sometimes a structural signal. In the phrase *a moving van,* the nature of the modification of *van* by *moving* is shown (a) by a rising intonation on the first syllable of *moving,* a falling intonation on the second syllable; and (b) a rising intonation on *moving* not falling until *van;* (a) means a van that does moving, (b) means a van in motion. Also occasionally he uses phonetic transcription to make clear structural differences which are apparent to the ear but are not reflected in our spelling: [sɛpərət, sɛpəret] for *separate.*

Fifth, and most important, he rejects meaning as a method of analysis. The simplest way to illustrate the fruitfulness of this approach is to cite his first example, Lewis Carroll's "Jabberwocky." As he points out, since this poem is nonsense, it cannot be analyzed on the basis of its meaning. Yet "any speaker of English will recognize at once the frames in which [the nonsense] words appear."[10] Evidently there is a structural framework which has a grammatical meaning independent of the lexical meanings of the words which are fitted into it; the structural meanings of a sentence plus the lexical meanings of its word units make what Fries calls the total linguistic meaning of the sentence. This is one of the most interesting and revealing chapters in the book and should demolish once and for all the notion that such languages as Latin have far more grammatical resources than does English.

The results of Fries's procedures are many and illuminating. Any proper appreciation of them, however, must be gained from firsthand acquaintance with his book. One of them may perhaps be suggested, since I have already touched upon it more than once. The traditional parts of speech are redefined, always, of course, in a functioning structure. Words are first divided into two groups of extremely unequal numbers: parts of speech and function words. The former, for the sake of brevity, may be roughly equated with nouns, verbs, adjectives, and adverbs. The latter, which in his material totaled only 154, are the kind of words which, along with such other structural devices as inflections, intonation, and position, make the grammar of "Jabberwocky" and the rest of English clear. Unlike the parts of speech, which are normally identified by various formal aspects, the function words are memorized by the native speaker of English, and their function is recognized from the word itself.

Much of the approach in this book is not original with Fries, and readers of *Language, Journal of the Linguistic Society of America* will find much in it that is familiar. Fries himself frankly recognizes his great indebtedness to others. And there are many matters of style, method, and detail to object to. But none of these matters is of much importance compared to the fact that Fries has presented to the "educated lay reader, [including] teachers in our schools and colleges,"[11] a description of the structure of English which that lay reader can read and which will give him a consider-

10 *Ibid.,* p. 70.

11 *Ibid.,* p. 7.

ably more complete understanding of how English works than any comparable book. To be sure, he'll find the going pretty hard; grammars are never easy reading, and Fries's book is harder than other grammars because the approach is new and the concepts often difficult. But no teacher who pretends to any acquaintance with the grammar of English can honestly ignore this book.

Any systematic study of a phenomenon inevitably raises the question of what is the use of it. About grammar the question has been asked with particular insistence of late. Fries does not shirk answering it. His final chapter, "Practical Applications," suggests six possible uses for his grammar. No criticism of his suggestions can be very meaningful except in the light of a rather full acquaintance with his system. It seems to me that his first suggestion, that his grammar should prove helpful in the teaching of English as a foreign language, is entirely plausible. The other points, however —except the last—are much less persuasive and entirely too reminiscent of the exaggerated claims made for the traditional prescriptive grammar: avoidance of ambiguous constructions, more accurate punctuation, greater variety in sentence structure, and better grasp of the devices for communicating meaning. In fact, he appears to contradict himself because just before presenting these points he has emphasized that native speakers of English master the grammar of their language at an early age, unaware of what they are doing, and

that they use that grammar unconscious of the varied and complex materials they are utilizing.

His final point occupies only a brief paragraph on the last page. It is so important that I shall quote it in full:

The chief use and value of a descriptive analysis of the structure of English, however, does not seem to me to lie in any of the five matters just discussed, or in all of them together. I believe fundamentally in *education* as distinct from *training*. Training seems to measure usefulness or value in terms of output or product, with the individual person as the means. His skills are developed so that he can do things. Education, in contrast with training, seems to stress the individual himself as the end, and measures usefulness and value in terms of contribution to the freedom and development of individual personality. From this point of view, I should insist that the chief value of a systematic analysis and description of the signals of structural meaning in English is the insight it can give concerning the way our language works, and through English, into the nature and functioning of human languages.[12]

This point of view is a reaffirmation of the original Greek philosophical approach to language, a curiosity about the nature of things, a desire for the liberation of the spirit through knowledge, of freedom from the bondage of authoritarianism in language. It is indeed progress in grammar if the author can help the educated lay reader to realize that language is his servant; that it is no tyrant that he must fear and subserve.

12 *Ibid.*, p. 296.

For discussion

A. In what sense does Dykema mean "formal" when he calls *The Structure of English* a formal grammar?

B. What parts of the traditional system of grammatical analysis are acceptable to Fries?

C. What, to Fries, is the chief value of an analysis of English?

D. In what ways does Fries limit what Dykema calls the classical procedure for defining a sentence?

E. What does Fries consider to be the total linguistic meaning of a sentence?

F. Explain Fries's conception of parts of speech and function words?

G. In establishing his form classes and function words, Fries's principal device is the diagnostic frame. He uses the following series of frames to establish a class of words.

1. (The) _____ is/was good.

2. _____s are/were good.

3. The _____ remembered the _____.

4. The _____ went there.

List twenty words which will fit into one or more of these frames. These are class I words according to Fries. The list is very like a list of nouns. List ten nouns which will not fit into any of these frames.

H. Roberts discusses the diagnostic frame in "The Relation of Linguistics to the Teaching of English" (p. 30). What are his objections to it?

GEORGE P. FAUST

Terms in phonemics

IN *The Structure of English,* Fries went from the sentence to the word. Even as he worked with his own assumptions, other linguists, using methods developed in describing some of the languages of the American Indian, were analyzing English in quite a different way. They believed that the grammarian should begin with the sound system, then analyze the making of words, and finally, investigate the relationship among groups of words. In short, one should describe phonology, morphology, and syntax in that order. One way to speak of the resulting grammar is to say that it is phonologically based. The next three articles talk about such a grammar.

In 1951, George Trager and Henry Lee Smith published *An Outline of English Structure,* a technical and theoretical work which devoted most of its ninety-one pages to a close analysis of English phonology and morphology. Its description of the sounds of English provided an orderly way to present many dialects of English. The Trager-Smith phonology won quick and widespread acceptance. Smith himself has said that he would prefer to have it called the Henry Sweet phonology, after the great English phonetician to whom all subsequent phonologists have been indebted. But whatever it should be called, it is the basis for the phonology chapters in a number of recent classroom texts on American English. Though the assumptions and procedures of Trager and Smith are in many ways quite opposed to those of Fries, textbook writers have chosen to regard their work as complementary, feeling, no doubt properly, that we must realize there is a difference between the scientific method and reasonable classroom procedure. The custom among teachers of English has been to use Trager and Smith for phonology, and Fries for syntax.

The spelling system of English, as we will see later, is a good deal more systematic than seems evident. Nevertheless, in talking about sounds as opposed to letters, it is obviously desirable to have a system in which each symbol represents only one sound and in which no sound is represented by more than one symbol. This is more or less accomplished by phonetics and by phonemics.

The Trager-Smith description of the sounds of English contains twenty-four consonants, nine vowels, the possibility of twenty-seven vowel combinations (diphthongs), and four phonemes each of stress, pitch, and juncture. The consonants, vowels, and

"Terms in Phonemics": From *College Composition and Communication,* February 1954, pp. 30–34. Reprinted with the permission of The National Council of Teachers of English and George P. Faust. Some of the footnotes from the original article have been omitted here.

most commonly used diphthongs are given below. The illustrative words for each sound represent the speech of a native speaker of English who lives in California. You may find some slight variations from your own speech.

Every field of study must have a special vocabulary to speed communication and make it precise. Part of one's technical education is to learn it. In the next few articles you will run into a terminological blizzard. It is not very important to memorize the terms themselves; what is important, is to understand what they indicate about the way language works. The first two articles, by George P. Faust of the University of Kentucky, follow Trager and Smith's *An Outline of English Structure* in discussing sounds and word formation in English.

CONSONANTS

/p/ The first sound in *pill, poor, prove*

/t/ The first sound in *take, till, tree*

/k/ The first sound in *kill, cup, cough*

/b/ The first sound in *boor, bill, bread*

/d/ The first sound in *dill, din, dread*

/g/ The first sound in *gill, grim, goose*

/f/ The first sound in *fill, fin, frame*

/v/ The first sound in *vine, vim, vale*

/s/ The first sound in *sip, sill, soul*

/z/ The first sound in *zip, zeal, zero*

/ŝ/ The sound spelled "sh" in *shill, shall, shake*

/ẑ/ The sound spelled "ge" in *"rouge,"* "s" in *treasure,* "ge" in *garage* (as it is sometimes pronounced)

/c/ The sound spelled "tch" in *watch* and "ch" in *chill*

/j/ The first sound in *jury, gin, Jack*

/θ/ The first sound in *theater, thick, thin*

/ð/ The first sound in *the, this, then*

/m/ The first sound in *man, move, mill*

/n/ The first sound in *nil, nudge, near*

/ŋ/ The last sound in *sing, bang, ring*

/l/ The first sound in *light, let, laugh*

/r/ The first sound in *rill, reek, roll*

/y/ The first sound in *you, year, yeast*

/w/ The first sound in *win, will, witch*

/h/ The first sound in *hill, him, who*

VOWELS

/i/ The vowel in *bit, miss, hill*

/e/ The vowel in *bet, mess, bread*

/æ/ The vowel in *bat, mass, plaid*

/ɨ/ A vowel commonly heard in both syllables of *children,* in the adverb *just* ("He was just leaving.") This vowel occurs mostly in unstressed syllables.

/ə/ The vowel in *duck, but, flood.* This vowel is also common in unstressed syllables. It occurs in each of the words in "some of the mud."

/a/ The vowel in *not, pot, hot.* (Many people have /ɔ/ in these words.)

/u/ The vowel in *foot, full, put.*

/o/ For some people, this is the vowel in *home* or *whole;* for others it is a diphthong.

/ɔ/ The vowel in *cough, bought, wash*

DIPHTHONGS

/iy/ *peel, me, lean, field*

/ey/ *say, hate, train, steak*

/ay/ *smile, I buy, cry*

/ɔy/ *boy, boil, loin, joy*

/aw/ *house, trout, lout, sound*

/uw/ *fool, new, tune, you*

/ow/ *go, groan, blow, rode*

/ah/ *pa, palm, calm*

/ɔh/ *saw, flaw, paw*

By means of phonemic analysis, structural linguists try to discover the sound-system of a language as it is consciously or subconsciously meaningful to the speakers. A new set of terms (and symbols) is forced upon them partly because they have formed new categories and developed new techniques and partly because the familiar terms have an aura of association that would act to block understanding if they were used in new senses. The difficulty is that the new terms themselves have blocked understanding between structuralists and teachers. The problem of this article is to remove some of the barriers and show some of the uses teachers can make of the present knowledge of English structure, with no attempt to go beyond phonemics.

But the barriers will not fall automatically with the explanation of a few technical terms. As I have tried to say earlier, we must first persuade ourselves to accept two basic tenets: (1) that speech is the primary form of language and underlies all writing, and (2) that the concern of structuralists is with the mechanisms of language as a medium, not with the "message" (meaning) carried by the medium.

These two tenets accepted, let us start by fastening attention on the *p*-sounds in the possible expression 'rapid pup.' We will follow the general practice of putting phonetic symbols in brackets, e.g., [p], and phonemic symbols between slashes, e.g., /p/. In a phonemic transcription of my speech without stress and intonation marked, we can set our expression down as /ræpid pǝp/. This is not phonetic, for among other things any competent phonetician could hear differences among the *p*-sounds as he listened to me. If he took the first as a phonetic norm, he might transcribe them in order as [p], [p'], and [p'], with ['] standing for aspiration (a puff of air that can be felt on the back of the hand held close to the mouth) and ['] indicating no release by reopening the lips. All three varieties are called allophones.

To put it as untechnically as I can, ALLOPHONES are phonetically similar sounds that never get in each other's way. As native speakers of English, we have learned to use the proper allophones automatically and to ignore them completely in our own speech and in the speech of others. This means that *if you know that a word has two pronunciations, they differ phonemically, not allophonically.* It is only when a foreigner fails to use the right allophones that we become vaguely conscious that something is wrong: The foreigner, we say, speaks English with an accent. In all this we are reacting quite normally, and no phonetically untrained reader should be disturbed if he fails to hear allophonic differences.

Allophones have COMPLEMENTARY DISTRIBUTION, the technical term that corresponds to "never get in each other's way." This is a tricky term to handle. Allophones tend to be restricted. That is, [p'] simply cannot appear at the beginning of a word because we have to reopen our lips to get on with the word. On the other hand, [p'] does on occasion replace [p'] at the end of a word. But we speakers react to /pǝp/ as the "same"

word, no matter which allophone is used, and any sense of difference here is likely to be referred to the speaker's attitude, not his dialect. Therefore, the allophones never collide, even when they alternate with one another, and they complement one another in such a way that in sum they take care of all the situations in which their phoneme occurs.

Complementary distrubution is one side of the coin, CONTRASTIVE DISTRIBUTION the other. Sounds contrast most obviously when the difference produces different words. Thus /p/ and /f/ contrast because 'pup' is not 'puff' (/pǝf/). *And one contrast anywhere in the language is enough to establish separate phonemes everywhere in the language.* It is known quite definitely that [p] between vowels is voiced in normal American speech and is thus very close to [b] in the same situation—at least as close to [b] phonetically as to initial [p']. But since [p] and [b] are assigned by speakers to different phonemes (cf. the contrast between /pet/ and /bet/), the phonetic similarity is inconsequential. You can test this for yourself. Just invite a friend to pat your 'rabid pup' and see whether his reactions are like those of the friends you have invited to pat your 'rapid pup.'

Here it is necessary to insist that the difference in meaning is the *result* of the difference in sound. Strangers who hear my weakly aspirated initial /p/ (an individual peculiarity) quite easily "misunderstand" me and think, for instance, that my middle initial is B instead of P. The sense of "misunderstand" here is that they have misclassified a sound, with resultant change of meaning.

An error of this sort points up one

extremely important difference between phonetics and phonemics. In phonetics a sound can be between a /p/ and a /b/ in the sense that it can have certain characteristics of each, such as the voicelessness of an initial /p/ and the relatively weak aspiration of an initial /b/. The phonetician tries to describe the sound actually produced. But in phonemics there are no gradations. *A sound is assigned to one phoneme or another, and there is no in-between stage.* The linguistic evidence goes to show that we hear in terms of phonemes and listen to only as much of a sound as we need to in order to assign it to an established phoneme. This is a fundamental reason why phonemic transcriptions don't need to distinguish among allophones.

We should now be ready for some definitions. A sound produced is a PHONE. It is a unique historical event, in theory as individual as a fingerprint. Obviously, only a microscopic sample of the phones produced ever get recorded, and yet the patterning of language is such that linguists can classify as confidently as though they had a statistically large sample. In great measure, this is because they have occasion to concentrate on only a few variations. The subclasses into which phones are fitted are ALLOPHONES, each of which, though in complementary distribution, is distinct from all others by at least one phonetic feature. At this level we are still in a region where sounds may be symbolized in phonetic transcription. Next, the allophones are gathered into one class, a PHONEME, which is distinguished by the phonetic similarity of its members and by its contrastive distribution with other phonemes.

To tie all three together, any phone may be called a phone (i.e., an individual sound) or an allophone (i.e., a member of an allophone) or a phoneme (i.e., a member of a phoneme). Imagine that I now hear you say "pup." The first sound was a phone, already past history. As long as it remains unclassified, I can call it nothing but a phone. Probably I will next classify it as a member of the phoneme /p/, and now I can call it either a phone or a phoneme. When finally I group it with other members of /p/ that have aspiration, I can also call it an allophone of /p/, and I can describe that allophone phonetically as [pʻ]. In the same kind of way, all other vowel-like or consonant-like phones can be identified as belonging to one or another of the thirty-three phonemes that make up this part of the English sound-system.

For teachers, the usefulness of having a working acquaintance with these phonemes is that it sheds valuable light on many spelling problems. All of us already know, in a relatively unsystematic way, that our students tend to reflect their pronunciations in their writing, but the remedies we have offered have sometimes been unrealistic, to a considerable extent because we have confused letters and sounds. One pronunciation of *often,* now well established, is supposed to be due to the letter *t* in the spelling—some people, apparently, never thought of *soften.* Once we realize that *used to* is regularly pronounced /yuwstuw/, not /yuwzd tuw/, we may be more sympathetic to the spelling *use to,* which is really very sensible, if not orthodox. Of course we should try to impress the conventional spelling but not, I suggest, at the cost of a pronunciation which may be unforced for some speakers but which I never happen to have heard attempted except by teachers. Again, probably many of us tear our hair over students who seem unable to pluralize words like *scientist*. But a great many standard speakers have /-s/ at the end of such words instead of /-st/, and to them the plural presumably sounds just like the singular.[1] It would strike an informed teacher as unreasonable to attempt to modify a standard pronunciation; it would be better to show the students that for spelling such words they cannot trust their ears. This is the type of situation which a knowledge of phonemics enables a teacher to handle sensibly.

To return to the sound-system, the set of phonemes referred to so far are called SEGMENTAL PHONEMES to distinguish them from another more recently discovered set, the SUPRASEGMENTAL PHONEMES. These consist of stresses, pitches, and junctures—the last being modes of transition from one speech-segment to another. Of course the fact of their existence is not news; the recent knowledge is of their contrastive distribution into phonemes, which has been worked out in considerable detail during the last ten years by Kenneth Pike[2] and others.

STRESS is familiar as what we call accent in dictionaries, where only three relative degrees are necessary, counting the unmarked as weak. (However, you should not expect dictionaries to be accurate on stress. For

example, they leave the second syllable of *cargo* unmarked, though it definitely has more stress than the second syllable of *sofa*—as much, in my speech, as the marked second syllable of *blackbird*.) Connected speech has a fourth degree of stress which overrides the others and which we use to establish word-groups. Customary symbols of stress are

$$/ \,', \,\char"5E, \,\grave{}\,, \,\char"2D8\, /,$$

called primary, secondary, tertiary, and weak.

Whêre's thĕ cárgò

illustrates the four phonemic stresses.

The very idea that relative levels of PITCH are contrastive is a novelty. Here there is nothing like a familiar dictionary to fall back on, and since the proof is somewhat complicated, about all that can be done here is to make the flat assertion that English has four phonemic pitches. The joke 'What are we having for dinner? Mother?' depends on the misuse of pitch levels. In the commonplace 'What are we having for dinner, Mother?' the vocative can be either at the lowest pitch or the next above, but it can never be at either of the two highest pitches. With next-to-top pitch, 'mother' becomes a separate question.

Pitches are usually symbolized by numbers: $/^{1,2,3,4}/$. Unfortunately, there are two systems in use, one that numbers from the top and one that begins at the bottom. Other devices, like dotted lines above and below the text, are also in use.

The phonemes of JUNCTURE, or TRANSITION, are classes of the ways we use to pass from one bit or stretch of linguistic material to the next. If this

1 A structurally more accurate way of putting this is that the final consonant cluster /-sts/ is non-existent in the speech of many Americans.

2 Kenneth L. Pike, *The Intonation of American English*, University of Michigan Press, Ann Arbor, 1945.

merely seems a clumsy way of saying something like "get from one phrase or sentence to the next," the reason is that the use of juncture helps to define terms like *phrase* and *sentence*. Therefore we cannot, without circular reasoning, use the terms in describing juncture. As a minor digression, let me point out that our standard practice has been to use circularity, though often at one or two removes. We may use *sentence* to help define *verb,* and then turn around and use *verb* to help define *sentence*. The structuralists try very hard not to fall into this sort of trap.

The four phonemes of juncture are symbolized by /+, |, ||, #/, called plus juncture, single bar juncture, double bar juncture, and double cross juncture, respectively. Plus juncture, which classically distinguishes 'night rate' from 'nitrate,' can be left behind with the observation that it always occurs at least between secondary stresses, and between a secondary and primary, unless one of the other three junctures is there. (This, of course, like all that follows, is a rule of the language, not of the structuralists; it is a phenomenon observed, not created.) The remaining junctures can be thought of as major, for they serve to establish what is probably the basic rule of English grammar. There is always one, and only one, primary stress between any pair of /|, ||, #/. This rule is completely accurate if the silence before speech is counted as a major juncture and if the speaker is not interrupted. For example, both these versions are accepted by listeners as normal English:

My ôlder brôther is a plúmber.
My ôlder bróther | is a plúmber.

Single bar juncture can be read as transition across a fairly minor break with pitch sustained to the point of juncture. It is never an uninterrupted speaker's final juncture. Double bar juncture is as familiar to us as the rising "question intonation," a thoroughly misleading term. The questions that end in double bar are those without question words, like 'Are you going?' and 'He's here?' In all but perhaps a very few dialects, questions like 'Where are you going?' do not end in double bar. Polite vocatives always end with double bar: 'I'm going, Mother.' Especially in rather slow speech, the rise of double bar is common within the conventional sentence:

The sôldiers in Koréa || wânted to gêt hóme.

Double cross juncture is marked by voice fade-out, and usually a lowering of pitch. It appears where periods have been used in the examples, and at the end of 'Where are you going?' It also appears, at least in some reading styles, before what we have been trained to call a non-restrictive subordinate clause at the end of a sentence.

The implications of the suprasegmental phonemes for teachers are important. Almost all marks of punctuation are juncture signals, as we demonstrate again and again by reading aloud mispunctuated student sentences to show that they sound queer. Some of us, perhaps, sometimes even deliberately misread the student's punctuation because it violates an editorial rule, not a linguistic principle. But almost nobody, within my knowledge, is equipped to give students a sensible explanation of punctuation in terms of major junctures and the arbitrary rules of editors.[3]

Reading styles differ within rather narrow limits, but for the sake of illustration we can arbitrarily pick one in which /#/ is symbolized by a period and /|||/ by a comma. No other junctures are marked by punctuation. If the student gives the reading "He wasn't there /|||/ therefore I didn't see him," the comma before *therefore* is right linguistically, however wrong it may be editorially. If he reads "I didn't go to the dance /#/ because I was too tired," the proper punctuation linguistically is into two sentences. In the past year and a half, I have marked comma faults and fragments RA for "Read aloud." When the student's reading has been right linguistically, I have been able to show him how to identify the situations in which he cannot trust to his ear for punctuation. Without claiming perfect results, I can say that I have been astonished at how readily students of all levels have taken to my explanations and how often they have asked me why punctuation was never explained to them that way in high school.

Over and above such editorial errors in punctuation, the suprasegmental phonemes are important in helping students understand why we group words as we do and how it happens that writing produced by the unwary is often ambiguous. Students can see (and hear) that junctures enclose word groups, and when they understand that the number of junc-

tures increases as the pace of reading slows, they can more and more guard their readers against misunderstanding. "After eating the baby fell asleep" (which I owe to a former colleague) tends to disappear. This is not simply a matter of punctuation, for often the student either alters the word order ("The baby fell asleep after eating") or makes a substitution ("After its meal the baby fell asleep"). The reason it disappears is that the student has discovered that

After êating the báby . . .

is a possible alternative to

After éating . . .

The sound system of English, then, has a rather direct bearing on what teachers do in the classroom. In particular, familiarity with the segmental phonemes should make for an understanding of spelling difficulties due to dialect and should kill once and for all the notion that unconventional phonemic spelling is a sign that the speller "doesn't speak good English" or "doesn't enunciate his words clearly": When the snow is deep, many of the best people wear

/ ártĭks/, not / árk + tĭks/.

And second, acquaintance with the suprasegmental phonemes can help us realize why naïve students punctuate as they do and manage to produce some of their howlers. It is not a question of studying speech for its own sake; it is a question of being able to put our fingers quite precisely on what is amiss and of being in a position to help each student accommodate himself to our traditional writing system and its editorial expectations.

---

[3] By far the best available explanation is that by A. H. Marckwardt in the Thorndike-Barnhart *Comprehensive Desk Dictionary* (Doubleday, 1951), pp. 21–24.

For discussion

A. Pronounce the following words: *lip, blip, plip, clip, atlas, fill, gulf, muscle.* You should be able to notice some distinction among the sounds of /l/. Leaving aside any technical explanation of what the differences are, show how complementary distribution will justify placing all the sounds in a single phoneme /l/.

B. Pronounce *significant* several times. What is the first consonant sound of the last syllable? It is possible that sometimes you will use /k/ and sometimes /g/? Does this mean that /k/ and /g/ are not separate phonemes in English? Why not?

C. In the Spanish word *dos* the grapheme *d* is pronounced like the initial consonant sound in *dough,* and in the word *lado* like the *th* of *lather.* In the Italian word *stadio* the first consonant sound is like the first consonant sound in *stadium,* and in the word *slitta* the first consonant sound is like the first consonant sound in *zip.* How then is a native speaker of Spanish likely to pronounce *ladder, fuddy-duddy,* and *radish?* How is a native speaker of Italian likely to pronounce *style* and *slap?* Basing your conclusion on this meager information, give the Spanish allophones of /d/ and the Italian allophones of /s/?

D. Two words commonly misspelled because of the way they are sometimes pronounced are *athlete* and *February.* Make a list of as many words of this type as you can.

E. Referring to the list in the introduction to this article, spell the following linguistic forms *phonemically*:

tint	chives	came	cot
drab	goal	book	caught
lop	fang	of	coot
that	check	cheap	cute
mess	lose	wood	judge

F. Indicate the heaviest stress in each of the following:

boiling point	briefcase
sourpuss	jumping jacks
grease monkey	lemon drop
cable car	escalate
onion peel	bloomer girl

G. Now indicate the secondary and—if there is one—the tertiary stress in each of the above.

H. Find two possible plus junctures in each of the following: /frəntir/, /pləmpay/, /naytreyt/, /wiθawtpeyšints/, /owldiŋglišgræmir/

GEORGE P. FAUST

Something of morphemics

IN "Something of Morphemics," Professor Faust continues his discussion of the Trager-Smith analysis, going from phonemics to morphemics, which includes ". . . everything from the smallest unit of meaning to the construction of the sentence." Since sentence analysis then becomes part of morphemics, and since many decisions about morphology will be based on differences in stress, pitch, and juncture, we may reasonably call the resulting analysis phonologically based.

Faust begins by distinguishing morphemics from morphology, and referential from differential meaning. Many of the terms he introduces in this discussion are morphological parallels to the ones he has used in his discussion of phonemics: *phoneme* and *morpheme; allophone* and *allomorph; segmental* and *suprasegmental phonemes;* and *segmental* and *suprasegmental morphemes.*

. . . As we approach morphemics, new terms will concern us, but they will seem like so much abracadabra unless the occasion for them is clear. I myself do not see how they could be dispensed with. Again, familiar terms used in new ways are sure to be traps unless the redefinitions of them are observed and absorbed. But as Professor Fries has observed, "The difference between the [structural] approach used here and the older approach lies much deeper than a mere matter of terminology."[1] There should be no worship of terms, nor fear either, for the terms themselves are not central except as they operate as

[1] *The Structure of English* (Harcourt, Brace & World, Inc., 1952), p. 2.

tools. In general, the structuralists seem to care relatively little for the terms and a great deal for accurate definition and consistent use. What is important is the discovery of a pattern or of a tool, a method, for bringing patterns to light.

MORPHEMICS, which includes everything in language (narrowly defined) from the smallest unit of meaning to the construction of the sentence, takes its name from a useful tool, the morpheme. The first stages of morphemics, up to syntax, are called MORPHOLOGY, and the first two steps in morphology are to identify morphs and classify them. A MORPH can be oversimply defined as an individual linguistic form which is an indivisible unit of mean-

"*Something of Morphemics*": From *College Composition and Communication*, May 1954, pp. 65–69. Reprinted with the permission of the National Council of Teachers of English and George P. Faust. Some of the footnotes from the original article have been omitted here.

ing. Someone who says "scramble" has used a morph. It seems to contain several forms—*am, ram, scram, ramble, amble.* But if any one of them is taken out, the remainder of the sounds is meaningless. We are forced to conclude that the "scramble" we heard is indivisible.

Any morph can be recorded as a phoneme or a pattern of phonemes. (Here it should be emphasized that no phoneme *qua* phoneme is a morph. To be a morph, a phoneme must in addition carry meaning.) Suppose you render the line "A rose is a rose is . . ." Each occurrence of *a* /ə/, *rose* /rowz/, and *is* /iz/ is a morph, but the second occurrence is not the same morph as the first, for, strictly speaking, no morph is ever repeated. This only means, of course, that the first pin of the paper is never the second, no matter how much alike they may be.

Determining whether a form is meaningful is a technical process that cannot be described here, but it is important to note that the structuralist does not need to be able to put his finger on the meaning. He only needs to know that it is there. And here is a good place to make, briefly, some distinction between referential meaning, which belongs to semantics, and differential meaning, which is a tool of structural linguistics. Given the knowledge that a form has meaning, it *is* important to the linguist to know whether its meaning is "same" or "different" as compared with another form. So, if he hears

"He's still"/hiyz stíl/

on one occasion and

"He's still here"/hiyz stíl híhr/

on another, he will want to find out whether the two forms he has recorded

as /stíl/ are "same" or "different." (As a native speaker, I say, "Different." Do we agree?)

Broadly speaking, structuralists arrive at morphemes by comparing morphs. A MORPHEME can be defined, again oversimply, as a class of morphs that are semantically similar and contrast with morphs belonging to other morphemes. Semantic similarity by itself might gather /red/, /yelow/, /bliw/ into one morpheme of color, but since they all contrast before /dres/, say, they belong to different morphemes.

Often there are differences among the members of a morpheme, usually phonemic, and it is useful to recognize subclasses, called allomorphs. An ALLOMORPH consists of like morphs that are in complementary distribution with all other members of their morpheme. For example, English has a morpheme of plurality which has a great many allomorphs. To take the three simplest and most obvious variants, consider *coats* /kowts/, *gloves* /gləvz/, and dresses /dresɨz/. In each case a member of the plural morpheme is present, as we can learn from experiment. The forms /s, z, ɨz/ differ phonemically but are in complementary distribution. That is, we do not say /kowtɨz/, and with our training, we probably cannot say /kowtz/. These three, along with many others also in complementary distribution, are set up as allomorphs of the plural morpheme. (The morpheme itself is recorded for conveniences as /Z$_1$/;[2] every such "cover symbol" should be

---

[2] For simplicity, the customary braces for morphemes are not used this article. The subscript distinguishes the plural morpheme from any others that may have any of the same phonemic shapes.

described in full somewhere.) *Allomorph* is so convenient a term that even morphemes with a single phonemic shape are said to have one allomorph.

The parallel of *morph, allomorph,* and *morpheme* with *phone, allophone,* and *phoneme* is obvious. Any morph may be called a morph (i.e., an individual linguistic form which is an indivisible unit of meaning) or an allomorph (i.e., a member of an allomorph) or a morpheme (i.e., a member of a morpheme). If I hear you say "Take your coats," the last meaningful unit, /s/, is a morph that immediately becomes past history. By comparison with other examples of /s/ with the same kind of meaning, I can set up what I think is a class. But a trained structuralist would very soon discover that my supposed class was only a subclass, an allomorph, of a morpheme that has many allomorphs.

The material considered so far has all consisted of segmental phonemes and has given us SEGMENTAL MORPHEMES. The suprasegmental phonemes produce SUPRASEGMENTAL MORPHEMES, whose meaningfulness is harder for us to grasp, partly—at a guess—because they have only recently been discovered. But apparently it is impossible for us to say anything in English without using at least three morphemes: one segmental, one of stress, and one of intonation (pitch and major juncture). The full phonemic transcription of one way of saying "Go" is

$$/^3\text{gów}^1\#/.$$

One morpheme is the segmental material, /gow/; one is the stress, /'/; and one is the intonation pattern, /³ ¹#/. The suprasegmental morphemes need not be examined here; their greatest value is in syntactic analysis.

After the morphemes are accounted for, the next step in morphology is to classify the segmental morphemes in what might be called "the grammar of the word." Briefly, the segments can be grouped into BASES, PREFIXES, and SUFFIXES. Bases are usually "free forms" like *sweet*—forms that occur without any prefix or suffix—but some are not, like *-ceive,* which always occurs with a prefix. Prefixes, which like suffixes are never free forms, need no comment. There are two kinds of suffixes, DERIVATIONAL and GRAMMATICAL. Derivational suffixes, like the *-ness* of *coolness,* tend to limit forms to a particular part of speech. (Does this account for our widespread objection to the use of *suspicion* as a verb?) Grammatical suffixes give us the inflections of the few remaining paradigms in English. Disregarding suprasegmental features, the WORD can now be defined as a single base with or without prefixes. By this definition, *incompatibility,* with its single base, is a word; *shotgun,* with two bases, is not. *It is of no linguistic importance that* shotgun *is written solid.*

The final step in morphology is the establishment of PARADIGMS, which can be viewed as sets of grammatical suffixes. These suffixes follow the base and derivational suffixes (e.g., either *help* or *helpfulness*). English has paradigms for pronouns, nouns, verbs, and adjectives. In at least the last three, "no suffix" must be recognized as a characteristic ending by contrast with the suffixes used. It is a peculiarity of the language that the noun suffixes for "plural" and "possessive" coalesce when they are both present and the plural morpheme is one of /s, z, ɪz/. Thus we get /kidz/ (alongside /menz/ where we might have expected /kidzɪz/.

The paradigm for MORPHOLOGICAL PRONOUNS, a notoriously irregular set, has been the occasion for a good deal of experimenting. The presentation we grew up with emphasizes person, number, gender and case in that order. One of the structural presentations reworks the order to gender, case, person, and number, with really no attention to the last two. The order of cases is also modified to subject, object, 1st possessive, 2nd possessive. Here is the paradigm: *Without Gender:* I, me, my, mine; we, us, our, ours; you, you, your, yours; they, them, their, theirs. *With Gender:* he, him, his, his; she, her, her, hers; it, it, its—. (Whether the forms of *who* are included is a matter of personal preference.)

The paradigm for NOUNS is: *Common Case:* Sg. (no suffix) /layf/, Pl. (/-Z₁/) /layvz/; *Possessive Case:* Sg. (/-Z₂/) /layfs/, Pl. (/-Z₁/ and /-Z₂/ merged) /layvz/.

The paradigm for VERBS is: *Infinitive and General Present:* (no suffix) /liv/, /rayz/; *3rd Singular Present:* (/-Z₃/) /livz/, /rayzɪz/; *Past:* (/-D₁/) /livd/, /rowz/; *Past Participle:* (/-D₂/) /livd/, /rizɪn/; *Present Participle:* ("-ing") "living," "rising."

The paradigm for ADJECTIVES is: *positive:* (no suffix) /layv/; *Comparative:* (/-ər/) /layvər/; *Superlative:* (/-ɪst/) /layvɪst/.

The reason for going into the paradigms fully is that they serve as definitions of parts of speech at the morphological level. If an item is inflectible within a paradigm—that is, if it appears with at least two appropriate

suffixes (including "no suffix")—it is a member of the part of speech defined by the paradigm.[3] Every item must qualify by this test to be included, which means that *poor* (*poorer, poorest*) is a MORPHOLOGICAL ADJECTIVE, but *excellent* remains unassigned. A MORPHOLOGICAL NOUN is defined as a linguistic item which is inflectible for singular/plural, or for common case/possessive, or for both. Similarly, a MORPHOLOGICAL VERB is inflectible for present/past, etc. *Man* is a noun because we write *man's* as well as because of *men;* it is also a verb because of *manned* and other verbal suffixation. What any one occurrence of the form *man* itself may be is a question of assigning it to a paradigm.

Roughly speaking, structural linguistics offers the same list of nouns and verbs as traditional grammar. It is not important why this is so. It is not even important what particular words, like *other* (cf. *others*), are included among nouns, say. What is important is the basis for the classification. We are thoroughly used to a system that often starts with philosophical definitions, and freshmen still know that "A noun is the name of . . ." At this point it is hard for me to see why, *philosophically* speaking, *rain* is not just as much of a noun in "It rained during the night" as in "Rain fell during the night." The difference to me now is purely linguistic. In the first,

---

[3] It is not true, as sometimes claimed, that morphological parts of speech cannot be identified without the help of syntax. Without anything to go on but "Boys will be boys" a linguist could find out from a completely naive informant that *boys* is the plural of *boy*. Contrast "Fuzz will be fuzz." If the linguist already knows that *they* is plural, he can take a short cut by trying "They will be boys."

rain has a suffix that belongs distinctly to the paradigm labeled *verb;* in the second, *rains,* with the plural morpheme, can be substituted for *rain* and produce an English sentence.

Structural definitions are no panacea in teaching, but my experience with using them has been encouraging. For the present, students who have mastered traditional grammar had better be left alone, unless they are exceptionally bright. But among those who never "learned grammar" in high school, I have found some who can match forms more easily than grasp the traditional definitions.

When we leave morphology for syntax, we come to an area where much has been done and much remains to be done. Professor Fries's analysis is so well known and speaks so adequately for itself that I need do no more than allude to *The Structure of English.* The highly technical Trager-Smith *An Outline of English Structure,* which I have been more or less following (but any mistakes are mine), is simply unreadable without training in structural linguistics. Yet it has been extraordinarily influential among structuralists, especially for its insistence on a separation of "levels" in analysis and for its report on how we use suprasegmental morphemes to determine constructions.

Separation of levels means, among other things, that parts of speech morphologically defined are not the same as parts of speech syntactically defined. If you hear "Today is Sunday," "Today's paper just came," and "He just came today," you can tell from the forms in the first two that *today* is a morphological noun. But in the second it is in some respects a SYNTACTIC ADJECTIVE, and in the last, fully a SYN-TACTIC ADVERB.[4] It is only at the syntactic level that adverbs, prepositions, conjunctions, question words (e.g., *when, why, what*), some auxiliaries, and some adjectives can be assigned to parts of speech. To avoid confusion, it is always best to prefix either *morphological* or *syntactic,* whichever is proper, to the name of the part.

Traditional definitions have been by meaning, by form, and by function. Definition by meaning is demonstrably unnecessary. By the separation of levels, it is now possible to take care of difficulties and confusions growing out of using a definition by form and definition by function simultaneously. As a resultant, we may well expect an end of such descriptions as "noun used as adjective" (e.g., in *state highway*) and "noun used as adverb" or "adverbial noun" (e.g., *home* in "He went home"). If the cleavage between levels were consistently represented in our schoolbooks, I feel sure we would be able to teach it easily.

Suprasegmental morphemes are either SUPERFIXES, patterns of stress with or without plus juncture intervening, or INTONATION PATTERNS, patterns of pitch and major juncture. Several superfixes have been discovered to be "phrase-making":

$$/\grave{}+\acute{}/, /\acute{}+\grave{}/, \text{ and } /\acute{}+\hat{}/.$$
$$(/\hat{}+\acute{}/ \text{ does not make phrases.})$$

Noun compounds have superfixes and are syntactic phrases (e.g., *shotgun* —shót + gùn—which was rejected as a morphological word). "A blackboard [blâck + bôard] isn't just a black

---

4 In terminology, the Trager-Smith analysis distinguishes less clumsily, but introduces more new terms: *morphological adjective = adjective; syntactic adjective = adjectival.* There are no *adverbs*—only *adverbials.*

board [blâck + bóard]" illustrates the difference between phrase and non-phrase, and so does "It's a come-down" (cóme + dôwn) in contrast with "He's come down" (côme + dówn). Intonation patterns make a number of distinctions, only one of which can be illustrated here. "²He's ³going¹#" uses the commonest morpheme, which can be described as "statement unless qualified by other signals." It contrasts with "²Is he ³góing³||," a pattern associated with questions that use no question-word. ("²He's ³góing³||," is a question because of the pattern; "²Where is he ²góing¹#" is a question because the pattern is qualified by the use of *where*.) Generally speaking, superfixes apply to phrases, while intonation patterns apply to larger constructions that might be called intonation clauses.

It has proved impossible to cover the ground of morphemics in even a simplified way. My apologies are due the reader for a crowded article which has found little room to point to applications useful to us as teachers. One thing is reasonably certain, and that is that many uses will be found as we gather a corps of middlemen—structuralists who know something about our teaching problems and teachers who are at home with structural linguistics.

For discussion

A. Derive an adjective, an adverb, and another noun from *act;* two adverbs from *length;* an adjective from *time;* an adjective and an adverb from *marvel;* and another noun from *friend.*

B. After his analysis of *An Outline of English Structure,* Faust sets up three word classes based upon inflection: nouns, verbs, and adjectives. Mark the words in the following sentences which are or can be inflected:
1. Noble Malcolm, poor but honest, patiently explained that he was an ideal prince.
2. The somewhat forbidding figure in olive drab muffled a slight cough as he crossed into Marlboro Country.
3. The Indian brave bravely braved the icy stream.
4. In a sly gesture of revenge, James chose a potted plant as a gift for his sternly teetotaling aunt.
5. The racer who won the race was a racist.
6. Her scarf blowing in the quickening breeze, Jeanine announced that she would see me again in lilac time.
7. The sick policeman looked sickly.

C. What is the morphemic difference between the noun *pervert* and the verb *pervert?* Between the noun *incense* and the verb *incense?*

D. What distinction does Faust make between referential and differential meaning?

E. List the morphs in *unkindlinesses* and *disagreements.*

F. Suppose you had to teach a student who knew very little English the various ways of pronouncing *-s* as an indication of the plural. Indicate a systematic arrangement of the way the different pronunciations of *-s* might be presented.

HENRY LEE SMITH, JR.

The teacher and the world of English

FOR A NUMBER OF YEARS, part of the time at the Foreign Service Institute in Washington, D.C. and now at the State University of New York at Buffalo, George L. Trager and Henry Lee Smith, Jr. have been working on a description of the organization of human knowledge. That their interest in communication goes far beyond what many people think of as language is clear from the first few paragraphs of "The Teacher and the World of English," in which Smith speaks as an anthropologist, a linguist, and an English teacher. He discusses gestures and snorts as well as the conventionally analyzed forms of communication, seeing in them cultural patterns which may be described by a trained observer as parts of a system. Up to a point, then, Smith is placing what Faust has said into a more elaborate philosophical framework.

Going further, however, he begins to apply what we have learned about the sound system to reach conclusions about grammar. Faust dealt only briefly with the suprasegmental morphemes, saying that their greatest value is in grammatical analysis. Smith now wants to use them in discussing relationships among words. For such a discussion, he must settle on a definition of *word*: a single base, with or without a prefix, with or without suffixes, whether inflectional or derivational, and with a superfix. With this definition, Smith sets up three word classes for English on the basis of inflection: nouns, verbs, pronouns. The adjective inflectional class discussed by Faust has been dropped. We must identify the rest of our word classes within phrases, which are *constructions* if a secondary stress goes with a primary (prêtty gírl) and *constructs* if there is no secondary stress (búbble gùm).

As construction or construct the phrase has two parts; our arrangements are binary. Whatever structure I observe has two constituents. For example, the immediate constituents of *pretty girl* are *pretty* and *girl*. If I have *a pretty girl,* the immediate constituents are *a* and *pretty girl,* the superfix becomes ˅ ´ and the construction becomes a construct. In this way, Smith shows the layering of constructions in English, and eventually assigns items to form classes based upon the superfix patterns.

In this procedure, the analysis of syntax is based upon phonology. As Smith points out, "John made Bill money" and "John made Bill captain" will be called syntactically the same because the superfix patterns and immediate constituents are identical. If they are to be distinguished, it must be on another level.

"The Teacher and the World of English": From *The English Journal,* vol. 47, n. 4, April 1958, pp. 181–188. Reprinted with the permission of The National Council of Teachers of English and Henry Lee Smith, Jr.

Today, more than ever before, vistas are opening that show us again the supreme importance of language. From one point of view it can be seen as man's first and greatest invention. Without it, human culture and human societies as we know them would be impossible; through it human beings have created their own unique adaptations. In short, language is truly the mark of our very humanity, for man is human by virtue of the kind of interaction that goes on through *human* communication systems, of which language is the queen. The very survival of the individual as well as the survival of the species is dependent upon language, and perhaps even more important, language *in* culture provides for the possibility of the development of individual consciousness and awareness of self, for the formulation of concepts, and for the creation and transmission of man's spiritual values, his art, and his literature.

Though I am primarily a linguist and an anthropologist, I speak today as one who has "English" as well as "Linguistics" in his academic title, and though I will be reporting in some respect on "research in progress," I am equally interested—and have been for over twenty years—in the application of the results of linguistic research to the teaching of the mother tongue from "literacy to literature." My experience has convinced me that a knowledge of the structure and the functioning of language and the other human communication systems is the essential basis for all really successful pedagogy in the area that has come to be called the "language arts." But even more important, I feel that to understand language and

the human communication process is in a very real sense to understand the essence of our humanity. Like other animals, man communicates through touch, taste, and smell; but only man can talk. Like other animals, man communicates his species membership and his position within his species by the very *set* and *quality* of his voice and bodily motions; but only man can talk.

Language is the most minutely structured, patterned, configured of all man's cultural systems, but there is system, order, and pattern in other communication systems than language. More and more clearly, we are seeing the importance of these other learned and patterned systems. More and more obvious does it appear that speech doesn't take place in a vacuum but is surrounded, as it were, by patterned bodily motions—the *kinesic* system—and by systematically analyzable vocalizations, or *paralanguage*. Here we include the *vocal qualifiers*, consisting of such phenomena as perceptibly measurable degrees of overloudness and oversoftness; degrees of drawl and "clipping" of portions of utterance; and degrees of increased or decreased height of pitch over the baseline established in the language itself. Paralanguage also includes laughing and crying "through" speech, the breaking of the voice, and the whole gamut of "tuts," clicks, sniffs, snorts, "uh's," "uh-uh's," and "uh-huh's," these latter termed the *vocal segregates*.

Kinesic and paralinguistic phenomena constitute separate patterned systems, which differ in their structure from culture to culture. However, of more real importance is the fact that in all cultures no one "just talks," but communication goes on only when there is a symphony of interplay of each system with each. As language is more than words, communication is more than language. Each system provides a means of *commenting* on the portions of the message that are being carried by the other systems, and for considerable stretches we may not talk at all but carry on our end of the interaction entirely through the other systems. And when we talk, we are reinforcing, emphasizing—maybe even negating— what we are saying by *how* we are saying it. Simultaneously, throughout the entire process, we are sending additional messages as to how we feel, who we think we are, and how we evaluate the person or persons with whom we are interacting. Communication is interaction, and the whole can be seen as a multileveled, complex, integrated package of interrelated and systematized phenomena. The more *congruently* the package is assembled, the more effective the interaction, and hence communication, will be.

Communication, then, is more than language, and language is far more than words on a printed page. Both the creator and the interpreter of literature and the plain writer and reader have only the letters of the alphabet and a sprinkling of punctuation conventions with which to represent this wonderfully complex symphony we have been describing. The artist has only the written language through which to transmit his understanding, his experiences, his emotions, his reactions, his ideas. The reader, if he has learned the same language and is a member of the same culture, can be moved to supply and even to recreate the artist's world, his beliefs and his intentions.

But even so marvellous an invention as writing is always *incomplete* and *inconsistent* in relation to the language that it symbolizes. It is a derived system and speech is always prior, even though spoken language is frequently influenced by written language. Granted that the written language in the hands of a skillful artificer can be made to carry much more than just a recording of linguistic events, writing as a system remains a sort of shorthand reminder to the native speaker of something that has been said or could be said in the language. As we all know, however, the written language is more immediately accessible than the spoken language; the written language has a permanence in contrast to the ephemeral character of speech; the written language is always more rigidly structured, more insistent on precision and clarity by the very virtue of the fact that it must stand alone. For these reasons, if for no others, it should be studied, understood, and mastered.

With a real understanding of the difference between the spoken and written language, it should be obvious that we should never allow our students to write "just the way they talk" any more than we should try to teach them to talk the way they *have* to learn to write. The failure to see and to understand the distinction between standard colloquial speech and the literary language and the failure to understand the relationship between speech and writing has been, I am convinced, the chief obstacle in imparting to our students both real literacy and a confident competence in speaking. Traditional grammar has been based, understandbly enough, on the literary language, but far too often the prescriptive rules which must be followed if we are to *write* acceptably have been used as a basis for how we should *talk*. The result, I'm afraid, has been to inject into our population a sort of mild schizophrenia which has produced many afraid to talk and totally unable to write.

THE MATTER OF USAGE

In trying to alleviate the situation, "traditionalists" and "structuralists" often almost come to blows over the term "usage." To those who link the term with grammar, it means *prescription;* to the linguist it means linguistic events which are to be *described* on all levels and in all contexts. Contrary to the belief of many, the linguist does not say "anything goes," or any way of talking or writing is "just as good" as any other. He simply states that for him, as a student of human behavior, *all* of language and speech, *every* linguistic event is data to be described and analyzed. As an anthropologist, he is just as much concerned with the contexts in which "them things" occurs as he is interested to find out when "those things" occurs. He is well aware that there are correlations between the *status* of individuals and their use of language; he notes dispassionately and with every means at his disposal which usages seem to be most *congruent* with culturally defined situations. He knows that in all cultures certain persons or classes of persons are highly regarded

while others are merely tolerated. The language of those with the status of "educated"—however the culture may understand this term—are those who by definition will be trustworthy informants as to acceptable and effective usage. Thus if our students are to be educated people, and they come to us unable to speak standard colloquial English, our educational system must teach them this level of language; if our students have little acquaintance with the literary language, every effort must be made to give them control of it as both readers and writers. By doing any less, we fail as educators and unless we accomplish this minimum successfully, we have no chance as *teachers* of English to instill an appreciation and understanding of the language and of the great things that have been thought and said in it.

As a structural linguist whose main interest over the years has been English, I have been greatly concerned about how little is really known about our most priceless possession. I have been even more concerned when I have seen the extent to which much that is taught about it is irrelevant, and more confusing than elucidating. I have been much interested and professionally preoccupied with the application of the results of linguistic research to the teaching of English throughout our educational system and to the problem of teaching Americans foreign languages and foreigners our language. My experience has convinced me that the basis of all really successful pedagogy in these areas is a knowledge of linguistic *structure*. But the application of linguistics is not the sole purpose for studying the structure of languages or of language;

it is a conviction of mine that the educated person should be aware of how his language really works as a matter of interest, concern, and value in and of itself.

If a knowledge of structure is essential, how are we to go about acquiring it? One thing the linguist has learned is that language—and I think this is true of all cultural systems—must be analyzed and described in and of itself, in terms of its own unique components—its sound, forms, and constructions. Language is language; the kinship system is the kinship system; the technological system is the technological system, and so on. Granted, language uniquely reflects and transmits the other systems of culture, but to try to get at the structure of language through other cultural systems only obscures the structure of all the systems. What I am saying here is that if we want to really understand how language relates to other systems of culture—the usual term for this is "meaning"—we first must know how language itself structures. I am also saying that we can get at meaning *only through structure,* and that we cannot get at *structure* through meaning.

Oftentimes statements like those I have just made are interpreted to the effect that the structuralist isn't interested in meaning; that he allows no room for all of the important values that language study really should carry. Nothing could be further from the truth. It is just because the linguist *is* interested in meaning that he is content to absent himself from felicity awhile. Quite true, he *does* object to meaning-based or philosophy-based attempts to define parts of the language, such as, "A noun is

the name of a person, place, or thing." Such a definition tells us nothing we didn't know, but a *structurally* based definition like, "A noun is a class of words that can be inflected for plural and possessive" *does* tell us something, particularly if we define our other word classes with similar criteria.

STRUCTURE OF SPOKEN ENGLISH

Since the linguist is aware that to understand the written language he must first understand the structure of the spoken language, and since he knows that traditional grammar is based on the literary language recorded in an incomplete and inconsistent writing system, he must first concern himself with completeness of description and consistency of description of the spoken language. This means he must know all the significant classes of sounds (phonemes) of the language and how these group themselves into words, constructions, and sentences. Failure to see all the significant entities at any level obscures the understanding of the structuring of each succeeding level. Rigorously, step by step, level by level, the linguist must advance, going to the next higher level for unanalyzed data to be treated systematically on the level that concerns him. Thus if we are concerned with phonemes, we go to words for our data, knowing that only when we have all our phonemes can we understand the structure of our words. To study our word-classes or parts of speech, we get our data from unanalyzed groups of words, knowing that only when we know how our words are classified can we attempt an analysis of occurrences of more than one word. To understand the patterning of constructions and sentences, we go to unanalyzed *discourse* for our data, building each set of statements on those that have gone before.

Throughout this technical and laborious process, the linguist classifies and arranges the data step by step, level by level, operating on the principle that certain events are the same as others and certain are different. Thus the word *pin* is determined as not the same as the word *bin* by virtue of the contrast between the initial phonemes, /p/ and /b/, not because one means a shiny, pointed metal object and the other a place to put coal or grain. By this procedure, the first sound in *pin* and the second sound in *spin,* even though they differ in quite a few respects, are classified as members of the same /p/ phoneme, since all "p's" *automatically* sound like the "p" in *spin* when an "s" precedes. And as a further check, the linguist finds that "k's" and "t's" pattern or "behave" in the same way.

Through the application of the criteria for establishing the phoneme classes the linguist finally arrives at an inventory for English which includes twenty-one consonants, nine short vowels, three semi-vowels (y, w, h), four significant degrees of loudness or *stress,* four significant levels of *pitch,* three *terminal junctures,* or ways to end stretches of utterance, and an *internal* or *plus* juncture, which is an open transition between vowel and/or consonant phonemes and contrasts with a normal or smooth transition.

Of the forty-five phonemes in the over-all pattern of English, I have time to exemplify only the stresses and the internal juncture and to examine how these phonological structure-points enter into patterns on the

higher levels of the linguistic structure. The functioning of these patterns has only recently been understood but at long last we have the basis for a truly systematic statement of many aspects of English grammar.

The four stresses are generally designated *primary* ('), *secondary* (ˆ), *tertiary* (`), and *weak* (ˇ). All four can be distinguished in the following examples:

1. Líght + hoùse + keêper (keeper of a light-house).
2. Lìght + hoúse + keèper (one who does light house-keeping).
3. Lìght + hóuse + keèper (a housekeeper light in weight).
4. A nêw + Yórker / is not a Nèw + Yórker.
5. Lòng + Ísland / is a lông + ísland.

The internal or plus juncture—versus the normal transition—can be heard in the following set of items, with normal transition exemplified first:

nítràte; níght + ràte; dýe + tràde

PHONOLOGY AND GRAMMAR

Now the combinations of patterns of these stresses and transitions are, as I have mentioned, the very blood and bone of English grammar. The way in which words are coupled, so to speak, in terms of the stresses they bear on either side of the juncture between them is the basis of how we can tell "what goes with what." But first we must draw the distinction between one word and more than one word. A single *word* in English is defined as having only one *base,* though it may have a *prebase*—usually called a "prefix"—and a number of *postbases,* or "stem-forming suffixes." These postbases then may be followed by *grammatical* or *inflectional* suffixes— the "endings" of nouns, verbs, and pronouns. Then each word, to be complete, must have a *stress pattern* or *word superfix*. Thus *bóyishnesses* is one word, consisting of the base *boy*— combined with the postbases *-ish-* and *-ness-*, terminated by the plural "ending" *-es* and completed by the stress pattern of primary stress followed by these weak stresses. But an item like *Whíte + Hoùse,* though it refers to a single, easily identified object in the culture outside the language, is not one word but two, since it combines two bases. *Whíte + Hoùse, whìte + hoúse, sêldom + rùns, rûns + séldom, sét + ùp, sèt + úp, úp + sèt, ùp + sét, a + bóy; táke'im* are all phrases, and the composition of phrases is in the province of *syntax.*

Before he can study phrases, the linguist must first have determined his *word classes,* or "parts of speech," which are determined in a language like English on the basis of which words can take inflectional suffixes. Only three such classes can be so set up for English—nouns, verbs, and pronouns; all other words are classified as *uninflectible.* It is in the classification of the uninflectible words that a complete phonology can be of the greatest help to us, and such a phonology—one that includes stresses and junctures— also gives us the clue to the way in which all these words—inflected and uninflectible alike—pair with each other. For the *key* to the phrase is that it always includes two parts; it is a binary arrangement. The *clue* to the phrase is the *phrase superfix,* a combination of *one* primary stress, one internal juncture or a normal transition, and another stress, not a primary. In other words, the word superfix may give up its primary stress when it enters into a phrase. Thus the word *white* combined with the word *house* (each with primary stresses) when put together under the phrase superfix of the shape '+' results in the phrase Whíte + Hoùse.

There are two kinds of phrases, the *constructs* and the *constructions.* The constructions are formed by phrase superfixes that have a *secondary* stress with their primary stress, and the constructs *never* have a secondary stress. Thus *gôod + bóy, Jôhn + rán, rûns + fást, sêt + úp* are all *constructions: úp + sèt, ùp + sét, sèt + úp, sét + ùp, ă + bóy, táke 'îm* are all *constructs.* Constructs may include constructions and *vice versa.* Thus the *construction gôod + bóy* can be combined with the word *a* under the construct superfix ⌣+' to result in the *construct ă + (gôod + bóy).* Further layerings of constructs and constructions can be exemplified by the utterance fraction *ă + nêw + áir + ràid + wàrden + pôst.* Here the procedure is to go first to the *internal* construct and follow the principle of binary composition throughout, always going to the end of the composition first. Thus *áir + ràid* is a construct under '+', the word *warden* is combined with *áir + ràid* under the construct superfix '+' to give the construct *(áir + ràid) + wàrden.* Then the construct *(áir + ràid + wàrden)* is put together with the word *post* under the construction superfix '+^ to give the nominal construction, *(air + raìd + wàrden + pôst).* Then going to the front of the composition, the word *new* is now combined with the construction *(áir + ràid + wàrden + pôst)* under the construction superfix `^+'` with the result, (*nêw + aîr + ràid + wàrden + pôst*). Finally the combination of constructs and constructions is combined with the word *a* under the *construct* superfix `ᵕ+'` and we have the construct *ă +* (*nêw + aîr + ràid + wàrden + pôst*). You will note the procedure has been purely mechanical; the *immediate constituents* of the utterance fraction have been established in a definite order and relationship, and every phonological juncture and stress has been assigned a syntactic role. No recourse to referential meaning has been resorted to, no pure "hunches" as to "what goes with what" have been followed.

As I mentioned earlier, the phrase superfix provides us with a means of classifying uninflectable words. For example, *of, in, out, up, to, our, down,* etc., have been classed both as "prepositions" and "adverbs" in such ways that only confusion has resulted. To "define" these words is extremely difficult; to *identify* them is extremely simple. If one of these uninflectable words enters into a *construction* it is an *adverbial* ("adverb," if you will). If it appears in a construct, it is a *prepositional*. Thus in *sét, + ùp, sèt + úp, úp + sèt,* and *ùp + stáirs, up* is a prepositional. In the construction *wént + úp, up* is an adverbial.

By further examination we find that nouns and verbs enter ultimately into constructions—the *subject-verb* construction or the *verb-object* construction (*Jóhn + rán, hît + Bíll*). Words that have been traditionally called adjectives and adverbs also appear only in constructions—prenominal, preverbal; adnominal and adverbal (e.g., *gôod + bóy, sêldom + rúns; trîp + abróad, rân + fást*). Pronouns in sub-

ject, object, or possessive cases appear almost without exception in constructs. The so-called relatives, interrogatives, and demonstratives form an interesting class of words (and constructs) which appear both under construct and construction superfixes.

I wish time permitted my going into the function of the intonation patterns—pitches and terminal junctures. I can only say that these give us the phonological basis for another syntactic pattern—the *arrangement,* and here we can handle perfectly mechanically such old bug-bears as the "dangling participle" and the "restrictive" and "non-restrictive" clauses. Suffice it to say in conclusion that syntax is dependent on phonology, or, to put it another way, just in so far as our phonology is incompletely understood, analyzed, and inventoried, so will our understanding of the composition of words, phrases, constructions, and sentences be incomplete. Not only will it be incomplete, but we will be forced to use criteria from *discourse* to make statements on the level of syntax. Much that is unsatisfactory in both traditional grammar and in recent linguistically oriented "positional grammar" or "pattern grammar" lies in the fact that a clear-level distinction between syntax and discourse analysis has not been made. For instance, such terms as "modification," "question sentence," "intransitive," "transitive," "direct object," "indirect object," "object complement," "statement," and so on are not matters of syntax but of the *distributional patterns* that are the concern of discourse. For example, *syntactically,* "John made Bill money" and "John made Bill captain" are identical, but on the level of discourse, the terms "indirect object," "direct object," and "object complement" are useful in making distinctions between *distributional* occurrences both within the sentence and between sentences in the discourse under analysis. To sum up, syntax stops with the syntactic analysis of the syntactic sentence or sentence fraction; discourse analysis concerns itself with further classification of relationships within the sentence and with distributional patterns of sentences and sentence fractions in actual discourse, spoken or written. From this last vantage point perhaps we can really tackle meaning!

For discussion

A. Draw a line *under* each *base* in the following, a line *over* each *derivational* suffix, and a line *through* each *inflectional* suffix in the following:

lawyers	school teachers
containment	rudest
outside	psycholinguists
authorize	relamizations
obscenities	Broadway
chickens	polysyllables
deadlier	fearlessly
reading	perpendiculous
journalistically	monographs
disappointed	lengthwise

B. Indicate the primary stress in each of the above.

C. Which of the above would satisfy the definition for single words in Smith's analysis?

D. On p. 188 Smith writes that three word classes can be determined by the inflectional suffixes they may take. Which items in the above list may be assigned to form classes on this basis?

E. Smith writes on p. 186 that to understand the written language the linguist must first understand the structure of the spoken language. How, according to Smith, does he acquire the understanding?

F. Mark the primary stress in each of the following. Then arrange them into two lists, one of *constructs* and one of *constructions*. You will have to use your own pronunciations as a guide, but the class results should be reasonably uniform. Assume normal pronunciation. For instance, in pronouncing "soapy water," *water* would normally receive more stress than *soapy,* though matters would be reversed if you were interested in conveying the idea that the water was not *clear,* but *soapy.* ("This is not clear wâter; it's soápy wâter.")

able man	red cap
cable car	redcap
goes out	growing boy
cook out	growing pains
pretty flower	sleeping pill
passion flower	sleeping beauty
new paper	brief case
newspaper	briefcase
flying field	broad way
flying Dutchman	Broadway

G. Indicate which of the italicized items in the following are adverbial and which are prepositional:

look *out*	sit *in*
look *out*	bréak *out*
drôp *in*	brêak *out*
rùn *down*	*in*sight
rûn *down*	*in* sight

OWEN THOMAS

Generative grammar: toward unification and simplification

THE WORK OF CHARLES FRIES, of Smith and Trager, and of many other grammarians makes a number of assumptions about what must be involved in the description of a language. Analysts are committed to each of these assumptions in varying degree, and their practice has not always followed their theory. Nevertheless, we may say that in the twenty-five years after the publication of Leonard Bloomfield's *Language* in 1933, American linguistics worked with the following assumptions:

1. The description of a language must be based upon a corpus, for instance, the Fries collection of telephone conversations.

2. Any utterance of a native speaker of a language that appears in the corpus must be described and is, therefore, in a sense grammatical. As Smith says, "Every linguistic event is data to be described and analyzed."

3. Faust and Smith indicate—and many contemporary textbooks of grammar show— that a grammar is a description of three sets of patterns in the corpus: phonological, morphological, and syntactic.

4. The description of a language involves dealing in succession with the phonology, the morphology, and the syntax. There is an additional assumption that one must not mix levels; for example, the syntax must not be called in to help describe the phonology. This assumption, however, is understood and discussed in varying ways.

5. There is (or it is possible to develop) a mechanical procedure for revealing the grammar of a language, such as Smith's use of superfixes to define structures and some of the parts of speech.

6. The importance of a structure may be judged by the frequency with which it occurs.

7. Language is binary. Any structure is divisible into two immediate constituents, as Smith points out. This assumption also is understood and discussed in a variety of ways.

8. There is no reason to consider that some structures are basic and some derived, that, for instance, the active voice underlies the passive.

"Generative Grammar: Toward Unification and Simplification": From *The English Journal,* vol. 51, n. 2, February 1962, pp. 94–99, p. 113. Reprinted with the permission of The National Council of Teachers of English and Owen Thomas. Some of the original footnotes from the article have been omitted here.

Scholars worked with a number of other assumptions, too, but they follow naturally from the ones mentioned here. Within a generation American linguistics, though concentrating heavily on phonology and morphology at the expense of syntax, developed a reputation as the most mature discipline among the behavioral sciences. Its influence became powerful, not only in anthropology (of which it is properly a branch) but also in psychology, history, philosophy, literary criticism, medicine, and, of course, the English curriculum. And though it usually takes a long time for the most advanced developments in a discipline to find their way into classroom texts, the normal cultural lag was dramatically abridged by the publication in 1956 of a high school text and a Freshman English text based upon structural linguistics.

In 1957, Noam Chomsky's *Syntactic Structures* rejected and replaced every one of the above assumptions:

1. The native speaker of English is a fertile source of examples of his own language. To limit him to a corpus other than himself is to sacrifice a chance for much valuable information. Every grammarian knows this, whether his theory suggests it or not.

2. Our frequent inability to manipulate properly any but the simplest English structures shows that we are not invariably grammatical in any meaningful sense of the word.

3. If we stop our analysis after describing the phonology, morphology, and syntax, we have perhaps organized our materials; but we have not produced a grammar. A grammar must specify the sentences in a language.

4. The sentence, rather than the sound, is the natural and proper place to begin work on a grammar.

5. Methodology, far from being a machine for discovering truth, is only a tentative way of looking for it. The scientist finds truth by hypothesis and deduction, and frequently cannot even describe the steps by which he has arrived at it.

6. No one has ever shown any statistical correlation between frequency of occurrence and grammatical importance. Fortunately few of us ever use such simple minded sentences as *Dogs bark*. These can be found in beginning language texts, and grammatically they are of great importance because they are usually kernel sentences around which elaborate statements are built.

7. Language can be considered binary only at certain levels.

8. The attraction of economy suggests that we think of *A dollar was found by him* as being structurally related to *He found a dollar*.

Syntactic Structures has naturally inspired much comment and study. In the next article, by Owen Thomas of the University of Indiana, some of Chomsky's points are reviewed.

Professor Thomas uses the experience of one of his summer classes to demonstrate that (a) there is little agreement on much of anything in traditional grammar; (b) everyone except the traditional grammarian points this out all the time; (c) nevertheless, traditional terminology is useful; (d) the structuralists, whether they are emphasizing syntactic patterns or phonological patterns, are difficult and demanding; (e) students resist descriptions that emphasize stress, pitch, and juncture, and immediate constituent parsing, and prefer descriptions that emphasize the sentence; and (f) the transformational–generative grammar of Noam Chomsky and others is understandable, convincing, and practical.

As summer school classes go, this one went pretty far, and one may conclude that, on the whole, things seem simpler in Indiana than in many other places. Nevertheless, we may take advantage of Professor Thomas's good luck to present a first answer to some questions: How does Chomsky define "grammar"? Which part is most closely related to the work discussed in the four previous essays? What is the position of definition in a transformational-generative grammar What is meant by "rule" in such a grammar?

The grammatical theories of Noam Chomsky, Morris Halle, and their followers are widely discussed but only rarely, if at all, are they applied to the teaching of English grammar in secondary schools. The reasons for this lack of application are many, varied, and complex, and even the primary reasons make an almost overwhelming list:

1. Chomsky, the generally acknowledged leader of the group, published the original statement of the theory less than ten years ago, and, consequently, the development of the theory is still in its early stages.

2. The explications of his theory have been directed more toward linguists, psychologists, and mathematicians than toward teachers of English grammar.

3. The criticisms of his theory by other linguists have generated more heat than light, and most secondary school teachers—who, after all, neither are nor need be linguists—have prudently rejected the opportunity to be burned.

4. The secondary school teacher, even if he should be curious, has no effective way of satisfying his curiosity since, almost without exception (according to the two-score catalogues I checked), departments of English offer no courses in comparative grammar.

Unfortunately, these reasons (and I have idealistically ignored the inertia of school boards and the conservatism of traditionally trained parents) have caused many teachers of English to assume that generative grammar—though perhaps "correct" in some mathematical sense—is pedagogically unadaptable to the needs of a secondary school curriculum.[1] Such an assumption, I feel, is false.

This personal feeling is based largely upon the response to a course, "English Grammar for Teachers," that I conducted in the summer of 1961 at Indiana University. The thirty students in the class were of widely varying backgrounds and experience. Some had just completed their second year of college work; others had been teaching for more than twenty years. All of them, however, although they didn't know it until the end of the eight-week session, were subjects in an experiment that the liberal adminis-

[1] The terms "transformational grammar" and "generative grammar" are sometimes used interchangeably. The latter term, however, seems to be supplanting the former. This trend was particularly noticeable at the recent (summer 1961) meeting of the Commission on English which debated some of the questions considered in this article.

tration of Indiana University permitted me to conduct. Briefly, and this is something of an over-simplification, we hoped to answer one question: what do secondary school teachers—not professional linguists—think of generative grammar?

The answer proved the validity of the question. Without exception, the students were convinced that certain deductions from the theories of Chomsky could be applied systematically to the teaching of grammar, not only in the secondary school but with an equal effectiveness in the elementary school.

Because of the unanimity of class opinion, it seems worthwhile to examine the structure of the course. Purposely, no text was assigned for general use during the first four weeks. Purposely also, the initial lectures were devoted to the history of the language and to the development of grammatical studies during the eighteenth and nineteenth centuries. The course, in short, was made to appear as non-controversial as possible. As a supplement to the lectures, the students were given daily assignments: "memorize the eight parts of speech, the four kinds of sentences, the six kinds of pronouns, and the four kinds of adjectives; diagram ten sentences; conjugate three verbs." Every Friday was given over to an informal clinic where we discussed the work of the preceding week. For the students, the initial clinic was a nearly shattering experience. Controversy forced its way into the syllabus.

TRADITIONAL GRAMMAR EXAMINED

Since no single text was assigned, the students had necessarily sought their definitions and diagraming rules in different books; without exception, these books were "traditional." The marked lack of agreement among these books (many of which were texts currently being used in various school systems) was surprising and, for most students, disconcerting. Some texts defined eight parts of speech; others admitted only seven (dismissing or ignoring the interjection). Some presented purely semantic definitions ("A noun is the name of a person, place, or thing"); others made a half-hearted bow toward structural definitions ("A noun is a word that names something"); and still others tried to combine the two types ("A noun is a word used to name a person, place, or thing"). Some listed four kinds of pronouns; others, six; and one, bravely, twelve. Some diagraming rules (which a few texts quietly ignored) called for left-slanting lines, some for right-slanting lines, some for perpendicular lines, and some for dashed lines. The students soon concluded that the traditionalists were not united, even on basic definitions, that—in fact—there was no single traditional grammar.

The second two weeks of the course were spent in determining why this lack of agreement existed. The lectures continued to be historical, although somewhat more controversial, and emphasized the contributions of Otto Jespersen, Holger Pedersen, Edward Sapir, and Leonard Bloomfield. Meanwhile, the students were consulting the initial chapters (those generally devoted to debunking the traditionalists) in works by structural linguists such as Charles C. Fries, James Sledd, and Harold Whitehall. These analyses, particularly Sledd's concise discussion, convinced the students that the inconsistencies of traditional grammar were fundamental. But curiously, the Friday clinic revealed that their initial dissatisfaction with the traditionalists was somewhat tempered, and they agreed (with Sledd) that traditional grammar—although Latinate and essentially inadequate to describe English—provides at least a useful terminology.

Probably the most important conclusion reached by the class during this period was that "form underlies meaning."[2]

At this point, and building on this axiom, we began a detailed study of Fries's method, which we supplemented from time to time with definitions taken from Sledd. The class was eager and excited; they expected to find, as they later revealed, a simple, self-consistent system to replace traditional grammar. They had no difficulty in accepting the essentials of Sledd's definitions since they were not aware that "mixing levels" is supposedly the unpardonable sin among structuralists. (They balked slightly, however, when Sledd introduced pitch and stress levels into some of his definitions.) They admitted, in theory, that Fries was right in emphasizing patterns and functions, but they re-

belled, in fact, when we came to a sentence analysis such as the following:[3]

$$D\ 3\ 3\ 1^a\ f\ D\ 1^b\ 4\ 2\ D\ 3\ 1^c\ f\ D\ 1^d\ f\ 2\ f\ 1^e$$
$$-F\quad -\ -\quad -F\quad +J+F-$$
$$it\qquad it\qquad\qquad it\qquad he\ he\qquad it$$

As one student said at a Friday clinic, "The high school pupil who understands *that* doesn't have to study grammar." They felt, in brief, that the cure was worse than the disease.

Thus halfway through the course, the students were wandering through two worlds, "powerless to be born." While in this uncomfortable state, they investigated—during the third two weeks—the pertinent literature in *College English, Educational Forum,* the *English Journal,* and the *NEA Journal.* They found the attacks, counter-attacks, and counter-counter-attacks of the traditionalists and the structuralists. (They found very little on Chomsky.) These investigations convinced them that they were not alone in their confusion and that the structuralists were as divided as the traditionalists, perhaps even more so.

At this point, then, most of the class felt that they could not conscientiously teach traditional grammar: the inconsistencies were too widespread and too basic. But they also felt that structural grammar—even assuming that the disagreements could be resolved—was far too complex to be readily adapted to the needs of secondary school pupils. Furthermore, they were antagonistic toward the emphasis, by the structuralists, on stress, pitch, and juncture, particularly as incorporated in "immediate constituent analysis" which splits the sentence, as one student said, "into a

---

2 This is one of the major points of disagreement between the structuralists and the traditionalists and probably stems (as Fries notes in *The Structure of English,* p. 7) from Jespersen: "But in syntax meaning is everything." Curiously, no traditionalist has noted that William Cobbett—as staunch a traditionalist as ever conjugated a verb—anticipated the structuralists in "Letter XII" of his *Grammar of the English Language* (originally published in 1818 and reprinted by Ward, Lock, & Bowden, Limited, London, n.d.) when he said: "the sense in which a word is used . . . determines what is the part of speech to which it belongs."

3 Fries, *Structure of English,* (1952), p. 268.

hodge of podges." They were, in short, ready for any theory that would justify traditional grammar or simplify structural grammar, particularly (in the latter case) if the theory redirected the emphasis toward the sentence as the most significant part of grammar.

With this attitude, they began their study of generative grammar, using the same text for the first time in the course: Chomsky's *Syntactic Structures*. Within one week they were agreed that his theory provided the necessary simplification of structural grammar (or rather, that his theory was simpler to understand than that of the structuralists) and that the resultant grammar could be adapted readily to the needs of secondary-school students. During the final week of the course, the class experimented —both in and out of class—with applications of Chomsky's theory.

What, then, is the theory? And how can his theory be applied to the teaching of grammar? Before answering these questions, we must consider his definition of grammar: a grammar is a device for generating the sentences of a language. Thus (to belabor the point), if a student understands the grammar of a language, he can construct grammatically correct sentences in that language. No grammar, however, can tell a student which of two grammatically correct sentences is *stylistically* better. Such judgments are outside the realm of grammar; they are solely matters of taste and must be taught accordingly.

"KERNEL" SENTENCES

After having defined the limits of his theory, Chomsky introduces a basic concept: that of a group of "kernel" sentences. A kernel sentence is "simple, active, declarative," and Chomsky feels that "all other sentences" are derived from kernel sentences by means of "transformations." Roughly, a "transformation" is a rule that either introduces new elements into kernel sentences (e.g., adjectives, negatives), or rearranges the elements of a kernel sentence (e.g., to produce an interrogative sentence), or both (e.g., to produce a passive sentence). Chomsky implies, therefore, that passive, interrogative, and negative sentences, and sentences containing, for example, adjectives, adverbs, and conjunctions, are all more complex or "sophisticated" than kernel sentences.

Not surprisingly, Chomsky's "kernel sentence" bears a strong resemblance to the simple "subject-verb-complement" sentence of traditional grammar. He states that a kernel sentence is composed of a "noun phrase plus a verb phrase." A "noun phrase" (symbol: NP) consists simply of an article (T) plus a noun (N), and the presence of the article is optional.[4] A "verb phrase" (VP) consists of an auxiliary (Aux) plus a main verb (V) plus a noun phrase (and this last "noun phrase" is of course, similar to the traditional "complement"); the noun phrase contained within the verb phrase is also optional. This may seem confusing at first reading, but the symbolic representation is straightforward and easy to understand:[5]

[4] More properly, I feel, the "article" should be called a "determiner" according to a definition such as that of Sledd in *A Short Introduction to English Grammar*, p. 207.

[5] This is the simplest possible presentation. Copyright laws being what they are, we cannot duplicate the presentation, and it must suffice to say that those rules, for example, pertaining to "noun phrase singular" (NP_s) are equally explicit, self-consistent, and easy to understand.

Sentence → NP + VP (where the arrow means "rewrite," i.e., "rewrite Sentence as NP plus VP")
NP → T + N
VP → Aux + V + NP

Thus, the following are "noun phrases":

> John, the boy, a dog, the men

And the following are "verb phrases":

> reads, eats the apple, may bury a bone, have bought the farm

Therefore, the following are "kernel sentences":

> John reads.
> The boy eats the apple.
> A dog may bury a bone.
> The men have bought the farm.

Chomsky thus simplifies the descriptions of English (such as that from Fries, quoted above) by limiting these descriptions to a relatively small number of simple sentences. All other sentences are "generated from" (i.e., built upon) these kernel sentences by applying certain constant and *invariable* transformations, and the constancy of the transformation is, for most teachers of English, a major feature of Chomsky's theory.

Thus, given a kernel sentence (e.g., "The men have bought the farm"), we may generate a passive sentence ("The farm has been bought by the men"), a negative sentence ("The men haven't bought the farm"), a "yes-or-no" interrogative sentence ("Have the men bought the farm?"), two "who-" interrogative sentences ("What have the men bought?" and "Who has bought the farm?"), and even combinations of these sentences (e.g., a negative-passive: "The farm hasn't been bought by the men"). Furthermore, with still

other transformations we may introduce adverbs, adjectives, and prepositional phrases into any or all of these sentences ("Who has finally bought the old farm on the hill?").[6]

These transformations, it is worth repeating, are invariable. Given a kernel sentence of a particular form (and Chomsky defines the required form precisely), then any and all related non-kernel sentences can be generated by applying the appropriate (and quite simple) transformation. One specific example will serve to illustrate these remarks. The "passive transformation" may be given in the following form:

To derive a passive sentence, we first need a kernel "string" containing the following elements: a noun phrase (NP), an auxiliary (Aux), a verb (V), and a second noun phrase (NP). These might be represented as follows:

$$[NP_1] + [Aux] + [V] + [NP_2]$$

To transform this string into a "passive string," the four basic elements are rearranged and three other elements are invariably added, as follows:

$$[NP_2] + [Aux] + be + en + [V] + by + [NP_1]$$

(The "en" which is added is the so-called "past participle morpheme.")

---

[6] There is quite obviously a relationship between Chomsky's kernel sentences and simple traditional diagraming, and even between those transformations which add adjectives and phrases to the kernel and those diagrams which indicate the subordinate position of adjectives and phrases. Transformations, however, indicate the exact nature of subordination; more importantly, they indicate the exact nature of the relationship between a kernel sentence and the associated passive, negative, and interrogative sentences.

Finally, the resultant string is converted into an English sentence by inserting appropriate parts of speech into the string.

Thus, given the kernel sentence:

[The man] + [has] + [eaten] + [the apple]

we may apply the transformation to produce:

[The apple] + [has] + be + en + [eaten] + by + [the man]

This, of course, reduces to: "The apple has been eaten by the man."[7]

Such is the nature of Chomsky's major contribution toward the simplification of grammar. In addition, he makes another, quite important contribution: he divides all of grammar into three parts. The first part presents those rules that pertain to kernel sentences ("phrase structure"), and here his theory will certainly draw upon the work of the structuralists. The second part presents rules that generate non-kernel sentences ("transformational structure"). And the third part presents the rules that are necessary to account for such irregular forms as "child, children" and "buy, bought" ("morphological structure"), and this part of his theory will probably draw upon the work of the historical grammarians (e.g., Jespersen).

The theory, then, is not too difficult for an adult to understand. And most persons acquainted with Chomsky's work, including the members of my

[7] For purposes of illustration, the transformation, as given, is somewhat simplified as the reader may see for himself by substituting, for example, a plural subject or object into the kernel. Such refinements, however, are easily and systematically handled through certain so-called "obligatory" transformations. The principle, at any rate, is invariable.

class, feel that his theories provide the only logical explanation currently available for the intuitive sense which most native speakers have of a relationship between active and passive, or positive and negative, or declarative and interrogative sentences. But we may legitimately ask whether transformations can be taught to secondary school pupils. This is essentially the same question we asked above: "how can Chomsky's theory be applied to the teaching of grammar?" To answer this question completely would be to write a text, or at least a syllabus, for a course on methods of teaching grammar. Obviously, nothing of that sort is being attempted here. But during the final meetings of my class, we reached agreement on a number of points that will probably be included in any text that is written.

APPLICATION TO SENTENCE STRUCTURE

We agreed, for example, that the study of grammar has one primary function: to enable a student to construct grammatically correct sentences. The most significant advance that an understanding of Chomsky's theory permits is the organization of this study according to increasing ("graduated") levels of sophistication in sentence construction. Thus, we should first teach the use of the kernel sentence (terminology is unimportant and should be subordinate to an understanding of the kernel form, i.e., to an understanding of a sentence that is "simple, declarative, active, with no complex verb or noun phrases"). The following sentences are typical kernel sentences:

The boy hit the ball.
The girl bought the dress.
The teacher ate the apple.
John loves Mary.

Conversely, the following sentences are *not* kernel sentences:

The ball was hit by the boy.
The girl didn't buy the dress.
Did the teacher eat an apple?
Who loves Mary?

Secondary school pupils, the class agreed, could construct kernel sentences of their own. Next they could be taught to construct passive sentences from their kernels, then, negative sentences, "yes-or-no" interrogative sentence, and "wh-" interrogative sentences. At each step, the teacher can point out the recurring elements of the resultant sentences (i.e., the underlying form). The repetition would familiarize the student—unconsciously, perhaps, but nonetheless effectively—with the basic form, and the ordering of the exercise—in gradually increasing levels of complexity—would enable the student to build his confidence systematically.

Students may then combine their sentences, for example the passive and the negative (and the teacher may note that the passive is formed before the negative is added). After (and sometimes during) exercises of this type, the teacher may introduce adjectives, adverbs, and prepositional phrases, noting that any of these may appear in any sentence form.[8]

Of course, in any presentation, certain definitions are required, but the

definitions should be introduced only when they are necessary, that is, only when a student needs a "label" to discuss the elements he is, in fact, using. Thus, "noun" and "verb" should be defined when the students are being taught the form of the kernel sentence. (I feel Sledd's definitions are quite appropriate.) In this way, those parts of speech that are simplest to define (and for the student to understand) are taught first, and the hard-to-define (and to understand) parts of speech as the "preposition" and the "conjunction," are postponed until the student has developed familiarity and confidence with the simpler and more important forms.

There are still other benefits to be derived from an understanding of Chomsky's theories. Transformations *per se,* as we have noted, probably cannot be taught to pre-college students; but from *any* transformation a teacher can deduce several invariable rules. For example, from the passive transformation we can deduce such rules as the following (and the list is by no means exhaustive):

1. There can be no passive voice unless a kernel sentence contains a subject and its object.
2. There can be no passive voice without an auxiliary verb or verbs. (If there is only one auxiliary, it must be a form of *to be.*)
3. The subject of the kernel sentence invariably follows the verb in the related passive sentence and is invariably introduced with the word "by."
4. The main verb in a passive sentence is invariably in the past participial form.

Similar rules, it is worth repeating, can be derived from any transformation, and the form of the transforma-

---

8 A method such as that advocated by D. M. Wolfe ("Grammatical Autobiography," *English Journal,* XLIX, 1 (January 1960), pp. 16–21) would be quite suitable for this kind of study.

tion guarantees that there are no exceptions to these rules.

In brief, then, Chomsky's theories are not difficult to understand. They are, in fact, a means of systematizing the almost countless "rules" of both traditional and structural grammarians. And most importantly, an understanding of Chomsky's theories permits a teacher to select and arrange grammatical elements in the most logical order and to build effectively upon preceding material. As teachers, we can hardly ask more of any theory.

For discussion

A. Answer the questions in the final paragraph of the introduction to this essay.

B. Some of the following sentences are transforms and some are kernels. Indicate which each is. If the sentence has been transformed, what is the kernel from which it comes?
1. Did John leave?
2. Mays hit another home run.
3. Aaron did not lose his memory.
4. The tall man left town.
5. Louise has not been approved by the board.
6. John may not go.
7. Josephine ran the show.
8. Marie crossed the bridge.
9. Geraldine ran off.
10. The money was spent by Gladys.
11. Where are the beans?
12. Naify has left.
13. Money isn't everything.
14. The farm was sold to Mr. Martin.
15. That problem is to be considered.
16. Alligators are a nuisance.
17. The poor are always with us.
18. Who likes blintzes?
19. The market dropped.
20. Has John gone?
21. Haas was dropped by the Forty-Niners.
22. The horse was led by Albert.
23. Has anyone seen Charlie?
24. Silence is not golden.

C. Given the kernel sentence "Ellie considered the problem," generate:
1. a passive sentence;
2. a "yes-or-no" interrogative sentence;
3. a "what" interrogative sentence;
4. a "who" interrogative sentence;
5. a negative interrogative sentence;
6. a sentence with an adjective in the noun phrase;
7. a sentence with an adjective in the verb phrase;
8. a sentence with one prepositional phrase in the noun phrase and another in the verb phrase.

Related Matters

We turn now to a few matters related to linguistics. Since we are in some way concerned with language when we talk, listen, read, write, think, or dream, the following section might be expected to cover quite a few matters. In a recent book, *The Study of Language: A Survey of Linguistics and Related Discipline in America* (1953), John B. Carroll of Harvard University treats extensively the association of linguistics with psychology, the social sciences, philosophy, education, communication, engineering, and speech. R. H. Robins of the University of London devotes a chapter to the same subjects in *General Linguistics: An Introductory Survey* (1964).

The essays we will now read are a little closer to the English classroom than are the subjects mentioned above, and the insights into language which may be gained from the earlier essays should be of use as we take up a few topics long familiar to all students in language courses—for instance, vocabulary, spelling, and dictionaries. We will also return to dialect geography and see how it can record cultural history, and we shall examine, to some extent, the language of literature. The section concludes with a discussion of linguistic relativity and determinism in a distinguished essay by Benjamin Lee Whorf.

DONALD J. LLOYD AND
HARRY WARFEL

Thirty years to a more powerful vocabulary

THOUGH IT IS WIDELY and quite reasonably believed that large vocabularies and large salaries go together, people who give elaborate attention to building their vocabularies rapidly in the hope that the effort will speed them along in the race for fortune are usually left at the gate. The depressing fact is that there are no "instant" vocabularies and not even any "do-it-yourself" vocabularies except those that are part of a more elaborate project involving education, experience, and time.

In this chapter from their book *American English in Its Cultural Setting*, Donald J. Lloyd (who wrote "The National Mania for Correctness" presented earlier) and Harry Warfel of the University of Florida tell why the instant vocabulary is an illusion. They discuss a number of things about language and about language learning which one does not normally associate with the idea of vocabulary building, and although they do not say so directly, they describe how we acquire our vocabulary formally, informally, and technically, as these terms are used in E. T. Hall's *The Silent Language* and discussed by Marckwardt in "Linguistics and English Composition" (see p. 22). We encounter again the idea that we must interpret the reality of our world in the terms which our language permits us.

Learning English words is quite a different matter from learning the structures of English. There are far more words to learn, particularly in a society like ours which is changing rapidly in almost every aspect and constantly adjusting its vocabulary to match and express the changes. The various speech communities within the English-speaking world do not share all the same words or use them in the same way. No matter how many nouns, verbs, adjectives, and adverbs we know and no matter how many senses we know for these words, there is always a multitude that we have never seen or heard and a multitude of different meanings attached to them. About the structures of English, on the other hand, the speakers of

English are in substantial agreement. Most of us know most of the structures of English and have known them from childhood. Words and their meanings are like the sands along the beach, easily tossed about by winds and waves; the structures are like the rocky backbone of the continent whose alterations have to be measured in centuries.

Popular books like *30 Days to a More Powerful Vocabulary* or *Increase Your Word Power* fool us in two ways: they give us the notion that there is something deficient about our vocabulary and lead us to think that a few more words tossed into it will fix everything up. Studies of the vocabularies of business executives show that they score about as high, for instance, as college professors; and it is probably true, as some people suggest, that you can pick the better of two mechanics by giving them a test on the terms used in their trade. The better mechanic will have a more precise and more extensive knowledge of the language of his trade. A big vocabulary is not a road to success. There is no evidence that the vocabulary comes first. The expert has a big vocabulary because he is experienced and competent.

Command and range of vocabulary and command and range of structures seem to result from two different kinds of ability, separate though not wholly unrelated to each other. In a group of people selected at random from the whole population according to their aptitude for learning words, a few people would come low on the scale, most people would group at the center, and a few people would place high, regardless of where they live, what their education or state of wealth

is, and what the color of their skin. Some people, no matter who or where they are, love to learn the names of things; some learn enough to get along and quit. A hill boy from the Cumberland mountains may relish every local term for farm tools, animals, flowers, trees, and for minute changes of the weather, even without any formal schooling. He may be a walking treasury of words that have never qualified for the dictionary, though they go back to Middle and Old English in a line of descent as honorable as any. A fairly well-off city boy, not much of a word lover but apt at making structures convey his meanings with common familiar terms, can get by with far fewer words quite well. Neither would ring the bell on a standard vocabulary test.

Persons with high I. Q.'s know more words than persons with low I. Q.'s, but that is not surprising, because an important part of the test on which the I. Q. is based is itself verbal. City people show up with higher quotients on these tests than country people, the children of the well-to-do come off better than the children of the poor, and whites do better than non-whites. An only daughter of well-to-do white city dwellers shows up best of all. Small wonder, since the tests are made up by well-to-do white city dwellers and favor their vocabulary. If she were tested on the vocabulary of the poorer non-white country people, she would run a sad race.

No successful means has ever been worked out for measuring a person's total vocabulary, but there has been a good deal of loose talk about vocabulary size. An ordinary person in any society knows about as many words as any other ordinary person in any other society; a gifted person knows more, and a less gifted person knows fewer. The ordinary person in any society has about the same control of structures; the more gifted control more, and the less gifted control fewer. Those gifted with words and those gifted with structures need not be the same people, for structure and vocabulary together express meaning; when you fall short on the one, you lean more heavily on the other. Modern scholars have the uncomfortable suspicion that the ordinary person in any society knows thousands more words than he has ever been given credit for, and that he adds to this store at a rate faster than has ever been calculated. As long as he moves in society he continues to add to his store of words. He probably increases at the fastest rate while he is young—simply because he starts out with none, and because all education is a learning of names for whatever the society finds worth naming. While a youngster is increasing his knowledge by reading, by taking courses, or by putting himself in the way of experience, he cannot fail to increase his vocabulary.

The English language uses many words of foreign origin. Before the eleventh century, English made new words out of native roots and stems, largely by combining materials already in use in the language, because the English-speaking people were relatively isolated on their islands. The Norman conquest which brought French rule to the English began a contact with other cultures which has never ceased. When two speech-communities meet in any kind of regular contact—in trade, in war, in day-to-day interchange of any kind—they trade words. When one society has prestige of any kind over another, the greater flow is from the respected group to the other. When any language is considered worth learning by another people—for its elegance, for the knowledge expressed in it, or for favors to be earned through knowing it—it forms a kind of mine of words to be exploited by the people who see its value. Thus the English-speaking people have borrowed freely from the French, Latin, and Greek, and at particular times for special reasons from German, Italian, Spanish, and most of the languages of the world. Borrowing is the respect that our people have paid to the accomplishments, the prestige, or the power of other nations.

All languages borrow. All languages have within their vocabulary many alien words; English does not differ from other languages in this respect. Since the eleventh century the English-speaking people have preferred to borrow. They came into the modern Global Period[1] of the language with no deep-seated or effective prejudice against borrowing. At all social levels, in all occupational groups, and in all intellectual disciplines the speakers of English drew from strange lands and peoples, from strange cultural complexes, and from strange systems of thought the words that seemed useful. They have borrowed with a more or less imperfect understanding of the other societies and languages, so that often the use of a word in English has little to do with its use in the language

[1] This is Lloyd and Warfel's term to help characterize the English language since about the middle of the sixteenth century, when explorers and settlers took it with them as they spread over the globe. American English, of course, falls entirely within this period.

it came from. They have borrowed into living and compulsive structures of thought and language that have always put their own stamp of meaning and form on the borrowings. Only words of limited use keep their original sound and meaning; once a word catches on and becomes public property it assimilates to English and loses its foreign quality. Thus we cannot distinguish between native and foreign words in use; only the etymologist, patiently checking the history of the word, can tell its origin. Still, the origin of a word has little to say about its present use. A word is, after all, only a slice of an utterance, a sequence of sounds whose meaning is a part of the total meaning of the utterance. All English words in general use are English, regardless of where they came from or when they came. They submit completely to the intentions of the English speech-communities which use them.

English is interesting, however, in having a "léarnèd" vocabulary which is associated mainly with writing and mainly borrowed from Latin, Greek, French, Italian, and German. Educated men and women, set apart from the uneducated by their interest in the arts and sciences and linked by this interest to the educated people of Europe, have an "international" vocabulary which is used, only slightly nationalized, in all the modern languages of Western Europe. As these intellectual disciplines advance, their practitioners (often without much actual knowledge of Latin or Greek) dip into the dictionaries of these languages for roots and stems that they can build into new forms of rather special meaning. Thus we have the "Schenectady Greek" of the electrical and electronics industry and the fancy new coinages of nuclear physics. This "vocabulary of learning" has to be mastered by anyone who wants to understand the arts and sciences: art, music, literature, the criticism and study of art and literature, the physical and biological sciences, the social sciences (anthropology, sociology, economics, history, education, and government), and all kinds of technologies. The prestige of these studies rubs off on the words used in them. Thus we have the peculiar notion that there is some special value in knowing and using "big words" for their own sake. We think we can take a short and easy way to education through word study and vocabulary building, whether or not we know anything about the arts and sciences in which those words are used.

The hard fact is that we talk as we live. Our vocabulary is not a dress that we put on our thoughts to make them socially acceptable. It is something more integral to our thinking. It is a private set of symbols that represent, for each of us, not things in the real world itself but the aspects of the world as we see it. We manipulate these symbols within the structures of the utterance; as long as we are talking to ourselves or within small groups, we can give them any meaning we choose. Thus children who play together often evolve a private language that sounds like gibberish to outsiders; thieves, lawyers, musicians, doctors, and used-car dealers, too, have special jargons that serve communication within the group without tipping off its secrets to the general public. The specific meanings we give to words are private. The meanings are always tied to the emotional circumstances we associate with our learning of the words. Since the normal use of language is in conversation, our employment of these private symbols is always a public matter. When we talk, we talk to other people; we have to come reasonably close to their meanings for our words in order to be understood. A constant cross-checking goes on within each speech-community in conversation, and this give and take of common talk keeps our private meanings for words pretty close to the meanings generally current in the whole group.

Mankind does not create a word and then look about for a meaning to attach to it. A human being is a living, growing, developing organism acting and reacting within total situations, themselves also always in flux. Each person comes to each new situation triply armed: with his own individual personality and character, with his experience in the world and in human society, and with the inherited fabric of his native language. As a person he has a running flow of unexpressed perceptions that are entirely his own. Some of his perceptions have come to other people and have been expressed in words; some of his perceptions could not have come to other men and women because the state of human society did not give rise to them. As John of Salisbury said in the twelfth century, we are pigmies standing on the shoulders of giants; we can see farther than they because they have lifted us up above their level. Each person, as an individual and as a member of human society, is experiencing beyond his own previous experience— often beyond the recorded experiences of other men.

Each person is pressing the language in two ways: he is pressing his own previous expression in language and he is pressing the previous expression of all dead and living users of the language. As far as he can, he uses the inherited vocabulary, nudging its range of meanings into a little wider compass; when that fails or when his knowledge of the inherited vocabulary fails him, he creates a new form to carry his new burden of meaning. In either case his private coinage must meet the public test; if other speakers have the same experience and find his term for it the handiest one to use, then it lives on. The experience may be too private to be communicated and may not be generally repeated. It may be only individually and not generally new, so that terms for it already exist. It may have been related, in ways he has not foreseen, to the general experience of men and women and expressed in familiar terms. Time may have shown it to be merely a partial observation of a whole new set of perceptions. If so, his term may last a while and pass out of use. In any case, vocabulary follows experience; it does not precede it.

Vocabulary building is a long process along two parallel lines. It is in one sense a slow maturing within a society, so that you learn its beliefs, customs, and concerns; and you learn the terms applied to what its necessities make it care about. In the other sense, it is an endless manipulation of these terms in language, of making and hearing utterances, of testing terms in structural patterns, so that you have a fair knowledge of the range of contexts in which each one occurs. This is the dual exploration by which children grow up into their parents' world, as the expanding reach of their senses brings more and more data to their brains. "What's this? What's that?" they ask, touching, handling, listening, and pointing. Their inquisitive minds take the proper order for vocabulary building—first the experience, then the word for it. In the endless chatter and inventive word play of children, the terms find their places in utterances. Children will use and overuse a word to the total distraction of adults, testing its reach in the language system. Their innocent acceptance of the relation between word and thing is wholesome for vocabulary building; children take concepts as given to them, directly and without subtlety. The unlettered adult continues this same uncritical association of word and thing. "Why do you call that thing a ratchet?" "Because that's its *name,* stupid."

Words follow experience. Without experience to tie them to, words are sheer empty verbalisms, sounds without sense. One good way to learn words is to put yourself into the situations where they are used and in the company of the people who use them, so that if you hear a term that is obscure you can ask how it is used and what it means to its users, like a child endlessly inquiring, "What's this, and what is it for?" In a garage you learn the parts of a car and their function; at an airport you learn about an airplane; you learn the vocabulary of art by contemplating works of art and seeking the answers to the questions they raise among artists and critics of art. You learn about drama by going to plays and joining in the talk in the lobby between the acts; you learn about music at concerts, by playing an instrument, by listening to records. You learn the vocabulary of philosophy by facing the problems of philosophy: what is existence, what can we know, and how can we know it?

The way to build your vocabulary is to build your experience, moving much among men and women and taking interest in their interests, with a courteous grave inquiry like that of a child. Before this flattering inquisitiveness the crustiest characters melt; the sailor displays his lines and nets, the mechanic explains the mysteries of a torque wrench or a stroboscopic timer, the scholar takes you through ancient manuscripts and shows you the brilliant illuminations or the rabbit drawn whimsically into a margin. In response to this inquisitiveness factories conduct guided tours, and museums lay out in displays the step-by-step creation of an etching or an epoch of civilization. Object and word go together; to put the two together for the inquiring stranger, a cook, baker, or candlestick-maker will pause in the day's occupations and explain what is what in his line of work. To put object and word together, the picture magazines run photographic essays, often of some grandeur, like "The World We Live In" series in *Life;* and "how-to-do-it" experts publish books and articles telling the novice what is involved in carpentry, bricklaying, or ceramics, and how to do it himself. It is a rare craftsman who brushes off a courteous interest in his craft.

The vocabulary of an educated person must go beyond this naïve sense of the relation of words to things. Words are symbols in language, not for the real world but for our ideas of the world; that is, they stand for concepts. They stand for thoughts, not things, even when they seem to have direct reference to objects. In language they sort into classes—into nouns, verbs, adjectives, and adverbs in English—and then they impose their class-meanings upon our perceptions, so that we see the world in the terms that our language permits. Other languages permit other perceptions; it is possible that if we are ever to get an accurate or complete representation of the world in language, we shall have to develop a super-language of languages, able to draw on the perceptions of all. In the meantime we get by with the perceptions our own language permits, classifying the events of the real world as well as we can within its framework. Our words stand for concepts that our people have developed; which word stands at any one time for which concept is determined by the utterances the words occur in. Our civilization is an elaborate structure of thought based on the relations between concepts; our arts and sciences are ordered statements of these relations. Scholarship as we know it is a professional search for new relations and systems of relations unperceived before.

The various intellectual disciplines that we study in college or out make heavy dependence on words because each one is a system of concepts expressed in words. In art, anthropology, chemistry, physics, biology, law, sociology, history, medicine, and in linguistics, we search for units that have not been perceived before; and when we think we see them, we give them names. We search for new relationships, new arrangements, and all kinds of manifestations other men have missed, and we give them names. Think of words like *gas, vitamin, phoneme, anesthesia,* and *allergy* as representing discoveries made by men whose minds looked into the world and found something new. These men chose or made up words that would let them talk about their discoveries. At the same time the investigators are looking at existing concepts to see whether they are real. Thus *ptomaine, phlogiston, ether,* and *rheumatism* have been examined and found to be grab-basket names for things that should not be classed together or names for things which seemed at first to be real but turned out in the end not to be.

When a student takes an introductory course in psychology, sociology, or physics, he spends a good deal of his time learning words, but not for the sake of his vocabulary. These are old studies in which a good deal of the basic thinking has been done before our time. We have to learn the basic concepts and their names so as to get quickly over what is known and on our way to the frontiers, where the line between what is definitely known and what is definitely not known is a shadowy half-world of the dimly perceived, the half-understood, and the tantalizing fragment.

We learn the basic jargon of each field. We must keep in mind that the persons in the field think that real perceptions of the way things are and work lie behind the jargon and are represented in language by the jargon. Otherwise, we are likely to think that a cute chatter made up of the terms is genuine knowledge. Scientists try to teach us their terms by putting us through the experiments, but we often come to the courses so full of popular misinformation and half-truths and so familiar with the sounds of the words, that we think it is all old stuff and we have nothing to learn. The problem is worse, perhaps, in psychology and sociology, since terms like *stimulus* and *response; personality, mesomorph,* and *other-directed; psyche, libido,* and *inferiority complex* are kicked around so much in public we forget that they have ever been precisely related to careful observations anywhere. As always, experience must come first, then a vocabulary that lets us talk about experience. A big vocabulary is a by-product of maturity.

Taking your body to where things are done is a good way to learn, and to learn words, but it has limitations. This is a big world full of societies of unmeasured antiquity and unimaginable complexity; so many things are going on that even a confirmed globe-trotter cannot look at all of them. Man is distinguished from the beasts by his ability to remember and record his experiences. Our society keeps its records in books; the people concerned with each part of human activity keep the records, many running back several thousand years. We can buy these books and own them for ourselves, or we can read them in libraries. The books can carry us where our bodies cannot go; the wonderful world of books is one we can travel without leaving our chairs. As single persons tied to our daily responsibilities and limited to a short life, we cannot get far beyond what our own five senses bring to us—what we can actually see, hear, touch, taste, and smell. With books our horizons stretch to the limits of the universe, over the whole span of recorded time, and into the minds of men of all eras and all countries. In our daily lives we meet the common run of men and women, but through books we can become acquainted with select men and women,

brilliant minds, daring and inventive discoverers, persons whose good or bad qualities have raised them to special eminence. The experiences we get through reading are just as real and just as much a part of us as those we get through our senses. The words we learn from reading—even if we have never heard them spoken and don't know how to pronounce them—enter our minds as honestly and as vividly as those we hear spoken in conversation.

When we say of a person that he is "well-read," we are saying something nice about him; we are giving him a title of respect. We do not mean merely that he has handled a lot of books of any kind; we mean that he has read books on many subjects and that the books have meant something to him. They have given him knowledge, and he has transmuted the knowledge in his own mind into wisdom. He knows a great deal, and he has thought about what he knows. He can enter into conversation with experts about their specialties. They recognize at once that he is using their language in their way. He understands how they feel about their work. But he has not read so as to become a bright and universal conversationalist; he has read for his own needs, his own development, and his own better knowledge about human beings in the world they live in. Of course he has a big vocabulary, and he uses it to think with, not as words only but as the tools of thought. There is no other worth-while use for a big vocabulary.

Standing in a library and looking at the thousands or millions of books, a youngster thinks: "How can I ever read all these?" Of course he cannot read them all. They are not all there for him, any more than all the bread, pies, and cakes in a bakery are all for him. The library serves many needs; it tries to have some books for almost everybody. The staff hopes that it can serve him by having all the books that he needs, or by telling him where he can find the books it does not have. His next question is, "Where shall I begin?" Of course he is not beginning; he already has a good deal of reading behind him. What he means is probably, "Where shall I start now to read the books that will be of the most use to me?" That question can be answered: start by reading the books that writers read.

What are those books? To begin with, there are six: the Bible, the plays of Shakespeare, Bulfinch's *Mythology,* Homer and the Greek plays, and Ruth Benedict's *Patterns of Culture.* Each person trying to become educated should own these books and have them on his own shelf, along with a good dictionary or two. He cannot know these six books too well. They are valuable to him because they are well-known, especially to people who write, so that other books are constantly referring to them. The human weakness that we have noticed before—our way of assuming that everybody knows what we know, except for the particular thing we are trying to explain at the moment—makes writers assume that everybody knows these books so well that it is safe to echo them, cite them, and reflect them in their writing. When Sigmund Freud, the great student of sick minds, thought he saw a complicated reaction of a son toward his father, a mixture of love, hate, and jealous competition for the affection of the mother, he cast about for something to call it. He chose a name from the Greek plays, the name of a king who had killed his father and married his own mother. He called it the Oedipus complex, confident that other people, too, knew the plays and would get his point.

Long before the Authorized Version of the English Bible appeared in 1611, the people of England had sneaked their translations and passed them from hand to hand. They read them in secret, often in great danger, hiding them from outsiders and poring over them by candlelight behind locked doors. The Bible meant to them the ordinary person's assertion of his right to know at first hand the word of God. The Roman Church published a Catholic Bible in English, the Rheims-Douai Version (1580–1610). From that time on, the English-speaking peoples have known and loved and studied the Bible. Both versions were quite beautiful in their phrasing, and so not only the Bible stories but the very twists and turns of language used in their telling have entered into our way of talking and writing and have become part of us. When William Jennings Bryan said, "You shall not crucify mankind upon a cross of gold," arguing merely about a gold standard for our money, he was talking to people who could be stirred deeply by the reference. Therefore, if for no better reason than to understand what you read, you need to know the Bible. You cannot know it too well.

About the same time, William Shakespeare was writing his plays. Even then the English-speaking peoples knew that they had something good. The plays have been acted and re-enacted, published and republished ever since; like the language of the Bible, the language of Shakespeare has become part of our heritage. For three and a half centuries, educated people have known them so well and have assumed that everybody knows Shakespeare so well that they freely quote, cite, and refer to the plays in their writing. You should buy those plays and read them, and you should do more; whenever any group of actors, no matter how good or bad, puts on a Shakespearean play in the movies, on the stage, or over television you should be there to see and hear them as dramatic performances, so that you can hear the living words of Shakespeare as he meant them to be heard—spoken by living men and women before an audience. You cannot know them too well.

Thomas Bulfinch's *The Age of Fable* (1855), often given the title *Mythology*, contains much of what we have left of the Classical tradition. Once all educated men and women knew Latin, and many of them knew Greek. They started the practice that still goes on of referring frequently and easily to Venus and Adonis, Aphrodite, Jupiter, Juno, Theseus and the Minotaur, Diana the Huntress, and Hercules the strong man. Bullfinch gathered all these myths up into a kind of dictionary and told them in brief and interesting form. Even if we know no more of Greece and Rome than we learn from Bulfinch, we at least know precisely what is being referred to when someone cites or quotes one of the ancient tales.

Homer's two rousing good stories about the Trojan War have been loved and read, quoted and translated since at least eight hundred years before Christ. Technically they are epic poems; but for our purpose, which is to understand better what we read, we can treat them as novels. The *Iliad* tells of Paris and Helen, Hector and Achilles, the siege of Troy, and the battles around the Greek beachhead before the city. It is still considered (especially by soldiers) the greatest war story of all time. The *Odyssey* tells of Odysseus' (Ulysses') ten-year struggle to get back home to Penelope in spite of battles, monsters on land and sea, and luscious and loving ladies who just liked to have him around. You can get these books in good, cheap, modern translations; they are interesting in and for themselves and they make good reading; more important, they are known and loved by authors who freely refer to them and assume that they can use them to make their points clear. They are keys to better reading.

The Greek plays of Sophocles, Aeschylus, and Euripides, which date from about 300 B.C., have been studied with few lapses since that time because of their deep insights into the acts and motives of men and women in trouble. In present-day terms they are good psychology besides being good drama; modern authors know them well and draw on them for references. They are still being acted in college, on Broadway and in the commercial theater, and on television. They have been used in operas. We have many good translations of them. They are quite short and easy and interesting to read, and they will leave you somewhat more civilized; the value in them which concerns us here is that they bring you better informed to other reading and better able to cope with it.

Ruth Benedict's *Patterns of Culture*

(1934) is a book that introduced the general public to the work of cultural anthropologists. It is a beautifully written display of the patterns of conduct within which members of human communities live, illustrated by the Pueblo culture of the American Southwest, the evil-magic-dominated society of the Dobu people of the Pacific, and the Kwakiutl Indians of the Pacific Northwest, with their wacky economic system that seems like a travesty of our own. From these groups Miss Benedict draws wise and penetrating extensions to the more complex society we live in. Sometimes called "cocktail anthropology," *Patterns of Culture* has become widely known, and it has introduced a general audience to the concepts of anthropology without swamping them in detail. Knowledge of it gives you a "stance" from which to cope with other modern works of history, economics, and sociology. You can get it in a paperbacked edition.

These six books can lead you to other books which give you a general cultural background. They touch all the arts and sciences at many points. You could find most or all of them on a list of ten best books such as people often make up, or a list of fifty or a hundred. (If you could carry only ten books with you to a desert island, one of the ten should be a notebook with blank pages in which you could set down your own thoughts.) People often find it worth while to find a list of a hundred great books, and systematically stock their shelves with

them in preparation for those long winter evenings when no company comes, the television breaks down, and there is nothing to do but read. You can find such lists in a book which is surely the reader's best friend, *Good Reading,* a volume published by the New American Library as a Mentor Book at fifty cents. The latest edition is a handy guide to more than 1250 books arranged by subject, with a comment on the nature and quality of each one. With this volume in your hand, you can read your way into any subject, from the older, standard books to the latest works just out.

The road to a big vocabulary is a long one, occasionally hard enough but pleasant and rewarding. It is not worth taking if you only want to dazzle your friends in conversation; people don't dazzle easily and they expect to have their say, too. If your aim is to walk the earth as an educated man or woman, at home and at ease with modern civilization, able to learn and teach as all educated men and women must, able to express yourself in terms that your hearers can understand and respect, then this is the road. Go through your days with an alert, sympathetic, inquiring mind, letting the people you meet teach you what they know; use your private hours to extend your acquaintance with men and affairs through reading. In thirty years or so you will have a more powerful vocabulary, and it will be where power must be to be of use to you—in your mind, available and at your command.

For discussion

A. Why are learning English words and learning English structures quite different matters?

B. Lloyd and Warfel write that "Command and range of vocabulary and command and range of structures seem to result from two different kinds of ability, separate though not wholly unrelated to each other." What are the two kinds of ability?

C. Lloyd and Warfel refer to coinages from Greek in the electronics industry as Schenectady Greek, because Schenectady is a center of the electrical business. We may also speak of Cape Kennedy Greek. Try to work out the meaning of the following—take advantage of the fact that your dictionary defines many prefixes and suffixes: *translunar space, agravic, photosphere, bioastronautics, jetavator, magnetohydrodynamics,* and *spatiography.*

D. The authors mention a number of different ways in which one's vocabulary grows. Using the terminology that Marckwardt borrows from Edward Hall's *The Silent Language,* which of these ways result from formal learning? From informal learning? from technical learning?

E. List as many words as you can in one of your own special vocabularies.

F. What five or six principal reasons do Lloyd and Warfel give for thinking that books like *30 Days to a More Powerful Vocabulary* do not provide a really useful way to build vocabulary?

SIR ARCHIBALD SLUTER

A defense of English spelling

For a variety of reasons—some good, some bad—the spelling system of English contains some irregularities, though not so many as you might think. However, since the bulk of the regularity is not always noticeable to a casual observer, most of us are frequently puzzled.

This puzzlement is nothing new. There was a time in the fourteenth century when the spelling system more nearly reflected the way people spoke. Since then, the writing system has wandered pretty far from the phonemic path, as anyone faced with a dozen spellings for the sound /ə/ can realize: r*u*b, s*o*n, d*ou*ble, fl*oo*d, d*oe*s, *a*rise, fount*ai*n, parl*ia*ment, vill*ai*n, dudg*eo*n, fam*i*ly, porp*oi*se. One is also struck by the possible volley of different sounds for the same spelling, as in d*o*, d*o*te, w*o*man, w*o*men, l*o*ve, sh*o*d.

The way of transgressors has not always been hard, however. Until long after the Renaissance, we frequently used a "spell-as-you-go" system. When Samuel Johnson wrote his famous letter to Lord Chesterfield, he twice spelled *address* with one *d*. He also occasionally used *persuit, butt, harased, imbecillity, ilness,* and *Boswel.* These days, the troubles caused by bad spelling may be serious. No maiden who spells *lose* with two *o*'s can hope to catch an English professor for a husband. And poor spellers can often cause trouble for those who come after them. For example, F. Scott Fitzgerald's indifference to orthography is partly responsible for continuing difficulties in establishing the text of *The Great Gatsby.* We still don't know whether in one place he meant *eternal* or *external,* and in another *orgiastic* or *orgastic.*

We have not, of course, lacked reformers. As early as 1200 A.D., an English monk named Orm wrote a series of metrical homilies in what was a serious try for phonetic spelling. He used a number of devices, the most evident of which is the doubling of any consonant which follows a short vowel. His manuscript, however, indicates that the power of his habitual spelling practices was so great that he could not always follow his own rules. And so it has gone ever since. In America, Noah Webster, Benjamin Franklin, Theodore Roosevelt, *The Literary Digest,* and the *Chicago Tribune* have all tried to improve our spelling habits. Webster was the most successful. Among many others, his spelling of *center* instead of *centre, plow* instead of *plough, draft* instead of *draught,* and *sentinel* instead of *centinel* are now standard in American English. He was not so lucky with *imagin, farewel, crum, fether, wo, ake,* and *skreen.*

The fact is that we still have a wide variety of spellings for a single sound and a wide variety of sounds for a single spelling, and would-be reformers have done little to alter this. It seems clear that the spelling system of English needs whatever defense and explanation it can get. In the following article, Sir Archibald Sluter, who, for many years, has worked with Paul Roberts on a study of English orthography, points out the immense amount of order there actually is in our spelling system and explains the vagaries there undoubtedly are.

It is a very common practice for people to deride English spelling, and it must be admitted forthwith that in many of its particulars it evokes derision, or in any event dismay. The culprit seems at first examination to be too far gone in sin to warrant either defense or attempted redemption. We are all familiar with the heinous -*ough* examples, wherein that peculiar spelling peculiarly denotes six different sounds, as in such words as *tough, bough, dough, through, cough,* and *hiccough.* Is this any way, we ask ourselves, to run a railroughed? And who among us will not recall Bernard Shaw's suggestion of *ghoti* as a plausible spelling for *fish* or the late Sir Arthur Quiller-Couch's witty poem "The Harbor of Fowey":

Yes, I have my own views:
But the teachers I follow
Are the lyrical Miews
And the Delphic Apollow.
Unto them I am debtor
For spelling and rhyme,
And I'm doing it bebtor
And bebtor each thyme.

But the orthographist, though he may smile with the layman at the quips that thus expose the absurdities in our writing system, cannot, with the layman, rest there. It is his duty, rather, to explore how far the charge that English spelling is simply chaotic be true. If he finds it altogether true, he might wish to suggest a remedy in the shape of some sort of spelling reform. If less than true, then in some measure he must assume the role of Counsel for the Defense. Since it is my view that English spelling is quite far from being chaotic and random, it is that role that I wish to play in the first part of my talk this evening. Having defended English orthography to the extent to which it seems to me defensible, I shall then undertake not to defend but to explain some of the vagaries that it unquestionably has.

We are sometimes told that English is so far from being systematic that, given the written form of a new word we cannot divine its pronunciation, or, hearing a new one, we cannot be at all certain how it should be rightly written. I submit to you, and shall endeavor to demonstrate, that this is only very partially accurate. Suppose I make up a word and spell it to you: K-E-C-K. Are you in any doubt at all how this should be uttered? You would not say /gek/ or /gēk/ or /keg/ or /kik/. You would say /kek/ and nothing else. Nor would you, if you are accustomed to reading English words, have any doubt about the sounds represented by the following combinations of letters:

P-O-C-K   T-A-F-F   B-R-U-P   N-I-M

K-I-L-E   L-O-K-E   D-E-E-V-E   T-R-A-P-E

Yes, but (I can hear you say) Professor Sluter is loading the dice. He has chosen very simple combinations of letters. Of course we know how to pronounce those. What about such spellings as the *-igh* of *sigh* or the *-eigh* of *weigh?* Well, my friends, I should reply first of all that it is these simple combinations that make up the vast bulk of our language—either by themselves or in company with other forms. Let us coin the word *brup* and say that it is a noun. Never mind what it means; say simply that it is *brup* and that is a noun. Shall we then have any hesitation in making, and correctly spelling, a related adjective *bruppy?* And shall we not proceed in perfect certainty and serenity to *bruppiness, brupful, brupfully, unbruppy, unbruppiness,* and, perhaps, *embrup, debrup,* and *brupdom,* making changes that are sometimes complicated (double the *p,* change the *y* to *i*) but whose regularity is demonstrated by the fact that we perform the operations without hesitation or debate?

But we can go a bit farther than that. Let us take the spelling I-G-H. I give you the invented word C-R-I-G-H-T. Are you in any doubt that it must be pronounced to rhyme with *bright* and *flight?* What alternative would there be? I give you B-E-I-G-H. Do you want to pronounce it any other way than /bā/? I give you P-L-E-M-N. Shall this not be /plem/? And, a point of some importance, shall we be surprised to find a *plemnable* or a *plemnation* in the wings, shall we not be directed by the spelling to the pronunciation of these, and can we then say that the *n* of *plemn* is a wholly useless and absurd appendage?

Bernard Shaw wished to ban, if not the bomb, at least the final *b* of *bomb,* spelling it *bom,* perhaps, or *bam.* Which would have the chief effect of concealing its relationship with *bombard,* as *autum* would eliminate con-nection with *autumnal, dam* with *damnation, vitəl* (were we to admit to our ordinary orthography the upstart schwa) with *vitality,* and so on. For our English spelling, because of the particular sound structure of our language, must play a difficult double role. It must give some reflection not only of the *sounds* but also of the *morphemes,* the units of meaning, of our language; and, in our language, because of the constant shifting of the accent and the effect of this shifting upon our vowel sounds, these do not always perfectly coincide. Thus the *o* of *Byron,* not needed to show the pronunciation of that proud name (for might we not write, without misleading, *Byren* or *Byran* or *Byrun* or even *Byrin* instead?) emerges, as it were, comes into its own in the adjective *Byronic. Byrenic, Byranic Byrunic, Byrinic* would be quite different words, and *Byrənic* (should we have been so heartless as to foist the schwa on a dead poet and spell him *Byrən*) would be impossible.

I am not saying that there are no English spellings which cannot be rendered unambiguously into speech. Of course not. In a number of places in our othography we use the same letter for two or more sounds, and there, indeed, uncertainty is possible. If I give you B-R-O-V-E, you will not know whether to rhyme it with *grove,* with *prove,* or with *love,* since the letter *o* before *v* may denote any of these three different sounds. If I give you T-H-E-A-D, you may hesitate between a pronunciation rhyming with *plead* and one rhyming with *bread.* B-O-U-C-H might make you toss between *touch* and *ouch,* though you would probably plump for the latter, because of the larger use of *ou* for the representation of that vowel sound. (How many others can you think of in which *ou* denotes the vowel sound of *touch?*) Or T-H-O-N might leave you uncertain whether to begin with the consonant of *than* or that of *thin*. Yet here too there is a large probability. In the initial position the consonant of *than* occurs only in what our American friends call *function words*. These are the little workers that pop about so busily in our sentences, pronouns (*they*), demonstratives (*this*), adverbs (*then*), and the article *the*. Since all of these are well known, we would normally assume that any newcomer with *th* cannot be of their number and would venture to begin *thon* like *thong* or *thought*.

Should you still disbelieve me when I say that unambiguous English spellings largely prevail over ambiguous ones, I can only urge you to try invention of the latter—made-up words whose spellings permit two or more pronunciations. I fancy you will scratch your head a bit before each addition to the list.

Let us now turn the coin over for a very brief examination of its obverse side. Can we confidently spell a word that we have only clearly heard? Not always, certainly, if it is an actual word of the language. If I give you *schism, quay, bourn, slough* you will not be able to tell me how they are properly spelled unless you have encountered them before and particularly learned their orthography. And this will be true also of much commoner words, like *bread, friend, many, gone, right, neighbor*. All of these—and a great many more—we had at one time to learn as exceptions to more general principles, and that is why our English youth must work so

very hard to master the orthography and why so many make shocking blunders and fail in their examinations. So much we must concede. But this does not mean that the regularities do not far outnumber the departures from the rule. I shall try to demonstrate.

This time I give you a word first in sound, not spelling. I pronounce for you the made-up word /kend/ and ask you to spell it. I shall be very much surprised indeed if you spell it any other way than *kend*. It is true that we use both *c* and *k* to represent the sound /k/, but we do not use *c* before *e*. It is further true that the sound /e/ has a number of possible representations: *e* in *bet*, *ea* in *head*, *ie* in *friend*, *a* in *many*. But *ea* does not occur before *nd* if memory (and Mr. Walker's dictionary) serve me, so you will not be tempted to *keand*. Nor can I really imagine the anomalous *friend* leading you to *kiend* or *many* to *kand*. No, /kend/ will be *kend*, unless of course we interpret it as the past tense of *ken*, in which case it will be *kenned*, and no questions asked. Again, morphology may play its part.

Or I give you /pīt/. Now here I can conceive of you going for *pight*. There are seventeen monosyllabic words in English in which the sound /īt/ is spelled *-ight*. Still, I think the more common I-consonant-E would prevail and induce you to *pite*. And I am sure that you would not render /rīb/ as *righb* or /bīf/ as *bighf*, for *gh* does not appear in this company. These must be *ribe* and *bife*.

I do not wish here either to claim too much for my client. There are some places in which two representations for a sound come near balance.

Thus, for /ā/ we use A-consonant-E pretty frequently but *ai* pretty frequently too, and we might be in considerable doubt whether to render /gād/ as *gade* or *gaid*. But usually there is probability—a usually overwhelming probability—and I question that there is any place in our English orthography where we are so in doubt about how to spell a word newly learned that our judgment, like a vagabond flag upon the stream, goes to and back, lackeying the varying tide, to rot itself with motion. We may often err, but we guess with confidence.

ENGLISH SPELLING

Well, I have tried to give my client, English orthography, so much defense as he is entitled to. For the rest, we must throw ourselves on the mercy of the court. But before judgment is passed, I should like to say something by way of explanation and extenuation. The accused may be in some measure guilty as charged, but the jury should not overlook the fact that he has had a long and difficult life.

There are a number of *general* reasons which account for the oddities of our spelling system, and I want to discuss some of them with you this evening. An obvious one is that our alphabet is not big enough for our language. We write our words with the Roman alphabet, which was borrowed from the Greek and modified to represent the sounds of Latin. I assume, though I am no classicist, that it was a proper and efficient vehicle for representing the sounds of Latin, but it isn't very good for English. It has just twenty-six characters,

whereas our language has more than twenty-six sound units, or *phonemes,* as they are called. Just how many more, I shan't say. It depends a bit on what authority one talks to, and the precise number does not bear significantly on our argument. But that there *are* more phonemes in English than twenty-six, all authorities agree, and therefore we must make some of our alphabetical symbols do double duty.

Thus we must put together the letter *s* and the letter *h* to signify the first consonant sound of *shirt* and the letters *c* and *h* for the first sound of *chirp.* Some of my colleagues think this latter to be composed of two consonant sounds, the initial sound of *too* followed by that of *shoe.* But even if it be, we have no ready way of rendering it, unless we confound confusion by writing *tsh: tshirp, tshin, tshuckle, tshurtsh.* Nor have we any single character for the last sound of *sing,* and we represent it with an *n* and a *g.* This device produces ambiguity in pairs like *singer* and *finger,* though, to be sure, the ambiguity is resolved if we take the morphology into account. Worse trouble confronts us in the combination of *t* and *h,* for not only does this not represent a /t/ sound followed by an /h/ sound, but it stands for two quite different single sounds—that of *than* and that of *thin.*

Yet these consonantal problems are niggling compared to those presented by the vowels. Counting diphthongs, I find no fewer than fifteen different vowel sounds in my pronunciation of English—those of *bill, bell, cap, cup, balm, treat, rain, know, hoot, put, saw, out, hide, boil,* and *fur.* To meet this vocalic complexity, we have in the Roman alphabet only *a, e, i, o,* and *u*. We must consequently resort to many dodges. One of them is the use of double letters: *ee, ai, ou, au,* and so on. Another is the employment of consonant letters to render vowel meaning; for example, the extra *l* that distinguishes *pall* from *pal*, the *l* that makes *balm* different from *bam*, the *r* which in *heard* not only means /r/ but also means that the vowel sound is not that of *head*. Of course we use the so-called silent *e* to distinguish *ride* from *rid*, *mete* from *met*, *rate* from *rat*, *rode* from *rod*, and *tube* from *tub*. Then we double consonants to separate *batter* from *bater*, *pinning* from *pining*, *stopping* from *stoping*.

But (the prosecution will argue) granted that we have to use complicated devices to redeem an inadequate alphabet, must we employ such a wide variety of them for single sounds? We use, for the sound /ē/, not only the E-consonant-E of *mete* but also *ea* in *meat* and *ee* in *meet*, not to mention single *e* in *he*, *ie* in *field*, *ei* in *seize*, and even *ay* in *quay*. Well, I could suggest that deciding on a single rendering of each phoneme would increase the number of homonyms in the language, those groups of words that sound alike and are spelled alike. But I really don't know that we would be in serious difficulties if we had to write "Wee'll meet at six and eet the meet and meet out the punishment." Anyway, I am no longer defending but explaining.

A part of the explanation is that English has been written for a longer time than other European languages. Nobody had written in French or Italian or German by the end of the seventh century; yet at this time English already had a quite respectable literature. Now when people begin to write their language, they must perforce try to put down those sounds that they hear in their speech. They must write phonetically. This the English (or the Saxons, as perhaps we must refer to them in that period) did when, after their conversion to Christianity in 597, they learned the Roman alphabet from their spiritual benefactors and set about using it to spell English words. We assume that the English of this period—Old English, as it is called—was quite a faithful representation of the way people talked.

But after people have been for a time in the habit of writing, a tradition of right writing develops. One tries to write as one's forefathers did. One is taught to do so. Therefore, there is a tendency for the writing system to stand still, for it not to change. Now this would cause no inconvenience if speech stood still too, but it doesn't. Speech changes as the centuries slip by, sometimes quite radically. Some sounds cease to be pronounced. Some that were different fall together, and some that were alike become different. When you see a pair of words like *meet* and *meat*, where different spellings are used for the same sound, you can be fairly sure that the sounds were once different. Where the same spelling is used for different sounds, as in *mean* and *meant*, it is likely that the sounds were once the same.

The "silent letters" are of several sorts. Some are not altogether silent. The *e* of *pine* tells us how to pronounce the preceding vowel, and we have seen how the *n* of *autumn* pipes up in *autumnal*. On the other hand, the *g* of *gnaw* and the *k* of *know* reflect no sound now pronounced, though they once did. Our ancestors had the ability, which we lack, to pronounce a /g/ or /k/ sound before /n/. Similarly the *gh* of *thought, weight, draught, sight* represented a sound not unlike that signified by *ch* in German *doch* and *ich*. Such a sound is still heard in some of the dialects of Scotland, though it has disappeared in most of English, leaving only its spelling behind.

A very important part of the explanation of the complexity of English spelling is the Norman conquest of 1066. For several centuries thereafter our country was ruled by people who either spoke French natively or who looked to France as the sole fount of civilization. For a century and a half after the conquest, English was scarcely written at all, and when it came again to the page it was set down by people schooled in French ways of orthography. It was at this time that we acquired, for example our *th* spelling; Old English had used the characters þ and ð from the old Runic alphabet for the sounds of *thin* and *then*. It was from the French scribes that we got our *gu* spellings as in *guess*, the *ch* of *chin*, the "soft g" of *gem* (as opposed to the hard one of *get*), *c* for the /s/ sound of *cent*, and many other oddities.

One peculiarity has its source in the nature of medieval writing. Medieval writing tended to be made with many up and down strokes so that such letters as *u, v, m, n*, were very easily confused. The word *some*, which was spelled *sum* in Old English script, in Middle English therefore looked something like this: ꙅ꙯꙯ꙮ. This was hard to read, and it became the practice to close the top of the *u* in order to mark the vowel letter off from a following *m, n*, or *v*: ꙅꙮ꙯꙯. But this in effect makes an *o* of the *u* and accounts for the use of *o* in

words like *some, son, love*, and a number of others.

The extensive borrowing of words and their spellings from French in the medieval period paved the way for later similar borrowing from the classical languages of the Renaissance era. Again, spellings as well as words were taken, and this explains the use of *ch* for /k/ in *character, ph* for /f/ in *phonograph, y* for /i/ in *myth*— all of these from Greek.

But if we must find a single outstanding villain to blame for the state of our spelling system, I think it must be that otherwise priceless boon, the fifteenth century invention of printing. Until this time, the writing, though well behind the changes taking place in sounds, still plodded valiantly after, trying to catch up. The writing of 1400 was not so good a representation of Middle English sounds as that of 800 was of Old English sounds, but it wasn't too far off the mark.

Printing changed that, though not immediately. Throughout the sixteenth century, spelling was still in flux, and indeed we are told that sixteenth century printers took advantage of the uncertainty to make their right-hand margins come out even, for example spelling *highness* as *highnes* if a shorter word were wanted, *highnesse* if a longer one. But by the seventeenth century, standardization set in, and since that period, changes have been very few. The standard that finally prevailed was a spelling that pretty well represented the sounds of two or three centuries earlier—the sounds of Middle English. This is largely the spelling that we have now.

In more recent times, many people have proposed reform of our spelling system, but with very little effect. The most successful reformer was the American Noah Webster, who, through his publications in lexicography, induced such improvements as the dropping of the *k* in *publick* and *magick*. He found, however, less response in us than in his countrymen, who now prefer *center* to *centre*, *traveler* to *traveller*, *tire* to *tyre*, and *jail* to *gaol*. Later efforts, such as that to supplant *though* with *tho*, *through* with *thru*, *dialogue* with *dialog*, have been rewarded with only very partial success, and anyway they do but nibble at the fringes.

Shall we ever reform our spelling system? Well, *ever* is a long time. I don't know about ever. But I doubt that the grandchildren of anyone now alive will see much change. We are a patient people and slow to change, and perhaps slowest to change in orthography. No doubt we will some day give up miles for kilometers and quarts for liters, and perhaps we shall even be persuaded to abandon pounds, shillings, and pence. But spell *phonograph* as *fonograf*? No. Unthinkable.

For discussion

A. What is Sluter's general answer to the idea ". . . that, given the written form of a new word we cannot divine its pronunciation, or, hearing a new one, we cannot be at all certain how it should be rightly written"?

B. Suppose I choose the spelling *k* to represent all appearances of the sound /k/ in English. I would then use it for the first sound in *cat*, *keen*, *queen*, and *chorus*, and for the final sound in *lick* and *physique*. Demonstrate why I cannot continue this procedure to develop a spelling system for English in which each letter represents only one sound.

C. What is Sluter's objection to spelling *bomb* either *bom* or *bam*? Give half a dozen other examples to illustrate his idea.

D. In most people's speech, *finger* and *singer* do not rhyme. Which of the two is composed of two morphemes?

E. The vowel sounds in *feet* may be spelled twelve different ways. Give examples of as many of them as you can. Then try for ten in the initial consonant sound of *cash*, and nine for the vowel sound in *rule*.

F. Account for *ghllaucyei rhaugn* as a spelling for *glassy rain* (*gh* as in *ghost*, for instance).

G. After pronouncing the following words, check your pronunciation with your dictionary: *halcyon, antithesis, cacoethes, periphrasis, solecism, atoll, larynx, Caribbean, Aloysius, inchoate, heinous, schism*.

H. List the various ways in which each of the following words may be pronounced: *hard, greasy, lingerie, root, bath, Tuesday, father, voice, turtle, dairy, balm, sister, vista, about, porch, mayonnaise, heart*.

I. What are the three principal reasons for the oddities of English spelling? Illustrate.

J. Why is it reasonable to retain the *gh* in *daughter, night*, and *light*?

J . J . L A M B E R T S

Spelling by folk etymology

WHEN A STUDENT SPELLS MOUNT TAMALPAIS as *tamale pie,* he demonstrates his ignorance, but he also demonstrates some learning. He certainly knows how to spell *tamale
pie,* and more or less how to pronounce *Tamalpais.* He has tried to spell what he
thought he heard. Sometimes he really does spell what he hears, but his spelling still
shows that he is making some kind of association between the familiar and the unfamiliar. Thus he may write of Czechoslovakia as *a Russian saddleite.*

This "catch-as-catch-can" etymologizing has been going on for a long time. Though it
didn't lead him to misspell the words, Samuel Johnson wrongly thought *motley* came
from *mothlike* and *chirp* from *cheer up.* He even wondered if perhaps *spider* didn't
come from "spy-dor—the insect that watches the door." This kind of thing finally led
Mark Twain to suggest that *Middletown* comes from a marrying of the *M* in *Moses* to
-iddleton. But perhaps Twain was too easily doubtful of superficially unlikely etymologies. Certainly the sources of *yankee, gringo, muskrat, calaboose, cockroach,* and what,
in Colorado, is commonly called the "Picketwire" River seem unlikely at first acquaintance.

J. J. Lamberts of the Arizona State University points out how this age-old linguistic operation can cause trouble in spelling.

The phenomenon of folk or popular etymology consists simply of re-
modeling the pronunciation or the
spelling of a word in terms of what
people incorrectly imagine to be its
derivation. That is, they make the
word over to resemble its supposed
source.

A typical example is the word *hangnail.* In OE this was *angnægl,* a compound of *ang* "painful" and *nægl*
"nail." By and by *ang* dropped out of
the language as a separate word and
the word *angnail* then seemed illogical. Someone apparently "corrected" this to *hangnail* on the plausible grounds that it hung next to the
nail. Or to cite a more recent instance,
early settlers encountered in the
American wilderness a rodent which
Algonquian Indians called a *wejak.*
Since it was to be found in the woods,

"Spelling by Folk Etymology": From *College English,* vol. 17, n. 8, May 1956, pp. 488–489.
Reprinted with the permission of The National Council of Teachers of English and J. J. Lamberts.

the pioneers reasoned that the Indians were talking bad English and that they were really trying to say *woodchuck*. The demands of logic, not too stringent, were satisfied and the creature from that time on was a *woodchuck*.

Teachers of spelling occasionally encourage students to break up troublesome words on the basis of an analogous fanciful meaning or association. A teacher once showed us how to spell *Connecticut* by pointing out that the river linked two states and crossed two more and was thus properly named "Connect-I-cut."

Such a quasi-etymological device is sometimes useful in producing acceptable spellings, but in the hands of the unskilled it can bear strange fruit indeed. In various situations students seem to go through some such word analysis as they grope for any kind of ready clew in reasoning out a spelling. This may go on oftener than we know. It is only when the method has failed that the reader meets a bizarre spelling which makes—to him, at least— little or no immediate sense.

Some tantalizing spellings that have turned up in my class papers point with varying degrees of clearness to the folk etymologizing of one word or another. Here are a few. I have included the immediate context and I have also ventured to suggest the association that may have been in the writer's mind.

"*Usuage* is grammar put into action. . . ." This is pretty clearly a confusion with the word *usual*. The person who makes this error—he is not alone —reasons that *usuage* is what people *usually* say. Because this is true it is difficult for him to see that there is anything wrong with the spelling.

"Menninger *compairs* man with a trout." Logic, such as it is, appears here too. When a person compares things, he puts them side by side, and the result is plainly a *pair*. Then why should not the verb be *compair?*

"The *perpetraitors* of this dasterdly [*sic*] crime." The "dasterdly" crime was happily a political one and the association with *traitor* in this particular situation is obvious.

"My first contact with this *playwrite.*" Now that the contemporary scene has almost no wheelwrights or wainwrights or millwrights, it scarcely occurs to most students that there can be a *playwright*. A person who *writes plays* must be a *playwrite*.

"Only by playing up the students' interests can the teacher hope to *aliven* the interest in classics." Why *enliven* something in order to make it *alive* was the logical point.

"I have a slight *incling* as to how. . . ." This is evidently a blend of two expressions: "I am *inclined* to think" and "I have an *inkling*." At any rate, the word *incline* has become mixed up in this.

"The immature were *foolhearty* and extravagant of life." The writer was faced with a choice between *hearty* and *hardy*. Is one a *hearty* fool or a *hardy* one? Since the first seemed to make better sense, that was the way it was written.

"Communication skills are . . . of *upmost* importance." Etymology is at work here. Analysis of *utmost* into its several degrees gives a positive *ut* which only a philologist would associate with *out*. Add to this the fact that by phonetic assimilation *utmost* is often actually pronounced as *upmost*. The marvel is that the unconventional spelling remains so rare.

"I believe that the president is not a war *mongrel* but is only trying his best to prevent war." I cannot imagine that the student who wrote this was so sophisticated as to think about letting "slip the dogs of war." But *monger* was unfamiliar to him. *Mongrel,* on the other hand, was a familiar word that could convey the idea of growling and other aspects of belligerence and consequently *mongrel* was the spelling that made sense.

"*Inverterate* smokers." Unless this is simply carelessness, it could easily pass for a reproachful reference to the spinelessness of habitual users of tobacco.

"The points I was *confussed* about." Here the idea of mental disturbance, of *fuss,* is apparent.

"A *ridiculose* poker game." What a wonderful aptness there is to this spelling in the situation in which it occurs. One doubts that this person spells this word the same way all the time. But here he seems to be suddenly stuck for the accepted spelling of the final syllable and an unexpected free association provides the interesting result. As a matter of fact, the occurrence of such nonce spellings lends plausibility to this entire theory.

Spellings of this kind are relatively infrequent in comparison to other types of unconventional orthography and only a few people seem to produce them fairly often. This suggests that the words themselves are not demons, but that the persons who resort to them have devised this system for themselves. To such persons these spellings are not wild guesses. Their orthography is fortified by logic. It has not occurred to them that there is very little logic about any English spelling, and with some surprise do they discover that their technique is unsatisfactory.

The only possible solution for the problem evidently lies in the ease with which it can be isolated. One simply singles out those who are addicted to it, and regardless of the many times that they apparently make the method yield results, one warns them that English spelling is such that nobody can be sure when a guess will prove to be fortunate and when it will be embarrassing. The instructor at this point suggests a more conventional approach, presumably the use of a good desk dictionary.

For discussion

A. Look up the etymology of the following words: *yankee, gringo, muskrat, calaboose, cockroach, welsh rarebit, crawfish, pantry, Purgatoire River,* and *Tamalpais.*

B. If you can, add some examples to Lamberts's examples of spelling by folk etymology.

HAROLD B. ALLEN

Pejorative terms for midwest farmers

OBSERVING AND DISPARAGING variations in the speech of others are ancient pastimes.
This fact is illustrated by the English word *solecism,* from *soloikos*—an attic Greek ad-
jective which described the backsliding dialect spoken by the colonists sent off to
Soloi, in Asia Minor.

Nowadays, we speak of *pejoration* and of *linguistic geography.* In the following article, Harold B. Allen of the University of Minnesota looks at some findings of linguistic
geography concerning pejorative terms for farmers in the Upper Midwest.

As Raven McDavid writes in his chapter "American English Dialects" in W. Nelson
Francis's *The Structure of American English* (a chapter upon which any brief discussion of American English dialects will almost certainly be based), "The principle upon
which all linguistic geography is built is the simple one of observing differences in
grammar, pronunciation, and vocabulary, determining the regional and social distribution of these differences, and seeking their historical and cultural explanations." This
explanation makes just about everyone a linguistic geographer. There is, however, an
undertaking which eventually will describe all American English dialects—the Linguistic Atlas Project. It has the cooperation of linguists throughout the United States
and Canada, and is the most extensive effort of its kind ever attempted.

The project was first set up in 1930 under the direction of Hans Kurath, who has
interpreted some of the Atlas data in "Area Linguistics and the Teacher of English"
(see p. 90). Atlases have been published, or are in preparation, for each of the areas
into which the United States—and Canada—have been divided.

Professor Allen is director of the Linguistic Atlas of the Upper Midwest, an area
which includes Minnesota, Iowa, the Dakotas, and Nebraska. Though yet unpub-
lished, the field work has been completed and the material is now being edited.

To prepare for the collection of materials which will be interpreted in the linguistic
atlas of a region, researchers select a number of communities for investigation. Then,
a field worker familiar with the social and cultural history of the region as well as with
phonetics, phonemics, and the entire analytic apparatus of contemporary linguistics,
visits these communities to collect data on pronunciation, vocabulary, and grammar.

"Pejorative Terms for Midwest Farmers": From *American Speech,* vol. 33, n. 4, December
1958, pp. 260–265. Copyright 1958 by Columbia University Press and reprinted with their
permission. Adapted from a paper read before the American Dialect Society, Madison, Wis.,
September 11, 1957.

As Allen points out, the persons interviewed represent a number of strata—chronological, social, and educational.

Subsequently, in marking maps to show the use of given items of pronunciation, vocabulary, or grammar within their area, investigators naturally notice how an item is distributed over a district. They can then draw lines on the map to show the limits of the area in which this item is dominant. Such a line is called an *isogloss*. A concentration of isoglosses establishes a *dialect boundary*.

The mapping of American English dialects is still far from complete, but we know enough to say that three dialect bands move across the country from east to west, reflecting both the original settlements in the Northern, Midland, and Southern part of the east coast as well as later migrations. Naturally, these bands—or at least parts of them—weave in and out as they cross the country. One result of this mapping is that we can no longer claim the existence of a "General American" speech.

Professor Allen here interprets the responses to the request of the Linguistic Atlas field workers for pejorative terms used to disparage people living in one part of the United States. A number of these terms are familiar to most of us; some reflect the homesteading period, and a few are seldom used items. The result is cultural history of the most convincing kind.

Apparently the development of town and city life has always induced a contrast between the social patterns of those who dwell outside the compact community and the patterns of those within it. It is a contrast almost always made to the disadvantage of the former. The classical Roman found in his native word *urbanus* much of the pleasant flavor today inhering in its derivative *urbane,* and when Cicero wrote of a *vox rustica* he was referring to no dulcet tones of a female Long Sam but rather to a speech that was harsh and displeasing.

Only in the past half century in this country has this contrast gradually diminished, diminished so much already that in many areas it now is present more in memory than in fact. The cultural lag between country dweller and city dweller began to shrink when the first model T's churned their way through the mud to bring the whole family to town for Saturday shopping and the movie.

Paved roads, mail-order companies and then chain stores in the small towns, radio and now television, to say nothing of the far-flung travels of farm youths in three foreign wars— all have conspired to make the visible and even audible difference well-nigh microscopic. That family-filled Buick Special crossing in front of you may belong to a city neighbor out for a drive; it may equally well belong to a wheat farmer from upstate. And you cannot tell readily by looking at its occupants or by listening to them talk.

Yet echoes of the old contrast between town and country do linger in our speech. They exist in the residue of disparaging names applied to people who live outside a settled community, names sometimes given by country dwellers to other country dwellers but usually applied by residents of town or city to their country cousins.

Fortunately for the cultural historian, the Linguistic Atlas fieldworkers have regularly been gathering the remaining evidence for this disparagement that for so long marked our culture. One item in the Atlas worksheets calls for words used to ridicule or disparage people living in the country. For readers of *American Speech* I need not go into detail about the methods by which the Atlas obtains information. I would remind readers only that the people interviewed are lifelong residents of their communities and that they represent three groups: Type I, old-fashioned and uneducated; Type II, middle-aged with high school training; and Type III, fortyish with a college degree or equivalent.

For the Upper Midwest Atlas 208 such informants were interviewed. The body of lexical data thus obtained has been supplemented by returns of a mail check list from 1,069 informants. Since the check list includes this particular item, then, there actually is evidence for these pejorative designations from a total of 1,277 persons. True, the difference in the validity of the two kinds of informants prevents adding their replies together, but the mailed evidence usually provides valuable corroboration for that obtained in the interviews and sometimes additional information not otherwise obtained.

As the table on page [233 f.] shows, a total of eighty-six different pejorative designations of rural dwellers was reported as in use in the five states of the Upper Midwest. Sixty-eight of these have high validity, for they were collected during personal interviews. Eighteen of these terms also were reported on the mailed check lists. In addition, the mail respondent supplied twenty-four other designations. Although some of these last may be

questioned, others are certainly significant if only because they are write-ins. As a rule, a voluntarily written addition to a questionnaire list has rather high validity. One is not likely to take the trouble to write in a word unless he knows it, uses it, and feels that its omission would leave out something important. *Hillbilly,* for instance, is such a write-in; so are *appleknocker, timber rat, hoosier, brush hog,* and *brush Yankee.*

Within the limits of this article I cannot offer a comprehensive analysis of all these replies. But it will be possible here to look, first, at the occurence of some familiar terms (both those distributed generally and those that show regional patterning); second, at those terms which reflect the homesteading period; and, third, at a few unusual terms with rather limited occurrence.

Of the many familiar terms reported the most common disparaging appellation is, as might be suspected without a survey, *hayseed.* This term came from 52.5 percent of the field informants and from an almost equal proportion, 52 percent, of the mail respondents. It is the only term to be reported as frequently by college graduates as by informants of Types I and II.

Next most frequent, surprisingly enough, is the word *farmer* itself, although as a disparaging term its effect is probably due to the context or to the intonation pattern. Precisely one third of the responses indicate this special connotation, but it may be observed that such responses occur more commonly in Northern than in Midland speech territory, with 38.5 percent reporting it in Minnesota and 77 percent in North Dakota, but only

13.5 percent in Nebraska. The contrary situation occurs with the third most frequent term, the still familiar *hick*, which was reported by 22 percent of the field informants and by 16 percent of the mail respondents. Town-dwelling Iowans and Nebraskans are much more likely to call their rural neighbors "hicks" than are Minnesotans or North Dakotans.

Iowans and Nebraskans also reveal a preference for the fourth most frequent term, *country jake*. Although the general field average is 14 percent, with that of the check lists a corresponding 13 percent, more than 18 percent of the Iowans use this in contrast with only 10 percent in Minnesota and North Dakota. The check lists sharpen this contrast: 23 percent in Iowa and a skimpy 4 percent in North Dakota. Perhaps an even stronger Midland preference is for the fifth most popular term, *clodhopper*. Twelve and two-tenths percent of all field informants and 11 percent of all mail respondents report using this word, but most of these are found in Midland territory, 16.3 percent in Iowa as against only 1.7 percent in Minnesota. Then in sixth place is the old-fashioned *rube*, widely scattered in 11 percent of the field records. Seventh is *yokel*. We oldsters who grew up on Mencken's *American Mercury* will recall this word nostalgically, but in truth it seems now more a literary term than a colloquialism. At least today only 3.5 percent of the records in Minnesota and Iowa report it; it did not turn up in the three Western states at all.

Then there are two terms widely known which in the Upper Midwest have only regional distribution. In this area, it should be pointed out, the principal isoglosses separating Northern from Midland speech cut off the northern third of Iowa and then extend diagonally across South Dakota to the northwestern corner. The eastern Platte River valley in Nebraska, however, is almost a Northern speech enclave as a result of its early settlement by pioneers from New York and northern Ohio. This settlement background is suggested by the data for the term *hayshaker*, which occurs in Minnesota, North Dakota, and northern Iowa, with only a single instance in southeastern Nebraska. (This informant's father and maternal grandmother were born in New York State.)

In direct contrast is another regional term, *hillbilly*. Almost certainly brought into the Upper Midwest by settlers hailing from Kentucky or other South Midland areas, *hillbilly* has been preserved in the Midland speech zone of southern Iowa and eastern Nebraska despite the absence of anything a Kentuckian would call a hill. This distribution pattern, I might add, corresponds with that of a number of lexical items known to be of South Midland origin. The percentages for *hillbilly* are 43 percent in Iowa, 11 percent in Nebraska, 4 percent in South Dakota, and none at all in Minnesota and North Dakota.

If the generally familiar terms heretofore discussed suggest the original settlement history and the related development of the village and town communities, two other sets of terms reflect special developments within the region. One of these took place in Minnesota, where much of the northern deforested land was allowed to be naturally reforested by a second growth of cedar and jack pine. Here can be found the subsistence farmer with his small cleared plot of unproductive soil. To him some townspeople have given the opprobrious name *jack pine savage* or *cedar savage*. Because of his type of house they have also called him a *shacker*. Further, because his low income may compel him to resort to hunting for food he is also known as a *shotgun farmer* or even, when the cost of ammunition may be too much for him, as a *rabbitchoker*.

The second special development within the area is familiar to us all from Western stories and movies. It is the pioneer migration of homesteaders into the cattle country of the Western plains, with the ensuing conflict between the cattlemen who sought to preserve the open range and the settlers who wanted to plow it up and put fences on it. This conflict legend has now been romanticized and exaggerated, but it certainly existed; and some of the bitterness of those days only a generation or two ago remains in the contemptuous terms the cattlemen applied to the incoming homesteaders who brought the plows that broke the plain.

Most common of the terms is *honyocker*, still a fighting word in the western Dakotas. "Them damned honyockers," an old Black Hills cattleman told me in profane contempt, "were always stealing our mavericks." This word almost invariably occurs with the *-er* suffix, and is rarely to be confused in form and never in meaning with the similar *honyock*. *Honyock*, in the sense "an uncouth countryman, especially of German or Bohemian origin," is principally found in eastern Nebraska, where many of the early settlers were of German or of Czech birth. Though surely of the same etymology, these terms must be differentiated.

Equally common and also apparently limited largely to the Dakotas is the self-explanatory appellative *sodbuster*, with the variant *soddy*. The term *soddy* may have a double origin, from *sodbuster*, on the one hand, and from the sod houses used as the first homestead dwellings, on the other. Old-timers I have interviewed offered both explanations. A less common term, one preserved now in Western fiction, is *nester*, reported twice in southwestern South Dakota. Also applied derisively by cattlemen to the homesteaders is the term *landsucker*, which field work turned up only once, in Haakon County, South Dakota. The informant said that the word is still commonly used by local ranchers.

As recently as 1913–14 a number of settlers and perhaps some migrants moved into the lower valleys of the southern Black Hills, in South Dakota, and there cleared the land by cutting down the jack pine and selling the trunks to be used as railway ties. Local cattlemen, who for years had profited through the use of these valleys as grazing land, viewed the whole proceeding with jaundiced eyes and promptly dubbed the invaders *tiehacks* and *wood ticks*. Apparently these terms remained localisms; they are now remembered with fond acerbity by the old cattlemen who still resent the fencing of the open range.

A few other terms of infrequent occurrence are of some interest. One, *bushwhacker*, is an old-timer itself. The last quotation in the sense of "a dweller in the backwoods" in the *Dictionary of Americanisms* is dated 1885. But it turns up still as a live designation in places as far apart as southern

Iowa and southern Manitoba and Ontario. The Canadian informants clearly considered the term one in everyday use.

In southeastern North Dakota I found the term *jackfish farmer,* applied to poor farmers who live along the Red River and add to their subsistence by catching jackfish, a kind of pike. In northeastern Nebraska other riverside dwellers, here along the Niobrara River, are locally called *river rats.* Then in central and north central Nebraska occur two other terms related to the geography of the region. When the first settlers appeared it was found that the soil was too sandy and climate too dry for a homesteader to make a living on the customary 160 acres. Enactment of the Kincaid Act increased the homesteader's allotment in such semiarid regions to 640 acres, an entire section. Homesteaders availing themselves of this law naturally became known as *Kincaiders,* a term sometimes though not always opprobrious. Then because of the area itself they also became known as *sandhillers,* a term still very much alive in Nebraska.

Dialectally important, though statistically insignificant, is the single occurrence of the old French *habitant,* with near-French pronunciation, used by the informant in Sprague, southeastern Manitoba. There the term seems to be applied only to the settlers from French-speaking Quebec and eastern Ontario who have moved into the cutover lands. If not used pejoratively it was certainly employed with a recognizable feeling of social superiority on the part of the speaker.

Many Upper Midwest informants remarked that words which poke fun at the farmer are no longer used in the same way as they were a generation ago. If used today, they are more likely spoken with consciously humorous intent. Hence to report upon their present-day occurrence in the speech of this area is to add a footnote to the passing of an era in the nation's history. With the increasing urbanization of rural culture the time is close when a dictionary that records any of these terms or meanings will have to use such a label as *hist.* or *archaic.* Desirably a linguistic atlas should be redone every half a century. How many of these eighty-six terms will appear in the records of Upper Midwest speech fifty years from now?

PEJORATIVE DESIGNATIONS OF RURAL DWELLERS IN THE UPPER MIDWEST

	Field	Check List		Field	Check List
1. appleknocker		x	10. cedar savage	x	x +
2. backwoodsman	x		11. clodbuster	x	
3. barn folks	x		12. clodhopper	x	x +
4. barnyard savage		x	13. cornhusker	x	
5. broncobuster	x		14. country boob	x	
6. brush hog		x	15. country bum	x	
7. brush Yankee		x	16. country bumpkin	x	x +
8. bushman	x		17. country cousin	x	
9. bushwhacker	x		18. country folk	x	x +

PEJORATIVE DESIGNATIONS OF RURAL DWELLERS IN THE UPPER MIDWEST—(*Continued*)

	Field	Check List			Field	Check List
19. country gentleman		x		55. jiggerboo	x	
20. country gawk	x			56. John farmer		x
21. country gook	x			57. Kincaider	x	x +
22. country guy	x	x +		58. landsucker	x	
23. country hick	x			59. lumberjack	x	x +
24. country ike	x	x +		60. mossback	x	x +
25. country jack	x			61. mountaineer	x	x +
26. country jake	x	x +		62. mountain boomer		x
27. country jay	x			63. nester	x	
28. country jig	x			64. oaf	x	
29. country jigger	x			65. old-timer		x
30. country lunk	x			66. puddle jumper	x	
31. country people	x			67. pumpkin husker		x
32. country punk	x			68. rabbitchoker	x	
33. country 'punkin'	x			69. rail splitter		x
34. countryman		x		70. rancher	x	x +
35. cowboy		x		71. river rat	x	
36. cowhand		x		72. rube	x	x +
37. farm boy		x		73. sand-hiller	x	x +
38. farmer	x	x +		74. shacker		x
39. goof	x			75. shotgun farmer	x	
40. habitant [ˌhæbi'tã]				76. slue foot	x	
41. hayseed	x	x +		77. sodbuster	x	x +
42. hayshaker	x	x +		78. soddy	x	
43. hick	x	x +		79. stubble jumper	x	
44. hick farmer	x			80. tiehack	x	
45. hillbilly	x	x +		81. timber rat		x
46. honyock	x	x +		82. white trash	x	
47. honyocker	x	x +		83. woodsman	x	
48. hoosier		x		84. wood tick	x	
49. jackfish farmer	x			85. yahoo	x	x +
50. jack pine farmer	x			86. yokel	x	
51. jack pine hillbilly		x			68	42 24
52. jack pine savage	x	x +		Phrase: from the sticks	x	x
53. jayhawk	x			+ denotes a term voluntarily added to the		
54. jayhawker	x			mail check list by the informant.		

For discussion

A. Allen points out that some of the pejorative words reflect special developments in the region. What developments do the following reflect: *cedar savage, honyocker, sodbuster, rabbitchoker, tiehacks, river rat, Kincaiders, habitant?*

B. See how many pejorative terms you can collect for each of the following:
1. a fraternity or sorority member
2. a non-member of a sorority
3. an intellectual
4. a college student who demonstrates on picket lines
5. a person who has a beard
6. a college professor
7. a teenager
8. a student who gets all "A"s
9. a student who gets all "D"s
10. a soldier or sailor
11. a Republican or Democrat.

C. Clip from a magazine or newspaper a picture of a long, upholstered article of furniture, which has arms and a back and which is used for sitting. Carry it with you for a couple of days, and from time to time show it to various people, asking what it is a picture of. Keep a record of the results, and of the age and approximate education of your informants.

ALBERT H. MARCKWARDT

Dictionaries and the English language

LIKE THE LINGUISTIC GEOGRAPHER, the lexicographer is an applied linguist—but with some differences. The work of a linguistic geographer is judged principally by other linguistic geographers. The work of the lexicographer, however, is on prominent public display, and judged by anyone who can obtain a dictionary. It is true, as Samuel Johnson said, that one needn't be a carpenter in order to judge a chair. Yet, where lexicography is involved, the lexicographer hardly has a chance to defend himself as a specialist.

That the lexicographer gets into trouble is not surprising, for he has an impossible task, a part of which is described in the following article by Albert H. Marckwardt. The subject is dictionaries, and, particularly, the controversial *Webster's Third New International*. The maker of dictionaries is supposed to write the biography—genealogical details and all—of the words in a language, a number of which are already well known to many people. A lexicographer of the English language can no longer, as his eighteenth-century counterpart did, simply say of a *cat* that it is "a creature well-known," or of a *dog* that it is "a quadruped well-known." Nor is his work ever done. Not only does he have an immense language to cope with, but each day it grows larger and larger. Therefore, it is not extraordinary that he occasionally misses a tree in the midst of such a dense forest. Johnson once unguardedly wrote that "*H* seldom, perhaps never, begins any but the first syllable." The members of the *Académie française* spent most of the year 1639 examining all French words beginning with *a*. They forgot *académie*.

None of us is perfect, not even the lexicographer, and critics have never spared him because he exhibits a natural human frailty. Some early reviewers were particularly hard on *Webster's Third New International Dictionary* (1961). Later writers, of unquestioned scholarship and competence have provided the publishers, G. & C. Merriam Company, with all the defense they need.

What may one reasonably ask from a dictionary, specifically a desk dictionary, which contains about as much language as most of us are willing to have constantly around? Naturally, the definitions are the most important thing, and no dictionary likely to be recommended by an English teacher will fail on this account. In other ways, however, there is a good deal of variety. Some dictionaries are somewhat daring

"Dictionaries and the English Language": From *The English Journal*, vol. 52, n. 5, May 1963, pp. 336–345. Reprinted with the permission of The National Council of Teachers of English and Albert H. Marckwardt.

about *Etymology,* a less than settled science in which a reckless and erroneous guess may become gospel, as, for instance, the derivation of *gringo* from "Green grow the rushes Oh." A dictionary should indicate alternate spellings and pronunciations, both between British and American English, and among the regional variations in America. Its pronunciation key should be as nearly phonemic as is commercially possible. It should not have a number of spellings for the same sound. A dictionary should be up-to-date. Language changes. And vocabulary changes much faster than either the sound system or syntax. A dictionary should cover compounds which can not be explained in terms of the parts, as, for example, the word *pork-barrel.* It should also cover some of the special vocabulary of the trades and the professions, and of games and sports. It must apply some usage labels, but these labels should not condemn what is, in fact, almost universal practice. A good dictionary should also do much more, but if it does the above, it is useful.

Now that much of the tumult and the shouting have subsided, and the controversy over *Webster's Third New International Dictionary* has attained the dignity of a casebook, it should be possible to consider both the dictionary and the varied reactions to it with a degree of detachment. Bergen Evans was quite correct in characterizing the storms of abuse provoked by the appearance of the new edition as a curious phenomenon. But how can it be explained? And more important still, what is there to be learned from it?

We must recognize, first of all, that a complete revision of our largest commercially produced dictionary of the English language has become a regularly recurring event in American life. Upon occasion the time table has varied a bit, but the following listing reveals an astonishing degree of regularity over the past century.

An American Dictionary of the English Language (Royal Quarto Edition, Unabridged)   1864
Webster's International Dictionary   1890
Webster's New International Dictionary   1909
Webster's New International Dictionary (Second edition)   1934
Webster's Third New International Dictionary   1961

Of the five Webster editions listed above, probably none has called forth such extremes of critical comment upon its appearance as the recent Webster Third. It was characterized as "a very great calamity." Its general tone was described as "a dismaying assortment of the questionable, the perverse, the unworthy, the downright outrageous." At the same time, other reviewers spoke of the work as "an intellectual achievement of the very highest order," and "a reference work which worthily carries on a tradition of great reference works."

These extremes of praise and blame are reminiscent of the reception of the 1828 edition of *An American Dictionary of the English Language,* compiled by Webster himself and the real parent of the long line of dictionaries which bear his name. At that time a reviewer in *The Southern Literary Messenger* denounced the treatment of pronunciation as horrible and the orthography as abominable. The English *Quarterly Review* judged it "a decided failure, conducted on perverse and erroneous principles," and in much the same vein as some of the critics of the Webster Third, complained that "we do not recollect ever to have witnessed in the same compass a greater number of crudities and errors, or more pains taken to so little purpose." But Webster's 1828 work has its admirers as well, particularly among the Germans, who praised the profound learning that it reflected.

The disparate comments on Webster's early work are of interest today only as a historical phenomenon, but those which have been applied to the Webster Third still give rise to considerable confusion. It is scarcely possible for both the critics and the admirers to be right in all that they say, and one may reasonably ask what a more dispassionate evaluation might be.

TWO TRADITIONS

In approaching such an appraisal, we must understand first of all that the American lexicographer in his concern with current English faces something of a dilemma. He is the inheritor of two traditions clearly in conflict, both of which have their roots in England.

The earlier tradition is that of Samuel Johnson, the compiler of the 1755 *Dictionary of the English Language,* who lent the first touch of sheer genius to English lexicography. In the preface of this great work, he pointed out that "every language has its improprieties and absurdities, which it is the duty of the lexicographer to correct or proscribe." According to him, the function of a diction-

ary was one, "by which the pronunciation of our language may be fixed and its attainment facilitated; by which its purity may be preserved, its use ascertained, and its duration lengthened." That Johnson was expressing the spirit of his age is shown by comments such as that of Lord Chesterfield, who wrote, "We must have a resource to the old Roman expedient in times of confusion and choose a Dictator. Upon this principle I give my vote for Mr. Johnson to fill that great and arduous post."

This concept of the lexicographer as a linguistic legislator or arbiter, if not absolute dictator, is still strong in the United States. It is frequently reflected, and indeed encouraged, by the slogans which dictionary publishers—not the editors, let me hasten to say—choose to advertise their wares. The very phrase, "Supreme Authority," which the G. and C. Merriam Company used to employ, supported this view of the dictionary; whether intentionally or not is open to conjecture.

The slightly later and opposed tradition is that of the lexicographer as the objective recorder of the language. For the English-speaking nations this concept was first realized on a substantial scale in what is now known as *The Oxford English Dictionary* but originally entitled *A New English Dictionary on Historical Principles.* Here the purpose is stated as follows:

The aim of this dictionary is to present in alphabetical series the words which have formed the English vocabulary from the time of the earliest records down to the present day, with all the relevant facts concerning their form, sense-history, pronunciation, and etymology. It embraces not only the standard language of literature and conversation, whether current at the moment or obsolete, or archaic, but also the main technical vocabulary, and a large measure of dialectal usage and slang.

Note that this statement contains not one word about fixing the language, about proscription or prescription of any kind. Operating on this basis, the lexicographer contents himself with setting down the record, leaving its interpretation to the reader. Needless to say, the prestige of the *Oxford English Dictionary* is enormous; it is generally conceded to be superior to the corresponding major dictionaries for the other western European languages. The principles on which it is based were formulated as early as 1859.

The conflict of principle which has been pointed out need not necessarily be troublesome. If the language involved is confined as to number of speakers and is the vehicle of a static and stabilized society, there is virtually no problem. An accurate description of the language as it is actually used, kept simple by the relative absence of variants, accurately designating social and regional status, will in itself serve prescriptive purposes. But this is not the case with English, which is spoken natively by some two hundred and seventy millions, spread over five continents of the globe. Under such circumstances, uniformity becomes a remote possibility. In the United States, at least, the language is that of a highly mobile society, both geographically and up and down the social scale. As a consequence the lines between class and regional dialects and the standard language inevitably tend to become blurred. Under such circumstances, the linguistic reporter and the legis-

lator are more likely to seem to be working at cross purposes.

Nevertheless, it is clearly evident that as the various editions of Webster march down the century, the statements of principle which are to be found in them move steadily away from the Johnsonian or prescriptive concept toward the descriptive position of the Oxford editors. Even as early as 1864, Chauncey A. Goodrich, the chief editor of the first major revision after Webster's death, asserted that, "The chief value of a dictionary consists in its Definitions; in giving a clear, full, and accurate exhibition, of all the various shades of meaning which belong, *by established usage,* to the words of a language."

Nor was the reportorial concept limited to the Webster series of dictionaries in this country. One of the principal competitors during the early years of the present century, Dr. Isaac K. Funk, wrote in the preface of the 1913 *Standard Dictionary of the English Language,* "The chief function of a dictionary is to record usage." It is true that this forthright statement of the descriptive function was followed by a somewhat unsuccessful attempt to reconcile it with the authoritarian concept, but nevertheless the principle had been stated.

1934 EDITION

The immediate predecessor of the new Webster Third was the 1934 edition. The following excerpt from its front matter (p. xvi) refers specifically to pronunciation, but it is a fair representation of the attitude of its editors toward all language matters:

The function of a pronouncing dictionary is to record as far as possible the pronunciations prevailing in the best present usage, rather than to attempt to dictate what that usage should be. In so far as a dictionary may be known and acknowledged as a faithful recorder and interpreter of such usage, so far and no farther may it be appealed to as an authority.

In the case of diverse usages of extensive prevalence, the dictionary must recognize each of them.

A somewhat broader treatment of the editorial function is to be found in the Introduction (p. xi) to the 1934 Webster:

Both Samuel Johnson and Noah Webster conceived it to be a duty of the dictionary editor to maintain the purity of the standard language. However, with the growth in literacy of the past century, and the increase in fiction and drama, in radio and motion pictures, of the use of dialect, slang, and colloquial speech, it has become necessary for a general dictionary to record and interpret the vocabularies of geographical and occupational dialects, and of the livelier levels of the speech of the educated.

It would be difficult to imagine a more cogent or forthright exposition of the descriptive function of the dictionary than these two statements of editorial policy. The first of them apparently satisfied the editors of the Webster Third, for they repeat it in their Introduction (p. 6a) with only one minor expansion: "best present usage" of the earlier edition now reads, "General cultivated conversational usage, both formal and informal." This offers additional support for the conclusion that with respect to the conflict between opposing lexicographical concepts, the descriptive had been wholly accepted, the prescriptive completely rejected in

1934. Whatever differences there may be between the 1934 and 1961 editions, they are not matters of policy or principle. They are instead differences in the way in which a principle common to both dictionaries has been realized.

Lexicographical policy is not ordinarily a matter of absorbing interest, but it has been necessary to deal with it at some length because the Webster Third has been criticized on occasion for repudiating, even sabotaging the principles of the second edition. Such charges serve only to reveal a total lack of awareness on the part of the critic as to what these principles were, how they have developed in this country, and how they reflect a steadily changing concept of the function of the dictionary. Actually, the furor over the Webster Third is a sad commentary on how inadequately the dictionary has been presented in the English classrooms of the nation and how insufficiently English teachers are informed about one of the principal tools of their profession.

PRACTICAL EDITORIAL DECISIONS

The extremes of public reaction to the new Webster must also be considered in terms of editorial decisions on a practical rather than a theoretical level. Such an understanding may best be attained by considering certain of the practical questions which confronted the editors, what the decisions on them were, and what the reasons for them may have been.

At the very outset of their preparations, the editors apparently felt an obligation to increase considerably the amount of evidence upon which the new dictionary was to be based. Dictionary evidence normally exists in the form of citation slips, the products of an extensive reading program. The citations are filed under their appropriate headwords, and in the editing process they constitute the raw material for the definitions and in fact for most of the word treatment.

At the time of the compilation of the second edition, the files in the Springfield offices held some 1,615,000 citation slips. In the years intervening between the two editions, as the result of what must have been a tremendous effort, this figure was nearly quadrupled. Just under 4,500,000 citations were added, resulting in a total of 6,000,000, a number approximately equalling the collection for the *Oxford English Dictionary*, but far more heavily concentrated on the language of the present day. In addition, the *Dictionary of American English* and the *Dictionary of Americanisms* had both been completed in the years 1944 and 1951 respectively, constituting a further increase in the size of the corpus available to the editors of the Webster Third. As a result, they found themselves with approximately 50,000 new words (words not entered in the Webster Second) and 50,000 new meanings for words already entered.

At this point physical and financial factors enter into consideration. For a number of reasons, undoubtedly based upon a century of business experience, the publishers are firmly committed to a single-volume dictionary. They had made the Webster Second as large, that is to say thick, as any one volume could possibly get and still assure a back that might withstand the rigors of long and constant use, particularly in schools and libraries.

Thus it was manifestly impossible to increase the number of pages by the ten or fifteen percent necessary to accommodate the new entries. If these were to be included, something had to come out. The kind of material that was removed forms the basis of some of the criticisms of the present edition.

The first excision consisted of the materials which, in earlier editions, had been placed below the horizontal line running across the page. These included archaisms, dialect forms, variant spellings, and proper names. To quote the editors, "Many obsolete and comparatively useless or obscure words have been omitted. These include, in general, words that had become obsolete before 1755 unless found in well-known major works of a few major writers." Incidentally, the significance of the date 1755 can scarcely escape one's attention. In the first place it was the publication year of Dr. Johnson's dictionary. Moreover, as a deadline for obsolescence, it marks an advance of two centuries and a half over the corresponding date of 1500 for the Webster Second. Thus, in word selection as well as in other matters, the emphasis is clearly placed upon the current state of the language.

Getting rid of the obsolete and the obscure did not in itself solve the space problem. Still other things had to go, and these taken together constitute the parts essential to a peripheral function of the dictionary long cherished by Americans—the encyclopedic function. In the process of elimination, the editors removed among other things:

1. The gazeteer section.
2. The biographical section.

3. Titles of written works and works of art.

4. Names of characters in fiction, folklore, and mythology.

5. Names of battles, wars, organizations, cities, and states.

6. Mottoes and other familiar sayings.

There have been further excisions as well. Color plates and illustrations are reduced in a proportion somewhere between one-fourth and one-third. Even the number of pages has gone down from 3210 to 2720.

ELIMINATION OF MATERIAL

This elimination of encyclopedic material has caused anguish. "Think, if you can," complains Wilson Follett, "of an unabridged dictionary from which you cannot learn who Mark Twain was, or what were the names of the apostles, or that the Virgin was Mary, the mother of Jesus of Nazareth, or what and where the District of Columbia is." Actually, this is not at all difficult. The great Oxford comes immediately to mind, as does Henry Cecil Wyld's *Universal Dictionary of the English Language,* or any of the great academy dictionaries of such languages as French or Spanish.

Nevertheless, Follett's reaction will be shared by many Americans. In the past, dictionaries published in this country have cheerfully served an encyclopedic as well as a lexicographic function, and ironically enough it was Noah Webster himself who was primarily responsible. His first dictionary, published in 1806 included tables of the moneys of most of the commercial nations in the world, tables of

weights and measures, ancient and modern, the divisions of time among the Jews, Greeks, and Romans, and an official list of the post-offices in the United States, to mention only a few of the extra features. Although the editors of the current volume have broken with their progenitor in cutting out these impedimenta, they have not at all departed from the essential principles of lexicography in so doing.

Undoubtedly they felt that the considerable increase in the number of illustrative citations would readily compensate for the loss of the peripheral material. Such citations do constitute the core of the reportorial dictionary. For instance, there were no citations for the adjective *oratorical* in the second edition; the Third has three. The second edition gave three identified citations for *chase,* verb. In the Third, there are four identified and seven unidentified citations.

According to the Preface of the current edition, "More than 14,000 different authors are quoted for their use of words or for the structural pattern of their words . . ." Many of these are contemporary. The reader is also informed that the verbal illustrations (citations apparently unidentified as to author) are "mostly from the twentieth century."

This innovation has met with something less than universal approval, a reaction not so much attributable to the editorial policy itself as to some of the advertising antics of the business office. The original brochure, announcing this edition as "one of the most remarkable literary achievements of all time," included among the list of authors cited such names as Billy

Rose, Fulton Lewis, Jr., Art Linkletter, Dinah Shore, Ted Williams, and Ethel Merman. In addition there were Harry Truman, Dwight D. Eisenhower, John F. Kennedy, and Richard Nixon, whose names were undoubtedly signed to reams of material which they did not compose. To the sympathetic this signalled a conscious attempt to include a wide range of current authors. To the critical it betokened a lack of discrimination and responsibility. Actually, the citations from such sources are few in number and small in proportion.

A point which must be taken into account here is that which was made at the very outset of this essay, namely that the life of a Webster edition is roughly calculated at twenty-five years. Thus, the overriding concern of the dictionary is quite appropriately the language in its current state. It is on these grounds that the editors may logically justify the preponderance of citations from current authors, irrespective of lasting literary merit. It may be assumed that in the 1986 edition many of them will be discarded, to be replaced by others from the 1970's and early 1980's. In this respect the Webster practice will differ sharply from that of the *Oxford English Dictionary,* for which no new edition was contemplated, although certainly only a small proportion of the authors cited in that work are literary giants of lasting reputation.

STATUS LABELS

Another departure in the Webster Third from the practice of earlier editions, which has given rise to considerable criticism, is the treatment of what are called *status labels.* Here

again some of the disapproval has its source in misunderstanding. Basically, the editors have developed a terminology which is at once semantically neutral and more precise than that which has been employed in the past. The label *illiterate* has been discontinued. It has become a term of censure rather than a dispassionate indication of the inability to read and write. The current replacements, *substandard* and *nonstandard* are matter-of-fact rather than pejorative and permit a gradation of acceptability, the latter indicating a wider range of occurrence than the former, although it is applied to a smaller number of words and expressions. American dialect ascriptions represent a great advance in precision over those of the second edition in that they reflect an adaptation of the terminology for the various dialect areas developed by Professor Hans Kurath, editor of the Linguistic Atlas and the most eminent linguistic geographer in the country. It was unfortunate, however, that the editors chose not to indicate those words current in all regions of the United States but not in England or other parts of the English-speaking world.

Another innovation in the Webster Third is the elimination of the label *colloquial.* There are two conceivable reasons for this: In the first place the term is ambivalent, signifying informality on the one hand and the spoken rather than the written medium on the other. It is customary now among students of the language to be somewhat more precise, recognizing not only colloquial but *casual* and *intimate* as further gradations of the spoken variety of the language, any of which not only may be but are regularly employed by speakers of un-questioned cultivation.

An even greater objection to the label *colloquial* is the persistence with which an unfavorable connotation has adhered to it. Dictionary users never interpreted the term in the way in which dictionary editors intended. It was not meant as a condemnation either in the Webster Second or in the various abridged dictionaries based upon it. The editors took great pains to say so, both in the prefatory material and in the definition of the word itself, but this went unheeded. So for the present edition the staff was faced with the alternative of finding an acceptable substitute less liable to misinterpretation, or of eliminating the label altogether. It chose the latter, partly perhaps because of the unsatisfactory experience of other dictionaries which had experimented with a substitute.

In general the changes in the choice and ascription of labels reflect an endeavor to achieve greater precision and objectivity. The attempt at precision undoubtedly finds some adherents, although there will be disagreements over the application of the labels in specific instances. The attempt at objectivity has, understandably enough, resulted in the disappearance of the censorious tone which, for many seemed to be part of the proper function of the labels *colloquial* and *illiterate*. To such persons, the lack of censure has been understood as a lowering of standards.

PRONUNCIATION

In dealing with pronunciation, the editors of the Webster Third had to contend with two factors which had not faced their predecessors. One was a new electronic development, namely voice amplification. The other was a new concept in the analysis of language, that of the phoneme or meaningful unit of sound.

Voice amplification affected the kind of pronunciation which the dictionary undertook to record. In pre-loud-speaker days, the second edition of Webster recorded what it called "formal platform speech," the speech of cultivated users of English, speaking formally with a view to being completely understood by their hearers. That there were other types of pronunciation wholly appropriate to less formal situations was readily conceded by the editors, but they evidently felt that their editorial responsibility could be discharged with the greatest amount of effectiveness and least confusion by indicating just the one.

The microphone has changed all this. Certain devices of articulation necessary for clarity when the speaker was forced to depend on lung power to make himself audible to the last row of a large auditorium are no longer necessary. Nor are they often employed today.

This change led the Webster editors into a complete revision of the manner in which evidence on pronunciation was collected. Where Webster Second had attempted a sampling, by means of written questionnaires, of the pronunciation of persons who did a considerable amount of public speaking, the Webster Third staff turned its attention directly to the language itself rather than to opinion about it. They listened to radio, television, and recordings; to speech in all parts of the country and in all types of situations. Again, as with the citations for word occurrences, forms, and meanings, the body of evidence was tremendously increased in range and scope, but certainly less skewed toward a single type of pronunciation.

In any English dictionary, and particularly one designed for use in the United States, a decision upon the particular system, or respelling, to indicate pronunciation always poses a problem. For a number of reasons, the American public has been unwilling to accept the International Phonetic Alphabet; nor is this a particularly economical device when a number of variants must be shown. The Webster Second continued with few changes the system of its predecessors, which was cumbersome in that a single sound was indicated by more than one transcription, and confusing in that a single character sometimes covered far more latitude than the user was likely to realize.

The editors of the current edition have attempted to take advantage of the phonemic concept, basic to present-day linguistic science. The general result has been the disappearance of a rash of diacritics which made the earlier dictionaries difficult to read and to interpret. Some useful characters have been taken over from the phonetic alphabet, notably the elongated *n* to indicate the usual sound of *ng*, and most important, the inverted *e* or schwa for the neutral vowel used in weakly stressed syllables. The latter, it must be confessed, is an innovation in which Webster followed some of its competitors. At all events, the public will no longer be misled into believing that the final vowel of *caucus* is somehow different from that of *fracas*.

Unfortunately the necessity of economizing on space has led to the excision of the authoritative treatments of the individual sounds of English which lent scholarly distinction to the second edition though perhaps read by only a few. Also, certain innovations of the Webster Third will cause annoyance until the public becomes accustomed to them. One of these may well be the indication of stress by a mark preceding rather than following the syllable. The removal of the pronunciation key from the bottom of the page is another. The use of a modified *d* character to indicate what the editors call, "the usual American pronunciation of *latter*," will seem to the critical like countenancing the slipshod, and it is possible that a *t* with a diacritic might have served quite as well without outraging quite so many sensibilities.

With pronunciation as with countless other features of the dictionary, the editors have attempted to present the facts of the language as they saw them. It is an honest presentation, maintaining the principles and the concept of the dictionary characteristic of previous editions, but carrying them out with greater consistency and basing them upon far more evidence. There have been errors of judgment, more often perhaps with respect to manner of presentation than in the interpretation of the facts which are reported, but this is inevitable in an undertaking of such magnitude.

My comments so far should have suggested, to a degree at least, the reasons for some of the changes which are to be found in the Webster Third. They have not yet given an answer to the question which was initially posed: why the extremes of praise and blame. The encomiums are easy to account for. They represent the approval of those who accept the descriptive principle and find in the current product a generally conscientious and more thorough implementation of it than is otherwise available.

CONTROVERSY

The chorus of protest is somewhat more complex in origin. It is in part the expression of a desire for linguistic authoritarianism, an attitude sincerely held by many which can be explained only in terms of a number of complex and interrelated factors in American cultural history. Added to this is the mistaken notion that the Webster Third represents a change in lexicographical principle, an error which is fostered by the more complete coverage and greater accuracy of the edition. The excision of certain kinds of nonessential material represented a sudden departure from a time-honored practice. Moreover, there is, as always, a tendency toward careless reading and inept comparison; upon occasion a judgment objected to in the third edition was already present in the second. This reflects a not uncommon situation. Even those who are willing to concede that language standards must ultimately rest upon usage are not infrequently distressed when they encounter a detailed and factual inventory of that usage. At such a point the normal reaction is to question the accuracy of the inventory and the soundness of the method upon which it is based.

An excellent illustration of this is to be found in the treatment of the very word that has given rise to so many headlines and caused so much acid comment—*ain't*. The statement which gave rise to the excitement, namely that *ain't* is used orally in most parts of the United States by many cultivated speakers, is merely a condensation of what has already been noted in Bagby Atwood's *A Survey of Verb Forms in the Eastern United States,* a study based upon the materials of the Linguistic Atlas of the United States and Canada. "Cultivated, our foot," comments the editor of the Chicago *Daily News;* yet the cultivated informants for the various regional atlases were selected on the basis of as rigorous a set of standards in terms of family background, education, and occupation as could be established.

The presumed role of structural linguistics in the Webster Third reflects a most unfortunate confusion, and ironically it is the editor of the dictionary who is in part responsible for it. In an article in *Word Study* prior to the publication of the dictionary, Dr. Gove unintentionally left careless and uninformed readers with the mistaken impression that Leonard Bloomfield in 1926 first stated the postulate that correctness rests upon usage. Despite the fact that Dr. Gove then went on to mention any number of areas in lexicography where linguistics had had no appreciable influence, the first part of his article appears to have left many readers with the mental image of a fifth column of structuralists burrowing their way through the Merriam-Webster files in Springfield.

This notion is wrong on two counts. First, the importance of usage in the establishment of a linguistic standard had been maintained by a host of scholars from the turn of the century on. They included Thomas Lounsbury, George P. Krapp, Louise Pound, Charles C. Fries, and Sterling A. Leonard, to mention only a few of the more distinguished. The structuralists accept this as a matter of course, but they did not invent the idea. Second, except for the treatment of pronunciation, structural concepts do not appear with any great frequency in the dictionary. Words are traditionally classified as nouns, adjectives, verbs, and so on. There was no attempt to substitute a scheme consistently based either upon form or function. This is a dictionary of words rather than of morphemes. I find it difficult to detect even a hint of structuralism in the handling of the definitions. Yet Dwight Macdonald[1] speaks of the "direct application" of structural linguistics "to making dictionaries," and the idea has been echoed by others.

It is the English-teaching profession which should be seriously disturbed by the dictionary controversy. If the Webster war has proved little or nothing about dictionaries, it has

[1] Dwight Macdonald, long one of our most articulate cultural assessors, wrote a review-article for *The New Yorker* (March 10, 1962) which presents most effectively the arguments of the detractors of the Webster Third.

demonstrated our ineptitude, if not absolute failure, in teaching our students what a dictionary is for, how it is made, and the proper way to use it. Much of the misunderstanding of principle, of the confusion of principle and practice, of the failure to read and interpret accurately can, with considerable justice, be laid at our door. After all, the embattled critics were once our students; had our teaching of the dictionary been soundly based, this comedy of errors should have been at least somewhat less comic.

To return to the dictionary itself, however, one can only say that by a more literal acceptance of its declared function, and by running counter more obviously to what people want or think they want in a dictionary and to what they think they have been getting, the Webster Third represents a calculated risk. Depending on one's point of view, it is either a courageous or a foolhardy venture into the latter half of the twentieth century. For the staff, who in the face of the public clamor must wonder if it has been at all worthwhile, there is only the dubious comfort in Macaulay's words, "The best lexicographer may well be content if his productions are received by the world in cold esteem."

For discussion

A. What are the two conflicting traditions in American dictionary making? Of which tradition was *Webster's Second International* (1934) an example?

B. How did *Webster's Third International* solve the problem of what was to be removed from *Webster's Second International*? Why did anything have to be removed? What takes up the space thus gained?

C. What is the justification for concentrating on language in its current state?

D. What changes have been made in the use of status labels? Why?

E. What were the new problems with which the editors of *Webster's Third International* had to contend in dealing with pronunciation?

F. What was the role of structural linguistics in *Webster's Third International?*

G. The last paragraph of the introduction to Marckwardt's article mentions a number of things a good dictionary should do. Make a list of these things, and check your own dictionary against it by looking up the following:

1. the etymologies of *posh, o.k., gringo, yankee,* and *schooner.*

2. the alternate spellings of *labor, theater, catalog, traveler, pretense, thru,* and *artifact.*

3. the alternate pronunciations of *bath, migraine, tube, new, loath, literature, fracas, trait, phonemic,* and *nuclear.*

4. the symbol in the prounciation key for the second vowel sound of *awful, offal,* and *dawdle.*

5. the most recent meaning of *beat, pad, camp, snow, joint, escalate, cool,* and *strike.*

6. the meaning of *slurb, exurbanite, sit-in, Bloody Mary, Molotov Cocktail, picture-tube,* and *miniaturization.*

7. the meaning of *soap opera, wet-back, Madison Avenue, ten-gallon hat, straw hat theater, carpet-bagger, cliffhanger, stovepipe hat, log-rolling,* and *dogface.*

8. the meaning of *mousetrap play, four bagger, texas leaguer, grand slam,* and *checkmate.*

9. the usage label applied to *irregardless, like* (used as a conjunction), *finalize, drank* (used as a past participle), and *ain't.*

DONALD P. COSTELLO

The language of "The Catcher in the Rye"

IT IS DOUBTFUL if a literary work can ever really accurately both reproduce the spoken dialect and be convincing. Sinclair Lewis, whose ear turned to tin in about the middle of his career, was generally considered to have reflected the spoken idiom in his early work. He himself wrote, however, that he would never think of using what people actually say for dialogue in his novels. He insisted that nobody would believe it. On the other hand, efforts of war novelists to gain verisimilitude by recording every bit of the obscenity which is as natural as breathing in large sections of any military establishment are eventually self-defeating because service-connected obscenities simply go unheard in their original context. They are usually the "uhs" and "ahs" that punctuate civilian conversation, even though occasionally a skilled practitioner can use a single obscenity as almost every part of speech within one sentence.

Nevertheless, convincing idiosyncracies of speech in literary monologues or dialogues are frequently a principal means by which a writer forms his characterizations. We do not meet Shylock until the third scene of *The Merchant of Venice,* and when we do meet him, his first three speeches average six syllables each. Each speech concludes with, "Well," and by the third "Well," Shylock is individualized; and Holden Caulfield is individualized with his "and alls."

As Donald P. Costello of Roosevelt University makes clear in "The Language of *The Catcher in the Rye,*" most critics thought J. D. Salinger recorded an authentic teenage idiom in the conversation and musing of Holden Caulfield. Doing this was, of course, not Salinger's principal intention. His intention was to create a complex individual character and dramatize his plight. One of the problems was to make the superficial destitution of teenage speech contribute to a characterization—that of Holden Caulfield. Costello talks about the way in which Salinger solved the problem.

A study of the language of J. D. Salinger's *The Catcher in the Rye* can be justified not only on the basis of literary interest, but also on the basis of linguistic significance. Today we study *The Adventures of Huckleberry Finn* (with which many critics have compared *The Catcher in the Rye*)

"*The Language of* The Catcher in the Rye": From *American Speech,* vol. 34, n. 3, October 1959, pp. 172–181. Reprinted with the permission of Donald P. Costello. Some of the footnotes in the original article have been omitted here.

not only as a great work of literary art, but as a valuable study in 1884 dialect. In coming decades, *The Catcher in the Rye* will be studied, I feel, not only as a literary work, but also as an example of teenage vernacular in the 1950s. As such, the book will be a significant historical linguistic record of a type of speech rarely made available in permanent form. Its linguistic importance will increase as the American speech it records becomes less current.

Most critics who looked at *The Catcher in the Rye* at the time of its publication thought that its language was a true and authentic rendering of teenage colloquial speech. Reviewers in the Chicago *Sunday Tribune,* the London *Times Literary Supplement,* the *New Republic,* the New York *Herald Tribune Book Review,* the New York *Times,* the *New Yorker,* and the *Saturday Review of Literature* all specifically mentioned the authenticity of the book's language. Various aspects of its language were also discussed in the reviews published in *America,* the *Atlantic,* the *Catholic World,* the *Christian Science Monitor,* the *Library Journal,* the Manchester *Guardian,* the *Nation,* the *New Statesman and Nation,* the New York *Times Book Review, Newsweek,* the *Spectator,* and *Time.* Of these many reviews, only the writers for the *Catholic World* and the *Christian Science Monitor* denied the authenticity of the book's language, but both of these are religious journals which refused to believe that the "obscenity" was realistic. An examination of the reviews of *The Catcher in the Rye* proves that the language of Holden Caulfield, the book's sixteen-year-old narrator, struck the ear of the con-

temporary reader as an accurate rendering of the informal speech of an intelligent, educated, Northeastern American adolescent.[1]

In addition to commenting on its authenticity, critics have often remarked—uneasily—the "daring," "obscene," "blasphemous" features of Holden's language. Another commonly noted feature of the book's language has been its comic effect. And yet there has never been an extensive investigation of the language itself. That is what this paper proposes to do.

Even though Holden's language is authentic teenage speech, recording it was certainly not the major intention of Salinger. He was faced with the artistic task of creating an individual character, not with the linguistic task of reproducing the exact speech of teenagers in general. Yet Holden had

[1] If additional evidence of the authenticity of the book's language is required, one need only look at the phenomenal regard with which *The Catcher in the Rye* is held by today's college students, who were about Holden's age at the time the book was written. In its March 9, 1957, issue, the *Nation* published a symposium which attempted to discover the major influences upon the college students of today. Many teachers pointed out the impact of Salinger. Carlos Baker, of Princeton, stated: "There is still, as there has been for years, a cult of Thomas Wolfe. They have all read J. D. Salinger, Wolfe's closest competitor." Stanley Kunitz, of Queens College, wrote: "The only novelist I have heard praised vociferously is J. D. Salinger." Harvey Curtis Webster, of the University of Louisville, listed Salinger as one of the "stimulators." R. J. Kaufman, of the University of Rochester, called *The Catcher in the Rye* "a book which has complexly aroused nearly all of them." See "The Careful Young Men," *Nation,* CLXXXIV (March 9, 1957), 199–214. I have never heard any Salinger partisan among college students doubt the authenticity of the language of their compatriot, Holden.

to speak a recognizable teenage language, and at the same time had to be identifiable as an individual. This difficult task Salinger achieved by giving Holden an extremely trite and typical teenage speech, overlaid with strong personal idiosyncrasies. There are two major speech habits which are Holden's own, which are endlessly repeated throughout the book, and which are, nevertheless, typical enough of teenage speech so that Holden can be both typical and individual in his use of them. It is certainly common for teenagers to end thoughts with a loosely dangling "and all," just as it is common for them to add an insistent "I really did," "It really was." But Holden uses these phrases to such an overpowering degree that they become a clear part of the flavor of the book; they become, more, a part of Holden himself, and actually help to characterize him.

Holden's "and all" and its twins, "or something," "or anything," serve no real, consistent linguistic function. They simply give a sense of looseness of expression and looseness of thought. Often they signify that Holden knows there is more that could be said about the issue at hand, but he is not going to bother going into it:

. . . how my parents were occupied and all before they had me (5.)[2]
. . . they're *nice* and all (5.)
I'm not going to tell you my whole goddam autobiography or anything (5.)
. . . splendid and clear-thinking and all (6.)

But just as often the use of such expressions is purely arbitrary, with no discernible meaning:

. . . he's my *brother* and all (5.)
. . . was in the Revolutionary War and all (6.)
It was December and all (7.)
. . . no gloves or anything (7.)
. . . right in the pocket and all (7.)

Donald Barr, writing in the *Commonweal*, finds this habit indicative of Holden's tendency to generalize, to find the all in the one:

Salinger has an ear not only for idiosyncrasies of diction and syntax, but for mental processes. Holden Caulfield's phrase is "and all"—"She looked so damn *nice*, the way she kept going around and around in her blue coat and all"—as if each experience wore a halo. His fallacy is *ab uno disce omnes;* he abstracts and generalizes wildly.[3]

Heiserman and Miller, in the *Western Humanities Review*, comment specifically upon Holden's second most obvious idiosyncrasy: "In a phony world Holden feels compelled to reenforce his sincerity and truthfulness constantly with, 'It really is' or 'It really did.' "[4] S. N. Behrman, in the *New Yorker*, finds a double function of these "perpetual insistencies of Holden's." Behrman thinks they "reveal his age, even when he is thinking much older," and, more important, "he is so aware of the danger of slipping into phoniness himself that he has to repeat over and over 'I really

2 Whenever *The Catcher in the Rye* is substantially quoted in this paper, a page number will be included in the text immediately after the quotation. The edition to which the page numbers refer is the Signet paperback reprint.

3 Donald Barr ("Saints, Pilgrims, and Artists,") *Commonweal*, LXVII (October 25, 1957), 90.
4 Arthur Heiserman and James E. Miller, Jr., "J. D. Salinger: Some Crazy Cliff," *Western Humanities Review*, X (1956), 136.

mean it,' 'It really does.' "[5] Holden uses this idiosyncrasy of insistence almost every time that he makes an affirmation.

Allied to Holden's habit of insistence is his "if you want to know the truth." Heiserman and Miller are able to find characterization in this habit too:

> The skepticism inherent in that casual phrase, "if you want to know the truth," suggesting that as a matter of fact in the world of Holden Caulfield very few people do, characterizes this sixteen-year-old "crazy mixed up kid" more sharply and vividly than pages of character "analysis" possibly could.[6]

Holden uses this phrase only after affirmations, just as he uses "It really does," but usually after the personal ones, where he is consciously being frank:

> I have no wind, if you want to know the truth. (8.)
> I don't even think that bastard had a handkerchief, if you want to know the truth. (34.)
> I'm a pacifist, if you want to know the truth. (44.)
> She had quite a lot of sex appeal, too, if you really want to know. (53.)
> I was damn near bawling, I felt so damn happy, if you want to know the truth. (191.)

These personal idiosyncrasies of Holden's speech are in keeping with general teenage language. Yet they are so much a part of Holden and of the flavor of the book that they are much of what makes Holden to be Holden. They are the most memorable feature of the book's language.

[5] S. N. Behrman, "The Vision of the Innocent, *New Yorker*, XXVII (August 11, 1951), 72.

[6] Heiserman and Miller, *op. cit.*, p. 135.

Although always in character, the rest of Holden's speech is more typical than individual. The special quality of this language comes from its triteness, its lack of distinctive qualities.

Holden's informal, schoolboy vernacular is particularly typical in its "vulgarity" and "obscenity." No one familiar with prep-school speech could seriously contend that Salinger overplayed his hand in this respect. On the contrary, Holden's restraints help to characterize him as a sensitive youth who avoids the most strongly forbidden terms, and who never uses vulgarity in a self-conscious or phony way to help him be "one of the boys. *Fuck*, for example, is never used as a part of Holden's speech. The word appears in the novel four times, but only when Holden disapprovingly discusses its wide appearance on walls. The Divine name is used habitually by Holden only in the comparatively weak *for God's sake, God,* and *goddam.* The stronger and usually more offensive *for Chrissake* or *Jesus* or *Jesus Christ* are used habitually by Ackley and Stradlater; but Holden uses them only when he feels the need for a strong expression. He almost never uses *for Chrissake* in an unemotional situation. *Goddam* is Holden's favorite adjective. This word is used with no relationship to its original meaning, or to Holden's attitude toward the word to which it is attached. It simply expresses an emotional feeling toward the object: either favorable, as in "goddam hunting cap"; or unfavorable, as in "ya goddam moron"; or indifferent, as in "coming in the goddam windows." *Damm* is used interchangeably with *goddam;* no differentiation in its meaning is detectable.

Other crude words are also often used in Holden's vocabulary. *Ass* keeps a fairly restricted meaning as a part of the human anatomy, but it is used in a variety of ways. It can refer simply to that specific part of the body ("I moved my ass a little"), or be a part of a trite expression ("freezing my ass off"; "in a half-assed way"), or be an expletive ("Game, my ass."). *Hell* is perhaps the most versatile word in Holden's entire vocabulary; it serves most of the meanings and constructions which Mencken lists in his *American Speech* article on "American Profanity." So far is Holden's use of *hell* from its original meaning that he can use the sentence "We had a helluva time" to mean that he and Phoebe had a decidedly pleasant time downtown shopping for shoes. The most common function of *hell* is as the second part of a simile, in which a thing can be either "hot as hell" or, strangely, "cold as hell"; "sad as hell" or "playful as hell"; "old as hell" or "pretty as hell." Like all of these words, *hell* has no close relationship to its original meaning.

Both *bastard* and *sonuvabitch* have also drastically changed in meaning. They no longer, of course, in Holden's vocabulary, have any connection with the accidents of birth. Unless used in a trite simile, *bastard* is a strong word, reserved for things and people Holden particularly dislikes, especially "phonies." *Sonuvabitch* has an even stronger meaning to Holden; he uses it only in the deepest anger. When, for example, Holden is furious with Stradlater over his treatment of Jane Gallagher, Holden repeats again and again that he "kept calling him a moron sonuvabitch" (43).

The use of crude language in *The Catcher in the Rye* increases, as we should expect, when Holden is reporting schoolboy dialogue. When he is directly addressing the reader, Holden's use of such language drops off almost entirely. There is also an increase in this language when any of the characters are excited or angry. Thus, when Holden is apprehensive over Stradlater's treatment of Jane, his *goddams* increase suddenly to seven on a single page (p. 39).

Holden's speech is also typical in his use of slang. I have catalogued over a hundred slang terms used by Holden, and every one of these is in widespread use. Although Holden's slang is rich and colorful, it, of course, being slang, often fails at precise communication. Thus, Holden's *crap* is used in seven different ways. It can mean foolishness, as "all that David Copperfield kind of crap," or messy matter, as "I spilled some crap all over my gray flannel," or merely miscellaneous matter, as "I was putting on my galoshes and crap." It can also carry its basic meaning, animal excreta, as "there didn't look like there was anything in the park except dog crap," and it can be used as an adjective meaning anything generally unfavorable, as "The show was on the crappy side." Holden uses the phrases *to be a lot of crap* and *to shoot the crap* and *to chuck the crap* all to mean "to be untrue," but he can also use *to shoot the crap* to mean simply "to chat," with no connotation of untruth, as in "I certainly wouldn't have minded shooting the crap with old Phoebe for a while."

Similarly Holden's slang use of *crazy* is both trite and imprecise. "That drives me crazy" means that he violently dislikes something; yet "to be crazy about" something means just the opposite. In the same way, to be "killed" by something can mean that he was emotionally affected either favorably ("That story just about killed me.") or unfavorably ("Then she turned her back on me again. It nearly killed me."). This use of *killed* is one of Holden's favorite slang expressions. Heiserman and Miller are, incidentally, certainly incorrect when they conclude: "Holden always lets us know when he has insight into the absurdity of the endlessly absurd situations which make up the life of a sixteen-year-old by exclaiming, 'It killed me.' "[7] Holden often uses this expression with no connection to the absurd; he even uses it for his beloved Phoebe. The expression simply indicates a high degree of emotion—any kind. It is hazardous to conclude that any of Holden's slang has a precise and consistent meaning or function. These same critics fall into the same error when they conclude that Holden's use of the adjective *old* serves as "a term of endearment."[8] Holden appends this word to almost every character, real or fictional, mentioned in the novel, from the hated "old Maurice" to "old Peter Lorre," to "old Phoebe," and even "old Jesus." The only pattern that can be discovered in Holden's use of this term is that he usually uses it only after he has previously mentioned the character; he then feels free to append the familiar *old*. All we can conclude from Holden's slang is that it is typical teenage slang: versatile yet narrow, expressive yet unimaginative, imprecise, often crude, and always trite.

Holden has many favorite slang ex-

pressions which he overuses. In one place, he admits:

"Boy!" I said. I also say "Boy!" quite a lot. Partly because I have a lousy vocabulary and partly because I act quite young for my age sometimes. (12.)

But if Holden's slang shows the typically "lousy vocabulary" of even the educated American teenager, this failing becomes even more obvious when we narrow our view to Holden's choice of adjectives and adverbs. The choice is indeed narrow, with a constant repetition of a few favorite words: *lousy, pretty, crumby, terrific, quite, old, stupid*—all used, as in the habit of teenage vernacular, with little regard to specific meaning. Thus, most of the nouns which are called "stupid" could not in any logical framework be called "ignorant," and, as we have seen, *old* before a proper noun has nothing to do with age.

Another respect in which Holden was correct in accusing himself of having a "lousy vocabulary" is discovered in the ease with which he falls into trite figures of speech. We have already seen that Holden's most common simile is the worn and meaningless "as hell"; but his often-repeated "like a madman" and "like a bastard" are just about as unrelated to a literal meaning and are easily as unimaginative. Even Holden's non-habitual figures of speech are usually trite: "sharp as a tack"; "hot as a firecracker"; "laughed like a hyena"; "I know old Jane like a book"; "drove off like a bat out of hell"; "I began to feel like a horse's ass"; "blind as a bat"; "I know Central Park like the back of my hand."

Repetitious and trite as Holden's vocabulary may be, it can, neverthe-

---

[7] Heiserman and Miller, *op. cit.*, p. 136.
[8] *Ibid.*

less, become highly effective. For example, when Holden piles one trite adjective upon another, a strong power of invective is often the result:

He was a goddam stupid moron. (42.)
Get your dirty stinking moron knees off my chest. (43.)
You're a dirty stupid sonuvabitch of a moron. (43.)

And his limited vocabulary can also be used for good comic effect. Holden's constant repetition of identical expressions in countless widely different situations is often hilariously funny.

But all of the humor in Holden's vocabulary does not come from its unimaginative quality. Quite the contrary, some of his figures of speech are entirely original; and these are inspired, dramatically effective, and terribly funny. As always, Salinger's Holden is basically typical, with a strong overlay of the individual:

He started handling my exam paper like it was a turd or something. (13.)
He put my goddam paper down then and looked at me like he'd just beaten the hell out of me in ping-pong or something. (14.)
That guy Morrow was about as sensitive as a goddam toilet seat. (52.)
Old Marty was like dragging the Statue of Liberty around the floor. (69.)

Another aspect in which Holden's language is typical is that it shows the general American characteristic of adaptability—apparently strengthened by his teenage lack of restraint. It is very easy for Holden to turn nouns into adjectives, with the simple addition of a -y: "perverty," "Christmasy," "vomity-looking," "whory-looking," "hoodlumy-looking," "showoffy," "flitty-looking," "dumpy-look-

ing," "pimpy," "snobby," "fisty." Like all of English, Holden's language shows a versatile combining ability: "They gave Sally this little blue butt-twitcher of a dress to wear" (117) and "That magazine was some little cheerer upper" (176). Perhaps the most interesting aspect of the adaptability of Holden's language is his ability to use nouns as adverbs: "She sings it very Dixieland and whorehouse, and it doesn't sound at all mushy" (105).

As we have seen, Holden shares, in general, the trite repetitive vocabulary which is the typical lot of his age group. But as there are exceptions in his figures of speech, so are there exceptions in his vocabulary itself, in his word stock. An intelligent, well-read ("I'm quite illiterate, but I read a lot"), and educated boy, Holden possesses, and can use when he wants to, many words which are many a cut above Basic English, including "ostracized," "exhibitionist," "unscrupulous," "conversationalist," "psychic," "bourgeois." Often Holden seems to choose his words consciously, in an effort to communicate to his adult reader clearly and properly, as in such terms as "lose my virginity," "relieve himself," "an alcoholic"; for upon occasion, he also uses the more vulgar terms "to give someone the time," "to take a leak," "booze hound." Much of the humor arises, in fact, from Holden's habit of writing on more than one level at the same time. Thus, we have such phrases as "They give guys the ax quite frequently at Pency" and "It has a very good academic rating, Pency" (7). Both sentences show a colloquial idiom with an overlay of consciously selected words.

Such a conscious choice of words

seems to indicate that Salinger, in his attempt to create a realistic character in Holden, wanted to make him aware of his speech, as, indeed, a real teenager would be when communicating to the outside world. Another piece of evidence that Holden is conscious of his speech and, more, realizes a difficulty in communication, is found in his habit of direct repetition: "She likes me a lot. I mean she's quite fond of me." (141), and "She can be very snotty sometimes. She can be quite snotty." (150). Sometimes the repetition is exact: "He was a very nervous guy—I mean he was a very nervous guy." (165), and "I sort of missed them. I mean I sort of missed them." (169). Sometimes Holden stops specifically to interpret slang terms, as when he wants to communicate the fact that Allie liked Phoebe: "She killed Allie, too. I mean he liked her, too" (64).

There is still more direct evidence that Holden was conscious of his speech. Many of his comments to the reader are concerned with language. He was aware, for example, of the "phony" quality of many words and phrases, such as "grand," "prince," "traveling incognito," "little girls' room," "licorice stick," and "angels." Holden is also conscious, of course, of the existence of "taboo words." He makes a point of mentioning that the girl from Seattle repeatedly asked him to "watch your language, if you don't mind" (67), and that his mother told Phoebe not to say "lousy" (160). When the prostitute says "Like fun you are," Holden comments:

It was a funny thing to say. It sounded like a real kid. You'd think a prostitute and all would say "Like hell you are" or "Cut the crap" instead of "Like fun you are." (87.)

In grammar, too, as in vocabulary, Holden possesses a certain self-consciousness. (It is, of course, impossible to imagine a student getting through today's schools without a self-consciousness with regard to grammar rules.) Holden is, in fact, not only aware of the existence of "grammatical errors," but knows the social taboos that accompany them. He is disturbed by a schoolmate who is ashamed of his parents' grammar, and he reports that his former teacher, Mr. Antolini, warned him about picking up "just enough education to hate people who say, 'It's a secret between he and I'" (168).

Holden is a typical enough teenager to violate the grammar rules, even though he knows of their social importance. His most common rule violation is the misuse of *lie* and *lay*, but he also is careless about relative pronouns ("about a traffic cop that falls in love"), the double negative ("I hardly didn't even know I was doing it"), the perfect tenses ("I'd woke him up"), extra words ("like as if all you ever did at Pency was play polo all the time"), pronoun number ("it's pretty disgusting to watch somebody picking their nose"), and pronoun position ("I and this friend of mine, Mal Brossard"). More remarkable, however, than the instances of grammar rule violations is Holden's relative "correctness." Holden is always intelligible, and is even "correct" in many usually difficult constructions. Grammatically speaking, Holden's language seems to point up the fact that English was the only subject in which he was not failing. It is interesting to note how much more "correct" Holden's speech is than that of Huck Finn. But then Holden is educated, and since the time of Huck there had been sixty-seven years of authoritarian schoolmarms working on the likes of Holden. He has, in fact, been overtaught, so that he uses many "hyper" forms:

I used to play tennis with he and Mrs. Antolini quite frequently. (163.)
She'd give Allie or I a push. (64.)
I and Allie used to take her to the park with us. (64.)
I think I probably woke he and his wife up. (157.)

Now that we have examined several aspects of Holden's vocabulary and grammar, it would be well to look at a few examples of how he puts these elements together into sentences. The structure of Holden's sentences indicates that Salinger thinks of the book more in terms of spoken speech than written speech. Holden's faulty structure is quite common and typical in vocal expression; I doubt if a student who is "good in English" would ever create such sentence structure in writing. A student who showed the self-consciousness of Holden would not *write* so many fragments, such afterthoughts (e.g., "It has a very good academic rating, Pency" [7]), or such repetitions (e.g., "Where I lived at Pency, I lived in the Ossenburger Memorial Wing of the new dorms" [18].

There are other indications that Holden's speech is vocal. In many places Salinger mildly imitates spoken speech. Sentences such as "You could tell old Spencer'd got a big bang out of buying it" (10) and "I'd've killed him" (42) are repeated throughout the book. Yet it is impossible to imagine Holden taking pen in hand and actually writing "Spencer'd" or "I'd've." Sometimes, too, emphasized words, or even parts of words, are italicized, as in "Now *shut up*, Holden. God damn it—I'm *warn*ing ya" (42). This is often done with good effect, imitating quite perfectly the rhythms of speech, as in the typical:

I practically sat down on her *lap,* as a matter of fact. Then she *really* started to cry, and the next thing I knew, I was kissing her all over—*any*where—her eyes, her *nose,* her forehead, her eyebrows and all, her *ears*—her whole face except her mouth and all. (73.)

The language of *The Catcher in the Rye* is, as we have seen, an authentic artistic rendering of a type of informal, colloquial, teenage American spoken speech. It is strongly typical and trite, yet often somewhat individual; it is crude and slangy and imprecise, imitative yet occasionally imaginative, and affected toward standardization by the strong efforts of schools. But authentic and interesting as this language may be, it must be remembered that it exists, in *The Catcher in the Rye,* as only one part of an artistic achievement. The language was not written for itself, but as a part of a greater whole. Like the great Twain work with which it is often compared, a study of *The Catcher in the Rye* repays both the linguist and the literary critic; for as one critic has said, "In them, 1884 and 1951 speak to us in the idiom and accent of two youthful travelers who have earned their passports to literary immortality."[9]

[9] Charles Kaplan, "Holden and Huck: the Odysseys of Youth, *College English,* XVIII (1956), 80.

For discussion

A. What illustrations does Costello give for his idea that Salinger thinks of his book as spoken rather than written?

B. What linguistic tricks does Holden use to reinforce his sincerity?

C. What do Holden's idiosyncrasies of speech reveal about his character?

D. Costello writes that *We had a helluva time* can mean either a good time or a bad time. This kind of statement, which depends upon what is said before and after for its complete meaning, is fairly common in speech. Give some other examples of similar ambiguity.

E. Give some examples of the way in which Holden changes nouns into adjectives and uses nouns as adverbs.

F. What is revealed about Holden by his mixing of levels of usage?

G. What is Holden's idea of correctness?

H. A good place to find spoken English in print is *The New York Times,* which regularly prints the full texts of interviews. Look one up and note what you consider to be deviations from written English.

I. *The Catcher in the Rye* was written some years ago. What words or expressions regularly used by Holden have disappeared from the language of the teenager today? What, if anything, has replaced them?

BENJAMIN LEE WHORF

Languages and logic

ENGLISH USUALLY PLACES an adjective modifier before the noun (*the white house*). French usually places it after (*la maison blanche*). By placing modifiers in different positions, we are likely to get quite different meanings (*secretary general—general secretary*). When we translate from one language to another, we must almost always sacrifice either beauty or accuracy. Different languages have sometimes been thought to be especially appropriate for use in different circumstances. It was a Renaissance commonplace that Adam first spoke to Eve in Italian, that for awhile they spoke in French, and that the Angel Gabriel spoke German when he expelled them from Eden.

This was perhaps fanciful, but it is no fancy that different languages divide areas of experience in a variety of ways. Any given language is likely to be rich in the areas of vocabulary which are important to the culture in which the language is spoken. *Grandfather,* in English, is the sign for two relationships: *mother's father* or *father's father.* Some languages have a word for each of these relationships. Seventy-five years ago, English reactivated the Old English *sibling* (relative) to express a relationship many languages have had for millennia—that among children having one or both parents in common. The best known example of this kind is the fact that the Eskimo has no single word for *snow,* but has instead a selection of terms which permit a brief, exact comment on what the snow conditions are. This does not mean that an experienced skier at Tahoe or Aspen cannot also tell you in English what the snow conditions are; it does mean that the snow vocabulary of English is not as rich as that of Eskimo, and, in fact, in Florida it is rather poverty stricken.

We may then agree that in a number of ways languages are different. They differ in their nomenclature for the same thing in the real world (*thimble* and *fingerhut*); they differ in the way they put sentences together; and they differ in the way they split up areas of possible observation. What does this imply? By means of language, is a particular conception of what the world is like passed from generation to generation? Do the grammar and vocabulary of a language determine the way in which its speakers see the world? Do we speak as we think, or do we think as we speak?

These questions, like many others, originated with the Greeks. But they were asked very insistently in the United States when linguists, in analyzing American

Indian languages, discovered dramatic differences from anything they had encountered in the study of Indo-European languages. Edward Sapir was one of these linguists. He felt that our language habits clearly predispose us to a certain view of the world. Benjamin Lee Whorf, one of his students, argued the idea vigorously. The combined concepts of linguistic relativity and linguistic determinism are called the Sapir-Whorf hypothesis, which has been the inspiration of much fruitful speculation and research in recent language study. The concept was not original with Sapir or Whorf, but it was vigorously reformulated and abundantly illustrated by them in some of the most graceful and persuasive language to be found in the literature of linguistics.

There is, however a problem. The questions we ask may lead us in a circle. To the question "How do we know different cultures have different world views?" the answer is "Because they have different languages." To the question "Why do different cultures have different languages?" the answer is "Because they have different world views." The thesis is unproved, and it seems possible that the similarities among languages will eventually be shown to outweigh the differences. We simply do not know whether some languages are more convenient for talking about flowers or physics than are others. But it seems certain that we tend to sort out our experiences in the way the categories of our language suggest.

In "Languages and Logic," Whorf comments most specifically on the nature of segmentation of experience in English (see p. 268 ff.). In the bulk of the rest of the article he uses his knowledge of Shawnee to show a different way of segmenting. In both ways he discovers pattern.

In English, the sentences "I pull the branch aside" and "I have an extra toe on my foot" have little similarity. Leaving out the subject pronoun and the sign of the present tense, which are common features from requirements of English syntax, we may say that no similarity exists. Common, and even scientific, parlance would say that the sentences are unlike because they are talking about things which are intrinsically unlike. So Mr. Everyman, the natural logician, would be inclined to argue. Formal logic of an older type would perhaps agree with him.

If, moreover, we appeal to an impartial scientific English-speaking observer, asking him to make direct observations upon cases of the two phenomena to see if they may not have some element of similarity which we have overlooked, he will be more than likely to confirm the dicta of Mr. Everyman and the logician. The observer whom we have asked to make the test may not see quite eye to eye with the old-school logician and would not be disappointed to find him wrong. Still he is compelled sadly to confess failure. "I wish I could oblige you," he says, "but try as I may, I cannot detect any similarity between these phenomena."

By this time our stubborn streak is aroused; we wonder if a being from Mars would also see no resemblance. But now a linguist points out that it is not necessary to go as far as Mars. We have not yet scouted around this earth to see if its many languages all classify these phenomena as dispar-

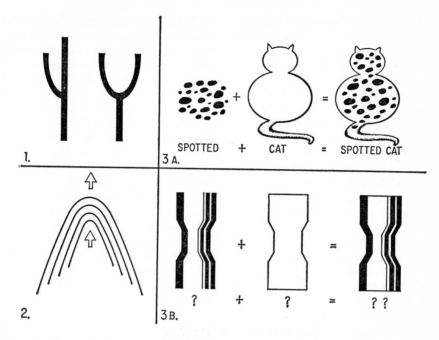

Figure 1. Suggested above are certain linguistic concepts which, as explained in the text, are not easily definable.

ately as our speech does. We find that in Shawnee these two statements are, respectively, *ni-l'θawa-'ko-n-a* and *ni-l'θawa-'ko-θite* (the θ here denotes *th* as in "thin" and the apostrophe denotes a breath-catch). The sentences are closely similar; in fact, they differ only at the tail end. In Shawnee, moreover, the beginning of a construction is generally the important and emphatic part. Both sentences start with *ni-* ("I"), which is a mere prefix. Then comes the really important key word, *l'θawa,* a common Shawnee term, denoting a forked outline, like Fig. 1, no. 1. The next element, *-'ko,* we cannot be sure of, but it agrees in form with a variant of the suffix *-a'kw* or *-a'ko,* denoting tree, bush, tree part, branch, or anything of that general shape. In the first sentence, *-n-* means

"by hand action" and may be either a causation of the basic condition (forked outline) manually, an increase of it, or both. The final *-a* means that the subject ("I") does this action to an appropriate object. Hence the first sentence means "I pull it (something like branch of tree) more open or apart where it forks." In the other sentence, the suffix *-θite* means "pertaining to the toes," and the absence of further suffixes means that the subject manifests the condition in his own person. Therefore the sentence can mean only "I have an extra toe forking out like a branch from a normal toe."

Shawnee logicians and observers would class the two phenomena as intrinsically similar. Our own observer, to whom we tell all this, focuses his instruments again upon the two phenomena and to his joy sees at once a manifest resemblance. Figure 2 illustrates a similar situation: "I push his head back" and "I drop it in water and it floats," though very dissimilar sentences in English, are similar in Shawnee. The point of view of linguistic relativity changes Mr. Everyman's dictum: Instead of saying, "Sentences are unlike because they tell about unlike facts," he now reasons: "Facts are unlike to speakers whose language background provides for unlike formulation of them."

Conversely, the English sentences, "The boat is grounded on the beach" and "The boat is manned by picked men," seem to us to be rather similar.

Each is about a boat; each tells the relation of the boat to other objects— or that's OUR story. The linguist would point out the parallelism in grammatical pattern thus: "The boat is $x$ed preposition y." The logician might turn the linguist's analysis into "A is in the state x in relation to y," and then perhaps into $fA = xRy$. Such symbolic methods lead to fruitful techniques of rational ordering, stimulate our thinking, and bring valuable insight. Yet we should realize that the similarities and contrasts in the original sentences, subsumed under the foregoing formula, are dependent on the choice of mother tongue and that the properties of the tongue are eventually reflected as peculiarities of

THE SHAWNEE LANGUAGE

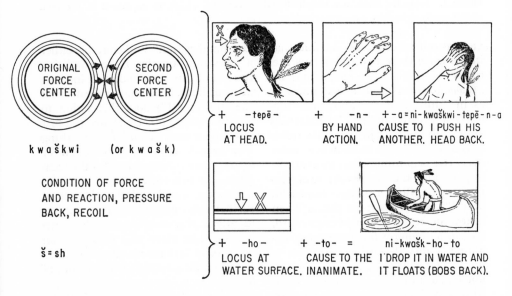

Figure 2. The English sentences "I push his head back" and "I drop it in water and it floats" are unlike. But in Shawnee the corresponding statements are closely similar, emphasizing the fact that analysis of nature and classification of events as like or in the same category (logic) are governed by grammar.

structure in the fabric of logic or mathematics which we rear.

In the Nootka language of Vancouver Island, the first "boat" statement is *tlih-is-ma;* the second, *lash-tskwiq-ista-ma.* The first is thus I-II-*ma;* the second, III-IV-V-*ma;* and they are quite unlike, for the final *-ma* is only the sign of the third-person indicative. Neither sentence contains any unit of meaning akin to our word "boat" or even "canoe." Part I, in the first sentence, means "moving pointwise," or moving in a way like the suggestion of the outline in Fig. 1, no. 2; hence "traveling in or as a canoe," or an event like one position of such motion. It is not a name for what we should call a "thing," but is more like a vector in physics. Part II means "on the beach"; hence I-II-*ma* means "it is on the beach pointwise as an event of canoe motion," and would normally refer to a boat that has come to land. In the other sentence, part III means "select, pick," and IV means "remainder, result," so that III-IV means "selected." Part V means "in a canoe (boat) as crew." The whole, III-IV-V-*ma,* means either "they are in the boat as a crew of picked men" or "the boat has a crew of picked men." It means that the whole event involving picked ones and boat's crew is in process.

As a hang-over from my education in chemical engineering, I relish an occasional chemical simile. Perhaps readers will catch what I mean when I say that the way the constituents are put together in these sentences of Shawnee and Nootka suggests a chemical compound, whereas their combination in English is more like a mechanical mixture. A mixture, like the mountaineer's potlicker, can be assembled out of almost anything and does not make any sweeping transformation of the overt appearance of the material. A chemical compound, on the other hand, can be put together only out of mutually suited ingredients, and the result may be not merely soup but a crop of crystals or a cloud of smoke. Likewise the typical Shawnee or Nootka combinations appear to work with a vocabulary of terms chosen with a view not so much to the utility of their immediate references as to the ability of the terms to combine suggestively with each other in manifold ways that elicit novel and useful images. This principle of terminology and way of analyzing events would seem to be unknown to the tongues with which we are familiar.

It is the analysis of nature down to a basic vocabulary capable of this sort of evocative recombination which is most distinctive of polysynthetic languages, like Nootka and Shawnee. Their characteristic quality is not, as some linguists have thought, a matter of the tightness or indissolubility of the combinations. The Shawnee term *l'θawa* could probably be said alone but would then mean "it (or something) is forked," a statement which gives little hint of the novel meanings that arise out of its combinations—at least to our minds or our type of logic. Shawnee and Nootka do not use the chemical type of synthesis exclusively. They make large use of a more external kind of syntax, which, however, has no basic structural priority. Even our own Indo-European tongues are not wholly devoid of the chemical method, but they seldom make sentences by it, afford little inkling of its possibilities, and give structural priority to another method. It was quite natural, then, that Aristotle should found our traditional logic wholly on this other method.

Let me make another analogy, not with chemistry but with art—art of the pictorial sort. We look at a good still-life painting and seem to see a lustrous porcelain bowl and a downy peach. Yet an analysis that screened out the totality of the picture—as if we were to go over it carefully, looking through a hole cut in a card—would reveal only oddly shaped patches of paint and would not evoke the bowl and fruit. The synthesis presented by the painting is perhaps akin to the chemical type of syntax, and it may point to psychological fundamentals that enter into both art and language. Now the mechanical method in art and language might by typified by no. 3A in Fig. 1. The first element, a field of spots, corresponds to the adjective "spotted," the second corresponds to the noun "cat." By putting them together, we get "spotted cat." Contrast the technique in Fig. 1, no. 3B. Here the figure corresponding to "cat" has only vague meaning by itself—"chevron-like," we might say—while the first element is even vaguer. But, combined, these evoke a cylindrical object, like a shaft casting.

The thing common to both techniques is a systematic synthetic use of pattern, and this is also common to all language techniques. I have put question marks below the elements in Fig. 1, no. 3B, to point out the difficulty of a parallel in English speech and the fact that the method probably has no standing in traditional logic. Yet examination of other languages and the possibility of new types of logic that has been advanced by modern logicians themselves suggest that this matter may be significant for mod-

ern science. New types of logic may help us eventually to understand how it is that electrons, the velocity of light and other components of the subject matter of physics appear to behave illogically, or that phenomena which flout the sturdy common sense of yesteryear can nevertheless be true. Modern thinkers have long since pointed out that the so-called mechanistic way of thinking has come to an impasse before the great frontier problems of science. To rid ourselves of this way of thinking is exceedingly difficult when we have no linguistic experience of any other and when even our most advanced logicians and mathematicians do not provide any other—and obviously they cannot without the linguistic experience. For the mechanistic way of thinking is perhaps just a type of syntax natural to Mr. Everyman's daily use of the western Indo-European languages, rigidified and intensified by Aristotle and the latter's medieval and modern followers.

As I said in an article, "Science and linguistics," in the *Review* for April 1940, the effortlessness of speech and the subconscious way we picked up that activity in early childhood lead us to regard talking and thinking as wholly straightforward and transparent. We naturally feel that they embody self-evident laws of thought, the same for all men. We know all the answers! But, when scrutinized, they become dusty answers. We use speech for reaching agreements about subject matter: I say, "Please shut the door," and my hearer and I agree that "the door" refers to a certain part of our environment and that I want a certain result produced. Our explanations of how we reached this understanding, though quite satisfactory on the everyday social plane, are merely more agreements (statements) about the same subject matter (door, and so on), more and more amplified by statements about the social and personal needs that impel us to communicate. There are here no laws of thought. Yet the structural regularities of our sentences enable us to sense that laws are SOMEWHERE in the background. Clearly, explanations of understanding such as "And so I ups and says to him, says I; see here, why don't you . . . !" evade the true process by which "he" and "I" are in communication. Likewise psychological-social descriptions of the social and emotional needs that impel people to communicate with their fellows tend to be learned versions of the same method and, while interesting, still evade the question. In similar case is evasion of the question by skipping from the speech sentence, via physiology and "stimuli" to the social situation.

The WHY of understanding may remain for a long time mysterious; but the HOW or logic of understanding—its background of laws or regularities—is discoverable. It is the grammatical background of our mother tongue, which includes not only our way of constructing propositions but the way we dissect nature and break up the flux of experience into objects and entities to construct propositions about. This fact is important for science, because it means that science CAN have a rational or logical basis even though it be a relativistic one and not Mr. Everyman's natural logic. Although it may vary with each tongue, and a planetary mapping of the dimensions of such variation may

be necessitated, it is, nevertheless, a basis of logic with discoverable laws. Science is not compelled to see its thinking and reasoning procedures turned into processes merely subservient to social adjustments and emotional drives.

Moreover, the tremendous importance of language cannot, in my opinion, be taken to mean necessarily that nothing is back of it of the nature of what has traditionally been called "mind." My own studies suggest, to me, that language, for all its kingly role, is in some sense a superficial embroidery upon deeper processes of consciousness, which are necessary before any communcation, signaling, or symbolism whatsoever can occur, and which also can, at a pinch, effect communication (though not true AGREEMENT) without language's and without symbolism's aid. I mean "superficial" in the sense that all processes of chemistry, for example, can be said to be superficial upon the deeper layer of physical existence, which we know variously as intra-atomic, electronic, or subelectronic. No one would take this statement to mean that chemistry is UNIMPORTANT—indeed the whole point is that the more superficial can mean the more important, in a definite operative sense. It may even be in the cards that there is no such thing as "Language" (with a capital L) at all! The statement that "thinking is a matter of LANGUAGE" is an incorrect generalization of the more nearly correct idea that "thinking is a matter of different tongues." The different tongues are the real phenomena and may generalize down not to any such universal as "Language," but to something better—called "sublinguistic" or "superlinguistic"—and NOT

ALTOGETHER unlike, even if much unlike, what we now call "mental." This generalization would not diminish, but would rather increase, the importance of intertongue study for investigation of this realm of truth.

Botanists and zoologists, in order to understand the world of living species, found it necessary to describe the species in every part of the globe and to add a time perspective by including the fossils. Then they found it necessary to compare and contrast the species, to work out families and classes, evolutionary descent, morphology, and taxonomy. In linguistic science a similar attempt is under way. The far-off event toward which this attempt moves is a new technology of language and thought. Much progress has been made in classifying the languages of earth into genetic families, each having descent from a single precursor, and in tracing such developments through time. The result is called "comparative linguistics." Of even greater importance for the future technology of thought is what might be called "contrastive linguistics." This plots the outstanding differences among tongues—in grammar, logic, and general analysis of experience.

As I said in the April 1940 *Review,* segmentation of nature is an aspect of grammar—one as yet little studied by grammarians. We cut up and organize the spread and flow of events as we do, largely because, through our mother tongue, we are parties to an agreement to do so, not because nature itself is segmented in exactly that way for all to see. Languages differ not only in how they build their sentences but also in how they break down nature to secure the elements to put in those sentences. This breakdown gives

units of the lexicon. "Word" is not a very good "word" for them; "lexeme" has been suggested, and "term" will do for the present. By these more or less distinct terms we ascribe a semifictitious isolation to parts of experience. English terms, like "sky, hill, swamp," persuade us to regard some elusive aspect of nature's endless variety as a distinct THING, almost like a table or chair. Thus English and similar tongues lead us to think of the universe as a collection of rather distinct objects and events corresponding to words. Indeed this is the implicit picture of classical physics and astronomy—that the universe is essentially a collection of detached objects of different sizes.

The examples used by older logicians in dealing with this point are usually unfortunately chosen. They tend to pick out tables and chairs and apples on tables as test objects to demonstrate the object-like nature of reality and its one-to-one correspondence with logic. Man's artifacts and the agricultural products he severs from living plants have a unique degree of isolation; we may expect that languages will have fairly isolated terms for them. The real question is: What do different languages do, not with these artificially isolated objects but with the flowing face of nature in its motion, color, and changing form; with clouds, beaches, and yonder flight of birds? For, as goes our segmentation of the face of nature, so goes our physics of the Cosmos.

Here we find differences in segmentation and selection of basic terms. We might isolate something in nature by saying "It is a dripping spring." Apache erects the statement on a verb *ga:* "be white (including clear, uncolored, and so on)." With a prefix *nō-* the meaning of downward motion enters: "whiteness moves downward." Then *tó,* meaning both "water" and "spring" is prefixed. The result corresponds to our "dripping spring," but synthetically it is "as water, or springs, whiteness moves downward." How utterly unlike our way of thinking! The same verb, *ga,* with a prefix that means "a place manifests the condition" becomes *gohlga:* "the place is white, clear; a clearing, a plain." These examples show that some languages have means of expression—chemical combination, as I called it—in which the separate terms are not so separate as in English but flow together into plastic synthetic creations. Hence such languages, which do not paint the separate-object picture of the universe to the same degree as English and its sister tongues, point toward possible new types of logic and possible new cosmical pictures.

The Indo-European languages and many others give great prominence to a type of sentence having two parts, each part built around a class of word —substantives and verbs—which those languages treat differently in grammar. As I showed in the April 1940 *Review,* this distinction is not drawn from nature; it is just a result of the fact that every tongue must have some kind of structure, and those tongues have made a go of exploiting this kind. The Greeks, especially Aristotle, built up this contrast and made it a law of reason. Since then, the contrast has been stated in logic in many different ways: subject and predicate, actor and action, things and relations between things, objects and their attributes, quantities and operations. And, pursuant again to grammar, the

notion became ingrained that one of theses classes of entities can exist in its own right but that the verb class cannot exist without an entity of the other class, the "thing" class, as a peg to hang on. "Embodiment is necessary," the watchword of this ideology, is seldom STRONGLY questioned. Yet the whole trend of modern physics, with its emphasis on "the field," is an implicit questioning of the ideology. This contrast crops out in our mathematics as two kinds of symbols—the kind like 1, 2, 3, x, y, z and the kind like $+$, $-$, $\div$, $\sqrt{}$, log $-$, though, in view of 0, $\frac{1}{2}$, $\frac{3}{4}$, π, and others, perhaps no strict two-group classification holds. The two-group notion, however, is always present at the back of the thinking, although often not overtly expressed.

Our Indian languages show that with a suitable grammar we may have intelligent sentences that cannot be broken into subjects and predicates. Any attempted breakup is a breakup of some English translation or paraphrase of the sentence, not of the Indian sentence itself. We might as well try to decompose a certain synthetic resin into Celluloid and whiting because the resin can be imitated with Celluloid and whiting. The Algonkian language family, to which Shawnee belongs, does use a type of sentence like our subject and predicate but also gives prominence to the type shown by our examples in the text and in Fig. 1. To be sure, *ni-* is represented by a subject in the translation but means "my" as well as "I," and the sentence could be translated thus: "My hand is pulling the branch aside." Or *ni-* might be absent; if so, we should be apt to manufacture a subject, like "he, it, somebody," or we could pick out for our English subject an idea corresponding to any one of the Shawnee elements.

When we come to Nootka, the sentence without subject or predicate is the only type. The term "predication" is used, but it means "sentence." Nootka has no parts of speech; the simplest utterance is a sentence, treating of some event or event-complex. Long sentences are sentences of sentences (complex sentences), not just sentences of words. In Fig. 3 we have a simple, not a complex, Nootka sentence. The translation, "he invites people to a feast," splits into subject and predicate. Not so the native sentence. It begins with the event of "boiling or cooking," *tl'imsh;* then comes *-ya* ("result") = "cooked"; then *-'is* "eating" = "eating cooked food"; then *-ita* ("those who do") = "eaters of cooked food"; then *-'itl* ("going for"); then *-ma,* sign of third-person indicative, giving *tl'imshya'isita'itlma,* which answers to the crude paraphrase, "he, or somebody, goes for (invites) eaters of cooked food."

The English technique of talking depends on the contrast of two artificial classes, substantives and verbs, and on the bipartitioned ideology of nature, already discussed. Our normal sentence, unless imperative, must

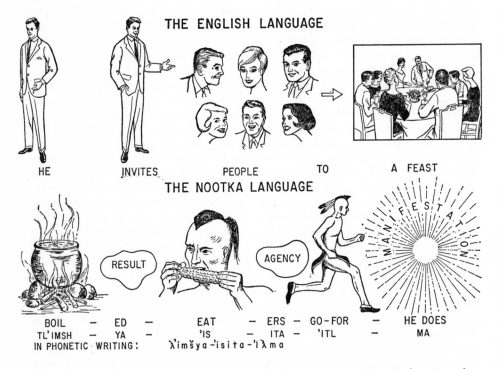

Figure 3. Here are shown the different ways in which English and Nootka formulate the same event. The English sentence is divisible into subject and predicate; the Nootka sentence is not, yet it is complete and logical. Furthermore, the Nootka sentence is just one word, consisting of the root *tl'imsh* with five suffixes.

have some substantive before its verb, a requirement that corresponds to the philosophical and also naïve notion of an actor who produces an action. This last might not have been so if English had had thousands of verbs like "hold," denoting positions. But most of our verbs follow a type of segmentation that isolates from nature what we call "actions," that is, moving outlines.

Following majority rule, we therefore read action into every sentence, even into "I hold it." A moment's reflection will show that "hold" is no action but a state of relative positions. Yet we think of it and even see it as an action because language formulates it in the same way as it formulates more numerous expressions, like "I strike it," which deal with movements and changes.

We are constantly reading into nature fictional acting entities, simply because our verbs must have substantives in front of them. We have to say "It flashed" or "A light flashed," setting up an actor, "it" or "light," to perform what we call an action, "to flash." Yet the flashing and the light are one and the same! The Hopi language reports the flash with a simple verb, *rehpi:* "flash (occurred)." There is no division into subject and predicate, not even a suffix like *-t* of Latin *tona-t* "it thunders." Hopi can and does have verbs without subjects, a fact which may give that tongue potentialities, probably never to be developed, as a logical system for understanding some aspects of the universe. Undoubtedly modern science, strongly reflecting western Indo-European tongues, often does as we all do, sees actions and forces where it sometimes might be better to see

states. On the other hand, 'state' is a noun, and as such it enjoys the superior prestige traditionally attaching to the subject or thing class; therefore science is exceedingly ready to speak of states if permitted to manipulate the concept like a noun. Perhaps, in place of the 'states' of an atom or a dividing cell, it would be better if we could manipulate as readily a more verblike concept but without the concealed premises of actor and action.

I can sympathize with those who say, "Put it into plain, simple English," especially when they protest against the empty formalism of loading discourse with pseudolearned words. But to restrict thinking to the patterns merely of English, and especially to those patterns which represent the acme of plainness in English, is to lose a power of thought which, once lost, can never be regained. It is the "plainest" English which contains the greatest number of unconscious assumptions about nature. This is the trouble with schemes like Basic English, in which an eviscerated British English, with its concealed premises working harder than ever, is to be fobbed off on an unsuspecting world as the substance of pure Reason itself. We handle even our plain English with much greater effect if we direct it from the vantage point of a multilingual awareness. For this reason I believe that those who envision a future world speaking only one tongue, whether English, German, Russian, or any other, hold a misguided ideal and would do the evolution of the human mind the greatest disservice. Western culture has made, through language, a provisional analysis of reality and, without correctives, holds resolutely to that analysis as final. The only correctives lie in all those other tongues which by aeons of independent evolution have arrived at different, but equally logical, provisional analyses.

In a valuable paper, "Modern logic and the task of the natural sciences," Harold N. Lee says: "Those sciences whose data are subject to quantitative measurement have been most successfully developed because we know so little about order systems other than those exemplified in mathematics. We can say with certainty, however, that there are other kinds, for the advance of logic in the last half century has clearly indicated it. We may look for advances in many lines in sciences at present well founded if the advance of logic furnishes adequate knowledge of other order types. We may also look for many subjects of inquiry whose methods are not strictly scientific at the present time to become so when new order systems are available."[1] To which may be added that an important field for the working out of new order systems, akin to, yet not identical with, present mathematics, lies in more penetrating investigation than has yet been made of languages remote in type from our own.

[1] *Sigma Xi Quart.*, 28:125 (Autumn 1940).

For discussion

A. In Whorf's opening example, in which he discusses *I pull the branch aside* and *I have an extra toe on my foot*, he shows that Shawnee makes such a pair of statements very similar. How might he talk about English *I pulled the wagon away* and *I pulled myself together?*

B. Discuss Whorf's belief that the sentences of Shawnee or Nootka combine terms in a "chemical" manner, while English combines its terms mechanically. Can you think of any English sentences which combine terms "chemically"?

C. What are some examples of useful English nouns that do not refer to three-dimensional objects? Give examples of sentences using such terms.

D. Give some examples in English where a simple word serves the function of a complete sentence.

E. List as many words as you can for the following small areas of the English vocabulary:
   1. timepieces
   2. deer
   3. bunions
   4. nudity
   5. humans between the ages of ten and twenty
   6. humans over sixty years old
   7. pineapples
   8. automobile body styles

F. What is behind Whorf's statement on p. 265 that it "may even be in the cards that there is no such thing as 'Language' (with a capital L) at all"?

G. Why does Whorf object to Basic English as an international language? How might he have felt about Esperanto?

H. On pp. 266–267 Whorf writes that *Whiteness moves downward* expresses in Apache what we would express by *It is a dripping spring*, and he claims that this represents a way of thinking entirely unlike our own. Why?

The Science of Language

A principal purpose of this book is to emphasize that the general study of language is part of our responsibility as students in the humanities. But this does not tell the whole story. The division into the specific disciplines through which today we seek out the secrets of our universe came after man developed language and literature. English as a professional study came even later, and little attention was paid to the characteristics of the disciplines by which it was surrounded. A result of this has been that while the English teacher considers the language to be part of *his* domain, anthropologists, philosophers, and others with a professional interest in it dispute his sovereignty in significant areas. There should be nothing surprising about this. Language is an interrelated series of patterns made by man, which, taken together, give the speaker of any language a way of thinking, feeling, and acting. It is an excellent example of what the anthropologist means by *culture*. Language is, therefore, quite properly a subject for the behavioral scientist. And one can say even more about science in language study.

As we have seen in many of the earlier articles in this book, the study of language often involves working with linguistic materials in a highly systematic way, which is determined by whatever theory of language the investigator may hold. The lexicographer, the dialect geographer, the structural linguist, the transformational linguist make statements which we may check for ourselves, since their conclusions are based upon operations that have been described for us. In this book we have read some highly integrated, general statements about language that rest upon observation of a mass of data.

General statements, however, sometimes remain exasperatingly hidden among the data. Very infrequently, the highly skilled and imaginative worker spots a hidden truth almost casually. When he does, he is called a genius—or perhaps a fool. Broadly speaking, even very temporary truth is not available by incantation, but the search for generalizations may be aided by a couple of things. It is helpful in any study to be able to limit the number of questions we ask at any given time. Beauty, said Pythagoras, is the reduction of the many to one. The crucial question among many linguists today is how to explain sentence formation. This is admittedly a pretty big question, but the attempt to answer it is providing lively discussion for students of language. After asking the question, the linguist usually has some tentative answers, which he checks. If the linguist is a good one, or if he is lucky, he may turn up a valid generalization which has never been made before, or which has never been elaborated upon before, or which was made so long ago that it may safely be rediscovered. The answers the linguist finds may be valid for many years, but in the long run they are temporary. His findings are destined to be expanded, partially replaced, or discarded.

The linguist, then, has a wide variety of data for his study: the results of the behavior of the speaker, the listener, and the learner of language. He describes his operations, and his experiments may, under proper conditions, be repeated. Increasingly, he works explicitly within a theory of grammar and language. At any given time he asks a limited number of questions. He uses well-developed techniques for eliciting information, and he has a methodology for checking the information he gets. He turns out always to be partially wrong, or at least incomplete, but he continues, adding—however minutely—to our store of knowledge about language. He is, in short, a scientist, and we may safely call the following section "Science and Language." It concentrates on the noisiest aspect of the current linguistic debate, and uses material from some academic spheres which border on linguistics to talk about a single radical problem: In English, with a limited number of sounds (about forty-five) and words (about half a million), we can produce an unlimited number of sentences and, theoretically, a single sentence of unlimited length. How can we account for this productivity?

NOAM CHOMSKY

The independence of grammar

"THE INDEPENDENCE OF GRAMMAR" is Chapter Two of Noam Chomsky's *Syntactic Structures* (1957), an early and still basic statement of the transformational-generative theory and its operation. For Chomsky the main task of linguistic analysis is to separate grammatical sentences from the ungrammatical and to study the structure of the grammatical ones. Accepting the native speaker's intuition about what is grammatical, a grammar will give ordered rules for producing all and only the grammatical sentences of a language. A grammar is adequate or inadequate as it performs or fails to perform this function; and a general theory of grammar is adequate or inadequate as it is applicable or inapplicable to a variety of languages.

How do we go about separating grammatical sentences from ungrammatical ones? As we saw in the section on grammar, Chomsky believes that there are some negative answers to this question. For one thing, it is perhaps wrong to assume that any utterance in a context has a determinate grammatical structure. Chomsky goes on to say that neither statistical frequency nor semantic significance determines whether a sentence is grammatical or ungrammatical. A sentence is grammatical or ungrammatical depending upon whether or not it has an underlying structure explained by the grammar.

As we have seen, transformational-generative grammar assumes that within an English sentence, however complex, we can observe a deep structure represented by one or more of a finite list of kernel sentences, all of which are simple and declarative. By one means or another, explicitly or implicitly, we must recognize the kernel and be aware of the manipulations to which it may be submitted. Our intuitive knowledge of these possibilities enables us to separate the grammatical from the ungrammatical. Our learned knowledge of the transformational-generative idea enables us to say why Chomsky's six illustrative sentences may be used to illustrate this point:

1. Colorless green ideas sleep furiously.
2. Furiously sleep ideas green colorless.
3. have you a book on modern music?
4. the book seems interesting
5. read you a book on modern music?
6. the child seems sleeping

"*The Independence of Grammar*": From *Syntactic Structures*, 1957, pp. 13–17. Reprinted with the permission of the publisher, Mouton & Co., The Hague, The Netherlands.

Chomsky calls (2), (5), and (6) ungrammatical in contemporary English. The second sequence obviously and severely fractures the word order for well-formed sentences. That there is an underlying difference between (4) and (6) may most easily be shown by placing *very* before *interesting* and *sleeping*. Clearly, the two sentences are only superficially identical in structure. We see in (3) that in some contexts *have* may take an object, and that when it does, subject + *have* may be transposed to form a yes–no question. In English, with many verbs that take objects, this is no longer possible (*John hit the girl. Mary bought a book*). If discussing the structure of a sentence involves considering the various manipulations to which that sentence may be put, then (5) is demonstrably ungrammatical. For all six sentences the determination of grammaticality has been made without semantic criteria.

. . . I will consider a *language* to be a set (finite or infinite) of sentences, each finite in length and constructed out of a finite sets of elements. All natural languages in their spoken or written form are languages in this sense, since each natural language has a finite number of phonemes (or letters in its alphabet) and each sentence is representable as a finite sequence of these phonemes (or letters), though there are infinitely many sentences. Similarly, the set of "sentences" of some formalized system of mathematics can be considered a language. The fundamental aim in the linguistic analysis of a language L is to separate the *grammatical* sequences which are the sentences of L from the *ungrammatical* sequences which are not sentences of L and to study the structure of the grammatical sequences. The grammar of L will thus be a device that generates all of the grammatical sequences of L and none of the ungrammatical ones. One way to test the adequacy of a grammar proposed for L is to determine whether or not the sentences that it generates are actually grammatical, i.e., acceptable to a native speaker, etc. We can take certain steps towards providing a behavioral criterion for grammaticalness so that

this test of adequacy can be carried out. For the purposes of this discussion, however, suppose that we assume intuitive knowledge of the grammatical sentences of English and ask what sort of grammar will be able to do the job of producing these in some effective and illuminating way. We thus face a familiar task of explication of some intuitive concept, in this case, the concept "grammatical in English," and more generally, the concept "grammatical."

Notice that in order to set the aims of grammar significantly it is sufficient to assume a partial knowledge of sentences and non-sentences. That is, we may assume for this discussion that certain sequences of phonemes are definitely sentences, and that certain other sequences are definitely non-sentences. In many intermediate cases we shall be prepared to let the grammar itself decide, when the grammar is set up in the simplest way so that it includes the clear sentences and excludes the clear non-sentences. This is a familiar feature of explication.[1] A cer-

1 Cf., for example, N. Goodman, *The Structure of Appearance* (Cambridge, 1951), pp. 5–6.

Notice that to meet the aims of grammar, given a linguistic theory, it is sufficient to have a partial knowledge of the sentences

tain number of clear cases, then, will provide us with a criterion of adequacy for any particular grammar. For a single language, taken in isolation, this provides only a weak test of adequacy, since many different grammars may handle the clear cases properly. This can be generalized to a very strong condition, however, if we insist that the clear cases be handled properly for *each* language by grammars all of which are constructed by the same method. That is, each grammar is related to the corpus of sentences in the language it describes in a way fixed in advance for all grammars by a given linguistic theory. We then have a very strong test of adequacy for a linguistic theory that attempts to give a general explanation for the notion "grammatical sentence" in terms of "observed sentence," and for the set of grammars constructed in accordance with such a theory. It is furthermore a reasonable requirement, since we are interested not only in particular languages, but also in the general nature of Language. There is a great deal more that can be said about this crucial topic, but this would take us too far afield.

On what basis do we actually go about separating grammatical se-

quences from ungrammatical sequences? I shall not attempt to give a complete answer to this question here, but I would like to point out that several answers that immediately suggest themselves could not be correct. First, it is obvious that the set of grammatical sentences cannot be identified with any particular corpus of utterances obtained by the linguist in his field work. Any grammar of a language will *project* the finite and somewhat accidental corpus of observed utterances to a set (presumably infinite) of grammatical utterances. In this respect, a grammar mirrors the behavior of the speaker who, on the basis of a finite and accidental experience with language, can produce or understand an indefinite number of new sentences. Indeed, any explication of the notion "grammatical in L" (i.e., any characterization of "grammatical in L" in terms of "observed utterance of L") can be thought of as offering an explanation for this fundamental aspect of linguistic behavior.

Second, the notion "grammatical" cannot be identified with "meaningful" or "significant" in any semantic sense. Sentences (1) and (2) are equally nonsensical, but any speaker of English will recognize that only the former is grammatical.

1. Colorless green ideas sleep furiously.
2. Furiously sleep ideas green colorless.

Similarly, there is no semantic reason to prefer (3) to (5) or (4) to (6), but only (3) and (4) are grammatical sentences of English.

3. have you a book on modern music?
4. the book seems interesting
5. read you a book on modern music?
6. the child seems sleeping.

(i.e., a corpus) of the language, since a linguistic theory will state the relation between the set of observed sentences and the set of grammatical sentences; i.e., it will define "grammatical sentence" in terms of "observed sentence," certain properties of the observed sentences, and certain properties of grammars. To use Quine's formulation, a linguistic theory will give a general explanation for what "could" be in language on the basis of "what *is* plus *simplicity* of the laws whereby we describe and extrapolate what is," (W. V. Quine, *From a Logical Point of View* [Cambridge, 1953], p. 54). Cf. §6.1.

Such examples suggest that any search for a semantically based definition of "grammaticalness" will be futile. There are deep structural reasons for distinguishing (3) and (4) from (5) and (6); but before we are able to find an explanation for such facts as these we shall have to carry the theory of syntactic structure a good deal beyond its familiar limits.

Third, the notion "grammatical in English" cannot be identified in any way with the notion "high order of statistical approximation to English." It is fair to assume that neither sentence (1) nor (2) (nor indeed any part of these sentences) has ever occurred in an English discourse. Hence, in any statistical model for grammaticalness, these sentences will be ruled out on identical grounds as equally "remote" from English. Yet (1), though nonsensical, is grammatical, while (2) is not. Presented with these sentences, a speaker of English will read (1) with a normal sentence intonation, but he will read (2) with a falling intonation on each word; in fact, with just the intonation pattern given to any sequence of unrelated words. He treats each word in (2) as a separate phrase. Similarly, he will be able to recall (1) much more easily than (2), to learn it much more quickly, etc. Yet he may never have heard or seen any pair of words from these sentences joined in actual discourse. To choose another example, in the context "I saw a fragile—," the words "whale" and "of" may have equal (i.e., zero) frequency in the past linguistic experience of a speaker who will immediately recognize that one of these substitutions, but not the other, gives a grammatical sentence. We cannot, of course, ap-

peal to the fact that sentences such as (1) "might" be uttered in some sufficiently far-fetched context, while (2) would never be, since the basis for this differentiation between (1) and (2) is precisely what we are interested in determining.

Evidently, one's ability to produce and recognize grammatical utterances is not based on notions of statistical approximation and the like. The custom of calling grammatical sentences those that "can occur," or those that are "possible," has been responsible for some confusion here. It is natural to understand "possible" as meaning "highly probable" and to assume that the linguist's sharp distinction between grammatical and ungrammatical[2] is motivated by a feeling that since the "reality" of language is too complex to be described completely, he must content himself with a schematized version replacing "zero probability, and all extremely low probabilities, by *impossible,* and all higher probabilities by *possible.*"[3] We see, however, that this idea is quite incorrect, and that a structural analysis cannot be understood as a schematic summary developed by sharpening the blurred edges in the full statistical picture. If we rank the sequences of a given length in order of statistical ap-

[2] Below we shall suggest that this sharp distinction may be modified in favor of a notion of levels of grammaticalness. But this has no bearing on the point at issue here. Thus (1) and (2) will be at different levels of grammaticalness even if (1) is assigned a lower degree of grammaticalness than, say, (3) and (4); but they will be at the same level of statistical remoteness from English. The same is true of an indefinite number of similar pairs.

[3] C. F. Hockett, *A Manual of Phonology* (Baltimore, 1955), p. 10.

proximation to English, we will find both grammatical and ungrammatical sequences scattered throughout the list; there appears to be no particular relation between order of approximation and grammaticalness. Despite the undeniable interest and importance of semantic and statistical studies of language, they appear to have no direct relevance to the problem of determining or characterizing the set of grammatical utterances. I think that we are forced to conclude that grammar is autonomous and independent of meaning, and that probabilistic models give no particular insight into some of the basic problems of syntactic structure.[4]

[4] . . . The relation between semantics and syntax . . . can only be studied after the syntactic structure has been determined on independent grounds. I think that much the same thing is true of the relation between syntactic and statistical studies of language. Given the grammar of a language, one can study the use of the language statistically in various ways; and the development of probabilistic models for the use of language (as distinct from the syntactic structure of language) can be quite rewarding. Cf. B. Mandelbrot, "Structure formelle des textes et communication: deux études," *Word* 10.1–27 (1954); H. A. Simon, "On a class of skew distribution functions," *Biometrika* 42.425–40 (1955).

One might seek to develop a more elaborate relation between statistical and syntactic structure than the simple order of approximation model we have rejected. I would certainly not care to argue that any such relation is unthinkable, but I know of no suggestion to this effect that does not have obvious flaws. Notice, in particular, that for any n, we can find a string whose first n words may occur as the beginning of a grammatical sentence S_1 and whose last n words may occur as the ending of some grammatical sentence S_2, but where S_1 must be distinct from S_2. For example, consider the sequences of the form "the man who . . . are here," where . . . may be a verb phrase of arbitrary length. Notice also that we can have new but perfectly grammatical sequences of word classes, e.g., a sequence of adjectives longer than any ever before produced in the context "I saw a—house." Various attempts to explain the grammatical-ungrammatical distinction, as in the case of (1), (2), on the basis of frequency of sentence type, order of approximation of word class sequences, etc., will run afoul of numerous facts like these.

For discussion

A. How does Chomsky define grammar? What makes a grammar adequate? How does he define a theory of language? What makes a theory adequate?

B. Chomsky rejects three explanations of *how* one may separate grammatical from ungrammatical sequences. What are the three explanations, and what are Chomsky's reasons for rejecting each?

ARCHIBALD A. HILL

Grammaticality

In "THE INDEPENDENCE OF GRAMMAR," Chomsky writes, "One way to test the adequacy of a grammar . . . is to determine whether or not the sentences that it generates are actually grammatical, i.e., acceptable to a native speaker, etc." But how do we find out what is acceptable to a native speaker?

Assuming that we have cornered one, we might simply say, "Can you say this in English?" However, since the native speaker is a product of his linguistic education and probably as wary of revealing ignorance as the next man, he may tell us that *Who do you want to see* is ungrammatical. Furthermore, man is variable in his assessment of grammaticality. Suppose one had just finished analyzing Macbeth's scene with Banquo, in which Macbeth says in a space of eighteen lines *Ride you this afternoon?*, *Goes Fleance with you?*, and *Is it far you ride?* It may not be an easy matter to strike *Read you a book on modern music?* from the roll of grammatical English sentences.

This difficulty does not make the last grammatical in contemporary English, but at least it illustrates that grammar changes as well as vocabulary, and perhaps it shows that the off-hand concept of grammaticality in an educated adult will be influenced by history as well as current events. His reaction may be motivated by one or more reasons. He may reject *Colorless green ideas sleep furiously* because it is nonsense. He may reject the abnormal arrangement of words in *Read you a book on modern music?*, and he will doubtlessly reject *Furiously sleep ideas green colorless* on both grounds.

Another thing worth remembering about the native speaker is that he has a strong tendency to inject sense into any bit of spoken English, no matter how unlikely. The redundancy level of language is high. There are, for instance, at least four signals for plurality in *Many children are there*. Anyone who has visited a foreign country in which the sentence intonation patterns are similar to those of English constantly thinks he is hearing English. Comedians who fake other languages in their routines usually rely almost exclusively on intonation patterns to make their acts convincing. The native speaker can frequently extract some kind of idea of grammaticality from almost any utterance. The making of operational tests of his intuitive response about gramaticality cannot be simple. Certainly, the person we question must be given some idea of what we mean by "grammatical."

"Grammaticality": From *Word*, vol 17, n. 1, April 1961, pp. 1–10. Reprinted with the permission of the Journal of The Linguistic Circle of New York and of Archibald A. Hill. Some of the footnotes from the original article have been omitted here.

In "Grammaticality," Archibald Hill, who also wrote "Correctness and Style in English Composition" (p. 49 ff.), describes the results he obtained from native speakers of English concerning the grammaticality of the six sentences discussed by Chomsky in the preceding article. For his experiments Hill adds four sentences to the list. He concludes that *Furiously sleep ideas green colorless* is not particularly hard to read, nor is it always read as a list. He notes that the intonation pattern influences the acceptance or rejection of a sequence, no matter how deviant otherwise. Because factual truth is widely considered a matter of grammar, *I never heard a green horse smoke a dozen oranges* was sometimes rejected. And finally, he discovered that native speakers vary widely in what they accept as grammatical. He has therefore devised another test, which fortifies his conviction that grammaticality is not demonstrable in the way in which Chomsky has suggested.

Among transformational analysts, it has become common to state that a grammar must generate all the grammatical sentences of a given language, and no ungrammatical sentences. It is also usual to say that naive expert speakers can be relied upon to reject all ungrammatical sentences, and that this convergent rejection can be used to build a theory of degrees of grammaticality. In the discussion of these beliefs which follows, I shall largely confine myself to Noam Chomsky's readily accessible *Syntactic Structures,* since Chomsky seems to speak for many of his fellow transformationists. On page 15 Chomsky lists six sentences which I quote verbatim:

1. Colorless green ideas sleep furiously.
2. Furiously sleep ideas green colorless.
3. have you a book on modern music?
4. the book seems interesting
5. read you a book on modern music?
6. the child seems sleeping.

Page 16 supplies two more, in the shape of a sentence frame with a blank to be filled by the words "whale," and "of." I have written out the two sentences, numbered them, and slightly changed the punctuation. For the original punctuation, see below.

7. I saw a fragile whale.
8. I saw a fragile of.

These sentences are accompanied by the following statements:

Sentences (1) and (2) are equally nonsensical, but any speaker of English will recognize that only the former is grammatical. (p. 15)

Similarly, there is no semantic reason to prefer (3) to (5) or (4) to (6), but only (3) and (4) are grammatical sentences of English. (*ibid.*)

. . . there are deep structural reasons for distinguishing (3) and (4) from (5) and (6) . . . (*ibid.*)

Yet (1), though nonsensical, is grammatical while (2) is not. Presented with these sentences, a speaker of English will read (1) with a normal sentence intonation, but he will read (2) with a falling intonation on each word; in fact, with just the intonation pattern given to a sequence of unrelated words. He treats each word in (2) as a separate phrase. Similarly, he will be able to recall (1) much more easily than (2), to learn it more quickly. . . . We cannot, of course, appeal to the fact that sentences such as (1) "might" be uttered in some sufficiently far-fetched context, while (2) would never be. . . . (p. 16)

. . . in the context "I saw a fragile—," the words "whale" and "of" may have equal (i.e. zero) frequency in the past linguistic experience of a speaker who will immediately recognize that one of these substitutions, but not the other, gives a grammatical sentence. (p. 16)

These statements, with their categorical pronouncements about the behavior of "any speaker of English," constitute predictions which invite experimental verification. Accordingly the eight sentences were copied onto cards, in exactly the form just given. To round out the number, I added two more sentences concocted by Martin Joos for a similar discussion:

(9) Those man left yesterday.
(10) I never heard a green horse smoke a dozen oranges.

The ten cards were shuffled into random order, and then given separately to ten informants. My informants were not, it is true, a reliable sample of the total English-speaking world, but it should be remembered that the statements to be tested applied to "any speaker." My informants were, however, fairly typical of the Academic community. They were professors, graduate students, one undergraduate business major, one secretary. Only three were in any sense linguists. The professors (except for two of the linguists) were teachers of English literature and composition. All were native speakers of English.

The first request to each informant was that he read aloud all the material on the cards. Rather interestingly, a number of the informants commented on the lack of punctuation in some sentences, and asked if they might "supply it" in their reading. They were told that they might do so in any fashion which seemed reasonable. The results of this request sharply contradicted Chomsky's statement that sentence (2) would be read with list intonation. Eight informants read (2) with a simple and single two-three-one double-cross pattern. Two broke the sentence into three phrases, with the breaks setting off *green* as the second phrase. It is interesting that one of those who used this pattern offered the spontaneous comment that the sentence "sounds like Modern Poetry." The second did not do so until questioned, but on the next day wanted the sentence quoted again, and then said "It not only sounds like Modern Poetry, it sounds like good Modern Poetry."

The next request to the informants was to reject any sentences which were ungrammatical, and to accept those which were grammatical. In the results of this voting, (9) "those man . . ." was the only sentence rejected by all ten informants. Sentence (2) "Furiously sleep . . ." was rejected by seven, accepted by three. The voting on (8) ". . . fragile of." was similar, seven rejecting, three (but not the same three) accepting. Sentences (5) "read you . . .?" and (6) ". . . seems sleeping." were each rejected by four, accepted by six. Sentence (10) ". . . green horse . . ." was rejected by three, accepted by seven. Sentence (1) "Colorless green ideas . . ." was rejected by one, accepted by nine. Sentence (3) "have you a book . . ." was accepted by all but one informant, who offered the qualification that it would be ungrammatical in his idiolect. This informant was one of the two linguists fully aware of differences in British and American dialects. Sentence (4) "the book seems . . ." was hesitated over before final acceptance by one informant. All others accepted without hesitation. Sentence (7) ". . . fragile whale," was accepted without hesitation by all informants.

Next, sentence (2) was read back with the three-phrase intonation pattern to all informants who had rejected the sentence, and these informants were then asked what the sentence now sounded like. Five then said that it sounded poetical. Two said that it sounded all right, but did not mean anything. A third said that it would be correct on one condition, that is, "if ideas are green, and can sleep." This informant had not applied the same conditions to (1).

Sentence (8) was also read back to the seven who rejected it, with primary stress and sentence-final intonation on *of*. Two then stated that such a reading made *of* a noun, and a third said that a pertinent question would then be "What's an *of*?"

There were also a few other comments. The one rejection of sentence (1) was from a student of literature, the informant who had accepted (2) because it sounded like poetry. One of the four who rejected sentence (5) "read you . . .?" commented that it would have been grammatical if it had begun with a capital, though he did not offer this comment about (4) which he had accepted. One of those who accepted (6) . . . "seems sleeping." offered the comment that it would have been rejected by Tennyson because it had too many *s*'s. Of the three who rejected (10) ". . . green horse . . ." two changed their votes when it was pointed out that the sentence was strictly true. The third agreed, but did not change his vote.

While the experiment described here is neither large-scale, nor exhaustive, it still yields significant results. Not only is Chomsky's statement that (2) can only be given as a list contradicted,[1] some of his other statements about it are also not borne out. In my experience informants did not find it hard to remember; they were intrigued by it. I am also told that one reader has even constructed a poem for the purpose of fitting (2) into it. I have not heard of any one who was similarly challenged by (1). As for the comments just given, one informant found (2) more acceptable on stylistic grounds than (1).[2]

Another conclusion is that the intonation-pattern influences acceptance or rejection. I would regard it as significant that a number of informants changed their votes on (2) and (8) when these sentences were read back

[1] It is interesting that Chomsky gives (in footnote 2, pp. 35–6) a rather different statement of the way ungrammatical sequences are read aloud. They are there stated to have "extra long pauses . . . contrastive stress and intonation, failure to reduce vowels and drop final consonants." It is not clear whether this is meant to be the same thing as giving list intonation, or something different. If different, one can be permitted to wonder if "extra long pauses" may not mean terminal junctures, and "contrastive stress" merely successive primary stresses on a sentence of several phrases. Such patterns, of course, occur on many quite grammatical sentences.

[2] It is an interesting, if unimportant, detail that it would be possible to argue that when sentence (2) is pronounced so as to treat both *green* and *colorless* as separate phrases, sentence (2) becomes at least a little more logical than sentence (1). Sentence (2) can be interpreted as meaning that two groups of ideas, one green, the other colorless, sleep furiously. In sentence one, a single group of ideas is stated to be with contradiction, both green and colorless.

with possible patterns. Somewhat similar, but less interesting to a linguist, is the fact that pointing out the truth of the negative sentence in (10) also influenced acceptance.

Moreover, the mere recording of these votes on a scale from most to fewest rejections does not tell the whole story. For instance, the extremes ran from one rejection to six. There was only one informant who rejected only one sentence. There were three who rejected only two, but only two of these agreed on the sentences rejected. Of the two who rejected the maximum of six, there was disagreement on two sentences.

A scale of grammaticality for any given group of sentences could, of course, be constructed by giving the sentences to a sample of naive expert speakers large enough to be statistically reliable. But in view of the idiosyncratic reactions and the many rationalizations having little to do with the real reasons for acceptance or rejection which our informants showed, it is unlikely that a scale built on percentages of acceptance would be very profitable. That is, it is to be doubted if any generally acceptable principles would emerge, and without such principles any new group of sentences would have to be tested afresh. The thought of testing all the sentences, possible and impossible in English, is too horrifying to be entertained for long.

In most of the passages in which Chomsky discusses grammaticality, it is also true that he is ultimately concerned not with sentences in isolation, but with series of sentences to which given transforms may or may not be applied. Thus if the attempt to define ungrammatical sentences in terms of

isolated sequences of words is given up, another kind of test immediately suggests itself. The test consists in putting sentences suspected of being ungrammatical in a relational or transformational framework, and testing their suitability to this frame. The test framework looks like this:

1. The plate is hot. The plate seems hot. The plate seems very hot.
2. The child is sleeping. The child seems sleeping. The child seems very sleeping.
3. The book is interesting. The book seems interesting. The book seems very interesting.
4. This hat is old. This hat seems old. This hat seems very old.
5. The wine was drunk by the guests. The guests drank the wine.
6. Golf is played by John. John plays golf.
7. The pie was eaten by John. John ate the pie.
8. John was drunk by midnight. Midnight drank John.
9. John is a man. Is John a man?
10. You have a book on modern music. Have you a book on modern music?
11. You read books on modern music. Read you books on modern music?
12. John can. Can John?

In these sets of sentences, set (2) is found in the series discussed by Chomsky on page 73. Set (3) is an expansion in accord with page 73, of a sentence found on page 15. Sets (1) and (4) were added.

In the second group, set (5) is given by Chomsky on page 80, where it is contrasted with set (8). Set (6) is given by Chomsky on page 78, with the statement that this set is more grammatical than the set "Golf plays John—John is played by golf." Set (7) was added.

In the final group, set (10) is derived from page 15, where it is made clear that Chomsky is concerned with the question as a transform of the declarative. Set (11) is similarly derived, but with a minor modification. Since a satisfactory declarative sentence could not be constructed from the question ("You read a book on modern music," might be taken as an imperative) the question form was revised to "Read you books on modern music?" Set (12) was added. Also, I revised punctuation throughout, to suggest sentence ends, and in some instances, sentence types.

The groups of sentences were then given individually to ten fresh informants. The informants were teachers of literature and composition except for one typist. The informants were told that the sentences were arranged in three groups, and that in each of these groups of four, the relations between sentences were the same throughout. The informants were asked to reject any set in which the relations were unsatisfactory, and the only other direction was that if any one sentence in a set seemed unsatisfactory, the whole set was to be rejected.

In one important way, the results were as expected. Sets (2), (8), and (11) were rejected by all informants, though one (a mediaevalist) rejected (11) only after considerable hesitation, and with a final statement that it was archaic, and so wrong. Still another rejected (11) only because he would not use it himself.

The surprises came in the sentences which were rejected by some informants (though not all), and the reasons given. Thus two informants rejected set (1) on the ground that things must either be hot or not hot, they can not seem hot. One informant rejected all the sets in group two, on the ground

that passives are weaker and less direct than actives. It was interesting that this informant then immediately added that sets (2), (8), and (11) were the primary examples of wrongness. Another informant rejected (2), (8), and (11) without hesitation, and then said that (3) seemed "a trifle odd," and that (6) was "awkward." The mediaevalist who said that (11) was archaic, said that (6) sounded as if it were translated from some foreign language.

It would seem that here also there are some significant results, and it is pleasant to be able to say that they are not all negative. The framework which tells the informant what the relationships are, also tells him how to treat the suspected sentence. Without such a framework he operates as Sapir long ago said we all operate, attempting to wring some kind of pattern, and some kind of meaning, out of the most unlikely material. What is significant in these results, then, is that sets (2), (8), and (11) were universally rejected, and that this rejection occurred in spite of the fact that the crucial sentences from (2) and (8) had previously been accepted by four informants out of ten, when the sentences had been presented in isolation. I should suggest, therefore, that universal rejection constitutes significant convergence, exactly the sort the analyst needs, and on which Chomsky hoped to found a theory of ungrammaticality. On the other hand, sentences which are not universally rejected do not show ungrammaticality either total, or to a significant degree. What appears here are occasional idiosyncratic and often nonlinguistic objections, like the one that nothing can "seem hot." Finally, sets like (9), objected to by no one, are also completely grammatical.

If my experimental results are verifiable, as I believe they are, I am at a loss to account for Chomsky's assertions that all speakers unhesitatingly reject certain sequences or pronounce them as mere lists. Chomsky has stated in an at least semipublic situation that these results are based on experiments several times repeated. I can only guess that there is some misunderstanding between us, or that one set of results is for some reason statistically unreliable.

It is worth pointing out, however, that there is an *a priori* theoretical reason why sentences in isolation would be unlikely to produce convergent rejection of those which are ungrammatical. The number of intonation patterns is small, and no utterance can be given without one of them occurring. It has, for instance, become a sort of commonplace among linguists that a normal child learns all the intonation patterns—and what they mean—before he is five years old. The lexicon of any language is not only so large that the individual speaker never learns it all, it is characteristically open to new coinages at any time. The result is that the normal speaker operates on the tacit assumption that he knows and can recognize all the intonation patterns, and can make full use of them in identifying grammatical structure. With vocabulary items, on the other hand, the equally normal assumption is that anything which turns up in a situation where the surrounding vocabulary items, and the intonation mark it as strange, is merely a word whose meaning is unknown. This second assumption is what explains the response of

those informants who heard "I saw a fragile of" read back with primary stress and final sentence-pitch on *of,* and said that such a reading made *of* a noun, or suggested the question "What's an *of?*". In short, a familiar intonation pattern takes precedence in identification over isolated word items made up of vowels and consonants. If the intonation is right, at least enough normal speakers will react to the sentence as grammatical though of unknown meaning, to prevent convergent rejection.

The Chomskyan approach—whether it is found in his writings or those of Lees or even Henry Lee Smith Jr.[3]—is

3 The Robert B. Lees passage to which I refer is in *Rules for English Pro-Nominalization,* IBM Research Center, 1960, p. 19, fn. 3:

"It is also important to recognize in this connection that, except for utterly impeccable, short sentences or for unintelligible gibberish, absolute judgments on grammatical acceptability cannot be given with assurance unless some independent knowledge has already been acquired about other formal features of English sentences and grammar relevant to the doubtful examples in question. Thus, e.g., we would reject the 'queer sentence'. '*John astounded the dark green.' with some conviction since we know from independent analyses that the distinction between 'animate' and 'inanimate' nouns is relevant in English sentence structures."

The example by Henry Lee Smith Jr. is from "Linguistics: A Modern View of Language," in *An Outline of Man's Knowledge of the Modern World,* edited by Lyman Bryson, McGraw-Hill, 1960, pp. 344–72. The example is found at page 355.

" 'The tall man smoked the black cigar' is an acceptable occurrence as a sentence, whereas . . . 'Tall the man cigar the smoked black' would be palpably impossible as an occurrence *and* as a sentence, since it violates grammatical patterns of the language."

The Lees sentence is the more interesting and important of the two, since it illus-

that a sentence can be proved to be ungrammatical on two conditions. The first of these is that the underlying segmental morphemes and words are fully identified, and the second is that the sequence in which these morphemes are presented is an impossible one. It is my contention that the first of these conditions is always unfulfilled when sentences are spoken. Every sentence gets a normal intonation pattern, and consequent irregularity of the sequence then simply contradicts the identification of the segmental morphemes. When a sentence consists of a normal sequence of words and morphemes with the exception of one intruder, and is furthermore provided with normal intonation, the tendency to abandon a semi-etymological identification of the

---

trates a belief which I presume to be seriously held. Yet I think it can be shown that the queerness of his sentence depends primarily on previous identification of *green* as the inanimate color adjective. For several hearers to whom I have read the sentence, the identification broke down, and *green* was identified as some other word. Some took it as the proper name *Green,* and some, part of a team-name, *Dark Green,* as in *Light Blue* for Cambridge. A large part of the queerness would disappear, certainly, if the last word, or the last two words, were capitalized.

The Smith example is more nearly trivial. Smith, a leading if not the leading exponent of phonologically based grammar and syntax, seems here to have been hasty, impelled by the necessity of giving an ungrammatical example in a popular article where he could not indicate the intonation. One wonders whether his meaning is not approximately "This is a sequence of words for which it would be difficult to find a suitable intonation pattern." One can be found, however. *Man cigar* can be read with the stress of a nominal compound, and the utterance as a whole read as two linked equations. The fact that the meaning remains unknown is irrelevant.

strange morpheme is very strong. That is, we follow the Joos law (cf. *Language,* Vol. 34, 1958; p. 286) and interpret the strange morpheme as the one which would do least violence to the context. Such a tendency also agrees with what lexicologists and other linguists have long known—that the meaning of a word can not be adequately known except in context. Thus a sequence like "look at the cross eyed. . . ." If filled with *of* will inevitably lead some hearers to re-identify an *of* as some kind of animal. Not until some other principle of ordering (such as alphabetical listing) is evident, can the naive expert speaker be relied upon to reject a sequence of words as being a non-sentence.

The assumption that morphemes and words are fully identifiable without out reference either to their syntactic position or the accompanying patterns of pitch, stress, and juncture, explains the ungrammaticality which Chomsky has ascribed to many of his sentences. Furthermore, belief in the absolute identifiability of morphemes forces Chomsky to rely on spelling in a fashion which is more than a little startling. In his "I saw a fragile *of*" it would appear that the letter sequence *o* and *f* is thought of as firmly identifying the preposition. No attention is given to the possibility that this pair of letters might spell a different word with a different pronunciation. There is here a curious parallel to a writer of a very different sort—Charlton Laird. Laird has recently maintained that it is possible to recognize the difference between "I scream" and "ice cream" without attention to the sound, because (among other things) "we guess at once that any word like *I* . . . which comes immediately before a word like *scream* is a subject. . . ."[4] Both Laird and Chomsky are relying upon spelling, both apparently without fully realizing that they are doing so. And both are forced to rely on spelling for the reason that there are only two systems which we can rely on for first identifications of a sentence heard or seen—the system of sound or the system of spelling. If we reject the one, we are forced to accept the other, with results which are confused and confusing if the reliance is not overtly realized.

A belief that sentences are merely strings of words, and that words in turn, are merely sequences of letters surrounded by white spaces, could certainly result in viewing grammaticality as a complex and difficult problem, and give to generative grammar the shakiness of any house without a firm foundation. It could also explain the hostility of many structuralists who maintain that language is basically a system of sound, only secondarily one of writing. But while it is sometimes true that controversy advances knowledge, at least a large part of the present controversy between structuralists and transformationists is unnecessary. It is ironical that transformationists, who are above all interested in processes, applicable to certain items, and giving certain results, should have been so insistent on judging items in isolation, with no attention to what the item was derived from, nor the process of derivation. It

4 Charlton Laird, *Thinking About Language*, Rinehart English Pamphlets (New York, 1960). The quotation is on page 56.

would almost appear that the insistence on the ungrammaticality of "Midnight drank John" marks abandonment of interest in transformations. Surely a transformationist ought to demand that such a sentence be judged only in the light of transforms of active to passive sentences, and the possible (or impossible) reversal of that process.

The transformationist should not ask whether an isolated sentence is grammatical. He should take sets of superficially similar sentences, and apply an identical transform to all of them, exhibiting the results. The sets, transforms, and results can be submitted to naive expert speakers, and acceptance, rejection, and responses can be expected to be reliable, as they can not when what is submitted to the naive expert speaker are isolated sentences. It is obvious that such a tool for eliciting reliable responses would be a powerful one for the transformationist, and that convergence would give him a foundation for generative grammar. It is less obvious that such testing would be no more than an application of a tool which has been basic in structural linguistics. The question asked by post-Bloomfieldian linguists has always been "are the items the same, or different?" and the answers have enabled structuralists to segment and describe much of language. With a more structural question, set in a more structural frame, the transformationists might reach some of the convergence which now they can only claim.

For discussion

A. How do the results of Hill's two experiments conflict with what Chomsky has said in "The Independence of Grammar?"

B. How does the intonation pattern influence one's judgment about grammaticality?

C. Why does Hill think that sentences in isolation are not likely to "produce a convergent rejection of those which are ungrammatical?"

D. What is Hill's case for the grammaticality of *Midnight drank John?*

NOAM CHOMSKY

Some methodological remarks
on generative grammar

WE CONTINUE THE DEBATE about grammar. The following remarks by Noam Chomsky originally appeared in the "Discussion" section of *Word* in answer to Archibald Hill's "Grammaticality" and to two other discussions about generative grammar, one by Roman Jakobson of the Massachusetts Institute of Technology, the other by Byron Bollinger of Harvard University.

It is probably worth saying again that the transformational–generative program is very ambitious. It attempts to account for a native speaker's skill in producing and understanding an indefinite number of different sentences and in knowing whether or not they are grammatical. A proper explanation of this skill must include some statements about man's ability to create language. A theory about language becomes a theory about learning, as will be illustrated at some length in George Miller's "The Psycholinguists," the last article in this book.

Furthermore, a worker in any discipline casts around for something to do only when he can do nothing else. Absolutely pure research is made necessary by our ignorance. It does not stem from total objectivity. With assumptions, hypotheses, and theories in abundance, the transformational-generative grammarian has plenty of materials that can be utilized. He works with all the assumptions attributed to him in the introduction to Owen Thomas's "Generative Grammar: Toward Unification and Simplicity" (p. 192), and with a number of others as well.

Chomsky here mentions some of these, and reviews what he attempted to demonstrate in his *Syntactic Structures* (1957). He also lists and discusses the kinds of data which might lead to meaningful comments about language learning, and he points out some ways in which underlying generalizations may be drawn from these data. This brings him to a direct discussion of Hill's "Grammaticality" and the difficulty of devising experiments for explaining a native speaker's intuitive observations about language. In the concluding section, Chomsky returns to a discussion of his use of the terms "grammatical," and "degree of grammaticalness," and describes a mechanism with which grammar may exercise increasing selectivity in a selection among sub-

"Some Methodological Remarks on Generative Grammar": From *Word*, vol. 17, n. 2, August 1961, pp. 219–239. Reprinted with the permission of the Journal of the Linguistic Circle of New York and of Noam Chomsky. Some of the footnotes from the original article have been omitted here.

categories of word classes in order to achieve maximum grammaticality. He can thus indicate how, for instance, *a cigarette away* is less grammatical than *a mile away* but more grammatical than *a phonetics away*.

These remarks are prompted by several critical discussions of recent work in descriptive syntax and syntactic theory carried out within the framework of generative grammar. I will try to clarify several issues that have, apparently, been the source of some misunderstanding and confusion as to the purposes and assumptions of this work, and to indicate how it can perhaps be extended into certain important but neglected areas.

It is useful, at the outset, to make a distinction between *data* and *facts*. The linguist's data consist of certain observations about the form and use of utterances. The facts of linguistic structure that he hopes to discover go well beyond these observations. A grammar of a particular language is, in effect, an hypothesis about the principles of sentence formation in this language. It represents a factual claim concerning the rules that underlie the data that have been collected. We judge the truth or falsity of this hypothesis by considering how well the grammar succeeds in organizing the data, how satisfying an explanation it provides for a wealth of empirical observations, how far-reaching are its generalizations, how successfully it accommodates new data. An enormous amount of data is available to any native speaker; the deeper facts of linguistic structure, however, remain hidden to him.

Similarly, a theory of linguistic structure is an hypothesis about linguistic universals. It asserts that the grammars of all human languages are constructed on such-and-such a specified plan. Such a theory should explicitly characterize the form of grammars (the schema for grammatical description) and should provide a method for selecting among alternative grammars, each compatible with the available data from some language (and each making a specific set of factual claims concerning this language). A theory of this sort can be verified in an indirect, but quite satisfactory way. We can ask whether, for each language, the most highly valued grammar of the specified form is confirmed in the sense described in the preceding paragraph.

A linguist who is exclusively concerned with linguistic data and not with the facts of language, in this broader sense, has severely limited the scope of his research.[1] A grammatical

[1] In his "Linguistic Science and Linguistic Engineering," *Word* XVI (1960) (henceforth, [LSLE]), Bolinger distinguishes between data-oriented and model-oriented approaches to linguistic description, the implication being that "model-oriented" studies are less concerned with the facts of language as such. The essential difference between the two approaches that Bolinger describes seems to me, rather, that his "data-oriented approach" limits its concern to a narrow subset of more immediately accessible facts; it does not attempt the precise formulation of deeper underlying generalizations.

It should be remembered, in this connection, that the most partial and limited set of explicitly formulated recursive (iterative) rules is, literally, far more extensive in coverage than the most immense collection of examples assembled and arranged by the data-oriented linguist. We return to this matter below.

description that gives nothing more than "a compact one-one representation of the stock of utterances in the corpus"[2] can be challenged only to the extent that the observations it summarizes or rearranges are defective. It claims little, and its interest is correspondingly limited.

In [SS][3] I was concerned with grammars that make a much stronger factual claim that this. A *generative grammar,* in the sense of [SS], is not a large collection of neatly organized examples, supplemented with comments about these examples and hints as to how to construct similar ones. Nor is it a discussion of efficient and compact notations (e.g., inventories of phonemes, morphemes, categories or construction types) in terms of which the utterances of a corpus can be represented. A generative grammar is a system of explicit rules that assign to each sequence of phones, whether of the observed corpus or not, a structural description that contains all information about how this sequence of phones is represented on each of the several linguistic levels—in particular, information as to whether this sequence of phones is a properly formed

or *grammatical* sentence[4] and if not, in what respects it deviates from well-formedness.[5] In particular, then, this grammar distinguishes a class of perfectly well-formed (fully grammatical) sentences. It is designed, in other words, to meet what Hockett has proposed as the basic test of significance for a grammar, namely, that it "generate any number of utterances in the language, above and beyond those observed in advance by the analyst—new utterances most, if not all of which will pass the test of casual acceptance by a native speaker."[6] To Hockett's

2 At one point (p. 366) in his *Methods in Structural Linguistics* (Chicago, 1951), Harris describes this as "the over-all purpose of work in descriptive linguistics." Later, however, he remarks (p. 372) that "the work of analysis leads right up to the statements which enable anyone to synthesize or predict utterances in the language." It is this set of statements that I am calling the grammar. I am not convinced that the last-quoted remark is really justified (that is, that any known procedures do provide an adequate grammar), but this is another question. At the moment I am only concerned to make the difference in aim explicit.

3 Throughout this article, [SS] will stand for *Syntactic Structures,* The Hague (1957).

4 In grammars of the type studied in [SS], part of the structural description of a phone sequence is its representation on the phrase structure level by a set of abstract strings that can be presented, equivalently, as a tree with labelled nodes. See [SS], and references there, for details. The fully grammatical sentences generated by the grammar are the ones represented by trees headed by a single node labelled S, where S is the distinguished initial symbol of the underlying constituent structure grammar. Transformational rules also play a part in assigning a phrase structure representation, in that theory, although the question exactly how they do so has not yet been satisfactorily answered. For discussion of this see my *Logical Structure of Linguistic Theory* (mimeographed, 1955, henceforth, [LSTL]), of which [SS] is essentially an excerpt, and "On the notion 'rule of grammar,'" *Proceedings of the Symposia on Applied Mathematics,* XIII (1961).

5 That is, sentences not generated directly can still be assigned a degree of grammaticalness, and a structural description which will indicate how they are related to directly generated sentences. A chapter of [LSLT] is devoted to this question, which is mentioned only in passing in [SS] (footnotes 2 and 7 of chapter 5). We return to this below in §5.

6 "Two Models of Grammatical Description," *Word* X (1954), reprinted in Joos, ed., *Readings in Linguistics* (Washington, 1957). See also Hockett's "A Note on 'Structure,'" *International Journal of American Linguistics* XIV (1948), also reprinted in Joos' *Readings.*

remark I should only like to add that a grammar must not merely specify an infinite class of properly formed utterances, but must also assign to each sequence of phones a structural description that provides a basis for explaining how this utterance is used and understood—that provides the structural information without which it is impossible to undertake this further task in a serious way.

Three theories of generative grammar are proposed for comparison and study in [SS]. The first (based on the notion of finite state Markov process or finite automaton) was shown to be too weak. The second was a formalized and somewhat generalized version of the theory of immediate constituents, reinterpreted as a theory of generative grammar. The third was a transformational model. I tried to show, by considering several kinds of linguistic data, that the immediate constituent theory was inadequate, and that the transformational theory seemed much more promising. Additional work that has appeared since then[7] seems to me to give support to this claim, which, I should like to emphasize again, is a factual claim concerning English and, more generally, the structure of natural languages—a claim that can be proven false in several ways; e.g., by the construction of grammars of a different form that are more successful in handling data of the kind that originally motivated the theory, by a proof that any grammar of this form must fail, for some natural language,

because of certain formal features of utterances in this language, etc.

The investigations of generative grammar described in [SS] were motivated in part by an interest in the problem of accounting for the ability of a speaker to produce and understand an indefinite number of new sentences (or for that matter, to recognize them as properly formed, or as deviating from well-formedness in one or another respect) ([SS], p. 15), a task that he performs regularly with great facility. A generative grammar can be regarded as an attempt to characterize certain aspects of this ability, and a particular theory of generative grammar is a proposal concerning its general and universal features.[8] If we hope to make significant progress towards these goals, the grammars we construct must be sufficiently precise so that we can deduce from them consequences that can be confronted directly with linguistic data of a rich and varied sort. This requirement is rarely met by either traditional or modern studies,[9] though this fact may

---

[7] E.g., [TAS] (which is, again, largely an excerpt from [LSLT]) and Lees' *Grammar of English Nominalizations* (Baltimore, 1960), henceforth referred to as [GEN].

[8] A theory of generative grammars can be regarded quite naturally as a proposal concerning certain fundamental and specific skills that the child brings to language learning. See my "Explanatory Models in Linguistics," *Proceedings of the International Congress on Logic, Methodology and Philosophy of Science* (August 1960), to appear, P. Suppes, editor (henceforth [EML]), for some further discussion.

[9] With some very limited exceptions, e.g., inflectional paradigms of the traditional sort. Given a list of lexical items, a paradigm gives explicit instructions for constructing a finite set of inflected forms. But it is clear that this is a relatively minor success.

It is on the level of syntax, of course, that the intuitive character of grammatical de-be obscured by the informality of linguistic descriptions, whether traditional or modern.

The study of precise generative grammars with explicit consequences (and the general form of such grammars) is in its infancy. Traditional grammars rely on the intelligence and linguistic intuition of the reader to provide the structural descriptions of items that do not appear in the collection of examples. There is little doubt that deep features of grammatical structure are unexpressed in a grammar addressed to an intelligent human who, in some totally unknown way, acquires the ability to produce and understand new sentences, having absorbed the information presented to him in a compendious traditional grammar. The study of generative grammars is, however, a natural outgrowth of traditional descriptive linguistics. Modern linguistics has, typically, been concerned with the much narrower problem of constructing several inventories of elements in terms of which utterances can be represented, and has given little attention to the rules that generate utterances with structural descriptions.[10]

Clearly if our goals are as described in §2, we will bring to bear data of many kinds in attempting to determine the validity of particular generative grammars or, more seriously, particular theories of generative grammar. Thus in [SS], [TAS][11] and elsewhere, I have been concerned with such data as

1. a. phonetic transcriptions;
   b. judgments of conformity of utterance tokens;
   c. judgments of well-formedness;
   d. ambiguity that can be traced to structural origins;
   e. judgments of sameness or difference of sentence type;
   f. judgments concerning the propriety of particular classifications or segmentations;

---

scriptions, and the defects of such descriptions, are most apparent, since it is here that the data cannot be enumerated in a finite list. However, I think that the preoccupation of modern linguistics with inventories rather than rules has had the effect of removing even significant aspects of phonology from the domain of linguistic research; for example, questions of the kind mentioned further below. For further observations on this see [EML], and Halle and Chomsky, *Sound Pattern of English* (forthcoming, henceforth, [SPE]).

10 In [TAS] (throughout this article [TAS], will designate the *Third Texas Conference on Problems in the Analysis of English*, A. A. Hill, editor) I noted a few exceptions

to this. In particular, Harris' morpheme-to-utterance rules can be reinterpreted as a model for generative grammar, and Hockett's Markov process model was explicitly designed as a sentence-generating grammar.

11 To avoid a possible misunderstanding, notice that I am suggesting that data of these kinds are relevant to determining the validity of grammars and linguistic theory, but not that these data should be utilized in the construction of or choice among grammars, insofar as this is specified by the theory of linguistic structure. The difference is fundamental. See [SS] and [EML] for further discussion. Thus we might try to develop a general theory of linguistic structure powerful enough to lead us from certain data about a language to a generative grammar of this language, limiting the data, in this context, to (a), (b), (c), that is, to the kind of data that we might regard as being available to the child who learns language. This might be a reasonable decision for someone whose motivation in studying generative grammars is to construct some sort of model for language learning. But such a person would still concern himself with such data as (d), (e), (f) in evaluating the success with which his theory of language learning duplicates the performance of the human.

and so on. By (a), I refer to the kind of data given by impressionistic phonetics of the usual kind, e.g., transcriptions of stress contours, etc. Category (b) includes the intuitive sameness-difference judgments that are fundamental to descriptive phonology, e.g., the observation that in my normal speech, *latter* and *ladder* are phonemically identical (i.e., tokens of them are) but *writer* and *rider* are phonemically distinct. To illustrate (c), I gave such examples as

2. colorless green ideas sleep furiously
3. furiously sleep ideas green colorless
4. the child seems sleeping
5. the book seems interesting

and several others. Thus I am as certain of the fact that (2) and (5) are well-formed (in a sense in which (3) and (4) are not) as I am of particular impressionistic phonetic transcriptions (e.g., of the various *light house keeper's*) or of particular judgments of sameness and difference. In connection with (d), I was concerned with such forms as *flying planes can be dangerous, I found the boy studying in the library,* etc. Examples of type (e) are of many kinds. Thus I discussed the problem of finding a grammatical explanation for the fact that *did you eat the apple, who ate the apple, what did you eat,* etc. are all naturally regarded as belonging to a special sentence type (as distinct from *you ate the apple,* etc.), and the problem of explaining the intuitively obvious difference between *the police suspected the man behind the bar, . . . questioned the man behind closed doors, . . . put the man behind bars.* Many other questions of the same kind were also raised, e.g., why *smóking mén* seems to mean "men who are on fire" rather

than "men who smoke." Concerning the propriety of segmentation and classification, it would be absurd not to use the fact that

6. [it ended late ([iDêndid + léyt], [D] = alveolar flap)

obviously contains at least four morphemes in evaluating a theory of morphemic analysis, or not to use the fact that *boy, horse, justice* are, in a certain clear sense, words of a different type from *compel, retain, bring,* etc., in determining the success of a theory of word classes.

Considerations of all of these kinds are familiar in traditional grammar. Considerations of kinds (a), (b), (f) are explicit in modern structural linguistics. Thus the methodological studies of American descriptivists are motivated by information of type (f), presumed known. If someone were to propose a theory of morphemic segmentation that led to the conclusion that (6) contains two morphemes, this consequence would, presumably, be regarded as grounds for rejecting the theory. The same is true of proposed methods (e.g., substitution procedures) for finding classes, for defining the phoneme, etc. These methodological studies (and the controversies to which they give rise) become utterly unintelligible if we do not make the perfectly justified assumption that they are an attempt to characterize precisely something that is, in part, intuitively given. The attempts to define "phoneme," "morpheme," etc. presuppose a set of clear cases of applicability or non-applicability of these terms, with reference to which the adequacy of the proposed definition can be tested. The same is true of an attempt to define "well-formed (grammatical) English sentence" (that is, the attempt to construct an English grammar), or the attempt to define "well-formed (grammatical) sentence in an arbitrary language L." In terms of the preceding discussion, these are attempts to discover and state the facts that underlie and account for the observed data. A refusal to use data such as (1) would eliminate linguistics as a discipline, just as surely as a refusal to consider what a subject senses or perceives would destroy psychophysics. In both cases, we are trying (though in very different ways) to find a basis for intuitive judgements. In both cases, furthermore, the difficulty of obtaining reliable and relevant reports is quite apparent.

It seems to me perfectly plain that an enormous amount of data of this sort is available to the native speaker (though it does not follow that it is easy to elicit such data). It is pointless to refuse to make use of such data in evaluating the success of a particular attempt to formulate the rules of some grammar (i.e., the rules that the native speaker must somehow have internalized when he has achieved the ability to produce and understand new sentences) or the principles that underlie grammatical structure in general.

It is data of the kinds mentioned above, it seems to me, that we are trying to characterize precisely, to account for and reduce to general underlying principles, when we study grammatical structure. A generative grammar can be thought of as a theory of the language that attempts to characterize and explain data of this sort. This point of view is discussed at length in [SS] (e.g., §§6, 8), [EML] and elsewhere, but I will illustrate

what I have in mind by a few examples.

In the case of data of type (1a), a generative grammar will attempt to exhibit general rules that underlie particular phonetic observations. It will try to show how the stress contours of English phrases and words are related to and determined by their immediate constituent structure and segmental phonemes;[12] it will offer an account of vowel reduction (as in the second syllable of *compensation,* but not *condensation,* in my speech) in terms of IC and syllable structure (cf. [EML] and [SPE]); it will try to explain why such items as *telegraph, aristocrat* (in the contexts #—#, —+y, —+ic), etc., have a particular set of variants, instead of others, by showing that this is a result of application of independently motivated rules (cf. [EML] and [SPE]); and so on, in innumerable similar cases. A generative grammar will be judged successful—that is, it will be judged to have brought to light the underlying facts of linguistic structure—to the extent that it shows how a relatively small number of simple and systematic rules account for a substantial quantity of such data. Cf. §1, above.

Similarly, in the case of data of the kind (1c), the generative grammar will attempt to exhibit interconnections among apparently independent judgments as to well-formedness and to state general rules from which a

12 Cf. Chomsky, Halle, Lukoff, "On Accent and Juncture in English," *For Roman Jakobson* (The Hague, 1956). A new version of this material, simplified, generalized, and incorporated into a much more general study of phonological processes, will appear in [SPE]. It is described in part in [EML] and (in an earlier version), in my contribution to the IVth Texas conference (1959).

large variety of such judgments (e.g., those mentioned above (6)) can be deduced as consequences. Cf. [SS], [TAS], [GEN], for many examples.

There is a second and independent way of approaching the study of data of kind (1). We can try to discover objective experimental techniques for characterizing these intuitive observations. Thus in the case of impressionistic phonetic observations of type (1a), we can try to discover objective acoustic or articulatory correlates to what the linguist hears as stress level, vowel quality, and so on. And in the case of data of kind (1c), we can try to construct behavioral tests that will correspond, in their results, to the intuitive judgments of well-formedness.[13]

Here, then, are two approaches to the data of linguistics. We can attempt to characterize the data by a generative grammar or by experimental tests. The two approaches are not alternatives. Obviously, both are justified and we should like to pursue them in such a way that they give convergent results. It is important to realize that each approach complements the other and that neither presupposes the other. Whichever approach we are pursuing, the criterion of success is provided by the data that give rise to the investigation; in this case, such data as (1).[14] Suppose, for example, that someone proposes that impressionistic judgments of stress level correspond to physical measures of intensity. He will quickly discover that "stress" as so defined does not at all correspond to the impressionistic transcriptions that constitute the phonetic record (1a). In the face of just this evidence, it would be absurd for him to conclude that the transcriptions are incorrect, that phonology is built on sand, etc. This lack of correspondence may simply show that he has chosen the wrong test.[15] Similarly,

[13] Linguists have in general not been much concerned with this approach to linguistic data. Thus even in the case of (1b), where a reasonably good test has been suggested (namely, the paired-utterance test proposed by Harris, op. cit., pp. 32f.), there is not a single paper in the linguistic literature devoted to an objective evaluation of its results, despite the fact that the relation of conformity (sameness-difference) among utterance tokens has been regarded, since the publication of Bloomfield's *Postulates,* as the cornerstone of structural linguistics. There is no doubt that this test will often fail to give the right results, in the form in which it is usually described. Some ways in which it can be improved have been suggested (e.g., in [SS], p. 96), but have not been systematically investigated.

[14] To some extent, of course, theoretical investigations or operational tests may lead us to reject some of the original data as irrelevant, or as probably incorrect or contaminated. We can expect that one result of systematic study, of either kind, will be to improve our understanding of what are the natural bounds of the discipline or what phenomena are relevant to deepening our investigation of linguistic structure.

[15] Continued failure of attempts to find a test might, ultimately, shake our confidence in the phonetic record, but it is not easy to say just when this would be justified. Thus we might discover that what the phonetician hears as stress level is determined in part not by the acoustic event but by an ideal stress pattern that is assigned to the utterance by the rules of a generative grammar—that is, the phonetician may be "hearing" something that is not present in the sound wave in full detail, but that is implied by the grammatical structure of the sound wave that he has understood in a certain way. I think, in fact, that this is not at all out of the question, in the case of stress levels. Cf. [SPE].

Similarly, a continued failure to elicit the judgment that (2), (5) are distinct in some significant way from (3), (4) might ultimately shake our confidence in this particular judgment, at least for certain speakers. It is, I suppose, conceivable that some

if the paired utterance test, administered in a certain way, fails to show that *writer* and *rider* are phonemically distinct in my speech, this is evidence that the proposed test requires revision. Or, if a test for grammaticalness (i.e. a test of (lc)) is proposed which fails to make the required distinction between (2), (5) on the one hand and (3), (4) on the other, we can conclude only that the test is poorly constructed.

In other words, we evaluate the success and relevance of an operational test (just as we evaluate the success of a generative grammar) by asking how well it corresponds to the given data. There is no difficulty in constructing a bad grammar. It is just as easy to construct a bad test. There is no interest in either.

I would like to turn now to some of the criticisms of [SS]. Consider first Hill's [G]. What Hill shows is that several tests that he has tried are quite bad. I do not see the importance of these negative results, nor do I see any reason to find them at all surprising.[16]

Thus if we ask a speaker the question "which of these sentences are grammatical?" giving him no idea how this question is to be interpreted, we will naturally expect the responses to be of no use in characterizing data of type (lc). Similarly, if we were to ask a speaker "what do you hear?" his responses would probably be of little phonetic relevance (they would have little relation to (la)); or if we ask "were these utterances the same or different?" not indicating how we intend this question, we would expect the result to correlate poorly with the classification of utterance tokens as phonemically identical or distinct (cf. (lb)). Lack of correspondence, in such

---

signing phrase final intonation to each, and that he will be able to recall (2) more easily than (3), to learn it more quickly, etc., despite the fact that they are equally new to him. I was careful *not* to suggest that these remarks offer a general criterion for grammaticalness—they would, for example, no doubt fail in the case of (4), (5). Later, on pp. 35–36, I made some further remarks on phonetic accompaniments to deviation from grammaticalness, again suggesting no general operational criterion. In fact, I know of none.

There is only one apparent conflict between [SS] and Hill's results, namely, he has found that his informants did not assign phrase final intonation to each word in (3), as I did. This lack of correlation is not at all surprising. In such quasi-operational tests as these, the instructions, the setting and so on can have a significant effect on what the subject does. It is for this reason, among others, that neither my comments nor his can be taken seriously as the description of an experimental procedure. Talk of "statistical reliability" ([G], p. 7) in connection with such informal suggestions as these betrays a misconception as to what is a serious scientific experiment. In any event, the question how the particular sequence of words (3) is read (nothing else is at stake) is surely too insignificant to justify a sustained discussion.

---

speakers of English are unaware of the difference between (2), (5) and similar examples, on the one hand, and (3), (4), (or "tall the man cigar the smoked black," with whatever intonation—cf. [Hill, "Grammaticality," *Word* xvii, 1961, henceforth] [G], footnote 4), etc., on the other. Such a person, if he exists, is likely to be about as successful in studying syntax as a deaf man would be as a phonetician.

16 Hill seems to have the impression that I have suggested these tests as general criteria of grammaticalness or degree of grammaticalness. But this not the case. In [SS], I made it clear at the outset (p. 13) that I was not proposing any general behavioral test. I did assert (p. 16, as an aside, in the context of a discussion of order of approximation) that a speaker of English will treat (3), but not (2), as a sequence of unrelated words, as-

cases, demonstrates nothing about the validity of such observations as (la), (lb), (lc). It merely indicates, as we should have expected in advance, that more subtle means will be necessary if we are to obtain relevant information about the speaker's awareness.[17]

Hill does suggest one test which might yield some useful data. In this test, two sets of utterances are presented to a subject who is asked, essentially, whether the same formal relation holds in the two sets. Hill regards this test as "more structural" than a direct test of grammaticalness, and considers it somehow more relevant to the "transformationist."[18] Insofar as I can reconstruct the reasoning that leads to this conclusion, it seems to me to be based on two confusions. The first has to do with the nature of transformational relations. Thus some of the sets that Hill presented in his test

contain sentences that are transformationally related to one another, but others do not. If Hill considers this test particularly relevant to transformational grammar, it may be in part because he has misinterpreted the technical use of the term "grammatical transformation" in [SS], [TAS], [GEN], and elsewhere, taking it to refer to any formally statable relation among sentences. I do not think it has ever been used in this sense.

Secondly, there is apparent in Hill's paper a confusion about the relation between the terms "generative grammar" and "transformational grammar." Hill seems to identify the two. Similarly, Bolinger regards Jakobson's comments about grammaticalness (to which I return below) as having some particular relevance to "transformationalists" ([LSLE], p. 377). In fact, neither Hill's nor Jakobson's comments have any direct bearing on the transformational model for generative grammar. They apply rather to generative grammar as such, that is, to the attempt to construct precise grammars with explicit consequences as to well-formedness of utterances. Grammaticalness is no specific concern of those who happen to think that the particular transformational theory proposed in [SS], [GEN] and elsewhere is the most promising specific characterization of generative grammars. It is, rather, the concern of anyone who is interested in syntax in the traditional sense, or in the problems discussed above in §2.

One final set of criticisms of transformational grammar presented in [G] also requires some clarification. Hill is under the impression that those of us who are exploring transformational models for generative grammar be-

---

[17] This is noted explicitly by Maclay and Sleator in their "Responses to Language: Judgements of Grammaticalness," *International Journal of American Linguistics* XXX (1960), 281. Their tests apparently gave somewhat better and more relevant results than the one that Hill describes. In his "Language, Purposive Behavior and Evolution" (mimeographed, 1958), Eric Lenneberg describes a test of grammaticalness applied to (2) and randomly chosen rearrangements of the words of (2) which, given to M.I.T. undergraduate language students with appropriate instructions (there stated), gave the expected results uneqivocally.

[18] It should be observed that this test, as presented, is not yet very useful. Thus it does not tell us which of the two sentences "the child is sleeping," "the child seems sleeping" is to be rejected as deviating from well-formedness. Furthermore, it does not seem to be generalizable to such distinctions as (2)–(3). However, it can perhaps be refined, and it should be considered as one of a battery of tests that may ultimately succeed in giving a characterization of grammaticalness.

lieve that sentences are primarily to be regarded as strings of printed words, and that we reject the view that "language is basically a system of sound, only secondarily one of writing." This, he believes may "explain the hostility of many structuralists." In [SS], [GEN], and elsewhere, a grammar is regarded as consisting of a syntactic component and a morphophonemic component. The former generates an infinite class of strings of minimal syntactically functioning units. Each such string, furthermore, automatically receives a structural description. The morphophonemic component converts each item given as output by the syntactic component into, ultimately, the phonetic representation of an utterance. Both [SS] and [GEN] are devoted primarily to the syntactic component. Other studies have been primarily devoted to the morphophonemic component of a generative transformational grammar.[19] The fact that the output of a generative grammar is a representation of speech is made quite clear in [SS] (e.g., p. 46) and [GEN], however.[20]

Jakobson, in his [BVGM], also indicates his dissatisfaction with the use to which such examples as

6. colorless green ideas sleep furiously
7. furiously sleep ideas green colorless

were put in [SS]. This criticism (which is cited with approval in Bolinger's [LSLE]) I find quite curious and puzzling. What Jakobson says about these examples, and about the question of grammaticalness and degree of grammaticalness in general, seems to me in full support of the position maintained in [SS]—in fact, it is in part no more than a paraphrase, in a slightly different terminology. It seems to me, therefore, that Jakobson (and Bolinger) must have completely misinterpreted the point of view expressed in [SS].

In [SS] examples (6) and (7) were used to illustrate the futility of (a) a search for a semantically based definition of "grammaticalness," or (b) an attempt to define grammaticalness in terms of order of approximation. Thus (6), but not (7), is clearly a well-formed sentence (or, at least, more like one than (7)), although (a) neither (6) nor (7) seems to be "meaningful"

---

19 In particular, Halle's *Sound Pattern of Russian* (The Hague, 1960). This is also the central topic in my "Transformational Basis for Syntax," to appear in the *Proceedings* of the IVth Texas conference, 1959, A. A. Hill, editor; and it is discussed in a section of [TAS].

20 What led Hill to conclude that transformational grammar is concerned primarily with writing rather than speech was apparently my remark in [SS] that "in the context 'I saw a fragile—,' the words 'whale' and 'of' may have equal (i.e., zero) frequency in the past linguistic experience of a speaker who will immediately recognize that one of these substitutions, but not the other, gives a grammatical sentence" (p. 16). The point in that context, was to show that judgment of well-formedness is not based on statistical order of approximation. This is rather obvi-

ous, and hardly deserves more than this casual comment. It is true that the phrasing of this observation makes use of an appeal to the literacy of the audience. It would have been possible to make the same point, more elaborately, without this appeal. That is, I could have stated that in the context Σ—(where Σ stands for a phonetic transcription of "I saw a fragile," with full intonation, etc.), /wéyl/ will be interpreted as the familiar lexical item *whale*, /əv/ will be rejected with stress 4, and, with stress 1, either rejected or treated as a new, unfamiliar lexical item, or as the quotation form *of*. I suppose that one could add even further qualifications, but there are other places where preciseness and rigor are likely to be more rewarding.

in any sense independent of grammatical structure and (b) the two are not differentiated in terms of statistical order of approximation. The same examples could be used to illustrate the impossibility of (c) defining "grammaticalness" in terms of a frame of "grammatical morphemes," since (8) has the same frame as (6) and (9) the same frame as (7) (note that it would be begging the question to argue that the morphemes *ly,* etc., are different in (6) and (8))

8. harmless seem dogs young friendly (—less — —s — —ly)
9. friendly young dogs seem harmless (—ly — —s — —less).

What Jakobson points out is that we can recognize the grammatical structure of (6) (but not (7)), and that "these grammatical relations create a meaningful sentence." He also observes that only (6) could appear in a poem,[21] that we know how to question

it, that we can recognize in it certain metaphors, etc. These remarks are precisely in support of the argument in [SS] that (6) but not (7) is grammatical, and that the basis for whatever meaningfulness we can assign to it is its independently recognizable grammatical structure. The fact that the independently recognized "grammatical relations create a meaningful sentence" is perfectly consistent with the claim in [SS] that grammaticalness is not attributed to an utterance by virtue of the fact that the utterance is recognized to be meaningful. To argue against this claim, one would have to maintain that there is an absolute semantic property of "meaningfulness" that can be assigned to utterances quite independently of any consideration of their grammatical structure—a property that can be shown to hold of (6) but not (7). It is difficult to believe that anyone would seriously uphold this view.

From consideration of such examples as (6), (7) (and many others of different kinds—cf. [SS], §9) it seems evident that perception of grammatical relations in a sentence does not depend on a prior and independent identification of semantic properties, and that the study of grammatical structure seems to be, in fact, quite independent of meaning. Furthermore, as noted in [SS], p. 101,

"it seems that the study of meaning is fraught with so many difficulties even after the linguistic meaning-bearing elements and their relations are specified that any attempt to study meaning independently of such specification is out of the question.[22] To put it differently,

---

[21] Hill, on the contrary, considers that (7) but not (6) could be a line of modern poetry ([G], p. 4). Both Hill and Jakobson refer to poems written to prove these (opposing) points. In fact, the question whether a sequence of words might appear in a poem is entirely beside the point, since it is perfectly plain that deviation from well-formedness is not only tolerable, in prose or poetry, but can even be effectively used as a literary device. We return to this below. It is by no means a novel observation. Cf., e.g., Empson, *Seven Types of Ambiguity* (Meridian), p. 34: "The demands of metre allow the poet to say something which is not normal colloquial English, so that the reader thinks of the various colloquial forms which are near to it, and puts them together; weighting their probabilities in proportion to their nearness. It is for such reasons as this that poetry can be more compact, while seeming to be less precise, than prose. It is for these reasons, too, among others, that an insensitivity in a poet to the contemporary style of speaking . . . is so disastrous . . . ."

[22] This is taken for granted in investigations that are actually concerned with meaning. Cf., e.g., Ziff, *Semantic Analysis* (Ithaca, 1960).

given the instrument language and its formal devices, we can and should investigate their semantic function (as, e.g., in R. Jakobson, "Beitrag zur allgemeinen Kasuslehre," *TCLP* (1936)); but we cannot, apparently, find semantic absolutes, known in advance of grammar, that can be used to determine the objects of grammar in any way."

Nothing in Jakobson's remarks gives any reason to revise these conclusions. He is saying that having recognized a sentence as grammatical and having identified its grammatical relations, a speaker can proceed to interpret it, determining how these formal elements and constructions are functioning, in this case. It will, in general, be easier to invent some sort of an interpretation for a grammatical than for an ungrammatical sequence, as Jakobson observes. This is basically the point of view expressed in [SS].[23]

In this connection, we can turn to Bolinger's discussion of what he regards as the semantic basis for transformational grammar ([LSLE], p. 377). He asserts that "knowing the meaning of *seem,* we can predict with some assurance that the structure *He is seeming* is not likely to occur." Under one interpretation, this remark is perfectly true. In just the same way we could say that knowing the meaning of *seem,* we can predict that this element will not appear in the context *I saw—boy,* or knowing the meaning of *in,* we can predict the ungrammaticalness of *I saw in boy,* etc.[24] The comment is useful, however, only if we are presented with some characterization of the meaning of *seem, in,* etc., stated without reference to their grammatical function, from which this function can be predicted.[25] In the absence of this, Bolinger's statement reduces to the observation, misleadingly expressed, that *seem* does not appear in the progressive. In general, study of the continuing controversy over the reliance of grammar on meaning seems to me to show that the issue is only verbal—that no substantive claim is being made by those who claim that such reliance is essential.

In apparent conflict with [SS], Jakobson also argues that the notion "degree of grammaticalness" is untenable. Here too, however, I can find only a terminological issue. Jakobson

[23] The temporal implications in this description should not be taken too literally. However, I think that a reasonable perceptual model would have the property that grammatical structure is identified independently of any semantic consideration, and a reasonable model for language learning would have the parallel property. This is a large topic in itself, and I will not attempt to pursue it here. I would merely like to emphasize that those who regard semantics as providing the basis, in some sense, for grammar, may not have realized how extreme and implausible is their claim, if stated quite openly. The claim must be that there are semantic absolutes, identifiable in noises independently of the grammatical structure (in particular, the lexical items) assigned to them. Perhaps some weaker claim than this is intended, but if so, it has never, to my knowledge, been clearly formulated.

[24] The phrase "likely to occur" is often used in place of some such technical term as "grammatical." Its use gives an appearance of objectivity which is, however, quite misleading. In the literal sense of these words, practically nothing can be predicted about what is likely to occur in speech.

[25] It should be emphasized again that in studies devoted to meaning, the argument is usually reversed. Thus it is common to find the claim that knowing, seeing, etc., are not processes supported by the observation that *know, see* (like *seem*) do not naturally occur in the progressive, in their usual senses.

recognizes ([BVMG],[26] final paragraph) that there is some sort of scale of "obliteration" of "syntactic forms and the relational concepts which they carry," and he would, of course, insist on the importance of the distinction between literal and figurative usage. It is precisely such observations as these that motivate the study of deviation from grammaticalness to which he expresses his objection. Clearly the only question is whether the study of these problems is a natural outgrowth of grammatical investigations—that is, the question is to what extent considerations of the kind that are fundamental to the study of principles of sentence formation can provide some systematic account of such phenomena. I think that to some extent they can, and the investigation of degrees of grammaticalness (or, if one prefers, the scale of obliteration of syntactic forms . . .) is an attempt to show how a simple generalization of some familiar notions can give some insight into these problems.

Since the point has been widely misunderstood, I would like to emphasize that I am using the terms "grammatical" and "degree of grammaticalness" in a technical sense (which is, however, not unrelated to the ordinary one). In particular, when a sentence is referred to as semi-grammatical or as deviating from some grammatical regularity, there is no implication that this sentence is being "censored" ([BVGM], p. 144) or ruled out, or that its use is being forbidden. Nor, so far as I can see, are there any "ontological" considerations involved

([LSLE], p. 377, [BVGM], p. 144), except insofar as these are reflected in grammatical categories and subcategories. Use of a sentence that is in some way semi-grammatical is no more to be censured than use of a transform that is remote from the kernel. In both cases, what we are attempting to do is to develop a more refined analysis of sentence structure that will be able to support more sophisticated study of the use and interpretation of utterances. There are circumstances in which the use of grammatically deviant sentences is very much in place. Consider, e.g., such phrases as Dylan Thomas' "a grief ago,"[27] or Veblen's ironic "perform leisure." In such cases, and innumerable others, a striking effect is achieved precisely by means of a departure from a grammatical regularity.

Given a grammatically deviant utterance, we attempt to impose an interpretation on it, exploiting whatever features of grammatical structure it preserves and whatever analogies we can construct with perfectly well-formed utterances. We do not, in this way, impose an interpretation on a perfectly grammatical utterance (it is precisely for this reason that a well-chosen deviant utterance may be richer and more effective—cf. footnote 21). Linguists, when presented with examples of semi-grammatical, deviant utterances, often respond by contriving possible interpretations in constructed contexts, concluding that the examples do not illustrate departure from grammatical regularities. This

---

[26] [BVMG] designates Jakobson's article, "Boas' View of Grammatical Meaning," *The Anthropology of Franz Boas, American Anthropologist* (1959).

[27] One of the examples analyzed in Ziff's interesting study of the problem of deviation from grammaticalness, "On Understanding 'Understanding'" (mimeographed, 1960).

line of argument completely misses the point. It blurs an important distinction between a class of utterances that need no analogic or imposed interpretation, and others that can receive an interpretation by virtue of their relations to properly selected members of this class. Thus, e.g., when Jakobson observes ([BVGM], p. 144) that "golf plays John" can be a perfectly perspicuous utterance, he is quite correct. But when he concludes that it is therefore as fully in accord with the grammatical rules of English as "John plays golf," he is insisting on much too narrow an interpretation of the notion "grammatical rule"—an interpretation that makes it impossible to mark the fundamental distinction between the two phrases. The former is a perspicuous utterance precisely because of the series of steps that we must take in interpreting it—a series of steps that is initiated by the recognition that this phrase deviates from a certain grammatical rule of English, in this case, a selectional rule that determines the grammatical categories of the subject and object of the verb "play." No such steps are necessary in the case of the nondeviant (and uninteresting) "John plays golf."

I am not, of course, suggesting that every difficult, interesting or figurative expression is semi-grammatical (or conversely). The important question, as always, is to what extent significant aspects of the use and understanding of utterances can be illuminated by refining and generalizing the notions of grammar. In the cases just mentioned, and many others, I think that they can. If this is true, it would be arbitrary and pointless to insist that the theory of grammatical structure be restricted to the study of such relatively superficial matters as agreement, inflectionally marked categories, and so on.[28]

In short, it seems to me no more justifiable to ignore the distinctions of subcategory that give the series "John plays golf," "golf plays John," "John plays and," then to ignore the rather similar distinctions between seeing a man in the flesh, in an abstract painting, and in an inkblot. The fact that we can impose an interpretation in the second case and sometimes even in the third, using whatever cues are present, does not obliterate the distinction between these three strata.

Examples such as these provide a motive for the study of degrees of grammaticalness. Thus in addition to such data as (1), we can try to account for the observation that such phrases as (10) are not as extreme in their violation of grammatical rules as (11), though they do not conform to the rules of the language as strictly as (12):

28 Notice that if we do, arbitrarily, limit the study of grammar in this way, we cannot even account for the difference between (6) and (9), on the one hand, and (7) and (8), on the other, since this difference can be expressed only in terms of categories that are established in terms of syntactic considerations that go well beyond inflection. But if we distinguish (6) from (9) by rules involving such syntactic categories as Adjective, Noun, etc., we can just as well distinguish "John plays golf" from "golf plays John" by rules involving such syntactic subcategories as Animate Noun, etc. These are simply a refinement of familiar categories. I do not see any fundamental difference between them. No general procedure has ever been offered for isolating such categories as Noun, Adjective, etc., that would not equally well apply to such subcategories as are necessary to make finer distinctions. I return to this below.

10. a grief ago; perform leisure; golf plays John; colorless green ideas sleep furiously; misery loves company; John frightens sincerity; what did you do to the book, understand it?

11. a the ago; perform compel; golf plays aggressive; furiously sleep ideas green colorless; abundant loves company; John sincerity frightens; what did you do to the book, justice it?

12. a year ago; perform the task; John plays golf; revolutionary new ideas appear infrequently; John loves company; sincerity frightens John; what did you do to the book, bite it?

Here too, we can find innumerable relatively clear cases, and we can attempt to express these distinctions in a generative grammar (and, more importantly, we can try to find some basis for them through the study of generative grammar).

The question then arises: by what mechanism can a grammar assign to an arbitrary phone sequence a structural description that indicates its degree of grammaticalness, the degree of its deviation from grammatical regularities, and the manner of its deviation (cf. §1). This is a natural question to ask within the framework of §2.

Suppose that we have a grammar that generates an infinite set of utterances with structural descriptions. Let us call the units in terms of which these utterances are represented by the neutral term *formatives* (following a suggestion of Bolinger's). Suppose, in addition, that we have an m-level hierarchy of categories of formatives with the following structure. On level one we have a single category denoted C_1^1, the category of all formatives. On level two, we have categories labelled $C_1^2, \ldots, C_{n_2}^2$. On level three, we have categories $C_1^3, \ldots, C_{n_3}^3$, where $n_3 > n_2$, and so on, until we reach the mth level with categories $C_1^m, \ldots, C_{n_m}^m$ ($1 < n_2 < \ldots < n_m$). On each level, the categories are exhaustive in the sense that each formative belongs to at least one, perhaps more (in the case of grammatical homonymy). We might also require that each level be a refinement of the preceding one i.e., a classification into subcategories of the categories of the preceding level.

Let us assume, furthermore, that the mth level categories are the smallest categories that appear in the rules of the generative grammar. That is, the members of C_1^m are mutually substitutable in the set of generated utterances. Many of them may contain just a single formative.

For concreteness, think of the formatives as English words.[29] Suppose we have a three-level hierarchy. Then C_1^1 is the class of all words. Let $C_1^2 =$ Nouns, $C_2^2 =$ Verbs, $C_3^2 =$ Adjectives, $C_4^2 =$ everything else. Let $C_1^3, \ldots, C_j^3$ be subcategories of Verbs (pure transitives, those with inanimate objects, etc.); subcategories of Nouns, and so on. Every sequence of words can now be represented by the sequence of first level, second level, third level categories to which these words belong. Thus "misery loves company" is represented $C_1^1 C_1^1 C_1^1$ on level one, $C_1^2 C_2^2 C_1^2$ (i.e., NVN) on level two, $N_{abstr} V_k N_{abstr}$ on level three (where these are the appropriate C_i^3's) One of the selectional rules of the generative grammars (i.e., in the transformational model of [SS],

---

29 This is merely an illustrative example.

one of the context-restricted constituent structure rules) will specify that V_k occurs only with animate subjects. Thus "misery loves company" will not be generated by the grammar, though "John loves company" will. However, "misery loves company" has a level two representation in common with a generated utterance, namely, NVN. We therefore call it semi-grammatical, on level two. "Abundant loves company," on the other hand, has only a level one representation in common with a generated utterance, and is therefore labelled completely ungrammatical.

Without going into details, it is obvious how, in a similar way, a degree of grammaticalness can be assigned to any sequence of formatives when the generative grammar is supplemented by a hierarchy of categories. The degree of grammaticalness is a measure of the remoteness of an utterance from the generated set of perfectly well-formed sentences, and the common representing category sequence will indicate in what respects the utterance in question is deviant.[30] The more narrowly the mth level categories circumscribe the generated language (i.e., the more detailed the specification of selectional restrictions) the more elaborate will be the stratification of utterances into degrees of grammaticalness. No utterances are "lost" as we refine a grammatical description by noting more detailed restrictions on occurrence in natural sentences. By

adding a refinement to the hierarchy of categories, we simply subdivide the same utterances into more degrees of grammaticalness, thus increasing the power of the grammar to mark distinctions among utterances.[31]

Thus a generative grammar supplemented with a hierarchy of categories can assign a degree of grammaticalness to each sequence of formatives. If we could show how a hierarchy of categories can be derived from a generative grammar, then the latter alone would assign degree of grammaticalness. There are, in fact, several ways in which this might be possible.

Notice, first, that a transformational grammar will have such symbols as Noun, Adjective, . . . (in addition to much narrower subcategories) at intermediate levels of representation, even if it is designed to generate only a narrow class of highly grammatical sentences, since these larger categories will simplify the descriptions of the domains of transformational rules. Thus we can expect to find a hierarchy of categories embedded within the constituent structure rules of the

---

[30] We can represent only one "dimension" of deviation from grammaticalness in this way. There are others. Cf., e.g., [SS], §5, footnote 2. In obvious ways, we could give a more refined stratification of utterances by considering their parts, but I will not go into this.

[31] What is the natural point where continued refinement of the category hierarchy should come to an end? This is not obvious. As the grammatical rules become more detailed, we may find that grammar is converging with what has been called logical grammar. That is, we seem to be studying small overlapping categories of formatives, where each category can be characterized by what we can now (given the grammar) recognize as a semantic feature of some sort. If this turns out to be true in some interesting sense when the problem is studied more seriously, so much the better. This will show that the study of principles of sentence formation does lead to increasingly deeper insights into the use and understanding of utterances, as it is continually refined.

transformational grammar. This might be the appropriate hierarchy, or a step towards its construction.[32]

We might approach the question of projecting a hierarchy of categories from a set of utterances in a different way, by defining "optimal k-category analysis," for arbitrary k. Suppose, for simplicity, that we have a corpus of sentences all of the same length. Let $C_1, \ldots, C_k$ be (perhaps overlapping) categories that give an exhaustive classification of the formatives appearing in the corpus. Each sentence is now represented by at least one category sequence. Each such category sequence, in turn, is the representation of many sequences of formatives, in particular, of many that may not be in the original corpus. Thus a choice of k categories extends the corpus to a set of sentences that are not distinguishable, in terms of these categories, from sentences of the corpus. It is natural to define the optimal k-category analysis as that which extends the corpus the least, i.e., which best reflects substitutability relations within the corpus. Given, for each k, the optimal k-category analysis, we might select the optimal k-category analysis as a level of the hierarchy if it offers a considerable improvement over the optimal k-1-category analysis, but is not much worse than the optimal k + l-category analysis (this could be made precise, in various ways). It is easy to see that there are circumstances under which the optimal k-category analysis might contain overlapping classes

(homonyms).[33] It is also easy to drop the restriction that all sentences be of the same length, and that the corpus be finite. Such suggestions as these, when made precise,[34] offer an alternative way in which the generative grammar itself may impose degrees of grammaticalness on utterances that are not directly generated, through the intermediary of the category hierarchy projected from the set of generated sentences.

This suggestion is schematic and no doubt very much oversimplified. Nev-

---

32 This possibility was suggested by some remarks of R. B. Lees.

33 In general, it is to be expected that overlapping of categories will lead to an extension of the set of generated sentences, since categories will now be larger. There-fore, in general an analysis with disjoint categories will be preferred, by the evaluation procedures suggested above, over an analysis with an equal number of overlapping categories. Suppose, however, that the overlap includes true homonyms—suppose, e.g., that the categories N and V are allowed to overlap in such elements as /riyd/ (read, reed), etc. We now have two ways of (namely, VTN or NTN), *the reed looks tall* (TNVA or TVVA), and so on, instead of just one (e.g., VTN and TVVA, if /riyd/ is assigned to V). We can select, in each case, the representation which is required, on independent grounds, by other sentences, i.e., VTN and TNVA, in this example. In this way we can reduce the number of generated sentences by allowing categories to overlap. Overlapping of categories will be permitted, then, when the gain that can be achieved in this way more than compensates for the loss resulting from the fact that categories are larger. We might inquire then whether homonyms can be defined as elements that are in the overlaps in the optimal set of categories on some level. Some evidence in favor of this assumption is presented in [LSLT].

34 This approach to degrees of grammaticalness was described in more detail in [LSLT]. It was presented, with some supporting empirical evidence, in a Linguistic Institute lecture in Chicago in 1954, and again in the discussions of the IVth Texas conference, 1959.

ertheless, such an approach as this to the problem of defining syntactic categories has many suggestive features, and offers some important advantages over the alternatives (e.g., substitution procedures)[35] that have been described

[35] It is often proposed that categories be defined in terms of particular sets of inflectional morphemes, but unless some general method is given for selecting the relevant sets (none has ever been proposed, to my knowledge), such definitions are completely ad hoc, and simply avoid the problem of discovering the basis for categorization.

in the literature (cf. [LSLT] for a detailed discussion—in particular, it allows for the possibility of setting up a hierarchy of categories and subcategories and for a principled and general solution to the problem of recognizing homonyms). I mention it here to indicate one way in which the further investigation of deviation from grammaticalness might be systematically pursued.

For discussion

A. What distinction does Chomsky make between *data* and *facts?* What are the two approaches to the data of linguistics?

B. On p. 294 ff. Chomsky lists and illustrates six kinds of data with which he has been concerned. Provide additional illustrations for each of the six kinds of data.

C. On p. 296 Chomsky suggests the development of rules which account for vowel reduction in certain form class shifts by derivation (*telegraph: telegraphy; monarch: monarchy*). Give six more examples. How might Sir Archibald Sluter defend this shift in pronunciation?

D. What are Chomsky's objections to Hill's test for grammaticality? Chomsky thinks Hill has misinterpreted the technical use of the term "grammatical transformation." In what way? How does Chomsky use this term? How does Chomsky distinguish generative and transformational grammar?

E. In his discussion of degrees of grammaticalness, Chomsky gives three lists of expressions. Add five more examples to each list. Explain why each item in the first list is less conforming than the parallel item in the third list.

F. Using Chomsky's mechanism for indicating degrees of grammaticalness, arrange the sentences on p. 275 in order of decreasing grammaticality.

A N G U S   M c I N T O S H

Patterns and ranges

IN THE UNLIKELY POSSIBILITY that a combination of sounds cannot be placed in any context in an English sentence, the combination is meaningless. Of course, simply by being put into an English sentence, it takes on some meaning, if only by absorption from the words around it, as in *The wang took her seat in the first row of the balcony.* Though I do not know much about wangs, I know that this particular female can sit in the first row of a balcony. Even though we do not know what *thill* means in the sentence *The thill broke,* we do know that it broke, although this does not tell us much, since *glasses, hearts, storms, the weather, backs,* and the *stockmarket* all break, as well as, in this case, a *buggy shaft.* If the situation of the combination of sounds is reversed, and the sounds appear indifferently in any position in an English sentence, the combination is still meaningless. "Collocability"—the ability to appear in a context—has been given no boundaries. In the following essay, Angus McIntosh, of the University of Edinburgh, and editor of *The Linguistic Atlas of Scotland,* discusses collocability.

Since economy is desirable in a linguistic description, McIntosh thinks that we ought to recognize lexical constraints upon grammatical patterning at the outset of our analysis. We should admit that in a pattern which simply calls for a noun class, many nouns will not fit. We are faced with the problem of determining what specific members of a form class will fit into what positions. For example, in the sentence *The man saw his brother,* we have grammatically, a determiner, a noun, a transitive verb, another determiner, and another noun. So far as the grammar is concerned the words are not important. Such, says McIntosh, is a grammatical level of meaning. The two noun positions, however, would not accept a great number of words we generally assign to the noun class.

One can say about this that our grammar may be presented with a much finer mesh than is assumed here. The descriptions and the rules for the generation of sentences may account for a number of subclasses. Nouns may be common (*cup*), proper (*Saul*), concrete (*cat*), abstract (*antagonism*), count (*one cowl, two cowls*), non-count (*some mush,* but not *two mushes*), divisible (*jury*), indivisible (*ignorance*). Any one noun belongs to a number of these subclasses. Non-count nouns, for instance, come in a variety of shapes and sizes: *ethics* and *phonemics; wood, silver,* or *plaster; knowledge,*

"Patterns and Ranges": From *Language,* vol. 37, n. 3, July–September 1961, pp. 325–337. Reprinted with the permission of The Linguistic Society of America, Incorporated. Some of the footnotes from the original article have been omitted here.

learning, or *progress;* and a mixture such as *measles, news, billiards,* or *information.* When the mesh becomes finer, the subtypes might include *tall* or *short, heavy* or *light,* and other distinctions, since a transformational-generative grammar will have a semantic component. Presumably, given genius, a lifetime, and sufficient funds, rules that would use these distinctions could be described. Nevertheless, after awhile the problems of division become very complex.

In talking of grammatical patterns and lexical ranges, McIntosh brings up a number of things that would have to be considered in weaving such a fine-meshed grammar. Like a number of earlier essays, this one involves the question of grammaticality.

Some combinations of sounds are acceptable English even though they have not been assigned a referent, as, for example, *thup.* So it is with sentences. Sometimes the grammatically eligible sentence waits for technological developments in order to have sense assigned to it; take, for instance, *Please plug in the blanket and turn it on,* which would have been nonsense to an electrician as well as a grammarian until very recently. When Bertrand Russell devised *Quadruplicity drinks procrastination* as grammar vacant of reference, he could not foresee that the results of Big Four Conferences would crowd his creation with meaning.

Sometimes, however, the conforming grammatical pattern seems to lack something more than a need for its use. In McIntosh's *The molten postage feather scored a weather,* we have difficulty extricating meaning from the parts, much less recognizing the possibility of a subject–predicate relationship. We are puzzled by the collocation of the items, not by the sentence pattern. McIntosh speaks of two kinds of collocability. The first involves recognizing whether synonyms are mutually replaceable to produce English. If one simply lists *short, low, small, little,* and *stubby* as alternate members of a class, he will get into trouble when he begins to freely substitute these words in *He took a _____ vacation. Apex, zenith, crown,* and *summit,* though reasonably synonymous, are not mutually substitutable before *meeting.* Somehow, the linguistic description of a language should show these differences.

With a second kind of collocation, we cast around for some way in which to recognize a meaning. Since we do not ask whether we have encountered a particular word before, it does not appear before us simply as a new word. Nor does it satisfy a grammatical pattern. McIntosh suggests that we rely on both the test of familiarity and a criterion of pattern, but not grammatical pattern. The pattern, however restrictive or expansive, is a "range," an inventory of what, for instance, may go with the verb *shrug.* When we use *shrug,* we add either *shoulders* or nothing. We do not shrug our stomachs. We would be surprised to see either the words *meow* or *neigh* following *dogs.*

Our determination of the acceptability of the collocation shows how far we will go in extending range. In the actual use of language, ranges are continually being extended, frequently dramatically. The daily use of words—even the trite—need not be scorned. We are comfortable in its presence. Our minds can relax, and the cliché is useful in the ritual of social communication where we are interested, not in exchanging ideas, but in simply indicating our recognition of the existence of other human beings. Nevertheless, we do occasionally depart from the totally familiar. And a reasoned recklessness with syntax is essential to the creation of literature.

McIntosh is led to suggest that there are four distinct stylistic modes:

1. normal collocations and normal grammar;

2. normal collocations and unusual grammar;

3. unusual collocations and normal grammar;

4. unusual collocations and unusual grammar.

Though he does not elaborate upon this point, there are obvious implications for exploring questions of style. A writer may do violence to a line while soothing our sense of syntax. An unusual collocation may illustrate a new value, at least for the moment. If the collocation sticks—and Shakespeare's English and the Bible have been particularly sticky—the daring act becomes acceptable, then common, through popular assimilation. We can even "coin words" as Shakespeare noted when he coined the expression. These facts, McIntosh concludes, make the search for simple definitions of word classes a sleeveless errand, but they do not prevent our distinguishing the grammatical from the ungrammatical.

Grammarians tend to be occupied primarily with the establishment and description of allowed patterns and with the rejection of whatever falls outside these. Some way of looking at language in which a distinction is made between grammar and lexis seems to be necessary if the patternings are to be economically stated or defined. For there is a difference between speaking about the eligibility of a particular CLASS OF UNIT[1] in some place or places in the grammatical structure of a language and about the eligibility of EXPONENTS of that class of unit in such a place or places in a particular sentence. And we can only preserve the simplicity of our gram-

matical description if we are prepared from the start to let it be understood that there are lexical factors, factors of collocational[2] eligibility, which (in different ways to be considered later) tend to rule out of actual use a large number of "sentences" (and smaller units) even though these seem to conform to all the rules of grammatical pattern. Grammarians do not, generally speaking, much concern themselves with the rejection of such 'sentences' as these, for whatever shortcomings they may have are considered to be grammatically irrelevant and more a matter for the lexicologist. There are of course marginal cases in the judgment of which the grammarian may feel doubtful whether he has or has not a claim to be involved; this is a difficult matter, to which I call attention but which I do not care to pursue.

In all this there are certain similarities between the problem of evaluating words and that of evaluating larger structural units, such as sen-

[1] See M. A. K. Halliday, "Categories of the Theory of Grammar," §3.1 and §5.1 (WORD, Vol. 17, No. 3, December 1961, pp. 241–292). The present paper owes much to the stimulus of Halliday's remarks on grammar and lexis, especially §§2.1, 6.3, 7.3–4, 8.1, and in private discussion. I take this opportunity of expressing my thanks also to two other colleagues, J. M. Sinclair and J. P. Thorne, for helpful comments on an earlier draft of this paper, which was presented in February 1961 at a staff seminar at the School of Applied Linguistics, Edinburgh University.

[2] See McIntosh's four variations given in the introduction, above.

tences. Is *histle* a word in English? Or *geed* or *plint?* The answer is that they are not, but we do not make it because we can indicate some lack of eligibility from the point of view of pattern or allowed shape. Their not being words has something to do with no referent ever having been associated with them.[3] We may say that they could be adopted as words if the need for extra words happened to arise; they have an orthographic (and implied phonological) shape which makes them eligible for such adoption, and it might be said to be a mere matter of chance whether this or that particular exponent "exists" or not. On the other hand *brdliou* or *pdilb* are ineligible as English words because they would not be exponents with an allowed shape.

At the rank of the sentence something of the same sort occurs. *The flaming waste-paper basket snored violently* awaits only, as we might put it, a need for its use, and it would not be difficult to devise one, e.g. to construct a fairy tale to fit into.[4] It answers in this sense to *histle* or *geed* or *plint.* But *Twenty because tomorrow the had a it* can have no use as a sentence because it has not the structure appropriate to any type of sentence. It therefore answers to *brdliou* or *pdilb.*

3 A formal indication of this being the case is that they would collocate no better or worse with one word than with another. And if, by the imposition of a GRAMMATICAL restriction, we were told that *plint* was to be assessed as a noun, there would still, for example, be no adjectives which we felt to be more appropriate or less appropriate than any others to qualify it.

4 An interesting lexical study could be made of the shifts of meaning undergone by words in fairy tales. An important point would be the very limited group of words so affected, all the rest remaining more or less stable and "normal."

Finally, we should note, we have obviously genuine sentences like *Jane has just come in* or *The old man seems to have gone out of his mind,* just as we have obviously genuine words like *basket* or *though.*

But it is worth while asking what it is that leads us to label these obviously genuine, and whether our criteria for passing judgment on words are the same as for passing judgment on sentences. When I say that *basket* and *though* are words, it is because I know from experience that they play some kind of role that I regard as sufficiently typical of words to justify their being so labelled; I remember having used them in this sort of way or having heard them or seen them written. But in evaluating sentences the situation is rather different, because I am usually prepared to pronounce on the genuineness of a sentence even when I cannot recall having used it or heard it or seen it written. Thus (even if these circumstances pertain) I still have no hesitation in maintaining that *Jane has just come in* is a genuine sentence.

So it would seem that there is a difference in my attitudes here. I can never say: Though I cannot recall ever having used it or heard it or seen it before, *basket* is certainly a word.[5] But with something which I am evaluating as a sentence I am not worried by the question, have I ever encountered this alleged sentence before?[6] It is sufficient that I should somehow be

5 I may of course encounter a hitherto unfamiliar form, e.g., in a technical work, and decide that it is a word, simply because I am persuaded that it would not otherwise occur, still less recur, in this work. But this is a different matter.

6 As elsewhere, I am assuming here that the sentence under scrutiny consists of one or more morphemes whose status as such is not in question.

satisfied that this sequence of words, taken as a sentence, would make perfectly good sense in some situation (or perhaps a large number of situations) which I can describe or envisage. Dictates of grammatical pattern obviously come in here, but in evaluating e.g. *Jane has just come in* I have certain additional requirements in mind. I shall return to these later.

We should note that the problems I am considering crop up only rarely in the day-to-day interchanges of accomplished users of a language. For such people use for the most part only sequences of genuine words; it is by no means usual for nonwords like *histle* or *plint* to be found dotted here and there among them; similarly such people use only sentences and normally avoid nonsentences. Nevertheless these problems assert themselves in our dealings with children and other learners of the language, so that many of us do encounter them; they are not mere theoretical possibilities. And we can say that we are at once suspicious or on our guard if we encounter, posing as a word, a form which we have never encountered so doing before, whereas we are continually confronted by sentences which we willingly accept as such though we have been confronted by them before. When we sit in judgment on sentences, we certainly require first of all to be satisfied as to grammatical pattern; this criterion is enough in itself to put *Twenty because tomorrow the had a it* outside the pale at once. But there are some sequences of words which satisfy our demands about pattern and which nevertheless we may hesitate to call sentences; they are not (it seems to me) all acceptable, and of those that are, some are more obviously acceptable than others.

We may consider some examples. We can pronounce in favor of *Jane has just come in* without hesitation. *The flaming waste-paper basket snored violently* is perhaps less readily acceptable, at least by the man in the street; he is likely to object that the situations where it would be appropriate are so few as to be negligible. This kind of consideration has linguistic importance of a statistical kind, but it scarcely entitles anyone to deny to our example the status of sentence. In any case we should certainly not object to it in the same kind of way as to *Twenty because tomorrow the had a it*. Are we then to say simply that we have three grades: the readily acceptable, the rarely needed but acceptable, and the impossible? And that, before we can unreservedly write off a sequence of words as a nonsentence, it must have the characteristic our last example has, of being grammatically unacceptable? I do not think that we can proceed in this way; even a detailed treatment of our three examples or of any similar ones would not cover the situation adequately. For there are other problematic cases of a rather different order.

Let us take the sequence *The molten postage feather scored a weather*. Does this, like the waste-paper-basket sentence,[7] only await a need for its use, or is there some objection to it that we could not make to the other? We can hardly object to it on the grounds of pattern, in the sense I have been using this term, for

[7] The great rarity of the collocation *waste-paper-basket sentence* must put us on our guard against a possible misconception. A very rare collocation may be perfectly clear in the appropriate context and may not involve us in any agonizing speculations about possible radical shifts of meaning of one or other of the words in it.

it corresponds in this respect to readily acceptable sentences such as *The aged chemistry professor caused a sensation.* Neverthless it differs from the wastepaper-basket sentence in one quite fundamental way. For we cannot easily, to put it in everyday terms, "attach enough meaning" to *the molten postage feather* or to *scored a weather* to be able to conceive of any situation (in a fairy tale or elsewhere) where it might be appropriate.[8] This is a way of saying that words have only a certain tolerance of compatibility, only a certain POTENTIAL of COLLOCABILITY, quite apart from any considerations of pattern in the grammatical sense. It need hardly be said that the edges of this range of tolerance are vague and unstable, and that the question of what we mean by compatibility is a complicated one.

We can look at the matter of collocability from two different points of view. In the first we judge according to whether a word (to take the simplest sort of case, where we focus our attention on one only as being the oddity) achieves the purpose we suppose it to be intended to be carrying out in a particular context. Thus in a certain real-life situation I may object to *bitter* and demand its replacement by *sour* when someone says to me, *This lemon* (which we have just cut in two and are both sucking) *is bitter.* I am not thereby denying the possibility of lemons ever being bitter, but I am maintaining that *bitter* is certainly no adjective to use to describe this lemon: I am charging my

companion with a lexical lapse. If he had said *This lemon is sweet,* I should probably not, curiously enough, have questioned his linguistic competence, but have doubted rather his gustatory judgment or even his sanity. But if he uses the word *bitter,* I may well assume that his reaction to the taste of the lemon more or less coincides with mine; so if I object I am then accusing him of the misuse of a word.

In cases like this collocation of *bitter* and *lemon* we encounter an extremely common problem of applied linguistics which tends to be pushed into the background by descriptive linguists. They handle a corpus of many possible sentences which, in varying degrees of detail, they classify according to, or use to illustrate, the characteristics of the structure and of the system of the text or the language under analysis. But what is usually quite taken for granted is that the reader (or listener) will without question accept all these sentences as such; it is more or less left to him, if he so wishes, to work out for himself a context or contexts into which they will fit. Apart from any shortcomings of this approach from the standpoint of learning a language, there is a theoretical consideration here. If one sentence differs significantly from another even though their structure is the same, this is a linguistic difference. And if a description merely lists them as alternative exponents of the same structure and says nothing in lexical terms about the nature of the difference, it is for no better reason than that descriptions of this kind are mostly made by grammarians and not lexicologists. A merely grammatical description is no more a complete linguistic description than is a merely lexical one.

This needs to be kept in mind more

---

8 The only situation that I can think of (other than in a paper about language) where it would be wholly appropriate would be on the lips of someone in a pathological state of mind, e.g. in a delirium, where regularity of grammatical pattern and eccentricity of collocation often go together.

than it is by those who are primarily preoccupied with grammatical structures as such. For even in grammar, the choice of one structure rather than another or of one member of a paradigm rather than of another is significant, so critical a matter indeed that it can on occasion be a matter of life or death. Yet a great deal which follows from this is entirely taken for granted and passed over in descriptive grammars. Both from the grammatical and the collocational point of view there is for the user of a language a continual problem of decision in such matters, an incessant process of choice or selection from a number of alternatives. For him it is clearly not enough to be able to "create" or "generate" an unlimited number of "good" sentences, i.e. of sentences all of which would be appropriate in imaginable contexts. It should not therefore be beneath the dignity of the linguist to try to understand the strictly linguistic problems which are connected with the final selection of particular clusters of lexical items in particular grammatical patterns in a given instance of a sentence as used in a live situation.

The second way of looking at the matter of collocability is the one we have been following in the previous pages. In evaluating a collocation, we often tend to assess it without reference to a given context, and to pass judgment on it according to whether we can imagine a possible setting or settings into which we could appropriately insert it. This, of course, gives us much greater scope and allows us to toy with various possibilities of 'meaning' of one or more of the words involved in a way which would not be feasible if we were tied to a single contextualized instance. Thus,

without such restriction, I can easily find numerous suitable settings for *This lemon is sweet,* e.g. where two women are discussing different fabrics for a cushion cover, or where somebody is exclaiming over a child's painting of still life. I shall proceed on the assumption that this kind of scrutiny is perfectly legitimate and try to show that it has its own merits. But it is not at all the same thing as evaluating an instance of a collocation in an actual context.

We come now to a rather critical point. Do we, in judging the eligibility of collocations, use the sort of criteria we used for the eligibility of words, or those we used for the eligibility of sentences? Since, in all these cases, it offers more scope to pronounce on their eligibility in possible contexts which we are free to excogitate, rather than in some given context, I shall adopt here the second or general rather than the first or particular approach. And for the sake of clarity I shall simplify the question of criteria somewhat by assuming throughout that we are working within the bounds of well defined syntactic units about whose grammatical structure we are not in doubt. In this way we shall get as little involved as possible in irrelevant syntactical complications, and there will thus be no question of this or that collocation being ineligible because it fails to satisfy the requirements of grammatical pattern.

The answer to our question must certainly be that we do not write off collocations as impossible simply because we have never encountered them before. For if we did, we could not give our blessing to any new sentence except one which was made up, by some different permutation, of old familiar phrases. And even here we should have to say that those phrases collocated in a new way and could not therefore be legitimately juxtaposed. Nevertheless we certainly do not give our blessing to all sequences of words or phrases, however acceptable they may be grammatically. So it is still not clear how we are able to decide in favour of one collocation and to reject another. For instance one may balk at *the molten postage feather* as a fit subject for any sentence. Yet one may have no difficulty in accepting *the aged chemistry professor* as perfectly reasonable, even though, in the experience of many of us, it may not have the advantage over the other of having been encountered before. And those to whom it is not new, did they not once encounter it for the first time, and did they not accept it there and then?

In taking different attitudes towards these two sequences we rely, I suggest, not only on the test of familiarity, but on criteria of pattern. But the underlying patterns which are relevant here are of a quite different order from the grammatical patterning of which I have spoken hitherto. Hereafter I shall therefore distinguish this new kind of speaking of RANGE, using "pattern" only in relation to grammar. There is for instance a range, however laborious it may be to define or describe, which is represented by the fairly strictly limited inventory of nouns which may without any question be qualified by the word *molten*. The set of alternative available possibilities which this inventory consists of is just as much a part of the form of the language as is a grammatical system, and a full account of this set goes a long way towards constituting the meaning of *molten*.[9] Now this meaning itself rests (though it will of course depend on other collocational relationships as well) to a considerable extent on a certain similarity of meaning of all the nouns in question;[10] this, in turn, is merely another way of saying that there are marked similarities between the collocational habits of each and all of these.[11] Therefore if (ignoring *postage* for the moment) an attempt is made to collocate *molten* with a noun of a quite different "family"[12] (that is, one with a very different set of collocational habits) such as *feather*, the only experience we can fall back on to deal with it is experience of that aspect of linguistic form which in one way or another has to do with the phenomenon of range.

Confronted with *molten feather* we are likely to attempt to draw on this experience. We shall do so both for its direct bearing on these two words and for what it can provide for us in the

9 Another way of saying this is that if there were no restrictions on the collocability of *molten* (or any other word we may care to select), it would then have no meaning other than "grammatical," i.e. what it had by virtue of whatever restrictions there still were as to the places in grammatical structure it was eligible to occupy.

10 Or perhaps rather what Ludwig Wittgenstein calls "a complicated network of similarities overlapping and criss-crossing: sometimes overall similarities, sometimes similarities of detail." See *Philosophical Investigations* 1.66 (Oxford, 1953).

11 It need not, incidentally, disturb us if some words seem to have more than one range, such as a dictionary would signalize by listing separate meanings in a succession of subheadings. This is precisely what we must expect, and we may often find it convenient to divide our range into subranges as circumstances and our intentions suggest.

12 Wittgenstein 1.67.

way of other previously encountered words and collocations which in one way or another may seem analogous. According to our personal experience and how we draw upon it, we may react in at least three different ways:

1. We may write the whole thing off as meaningless.

2. Because we recall having encountered this kind of possibility before, we may search around for some hitherto unexperienced meaning of one or other of the two words, in the hope that this single adjustment will put everything right. Thus *molten pig* would become clear to a child when (but only when) he became aware of the relevant meaning of *pig*. So we might seek to discover or postulate some similar use of *feather* with a subrange of collocability which (though it was hitherto unknown to us) would at once align it with that group of nouns which may be qualified by the word *molten*. In particular we might examine hopefully the rare use where *feather* designates a kind of iron wedge used for splitting stones.[13] Alternatively (clutching at another quite different formal characteristic of the language) we might seek to discover some connection between *molten* and *moult* which would lead to our being satisfied with the collocation.

Another related approach would be to decide that no amount of adjustment of this sort with respect to one of the words would be sufficient, and to try to tackle *molten feather* in the light of such phrases as *Bloody Mary* or *black velvet* or *cat's eyes* or *red herring,* on the hypothesis that our difficulty may well spring from the fact that, as in so many other cases, the lexical item and the word are not coextensive.

3. In accordance with an intuitive understanding of "range-extending" tendencies which are characteristic of language,[14] we may seek to read into one or the other of the words some plausible extension of a familiar meaning, i.e. an extension of collocational range which we might be ready to accept on account of analogous phenomena with which we are already familiar in connection with other words, particularly other words whose collocational habits associate them fairly closely with *molten* itself.

Thus we know that *flaming, burning, incandescent,* and others have, for whatever reason, a broader range of collocation than that which we have hitherto associated with *molten.* We might therefore seek to interpret *molten* in some such terms as "radiant liquefaction," arguing perhaps that if Herrick can use *liquefaction* of Julia's clothes, then a hotted-up version of the same image may well be applied here to *feather.* Whatever we may do on these lines, we shall be attempting to understand our collocation by postulating an extension of range for which we can find reasonably close parallels.

In practice, of course, in coming to a conclusion on any of these lines about *molten feather* in an actual instance, we should always be guided by collocational evidence of a more varied sort. What this molten feather

---

[13] See the *Oxford English Dictionary* s.v. *feather* sb. 16b.

[14] There are of course pattern-extending tendencies also, which amounts to saying that grammar does not remain fixed either, but we are not concerned with these here; they form an ill-explored branch of the history of English.

"is" (if it is anything) will be decided not only on the basis of possibilities we can think of in the various ways suggested above, but also on the basis of such evidence as the kind of verb our phrase is in subject relation with, and numerous similar factors. For the assessment of a collocation in the last resort involves in one way or another all other lexical items in the context, and there is scarcely a limit to the remove at which these may affect our interpretation of the word we happen to be specially preoccupied with. Furthermore various circumstances in the situational context are likely to be relevant.

There is, fortunately, no need for us to come to a final conclusion about the validity of *molten postage feather* or of *scored a weather,* each judged in isolation, but there would be few who would accept these in a subject-predicate relationship; in other words, this "sentence" must be judged in a way quite differently from our waste-paper-basket sentence. And if (as seems likely) we reject it, it is because of departures from tolerated ranges of collocability, and neither because it violates pattern on the one hand nor because it "only awaits a need" on the other.

It is always dangerous to assert that a short sequence of this sort could in no circumstances constitute an acceptable sentence, but longer sequences can easily be produced which would daunt the most ingenious devisers of plausible contexts. And an account of a situation where even the present example might grudgingly be given acceptance would almost certainly involve at the same time the postulating, for certain of the lexical items, of meanings for which there was nowhere any previous evidence. The fictional situation devised would have to include "meanings" which, however plausible, were themselves also fictional. In other words no mere description of a context for our example will in itself clear up anything; we shall be asked at the same time to accept that in this context these lexical items have certain rather odd meanings. And we shall run the risk of overlooking the purely fictional nature of these alleged meanings, partly through being spellbound by the oddity of the situation described, and partly because it will have been specifically designed to make the meanings as plausible as possible.

It is typical of such cases that even though every effort is made to invent a situation which will do least violence to the use of lexical items, it is impossible to invent one in which no violence is done at all. In such a case this feature of oddity of use of lexical items must itself therefore be accepted as one of the characteristics or ingredients of the situation which has been devised. I would suggest that we do not encounter this kind of difficulty when dealing with the waste-paper-basket sentence, because we feel that there is nothing in it which is beyond our normal experience of "range-extending" tendencies.

With these matters in mind, let us turn to the question of what goes on in the matter of collocations when language is actually being used. When we speak or write, we have to strike a rather delicate balance. If we stick entirely to familiar collocations, then, to put it mildly, we run a grave risk of being trite. Indeed we can only escape this danger by departing from the familiar at some dimension or other, phrase, clause, or whatever it may be; anything new we have to say will demand this. It is important to stress the word "dimension." For different users of language (and indeed different traditional styles of language) vary as to the point at which they tend to kick off into the void; below a certain dimension their collocations may be very "ordinary," but the collocation of these collocations may be much more daring and unusual.[15]

At whatever point we kick off, if we depart too far from some sort of tolerated range, we run the risk of being obscure. The balance we have to strike is therefore between triteness and obscurity. I am not concerned here with the somewhat similar way in which one can be cautious or daring about grammatical patterns. But I wish to note this similarity and to point out that collocational caution or abandon and grammatical caution or abandon may or may not march in step. For instance, my colleague Halliday has made me aware of the contrast there is in many poems of W. B. Yeats between the normality of most

[15] It is in contexts like this that it is useful to keep in mind the distinction between the general and the special approach. One might say for example that *sour lemon* is a familiar enough collocation but that if the whole phrase is used in an unfamiliar context its impact may be considerable, e.g. if I use it in reference to my uncle. Strictly speaking, then, it seems that we should distinguish between familiarity from the point of view of the forms involved and from the point of view of the referent. In practice this is not important, because (unless "uncle" figures only in the situational context and not in the text) at the dimension where we are dealing with *uncle* and *sour lemon* as themselves a collocation, we shall already have made a distinct step towards the unusual.

of his grammatical patterns and the unusualness of many of his collocations. When something of this sort is going on, the possibility of a fairly precise analytical way of handling it is clearly of importance for anyone making an approach to the analysis of style.

So, to put the matter with considerable crudity, we can already say on this basis that there is the possibility of four obviously distinct stylistic modes: normal collocations and normal grammar, unusual collocations and normal grammar, normal collocations and unusual grammar, unusual collocations and unusual grammar. This of course is only a beginning. For that which is collocationally unusual may or may not involve individual words which are themselves unusual; contrast *flaming waste-paper basket* with *indesinent hebetude*. And we should make a distinction between that which is normal in the sense of "already familiar" and in the sense of "not hitherto encountered but normal according to criteria of range"; I shall give an example of this kind of collocation later. I do not propose to elaborate here on these stylistic modes and their variations; I merely suggest them as part of a useful basic framework with the help of which, it seems to me, one might profitably explore many fundamental stylistic problems.

The question of the limitations imposed on CHOICE by the dictates of tolerated range is one of some interest. Since we are dealing with collocations, I am not primarily concerned here with the choice or use of the intrinsically rare word and the numerous different reasons there may be for such a choice. Nevertheless this is an important aspect of style and it is worth while to keep in mind the various effects intended or achieved by the use of such words. We might take note likewise of different kinds of intrinsically rare grammatical patterns that the effects achieved by these too may be very diverse. For here, as with vocabulary, a given peculiarity of this sort may be one of many different kinds and the effect or "flavor" will vary accordingly. This of course is a commonplace and would not be worth mentioning were it not that such problems, despite being familiar, are rarely if ever subjected to rigorous scrutiny within a proper analytical framework.

In pursuing a little further the question of collocations, normal and unusual, I shall take the position that the meanings a given word has (however we may define meaning) are in some direct way associated with our experience of that word in a variety of contexts, our association of that word with other words which have, in our experience, a somewhat similar range, and our association of the word with other words of similar shape, often but not always etymologically related. Such similarly shaped words may well play diverse grammatical roles, so they will not necessarily have at all the same range; the association, by thus straddling grammar, may therefore lead us to draw conclusions about a word with one such range from another with another range.

The experience and associative habits of no two people are exactly the same, though we tend to have a good deal in common with others in all this, for the obvious reason that we necessarily share much of our linguistic experience with them. Even so there are notable discrepancies, as we may gather from the chastening experience of looking at a large dictionary, which tells us something of the combined lexical habits of many people. In so doing, it lists sometimes words of which I have had no previous experience, sometimes words which turn out to be capable of meaning things I did not know they could, i.e. which can stand in certain collocational relationships of which I was hitherto unaware. We should also note that the dictionary does not accept anything that falls below a certain generality of experience: it does not cover those private (e.g. family) words or collocations which are only shared within a small circle. And of course it cannot provide us, by paraphrase or definition or in any other way, with anything like all the numerous delicately discriminated shades of meaning which a word may have in (say) ten thousand different instances. All it can do is to list (and perhaps connect) different meanings in rough classes, each class representing what I call a USE, i.e. a group of instances classed together because the meaning therein seems to require or justify a definition or paraphrase different from that of some other class.

Broadly speaking, I would regard a normal collocation as one which, when we encounter it, we can readily assign to one or another of the classes with which we, as well as the larger dictionaries in their overtly more ordered fashion, in some sense operate. By "readily" I mean without any feeling that by so doing we are in any striking or significant way extending (as distinct from so to speak filling in) that class by admitting our instance to membership. I use the words "normal" and "unusual" rather than "familiar" and "unfamiliar" because the latter would tend to imply that we required some yardstick of previous experience of the instance itself; this, as I have suggested, is not the case. Previous experience of this sort does indeed validate some collocations which, judged purely on some rather vague criterion of normal expected range, might otherwise appear odd (e.g. *He was in a blue funk*), just as it validates instances of some rather odd grammatical patterns (e.g. *He came a cropper*).[16] But this particular kind of experience is not the crucial factor in many cases.

For, to go back to a point made earlier, absence of previous experience—for instance of *rhododendron bush* and *died* as exponents of a subject-predicate relationship—does not prevent me from saying with complete confidence in an appropriate situation: *The rhododendron bush died*. As I have suggested, there are complicated rules of range operating here which are based on a knowledge on our part of the "kind of verb" which can serve as a predicate to what we might describe, if we spoke of it at all, as "this sort of subject." There is of course, for such knowledge, a basis of experience of instances. If we have not actually noted down all previously encountered examples bearing on this problem, we must still recognise the relevance here of the notebook of memory. But there is a further element in our knowledge than that implied by the mere possession of an inventory of instances; this we should not overlook any more than we should overlook, in the field of grammar, the importance of a knowledge which is more than mere crude inventory-information about paradigmatic phenomena.

In what we are concerned with, this kind of knowledge has to do with the ways in which we order the information we have acquired from the observation of instances. It has to do with our understanding of la langue, an understanding only small fragments of which may be called into play when we produce any single appropriate sentence. We draw upon this both in such production and also in evaluating and attempting to understand what others produce. To take a very simple example, it is a fragment of this knowledge which forbids me to say (except in some kind of a whimsical register): *The rhododendron bush passed away*. And for pedagogical purposes we must necessarily sometimes isolate such a fragment and formulate it separately. We can then treat by themselves, when need arises, just such problems as that of the difference between the ranges of *die* and of *pass away*.

It is necessary to say this because there is too often a tendency for people dealing with a language to retreat from the handling of the trickier kinds of difficulty of this sort, suggesting as they do so that some difficulties are just not amenable to rigorous treatment in comparative isolation. They often speak as though only a total possession of the whole Sprachgefühl in all its sophistication can be of much avail in solving a person's difficulties with such things as the choice between *gehen* and *fahren* in German or *ser* and *estar* in Spanish.

---

[16] Examples such as these may well give us trouble the first time they are encountered; they then differ in this respect from *the aged chemistry professor*.

It is true that there are complex and far-reaching problems of range in the more complicated aspects of such cases. But it is not true to maintain that they cannot profitably be isolated, and thereafter handled in such a way, for the benefit of children or foreigners, as to make up in a large measure for the fact that such learners have not had full "natural" opportunities to accumulate (as a mature native has) a sufficiency of ordered information relevant to a mastery of the problem in question.

We may also regard this systemic knowledge of range as crucial when we are considering certain aspects of the use of English by experienced native speakers or writers. For it is very much tied up with the generative or range-extending process whereby it is possible at all for unusual collocations to be added to those already experienced.[17] A great number of new collocations which, though new, we readily include in the category "normal" are perhaps of merely minor interest. These are examples of the "range-filling-in" type, where, though we have never encountered them before (and we may well not suspect this at all), the nature of the range in which they fall is virtually unmodified by the new instance. An example would be that where I merely added *rhododendron bush* to my previous experience of plant names which col-

locate with *die* in a subject-predicate relation.

It would not be just, I think, to classify within this "normal" category all such cases as pass unnoticed when we first encounter them. For it is almost certainly true that a great many range-extending collocations are of a kind which also pass unnoticed in this way. If this were not so, it would hardly be possible to explain the enormous range drift, affecting so very much of the lexis, which has taken place and is at present taking place in English. If we were to make boggling or raised eyebrows the criterion for range-extending instances, it would have to be objected, I think, that these indications of something odd having happened simply do not occur often enough, in our individual experiences, to account for more than a small proportion of the drift. This amounts to saying that the dictates of range are such as to permit the admission of new exponents on the very margin of tolerability without our even feeling that these are in any way dubitable. Sometimes of course we may find that there is disagreement about what is dubitable, and it is no accident that what is not felt to be at all marginal or odd by younger speakers may well be felt by the elderly to be barely on or even well beyond the edge of acceptability.[18]

At other times we are aware of instances which seem daring and innovatory, which seem (though we may

[17] A matter quite as important as range-extending is the process whereby range is constricted though the abandoning of previously familiar uses, or the more complicated but also more common situation where the range is constricted at one point but extended at another. In all this there are parallels to what happens with grammatical patterns.

[18] This of course applies also to lexical items as such and to grammatical patterns as well. Furthermore, in the case of lexis-range and pattern constriction, it may be the young who question the acceptability of something which is regarded as normal by the elderly.

not put it so) to involve a real extension of range. Some instances of this kind may quickly affect a considerable proportion of the speakers of a language; for instance we may begin to be aware that many people are using the word *smashing* with a strange meaning or in a strange way, as perhaps in *We had a smashing time yesterday evening*. This implies that we are aware of having begun to hear the word *smashing* in environments (situational as well as linguistic) which hitherto we should certainly have considered inappropriate not only because of their being out of our previous experience but also because of being beyond what our range-sense would regard as even marginally tolerable.

Other instances of unusual collocations may be much more OCCASIONAL, even perhaps unique. These are the kind which tend to be of such importance in literature, and especially in poetry. They are part of the machinery whereby the prose writer or the poet strives, over a larger or smaller stretch of text, to convey something which he cannot achieve by normal means, and he thereby sets us a problem in which we can lean on no experience of directly relevant instances. It may be of course that in a given case we are in the presence of the very birth of something which thereafter passes into general use and from then on forms part of the normal inventory of collocations involving the words in question; so with various phrases adopted into the language from Shakespeare and the Bible. It would be an interesting study to attempt to determine what there was about them that led to their adop-

tion on this scale while others, often no less striking, passed virtually unnoticed. In cases of this latter sort the flavor of the collocation, unsullied by subsequent general employment, will tend to remain sharp and distinctive. But in either event we encounter the same general problem of the nature of the impact of unusual collocations at the time of their first use.

This problem is complicated by a factor which cannot be treated here, but which I mention because it is often lost sight of. If, contrary to normal practice, two words A and B are collocated, there is a common tendency to assume that the resultant phrase exemplifies a rare use of A only or of B only, i.e. that the oddity belongs somehow to one of the forms and not to both. It is true that there are often good reasons for looking at the matter in this way; very often everything in a whole sentence seems quite normal except one word which sticks out from all the others. When this happens, the reaction we have is based on attitudes about the expected or tolerated range of words and we can easily persuade ourselves that only one word is behaving in a curious way collocationally. But we must not forget that to look at the matter in this way is illusory; the collocational oddity must involve at least one other word quite intimately, and we are led astray simply by the fact that (though this is so) the meaning of this other word does not seem to be affected to anything like the same degree. This may well be, and it is part of the fascination of the whole business, but to concentrate exclusively on the word in question is not to exhaust the interest of the collocation.

I shall conclude with one or two remarks about structurally very simple collocations in which we can most easily ask ourselves where the oddity lies, and why it should seem to be concentrated on one word in many cases. If I encounter for the first time the collocation *steel postage-stamp,* I am likely, I think, to modify my views (if I may so put the matter in everyday terms) about postage-stamps rather than about steel. And so with *rubber book* or *transparent dog* or *talking bear.* But with *hammering weekend,* in similar circumstances, I feel that it would be the adjective to which I should have to adjust, and a weekend would remain much the same thing in my mind as before. And so perhaps with *constipated river* or *witty putt.* Profitable work could be done on the factors which operate to focus our attention on particular words in this way on some occasions and to produce quite different reactions on others, such as in those cases where the oddity seems to lie in the phrase as a whole, and the somewhat eccentric implied relationship, rather than anything remarkable which seems to have happened to the meaning of either word. My own collocation *waste-paper-basket sentence* will serve as an example of something in this kind. An investigation of this problem would certainly have to pay due attention to two factors: the role which the items concerned play in the grammatical structure, and the "power" of each item in informational terms, i.e. the relative degree of restriction of their accepted collocational range.

What I have tried to deal with is one or two aspects of the problem of the choice or decision which confronts us continually in using language, even within a prescribed framework of grammatical patterns. In particular I have tried to deal with the factor of RANGE, and to suggest that the term might profitably be used in connection with lexis in a sense whereby it then answers to what, on the grammatical side, I have labeled PATTERN. Pattern has to do with the structures of the sentences we make; range has to do with the specific collocations we make in a series of particular instances. Since collocations, in larger and larger units, are the material out of which instances of sentences are made, it is these considerations of range which we must take into account, within the dictates of pattern, in dealing with the text of actual sentences. I have thus attempted to bring into the open a number of questions that tend to be overlooked by those who focus their attention on matters of grammatical pattern to the exclusion of almost everything else.

For discussion

A. Lawrence Durrell, the author of *The Alexandrian Quartet,* has written both a poem and a book called *Bitter Lemons.* Is this an acceptable collocation to McIntosh?

B. McIntosh writes that *The flaming waste-paper basket snored violently,* and *The molten postage feather scored a weather* must be judged in different ways. What are these different ways?

C. McIntosh feels that his discussion has two clear implications for the teaching of English as a second language. What are they?

D. When we see a new collocation, we are apt to attribute its strangeness to one of its items, not both. McIntosh then contrasts a collocation like *steel postage-stamp* with one like *hammering weekend*. List ten collocations which you believe to be like *steel postage-stamp*, and ten which you think are like *hammering weekend*.

E. Following are some tried and true collocations in English. What normally goes in the blank is obvious. By changing the word order or putting something unusual in the blank, or both, extend the range of each item (e.g., Time wounds all heels).
1. He bogged _____.
2. A rough and _____ answer.
3. Familiarity breeds _____.
4. He is every _____ a gentleman.
5. A straight line is the shortest distance between _____.
6. Hitch your wagon _____.
7. Two is company. Three _____.
8. All's _____ that _____.
9. All is not _____ that _____.
10. A penny saved is _____.

F. Which of McIntosh's stylistic modes are represented in each of the following?

> Irks care the crop-full bird? Frets
> doubt the maw-crammed beast?
> ROBERT BROWNING, "Rabbi Ben Ezra"

> "Things are in the saddle and ride mankind."
> RALPH WALDO EMERSON

> "It is about a cigarette from here."
> GREEK PEASANT answering the question:
> "How far to Patras?"

> The hand that rounded Peter's dome,
> And groined the aisles of Christian Rome,
> Wrought in a sad sincerity;
> Himself from God he could not free.
> RALPH WALDO EMERSON, "The Problem"

> Sad-eyed in October, 1936, was nimble, middle-sized
> *Life*-President Clair Maxwell as he told newshawks
> of the sale of the fifty-three-old gagmag to *Time* . . .
> Where it will all end, knows God!
> WOLCOTT GIBBS, "Time . . . Fortune . . . Life . . . Luce"

> . . . I'm a plain man, and in a single station,
> But Oh! ye lords of ladies intellectual,
> Inform us truly, have they not henpecked you all?
> BYRON, Canto I, "Don Juan"

> Where, like a pillow on a bed,
> A pregnant bank swelled up to rest
> The violet's reclining head,
> Sat we two, one another's best.
> JOHN DONNE, "The Ecstasy"

As when to them who sail
Beyond the Cape of Hope, and now are past
Mozambic, off at sea north-east winds blow
Sabaean odors from the spicy shore
Of Araby the blest, with such delay
Well pleased they slack their course, and many a league
Cheered with the grateful smell old ocean smiles;
JOHN MILTON, "Paradise Lost"

GEORGE A. MILLER

The psycholinguists:
on the new scientists of language

As has already been pointed out, the transformational-generative grammarian wishes to account for the linguistic creativity of a language user. The grammarian wants to explain our ability to distinguish intuitively degrees of grammaticalness (*a mile away* as grammatically different from *a cigarette away*). He wants to characterize our ability to understand sentences which may never have been used before (*The baby is dropping her pacifiers into the mouth of her wooden hippopotamus*). And he wants to explain our ability to observe differences in superficially apparently identical structures (*bat boy, arm band*).

Nevertheless, Chomsky and others have repeatedly emphasized that their grammar is not "in itself" a model of the language user. It is not a verbal presentation of whatever grammar machine resides in the speaker's head. The explanation is first of the grammar, not of the biology or the psychology. The language-user's linguistic performance has been abstractly generalized, not operationally described.

Despite this disclaimer, however, transformational-generative grammar has been very appealing to many scholars interested in explaining the psychological processes that go on when people use sentences. One of these is George A. Miller, Professor of Psychology at Harvard University, the author of an early book on psycholinguistics (*Language and Communication,* 1951), and more recently both an independent and a co-contributor with Chomsky to fundamental research in psycholinguistics working from a transformational-generative base. The following article was originally published in *Encounter,* an English magazine of international interest published for the layman. In it, Professor Miller discusses the principal problems of contemporary psycholinguistics within the theoretical framework elaborated upon in earlier articles by Chomsky. One implication of Professor Miller's discussion is that transformational-generative grammarians have perhaps come closer to the model of a language user than they have claimed. He also illuminates the challenging features of language study in a wide context, resetting and illustrating again most of the ideas discussed in the preceding essays of this section.

"The Psycholinguists": From *Encounter,* vol. 23, n. 1, July 1964, pp. 29–37. Reprinted with the permission of the publisher and George A. Miller. Some of the footnotes in the original essay have been omitted here.

Psychologists have long recognised that human minds feed on linguistic symbols. Linguists have always admitted that some kind of psycho-social motor must move the machinery of grammar and lexicon. Sooner or later they were certain to examine their intersection self-consciously. Perhaps it was also inevitable that the result would be called "psycholinguistics."

In fact, although the enterprise itself has slowly been gathering strength at least since the invention of the telephone, the name, in its unhyphenated form, is only about ten years old. Few seem pleased with the term, but the field has grown so rapidly and stirred so much interest in recent years that some way of referring to it is urgently needed. *Psycholinguistics* is as descriptive a term as any, and shorter than most.

Among psychologists it was principally the behaviourists who wished to take a closer look at language. Behaviourists generally try to replace anything subjective by its most tangible, physical manifestation, so they have had a long tradition of confusing thought with speech—or with "verbal behaviour," as many prefer to call it. Among linguists it was principally those with an anthropological sideline who were most willing to collaborate, perhaps because as anthropologists they were sensitive to all those social and psychological processes that support our linguistic practices. By working together they managed to call attention to an important field of scientific research and to integrate it, or at least to acquaint its various parts with one another, under this new rubric.

Interest in psycholinguistics, however, is not confined to psychologists and linguists. Many people have been stirred by splendid visions of its practical possibilities. One thinks of medical applications to the diagnosis and treatment of a heterogeneous variety of language disorders ranging from simple stammering to the overwhelming complexities of aphasia. One thinks too of pedagogical applications, of potential improvements in our methods for teaching reading and writing, or for teaching second languages. If psycholinguistic principles were made sufficiently explicit, they could be imparted to those technological miracles of the twentieth century, the computing machines, which would bring into view a whole spectrum of cybernetic possibilities. We could exploit our electrical channels for voice communications more efficiently. We might improve and automate our dictionaries, using them for mechanical translation from one language to another. Perhaps computers could print what we say, or even say what we print, thus making speech visible for the deaf and printing audible for the blind. We might, in short, learn to adapt computers to dozens of our human purposes if only they could interpret our languages. Little wonder that assorted physicians, educators, philosophers, logicians, and engineers have been intrigued by this new adventure.

Of course, the realisation of practical benefits must await the success of the scientific effort; there is some danger that enthusiasm may colour our estimate of what can be accomplished. Not a few sceptics remain unconvinced; some can even be found who argue that success is impossible in principle. "Science," they say, "can go only so far. . . ."

The integration of psycholinguistic studies has occurred so recently that there is still some confusion concerning its scope and purpose; efforts to clarify it necessarily have something of the character of personal opinion.[1] In my own version, the central task of this new science is to describe the psychological processes that go on when people use sentences. The real crux of the psycholinguistic problem does not appear until one tries to deal with sentences, for only then does the importance of productivity become completely obvious. It is true that productivity can also appear with individual words, but there it is not overwhelming. With sentences, productivity is literally unlimited.

Before considering this somewhat technical problem, however, it might be well to illustrate the variety of processes that psycholinguists hope to explain. This can best be done if we ask what a listener can do about a spoken utterance, and consider his alternatives in order from the superficial to the inscrutable.

The simplest thing one can do in the presence of a spoken utterance is to listen. Even if the language is incomprehensible, one can still *hear* an utterance as an auditory stimulus and respond to it in terms of some discriminative set: how loud, how fast, how long, from which direction, etc.

Given that an utterance is heard, the next level involves *matching* it as a phonemic pattern in terms of phonological skills acquired as a user of the language. The ability to match an input can be tested in psychological experiments by asking listeners to echo what they hear; a wide variety of experimental situations—experiments on the perception of speech and on the rote memorisation of verbal materials—can be summarised as tests of a person's ability to repeat the speech he hears under various conditions of audibility or delay.

If a listener can hear and match an utterance, the next question to ask is whether he will *accept* it as a sentence in terms of his knowledge of grammar. At this level we encounter processes difficult to study experimentally, and one is forced to rely most heavily on linguistic analyses of the structure of sentences. Some experiments are possible, however, for we can measure how much a listener's ability to accept the utterance as a sentence facilitates his ability to hear and match it; grammatical sentences are much easier to hear, utter or remember than are ungrammatical strings of words, and even nonsense (*pirot, karol, elat,* etc.) is easier to deal with if it looks grammatical (*pirots karolise elatically,* etc.). Needless to say, the grammatical knowledge we wish to study does not concern those explicit rules drilled into us by teachers of traditional grammar, but rather the implicit generative knowledge that we all must acquire in order to use a language appropriately.

Beyond grammatical acceptance comes semantic interpretation: we can ask how listeners *interpret* an utter-

[1] My own opinions have been strongly influenced by Noam Chomsky. A rather technical exposition of this work can be found in Chapters 11–13 of the second volume of the *Handbook of Mathematical Psychology,* edited by R. D. Luce, R. R. Bush, and E. Galanter (Wiley, New York, 1963), from which many of the ideas discussed here have been drawn.

ance as meaningful in terms of their semantic system. Interpretation is not merely a matter of assigning meanings to individual words; we must also consider how these component meanings combine in grammatical sentences. Compare the sentences: *Healthy young babies sleep soundly* and *Colourless green ideas sleep furiously*. Although they are syntactically similar, the second is far harder to perceive and remember correctly—because it cannot be interpreted by the usual semantic rules for combining the senses of adjacent English words. The interpretation of each word is affected by the company it keeps; a central problem is to systematise the interactions of words and phrases with their linguistic contexts. The lexicographer makes his major contribution at this point, but psychological studies of our ability to paraphrase an utterance also have their place.

At the next level it seems essential to make some distinction between interpreting an utterance and understanding it, for understanding frequently goes well beyond the linguistic context provided by the utterance itself. A husband greeted at the door by "I bought some electric light bulbs to-day" must do more than interpret its literal reference; he must understand that he should go to the kitchen and replace that burned-out lamp. Such contextual information lies well outside any grammar or lexicon. The listener can *understand* the function of an utterance in terms of contextual knowledge of the most diverse sort.

Finally, at a level now almost invisible through the clouds, a listener may *believe* that an utterance is valid in terms of its relevance to his own conduct. The child who says "I saw five lions in the garden" may be heard, matched, accepted, interpreted, and understood, but in few parts of the world will he be believed.

The boundaries between successive levels are not sharp and distinct. One shades off gradually into the next. Still the hierarchy is real enough and important to keep in mind. Simpler types of psycholinguistic processes can be studied rather intensively; already we know much about hearing and matching. Accepting and interpreting are just now coming into scientific focus. Understanding is still over the horizon, and pragmatic questions involving belief systems are presently so vague as to be hardly worth asking. But the whole range of processes must be included in any adequate definition of psycholinguistics.

I phrased the description of these various psycholinguistic processes in terms of a listener; the question inevitably arises as to whether a different hierarchy is required to describe the speaker. One problem a psycholinguist faces is to decide whether speaking and listening are two separate abilities, co-ordinate but distinct, or whether they are merely different manifestations of a single linguistic faculty.

The mouth and ear are different organs; at the simplest levels we must distinguish hearing and matching from vocalising and speaking. At more complex levels it is less easy to decide whether the two abilities are distinct. At some point they must converge, if only to explain why it is so difficult to speak and listen simultaneously. The question is where.

It is easy to demonstrate how important to a speaker is the sound of his own voice. If his speech is delayed a fifth of a second, amplified, and fed back into his own ears, the voice-ear asynchrony can be devastating to the motor skills of articulate speech. It is more difficult, however, to demonstrate that the same linguistic competence required for speaking is also involved in processing the speech of others.

Recently Morris Halle and Kenneth Stevens of the Massachusetts Institute of Technology revived a suggestion made by Wilhelm von Humboldt over a century ago. Suppose we accept the notion that a listener recognises what he hears by comparing it with some internal representation. To the extent that a match can be obtained, the input is accepted and interpreted. One trouble with this hypothesis, however, is that a listener must be ready to recognise any one of an enormous number of different sentences. It is inconceivable that a separate internal representation for each of them could be stored in his memory in advance. Halle and Stevens suggest that these internal representations must be generated as they are needed by following the same generative rules that are normally used in producing speech. In this way the rules of the language are incorporated into the theory only once, in a generative form; they need not be learned once by the ear and again by the tongue. This is a theory of a language-user, not of a speaker or a listener alone.

The listener begins with a guess about the input. On that basis he generates an internal matching signal. The first attempt will probably be in error; if so, the mismatch is reported and used as a basis for a next guess, which should be closer. This cycle repeats (unconsciously, almost certainly) until a satisfactory (not necessarily a correct) match is obtained, at which point the next segment of speech is scanned and matched, etc. The output is not a transformed version of the input; it is the programme that was followed to generate the matching representation.

The perceptual categories available to such a system are defined by the generative rules at its disposal. It is also reasonably obvious that its efficiency is critically dependent on the quality of the initial guess. If this guess is close, an iterative process can converge rapidly; if not, the listener will be unable to keep pace with the rapid flow of conversational speech.

A listener's first guess probably derives in part from syntactic markers in the form of intonation, inflection, suffixes, etc., and in part from his general knowledge of the semantic and situational context. Syntactic cues indicate how the input is to be grouped and which words function together; semantic and contextual contributions are more difficult to characterise, but must somehow enable him to limit the range of possible words that he can expect to hear.

How he is able to do this is an utter mystery, but the fact that he can do it is easily demonstrated.

The English psychologist David Bruce recorded a set of ordinary sentences and played them in the presence of noise so intense that the voice was just audible, but not intelligible. He told his listeners that these were sentences on some general topic—sports, say—and asked them to repeat what they heard. He then told them they would hear more sentences on a different topic, which they were also to repeat. This was done several times. Each time the listeners repeated sentences appropriate to the topic announced in advance. When at the end of the experiment Bruce told them they had heard the same recording every time—all he had changed was the topic they were given—most listeners were unable to believe it.

With an advance hypothesis about what the message will be we can tune our perceptual system to favour certain interpretations and reject others. This fact is no proof of a generative process in speech perception, but it does emphasise the important role of context. For most theories of speech perception the facilitation provided by context is merely a fortunate though rather complicated fact. For a generative theory it is essential.

Note that generative theories do not assume that a listener must be able to articulate the sounds he recognises, but merely that he be able to generate some internal representation to match the input. In this respect a generative theory differs from a motor theory (such as that of Sir Richard Paget) which assumes that we can identify only those utterances we are capable of producing ourselves. There is some rather compelling evidence against a motor theory. The American psychologist Eric Lenneberg has described the case of an eight-year-old boy with congenital anarthria; despite his complete inability to speak, the boy acquired an excellent ability to understand language. Moreover, it is a common observation that utterances can be understood by young children before they are able to produce them.

A motor theory of speech-perception draws too close a parallel between our two capacities as users of language. Even so, the two are more closely integrated than most people realise.

I have already offered the opinion that productivity sets the central problem for the psycholinguist and have even referred to it indirectly by arguing that we can produce too many different sentences to store them all in memory. The issue can be postponed no longer.

To make the problem plain, consider an example on the level of individual words. For several days I carried in my pocket a small white card on which was typed UNDERSTANDER. On suitable occasions I would hand it to someone. "How do you pronounce this?" I asked.

He pronounced it.

"Is it an English word?"

He hesitated. "I haven't seen it used very much. I'm not sure."

"Do you know what it means?"

"I suppose it means 'one who understands.' "

I thanked him and changed the subject.

Of course, understander *is* an English word, but to find it you must look in a large dictionary where you will probably read that it is "now rare." Rare enough, I think, for none of my respondents to have seen it before. Nevertheless, they all answered in the same way. Nobody seemed surprised. Nobody wondered how he could understand and pronounce a word without knowing whether it was a word. Everybody put the main stress on the third syllable and constructed a meaning from the verb "to understand" and the agentive suffix *"er."* Familiar morphological rules of English were applied as a matter of course, even though the combination was completely novel.

Probably no one but a psycholinguist captured by the ingenuous behavioristic theory that words are vocal responses conditioned to occur in the presence of appropriate stimuli would find anything exceptional in this. Since none of my friends had seen the word before, and so could not have been "conditioned" to give the responses they did, how would this theory account for their "verbal behaviour"? Advocates of a conditioning theory of meaning—and there are several distinguished scientists among them—would probably explain linguistic productivity in terms of "conditioned generalisations."[2] They could argue that my respondents had been conditioned to the word understand and to the suffix -er; responses to their union could conceivably be counted as instances of stimulus generalisation. In this way, novel responses could occur without special training.

Although a surprising amount of psychological ingenuity has been invested in this kind of argument, it is difficult to estimate its value. No one has carried the theory through for all the related combinations that must be explained simultaneously. One can speculate, however, that there would have to be many different kinds of generalisation, each with a carefully defined range of applicability. For example, it would be necessary to explain why "understander" is acceptable, whereas "erunderstand" is not. Worked out in detail, such a theory would become a sort of Pavlovian paraphrase of a linguistic description. Of course, if one believes there is some essential difference between behaviour governed by conditioned habits and behaviour governed by rules, the paraphrase could never be more than a vast intellectual pun.

Original combinations of elements are the life blood of language. It is our ability to produce and comprehend such novelties that makes language so ubiquitously useful. As psychologists have become more seriously interested in the cognitive processes that language entails, they have been forced to recognise that the fundamental puzzle is not our ability to associate vocal noises with perceptual objects, but rather our combinatorial productivity—our ability to understand an unlimited diversity of utterances never heard before and to produce an equal variety of utterances similarly intelligible to other members of our speech community. Faced with this problem, concepts borrowed from conditioning theory seem not so much invalid as totally inadequate.

Some idea of the relative magnitudes of what we might call the productive as opposed to the reproductive components of any psycholinguistic theory is provided by statistical studies of language. A few numbers can reinforce the point. If you interrupt a speaker at some randomly chosen instant, there will be, on the average, about ten words that form grammatical and meaningful continuations. Often only one word is admissible and sometimes there are thousands, but

2 A dog conditioned to salivate at the sound of a tone will also salivate, though less copiously, at the sound of similar tones, the magnitude declining as the new tones become less similar to the original. This phenomenon is called "stimulus generalisation."

on the average it works out to about ten. (If you think this estimate too low, I will not object; larger estimates strengthen the argument.) A simple English sentence can easily run to a length of twenty words, so elementary arithmetic tells us that there must be at least 10^{20} such sentences that a person who knows English must know how to deal with. Compare this productive potential with the 10^4 or 10^5 individual words we know—the reproductive component of our theory—and the discrepancy is dramatically illustrated. Putting it differently, it would take 100,000,000,000 centuries (one thousand times the estimated age of the earth) to utter all the admissible twenty-word sentences of English. Thus, the probability that you might have heard any particular twenty-word sentence before is negligible. Unless it is a cliché, every sentence must come to you as a novel combination of morphemes. Yet you can interpret it at once if you know the English language.

With these facts in mind it is impossible to argue that we learn to understand sentences from teachers who have pronounced each one and explained what it meant. What we have learned are not particular strings of words, but *rules* for generating admissible strings of words.

Consider what it means to follow a rule; this consideration shifts the discussion of psycholinguistics into very difficult territory. The nature of rules has been a central concern of modern philosophy and perhaps no analysis has been more influential than Ludwig Wittgenstein's. Wittgenstein remarked that the most characteristic thing we can say about "rule-governed behaviour" is that the person who knows the rules knows whether he is proceeding correctly or incorrectly. Although he may not be able to formulate the rules explicitly, he knows what it is to make a mistake. If this remark is accepted, we must ask ourselves whether an animal that has been conditioned is privy to any such knowledge about the correctness of what he is doing. Perhaps such a degree of insight could be achieved by the great apes, but surely not by all the various species that can acquire conditioned reflexes. On this basis alone it would seem necessary to preserve a distinction between conditioning and learning rules.

As psychologists have learned to appreciate the complexities of language, the prospect of reducing it to the laws of behaviour so carefully studied in lower animals has grown increasingly remote. We have been forced more and more into a position that non-psychologists probably take for granted, namely, that language is rule-governed behaviour characterised by enormous flexibility and freedom of choice.

Obvious as this conclusion may seem, it has important implications for any scientific theory of language. If rules involve the concepts of right and wrong, they introduce a normative aspect that has always been avoided in the natural sciences. One hears repeatedly that the scientist's ability to suppress normative judgments about his subject-matter enables him to see the world objectively, as it really is. To admit that language follows rules seems to put it outside the range of phenomena accessible to scientific investigation.

At this point a psycholinguist who

wishes to preserve his standing as a natural scientist faces an old but always difficult decision. Should he withdraw and leave the study of language to others? Or should he give up all pretence of being a "natural scientist," searching for causal explanations, and embrace a more phenomenological approach? Or should he push blindly ahead with his empirical methods, hoping to find a causal basis for normative practices, but running the risk that all his efforts will be wasted because rule-governed behaviour in principle lies beyond the scope of natural science?

To withdraw means to abandon hope of understanding scientifically all those human mental processes that involve language in any important degree. To persevere means to face the enormously difficult, if not actually impossible task of finding a place for normative rules in a descriptive science.

Difficult, yes. Still one wonders whether these alternatives are really as mutually exclusive as they seem.

The first thing we notice when we survey the languages of the world is how few we can understand and how diverse they all seem. Not until one looks for some time does an even more significant observation emerge concerning the pervasive similarities in the midst of all this diversity.

Every human group that anthropologists have studied has spoken a language. The language always has a lexicon and a grammar. The lexicon is not a haphazard collection of vocalisations, but is highly organised; it always has pronouns, means for dealing with time, space, and number, words to represent true and false, the basic

concepts necessary for propositional logic. The grammar has distinguishable levels of structure, some phonological, some syntactic. The phonology always contains both vowels and consonants, and the phonemes can always be described in terms of distinctive features drawn from a limited set of possibilities. The syntax always specifies rules for grouping elements sequentially into phrases and sentences, rules governing normal intonation, rules for transforming some types of sentences into other types.

The nature and importance of these common properties, called "linguistic universals," are only beginning to emerge as our knowledge of the world's languages grows more systematic. These universals appear even in languages that developed with a minimum of interaction. One is forced to assume, therefore, either that (*a*) no other kind of linguistic practices are conceivable, or that (*b*) something in the biological makeup of human beings favours languages having these similarities. Only a moment's reflection is needed to reject (*a*). When one considers the variety of artificial languages developed in mathematics, in the communication sciences, in the use of computers, in symbolic logic, and elsewhere, it soon becomes apparent that the universal features of natural languages are not the only ones possible. Natural languages are, in fact, rather special and often seem unnecessarily complicated.

A popular belief regards human language as a more or less free creation of the human intellect, as if its elements were chosen arbitrarily and could be combined into meaningful utterances by any rules that strike our collective fancy. The assumption is implicit, for example, in Wittgenstein's well-known conception of "the language game." This metaphor, which casts valuable light on many aspects of language, can, if followed blindly, lead one to think that all linguistic rules are just as arbitrary as, say, the rules of chess or football. As Lenneberg has pointed out, however, it makes a great deal of sense to inquire into the biological basis for language, but very little to ask about the biological foundations of card games.

Man is the only animal to have a combinatorially productive language. In the jargon of biology, language is "a species-specific form of behaviour." Other animals have signalling systems of various kinds and for various purposes—but only man has evolved this particular and highly improbable form of communication. Those who think of language as a free and spontaneous intellectual invention are also likely to believe that any animal with a brain sufficiently large to support a high level of intelligence can acquire a language. This assumption is demonstrably false. The human brain is not just an ape brain enlarged; its extra size is less important than its different structure. Moreover, Lenneberg has pointed out that nanocephalic dwarfs, with brains half the normal size but grown on the human blueprint, can use language reasonably well, and even mongoloids, not intelligent enough to perform the simplest functions for themselves, can acquire the rudiments. Talking and understanding language do not depend on being intelligent or having a large brain. They depend on "being human."

Serious attempts have been made to teach animals to speak. If words were conditioned responses, animals as intelligent as chimpanzees or porpoises should be able to learn them. These attempts have uniformly failed in the past and, if the argument here is correct, they will always fail in the future—for just the same reason that attempts to teach fish to walk or dogs to fly would fail. Such efforts misconstrue the basis for our linguistic competence: they fly in the face of biological facts.[3]

Human language must be such that a child can acquire it. He acquires it,

[3] The belief that animals have, or could have, languages is as old as man's interest in the evoltuion of his special talent, but the truth of the matter has long been known. Listen, for example, to Max Müller (*Three Lectures on the Science of Language*) in 1889: "It is easy enough to show that animals communicate, but this is a fact which has never been doubted. Dogs who growl and bark leave no doubt in the minds of other dogs or cats, or even of man, of what they mean, but growling and barking are not language, nor do they even contain the elements of language."

Unfortunately, Müller's authority, great as it was, did not suffice, and in 1890 we hear Samuel Butler ("Thought and Language," in his *Collected Essays*) reply that although "growling and barking cannot be called very highly specialised language," still there is "a sayer, a sayee, and a covenanted symbol designedly applied. Our own speech is vertebrated and articulated by means of nouns, verbs, and the rules of grammar. A dog's speech is invertebrate, but I do not see how it is possible to deny that it possesses all the essential elements of language."

Müller and Butler did not argue about the facts of animal behaviour which Darwin had described. Their disagreement arose more directly from differences of opinion about the correct definition of the term "language." To-day our definitions of human language are more precise, so we can say with correspondingly more precision why Butler was wrong.

moreover, from parents who have no idea how to explain it to him. No careful schedule of rewards for correct or punishments for incorrect utterances is necessary. It is sufficient that the child be allowed to grow up naturally in an environment where language is used.

The child's achievement seems all the more remarkable when we recall the speed with which he accomplishes it and the limitations of his intelligence in other respects. It is difficult to avoid an impression that infants are little machines specially designed by nature to perform this particular learning task.

I believe this analogy with machines is worth pursuing. If we could imagine what a language-learning automaton would have to do, it would dramatise—and perhaps even clarify—what a child can do. The linguist and logician Noam Chomsky has argued that the description of such an automaton would comprise our hypothesis about the child's innate ability to learn languages or (to borrow a term from Ferdinand de Saussure[4]) his innate *faculté de langage*.

Consider what information a language-learning automaton would be given to work with. Inputs to the machine would include a finite set of sentences, a finite set of non-sentences accompanied by some signal that they were incorrect, some way to indicate that one item is a repetition or elaboration or transformation of another, and some access to a universe of perceptual objects and events associated with the sentences. Inside the machine there would be a computer so programmed as to extract from these inputs the nature of the language, *i.e,* the particular syntactic rules by which sentences are generated, and the rules that associate with each syntactic structure a particular phonetic representation and semantic interpretation. The important question, of course, is what programme of instructions would have to be given to the computer.

We could instruct the computer to discover any imaginable set of rules that might, in some formal sense of the term, constitute a grammar. This approach—the natural one if we believe that human languages can be infinitely diverse and various—is doomed from the start. The computer would have to evaluate an infinitude of possible grammars; with only a finite corpus of evidence it would be impossible, even if sufficient time were available for computation, to arrive at any unique solution.

A language-learning automaton could not possibly discover a suitable grammar unless some strong *a priori* assumptions were built into it from the start. These assumptions would limit the alternatives that the automaton considered—limit them presumably to the range defined by linguistic universals. The automaton would test various grammars of the appropriate form to see if they would generate all of the sentences and none of the non-sentences. Certain aspects would be tested before others; those found acceptable would be preserved for further evaluation. If we wished the automaton to replicate a child's performance, the order in which these aspects would be evaluated could only be decided after careful analysis of

4 Ferdinand de Saussure (1857–1913), a French-Swiss scholar and teacher, whose *Course in General Linguistics* (1916) is one of the most influential books in modern linguistics.

the successive stages of language acquisition in human children.

The actual construction of such an automaton is, of course, far beyond our reach at the present time. That is not the point. The lesson to learn from such speculations is that the whole project would be impossible unless the automaton—and so, presumably, a child—knew in advance to look for particular kinds of regularities and correspondences, to discover rules of a rather special kind uniquely characteristic of human language in general.

The features that human infants are prepared to notice sharply limit the structure of any human language. Even if one imagines creating by decree a Newspeak in which this generalisation were false, within one generation it would have become true again.

Psycholinguistics does not deal with social practices determined arbitrarily either by caprice or intelligent design, but with practices that grow organically out of the biological nature of man and the linguistic capacities of human infants. To that extent, at least, it is possible to define an area of empirical fact well within the reach of our scientific methods.

Another line of scientific investigation is opened up by the observation that we do not always follow our own rules. If this were not so, of course, we would not speak of rules, but of the laws of language. The fact that we make mistakes, and that we can know we made mistakes, is central to the psycholinguistic problem. Before we can see the empirical issue this entails, however, we should first draw a crucial distinction between theories of language and theories of the users of language.

There is nothing in the linguistic description of a language to indicate what mistakes will occur. Mistakes result from the psychological limitations of people who use the language, not from the language itself. It would be meaningless to state rules for making mistakes.

A formal characterisation of a natural language in terms of a set of elements and rules for combining those elements must inevitably generate an infinitude of possible sentences that will never occur in actual use. Most of these sentences are too complicated for us. There is nothing mysterious about this. It is very similar to the situation in arithmetic where a student may understand perfectly the rules for multiplication, yet find that some multiplication problems are too difficult for him to do "in his head," *i.e.,* without extending his memory capacity by the use of pencil and paper.

There is no longest grammatical sentence. There is no limit to the number of different grammatical sentences. Moreover, since the number of elements and rules is finite, there must be some rules and elements that can recur any number of times in a grammatical sentence. Chomsky has even managed to pinpoint a kind of recursive operation in language that, in principle, lies beyond the power of any finite device to perform indefinitely often. Compare these sentences:

(R) *Remarkable is the rapidity of the motion of the wing of the hummingbird.*
(L) *The hummingbird's wing's motion's rapidity is remarkable.*
(E) *The rapidity that the motion that*

the wing that the hummingbird has has has is remarkable.

When you parse these sentences you find that the phrase structure of (R) dangles off to the right; each prepositional phrase hangs to the noun in the prepositional phrase preceding it. In (R), therefore, we see a type of recurring construction that has been called right-branching. Sentence (L), on the other hand, is left-branching; each possessive modifies the possessive immediately following. Finally, (E) is an onion; it grows by embedding sentences within sentences. Inside "The rapidity is remarkable" we first insert "the motion is rapid" by a syntactic transformation that permits us to construct relative clauses, and so we obtain "The rapidity that the motion has is remarkable." Then we repeat the transformation, this time inserting "the wing has motion" to obtain "The rapidity that the motion that the wing has has is remarkable." Repeating the transformation once more gives (E).

It is intuitively obvious that, of these three types of recursive operations, self-embedding (E) is psychologically the most difficult. Although they seem grammatical by any reasonable standard of grammar, such sentences never occur in ordinary usage because they exceed our cognitive capacities. Chomsky's achievement was to prove rigorously that any language that does *not* restrict this kind of recursive embedding contains sentences that cannot be spoken or understood by devices, human or mechanical, with finite memories. Any device that uses these rules must remember each left portion until it can be related to its corresponding right portion; if the memory of the user is limited, but

the number of admissible left portions is not, it is inevitable that some admissible sentences will exceed the capacity of the user to process them correctly.

It is necessary, therefore, to distinguish between a description of the language in terms of the rules that a person *knows* and uses and a description of that person's *performance* as a user of the rules. The distinction is sometimes criticised as "psycholatry" by strict adherents of behaviourism; "knowing" is considered too mentalistic and subjective, therefore unscientific. The objection cannot be taken seriously. Our conception of the rules that a language-user knows is indeed a hypothetical construct, not something observed directly in his behaviour. But if such hypotheses were to be forbidden, science in general would become an empty pursuit.

Given a reasonable hypothesis about the rules that a language-user knows, the exploration of his limitations in following those rules is proper work for an experimental psychologist. "Psychology should assist us," a great linguist once said, "in understanding what is going on in the mind of speakers, and more particularly how they are led to deviate from previously existing rules in consequence of conflicting tendencies." Otto Jespersen made this request of psychology in 1924; now at last the work is beginning.[5]

One example. Stephen Isard[6] and I asked Harvard undergraduates to

[5] *The Philosophy of Grammar* (Allen and Unwin, London, 1924, p. 344).
[6] G. A. Miller and S. Isard, "Some Perceptual Consequences of Linguistic Rules," *Journal of Verbal Learning and Verbal Behavior* (1963), vol. 2, pp. 217–228.

memorise several sentences that differed in degree of self-embedding. For instance, the twenty-two words in the right-branching sentence, "We cheered the football squad that played the team that brought the mascot that chased the girls that were in the park," can be re-arranged to give one, two, three, or four self-embeddings; with four it becomes, "The girls (that the mascot (that the team (that the football squad (that we cheered) played) brought) chased) were in the park." One self-embedding caused no difficulty; it was almost as easy to memorise as the sentence with none. Three or four embeddings were most difficult. When the sentence had two self-embeddings—"The team (that the football squad (that we cheered) played) brought the mascot that chased the girls that were in the park" —some subjects found it as easy to memorise as sentences with zero or one embedding, others found it as difficult as sentences with three or four. That is to say, everybody can manage one embedding, some people can manage two, but everybody has trouble with three or more.

Records of eye movements while people are reading such sentences show that the trouble begins with the long string of verbs, "cheered played brought," at which point all grasp of the sentence structure crumbles and they are left with a random list of verbs. This is just what would be expected from a computer executing a programme that did not make provision for a sub-routine to refer to itself, *i.e.*, that was not recursive. If our ability to handle this type of self-embedded recursion is really as limited as the experiment indicates, it places a strong limitation on the kinds of theories we can propose to explain our human capacities for processing information.

On the simpler levels of our psycholinguistic hierarchy the pessimists are wrong; much remains there to be explored and systematised by scientific methods. How far these methods can carry us remains an open question. Although syntax seems well within our grasp and techniques for studying semantic systems are now beginning to emerge, understanding and belief raise problems well beyond the scope of linguistics. Perhaps it is there that scientific progress will be forced to halt.

No psychological process is more important or difficult to understand than understanding, and nowhere has scientific psychology proved more disappointing to those who have turned to it for help. The complaint is as old as scientific psychology itself. It was probably first seen clearly by Wilhelm Dilthey, who called for a new kind of psychology—a kind to which Karl Jaspers later gave the name *"verstehende Psychologie"*—and in one form or another the division has plagued psychologists ever since. Obviously a tremendous gulf separates the interpretation of a sentence from the understanding of a personality, a society, a historical epoch. But the gap is narrowing. Indeed, one can even pretend to see certain similarities between the generative theory of speech perception discussed above and the reconstructive intellectual processes that have been labelled *verstehende*. The analogy may some day prove helpful, but how optimistic one dares feel at the present time is not easily decided. Meanwhile, the psycholinguists will undoubtedly continue to advance as far as they can. It should prove interesting to see how far that will be.

For discussion

A. What is Miller's definition of psycholinguistics? What does he mean by "productivity"?

B. What, according to Miller, are the six things a listener can do about any utterance?

C. What is the point of Miller's comment (p. 332), "For most theories of speech perception the facilitation provided by context is merely a fortunate though rather complicated fact. For a generative theory it is essential."

D. What does a motor theory of speech perception assume, and what is Lenneberg's evidence against it? Explain Miller's statement (p. 332), "A motor theory of speech perception draws too close a parallel between our two capacities as users of language. Even so, the two are more closely integrated than most people realize."

E. What distinction is made between conditioning and learning rules? What is the difficulty for the psychologist of the idea ". . . that language is rule-governed behavior characterized by enormous flexibility and freedom of choice"?

F. Conduct the UNDERSTANDER experiment. Do your results correspond with Miller's?

G. What does Miller give as language universals? What are the implications for his argument?

H. Why have all attempts to teach animals to speak failed?

I. Limiting yourself to the range defined by linguistic universals, give the *a priori* assumptions Miller would build into his language-learning automaton from the start in order to find a suitable grammar.

J. Why does Miller make a careful distinction between the theory of a language and the theory of a user of the language?

K. Write five right-branching sentences, five left-branching sentences, and five self-embedding sentences. Make them as long as you can.